Inside Jokes

Inside Jokes

Using Humor to Reverse-Engineer the Mind

Matthew M. Hurley, Daniel C. Dennett, and Reginald B. Adams, Jr.

The MIT Press
Cambridge, Massachusetts
London, England

For information about special quantity discounts, please email special_sales @mitpress.mit.edu

This book was set in Stone Sans and Stone Serif by Toppan Best-set Premedia Limited. Printed and bound in the United States of America.

Library of Congress Cataloging-in-Publication Data

Hurley, Matthew M., 1977–.
Inside jokes: using humor to reverse-engineer the mind / Matthew M. Hurley, Daniel C. Dennett, and Reginald B. Adams.
  p. cm.
Includes bibliographical references and index.
ISBN 978-0-262-01582-0 (hardcover: alk. paper)
1. Laughter—Psychological aspects. 2. Laughter—Philosophy. 3. Wit and humor—Psychological aspects. 4. Wit and humor—Philosophy. I. Dennett, Daniel Clement. II. Adams, Reginald B. III. Title.
BF575.L3H89   2011
152.4'3—dc22

2010044707

10 9 8 7 6 5 4 3 2 1

Contents

Preface

In April 1975, Martin Gardner reported, in his *Scientific American* magazine column "Mathematical Games," that a new computer chess program invented at MIT "had established, with a high degree of probability, that pawn to king's rook 4 is a win for White." Tragedy! If this were so, the noble game of chess would be killed for all time, no more challenging than tic-tac-toe. Even if the algorithm purportedly discovered by the program was tediously complicated, something no human chess-player could hope to memorize, the mere knowledge that there was a mindless recipe for winning any game of chess would drain all the glory, all the art, out of the contest. Who would want to devote years to honing skills, enduring grueling tournaments, hunting for exquisite new strategies, all the while knowing that there was an easier way to win, a cheap trick that could not be thwarted? Nobody knows how many readers were taken in, but surely Gardner's unwelcome news struck at least momentary dread in the hearts of some chess-lovers, before they tumbled to the date and chuckled with relief. April Fools'!

Late one night a few years later, the sex researchers William Masters and Virginia Johnson, authors of *Human Sexual Response* (1966), were analyzing their voluminous data on orgasm and noticed a subtle but striking pattern: they had discovered, to their amazement, that the uttering of a simple verbal formula, a string of words (in any language) that exhibited an arcane pattern based on the Fibonacci series, would bring any normal postpubescent human to orgasm within a minute. They rechecked their data, ran just a few confirmatory experiments, and then . . . destroyed their notes, salted their data with misleading falsehoods to conceal the pattern from future eyes, and took a solemn vow not to reveal the secret they had uncovered. Thanks to their heroic sacrifice, sex as we know it lives on.

In early 2010, Hurley, Dennett, and Adams put the finishing touches on their evolutionary/neurocomputational model of humor and wondered if, just possibly, they had cracked the mystery that had baffled intrepid analysts and researchers for several millennia: it seemed they might have not only uncovered the neural mechanisms of humor but in the process devised a foolproof recipe for generating humorous *stimuli* of all varieties, from slapstick to witty retorts, from dirty jokes to high comedy. Set the dial and turn the crank and out comes Oscar Wilde, Charlie Chaplin, W. C. Fields, P. G. Wodehouse; nudge the dial and turn the crank again and out comes Steve Martin, Jim Carrey, Dave Barry, Gary Larson . . . Reductionistic science has triumphed again, and humor, as we know it, will soon be dead.

OK, we lied about Masters and Johnson. And we lied about the humor recipe. Not only does the theory in this book not uncover such a recipe, it shows why it is extremely unlikely that anybody—or any bank of computers—will ever find one. Art really is different from science, and comedy is art, like music and, well, art. Art does involve a kind of technology (*techne* in Greek, *technique* that one can master), but all the technique in the world only takes the would-be artist partway; our model helps explain why this is so, why the neural mechanisms engaged by humor—and they are, at bottom, "just" fantastically complex mechanisms, no *wonder tissue* involved at all—are quite systematically tamperproof. Nobody can *prove* that there will never be an algorithm for perfect chess; it is known that chess, which is a finite game, is officially vulnerable to brute-force, exhaustive, algorithmic solution, but it is also clear that no physically possible computer could complete that algorithmic search. That does not rule out the (tragic) possibility that there is a discoverable shortcut. Similarly, nobody can *prove* that there is no shortcut to humor, but the vast space of possible humor is much, much larger and more complicated than the space of chess, and changing all the time, so nobody should be too worried. Still, we appreciate that many people will confront our book with mixed emotions: curiosity—why on earth is there humor at all? how *could* it work?—competing with the hope that mystery will triumph, that nimble art will scamper out of the path of the lumbering juggernaut of science yet again. We share those mixed emotions and are happy to report that, if we are right, both will be gratified. We will explain why humor exists, how it works in the brain, and why comedy is an art. Let's begin with the first of these questions.

There was an old woman who lived in a shoe.
She had so many children she didn't know what to do . . .
(Their rooms were piled high with the playthings of boys:
comic books, fishing rods, discarded toys,
model planes, model trains and the dirt that goes with them
and huge piles of laundry that flowed out to the kitchen.
And try as she may to get them to sweep—
she'd scold them, and threaten, implore them, and weep;
she'd given them dust-cloths, and vacuums and brooms—
she just could not get them to clean up their rooms.)
So she gave them some broth, without any bread,
and whipped them all soundly, and put them to bed.
. . . and, then, one night the old woman got a new idea:

She made them pajamas and bed socks of Swiffer cloth, and the next night while they slept she hid lots of candies around in their rooms, under the beds, under the piles of toys and clothes. In the morning when the children discovered the first of these candies, they went on a gleeful rampage, piling and sorting their belongings in the hunt for all the candies. By noon they were stuffed with candy—and their rooms were as orderly and clean as Martha Stewart's front parlor.

That may be an unlikely story, but we propose that Mother Nature—natural selection—has hit upon much the same trick to get our brains to do all the tedious debugging that they must do if they are to live dangerously with the unruly piles of discoveries and mistakes that we generate in our incessant heuristic search. She cannot just order the brain to do the necessary garbage collection and debugging (the way a computer programmer can simply install subroutines that slavishly take care of this). She has to bribe the brain with pleasure. That is why we experience mirthful delight when we catch ourselves wrong-footed by a concealed inference error. Finding and fixing these time-pressured mis-leaps would be constantly annoying hard work, if evolution hadn't arranged for it to be fun. This wired-in source of pleasure has then been tickled relentlessly by the *supernormal stimuli* invented and refined by our comedians and jokesters over the centuries. We have, in fact, become addicted to this endogenous mind candy in much the way long-distance runners become addicted to the endorphins their strenuous efforts pump into their blood streams. Humor, we will try to show, evolved out of a computational problem that arose when our ancestors were furnished with open-ended thinking.

This book grew out of Matthew Hurley's dissertation at Tufts University, completed in 2006, supervised by his two coauthors, Daniel Dennett and Reginald Adams, Jr. Since then it has undergone substantial revisions and enlargements, but the central novelties are Hurley's and the essential details of the theory remain unchanged since its earlier dissertational form. Humor has been a major research interest of Adams for years, and he led the way into the vast literature on humor for his coauthors, correcting myopic interpretations and misapprehensions, and holding their feet to the fire when their ideas were less clear and precise than they should be. For Dennett, this project discharges a promise unkept for almost twenty years. Here, at long last, is "a proper account of laughter" (and amusement) that "moves beyond pure phenomenology" (*Consciousness Explained*, 1991, pp. 64–66) that he can endorse wholeheartedly.

This is a book about humor, but it's not *just* about humor. It is a book about the epistemic predicament of agents in the world and a class of models of cognition that can successfully deal with that predicament. It argues that emotions govern *all* our cognitive activities, large and small, and that humor is thus a rich source of insights into the delicate machinery of our minds. Armed with the right theory, we can use humor as a sort of mind-reading device, exposing both the covert knowledge and the inner workings of the amused mind. Our theory draws extensively on earlier work in the field, but it adds a perspective, both evolutionary and computational, that has been largely missing. Humor cannot be just a happy accident of our biology, and the problem it is designed—by evolution—to solve must be a problem that is unique to our species (though we may see primitive or proto-versions of humor in other species). The theory we present attempts to answer questions that earlier work didn't even ask, and it is probably not quite right but it gives us all something to fix that is, we think, a significant advance over the earlier efforts.

We are indebted to a number of people for their contributions throughout the development of the ideas presented in this book. First, we would like to thank the late Alexander (Sasha) Chislenko whose own theory of humor—a kind of surprise theory (personal communication, 1998)—first inspired Matthew to look for an evolutionary answer to the riddle. Our theory differs from his, but if it wasn't for Sasha's insights this project might never have been undertaken.

As the project progressed, we received extensive insightful comments and discussions from David Huron, Deb Roy, V. S. Ramachandran, Justina Fan, Leo Trottier, Alexander Ince-Cushman, Paul Queior, Seth Frey, Lindsay

Dachille, Eric Nichols, Barry Trimmer, Keith Morrison, and several anonymous reviewers for MIT Press, all of whom read and remarked on early drafts; likewise, David Krakauer, Donald Saari, Gil Greengross and others engaged in thoughtful discussion of our theory with us at the Santa Fe Institute colloquium on May 3, 2010, and the May 5, 2010, colloquium sponsored by the Computer Science Department at the University of New Mexico. Numerous others have offered useful reactions to our theory. We are very grateful for all these exchanges. Additional thanks go to a number of friends and colleagues from around the world who provided discussion about terms in other languages that have two senses that are similar to the two main senses of the English word "funny" (see chapter 3). These people are: Rodrigo Correa, Gaston Cangiano, Priscilla Borges, Gilles Fauconnier, Ina Lieckfeldt, Bettina Seidl, Doreen Kinzel, Athina Pantelidou, Van Agora, Vera Szamarasz, Csaba Pleh, Miro Enev, Kaloyan Ivanov, Adriana Belencaia, Yuliya Yaglovskaya, Takao Tanizawa, Toshiyuki Uchino, Heejeong Haas, Angie Huh, Ally Kim, David Moser, Stephanie Xie, Jenny Prasertdee, Johan Vaartjes, Katerina Lucas, and Güven Güzeldere. Douglas Hofstadter and the Center for Research on Concepts and Cognition (CRCC) at Indiana University provided much appreciated support during a large part of the writing of this manuscript; we thank Doug as well as Helga Keller from the CRCC, and also Teresa Salvato at the Center for Cognitive Studies at Tufts University for their help and support. We owe our gratitude also to Tom Stone, Philip Laughlin, Judy Feldmann, and the rest of the team at MIT Press who helped bring the manuscript to production. Lastly, but most importantly, all of us would like to thank our families for their constant support throughout the process of writing, especially Justina Fan, Susan Dennett, and Katharine Donnelly Adams.

Matthew M. Hurley
Daniel C. Dennett
Reginald B. Adams, Jr.
2011

1 Introduction

The most exciting phrase to hear in science, the one that heralds new discoveries, is not "Eureka!" (I found it!) but "That's funny. . . ."
—Isaac Asimov

Comedy is half of life, according to the theater. (The other half is tragedy.) A large portion, in any case, of people's time is spent attempting to get each other to laugh. Stories are told, jokes recounted, and witticisms cracked whenever possible. In only the most solemn occasions is humor deemed inappropriate, and innovators are pushing the envelope of propriety all the time. When we find humor in a situation, we feel compelled to share it with others. Today, our taste for comedy apparently outstrips our taste for tragedy. Much of our entertainment industry, in every medium (aside from music), consists of humor. If there is not enough comedy in our daily lives, we turn to our televisions and let professional comedians fill the gap, almost in the way we insist on filling our waking hours with recorded music. Like music, alcohol, tobacco, caffeine, and chocolate, humor is a modern human addiction. And if we are to understand humor, we need to adopt a biological perspective from which we can observe—and formulate testable hypotheses about—the evolution of this addiction.

Every cell in our bodies needs sugar—glucose—the fuel that keeps us alive. A good source of glucose is fructose, the sugar in ripe fruit, which the liver can readily convert to glucose. As it turns out, the common natural sugar with the highest subjective sweetness rating—the one the sweetness sensors in our tongues are most tuned to detect—is fructose. So evolution has engineered a powerful fructose-harvesting system and given it a high priority—our cells operate on the rough principle: Whenever the opportunity to harvest fructose is detected, act on it. Honey, which is mainly glucose and fructose, is a particularly good opportunity for harvesting. It is hard to believe that the yumminess of chocolate cake or maple syrup or strawberry jam all boils down, almost literally, to the deeply practical glucose imperative, but it does. That's the way to understand why we have a sweet tooth. Why do we have a funny bone, a similar craving for, and appreciation of, humor? For a similarly practical reason: We *need* to devote serious time and energy to doing something which, if we didn't do it, would imperil our very lives. . . . Nature has seen to it that we act vigorously on this need, by rewarding that action handsomely.

The phenomena of evolution are not as simple as they are often portrayed. It is not just a matter of the natural selection of "genes for" this or that—whichever feature of living things catches the attention and curiosity of the researcher. In particular, it is important to consider not just the ends but the means, the organic machinery that is going to do the work, whatever it is. The How questions of biology are just as important as the Why questions (Francis 2004), and some evolutionary puzzles are systematically unanswerable without information about the constraints on the performance of the system, and even an educated guess about those constraints depends on having at least a crude model of the machinery. The evolution of our "sense of humor," we will show, could not possibly be explained without hypotheses about the functional architecture of our brains, for the simple reason that what different humorous items have in common is *only* the similar effects they have on those brain systems and the resultant *subjective* experiences. At various points in this book we draw attention to physical complications that really matter, but just as often we slide over complications that we deem—perhaps too riskily—to be ignorable for our purposes. In particular, we set aside for another occasion questions of the complex and dynamical role of development in the relations between genes, organisms, and environment.

As prominent as humor is in our lives, it is at least equally as mysterious. Why does humor exist at all? Why is this category of our experience such a salient feature of our lives? Another question: Why is humor enjoyable? Why shouldn't we simply detect jokes without feeling anything? And why do we laugh (as opposed to belching or scratching our ears, say) when something is funny? These questions are vexing, and our inability to answer them with ease seems at first to be due to our inability so far to answer the question that has led to most of the existing research in humor: What is the *essence* of humor? What features are both necessary and sufficient to differentiate between those things that are funny and those that are not? We will argue that this question is ill posed; as usual in the post-Darwinian world of biology, it is a mistake to concentrate on finding presumed essential features since one is more likely to find lineages of similar items, evolving according to changing selectional pressures.

The essentialist quandary has two faces. We've just mentioned the difficulty with defining the features for the category of interest, but on the other side there is danger of conflict with nearby categories that may share some of the same features: In the space of human cognitive traits in the neighborhood of humor we also find such categories as nonhumorous riddles, wordplay, and problem solving, as well as other kinds of appreciation of wit and intellect such as the happiness one feels when witnessing a virtuoso performance. Humor experiences blend in with many of these other kinds of experience without clear boundaries between them. Wordplay can be fun without being funny, and so can fishing or gardening or doing one's job. In every case, there can be relatively intense periods where one's emotion borders on glee, and one may even laugh out of sheer pleasure. There is little prospect of drawing a boundary that separates the subspecies *funny* from the genus *delightful*. They are all cognitive joys of one sort or another. Such categories are notoriously difficult to provide with essences (Wittgenstein 1953; Lakoff 1987). We can replace the essentialist question with an improvement: What makes us feel that some things are funny?

This question calls for some sort of causal answer, in terms of processes going on in our minds, and it is our goal to provide a preliminary sketch of not just a cognitive model, but an emotional and *computational* model of humor. This may seem at first to be not just outrageously ambitious, but positively incoherent. The very idea of a *computational* entity that has a sense of humor has long been considered impossible. Even in science-fiction stories that involve artificially intelligent agents (such as the character Data from *Star Trek*), such characters are typically portrayed as lacking the capacity for emotions in general, and especially for particular behaviors such as humor generation and appreciation.[1] The writers of such stories apparently believe that it is not possible to give these traits to a nonbiological computational agent—or else they are tactically conceding this point of ambient prejudice since overcoming it would require too much expository and justificatory effort. We propose to tackle this prejudice

---

1. But see *Star Trek: The Next Generation*, episode 30: "The Outrageous Okona," in which Data attempts to acquire humor.

head on, arguing that a truly intelligent computational agent could not be engineered *without* humor and some other emotions. These emotions—or their functional equivalents—are requirements of any agent, biological or not, that has human-level intelligence.

When we use the word *computational* here, we intend it more broadly than is typical in cognitive science. We do not yet intend to build a practical testable model, say via neural-network architecture; rather, we are beginning where good design always begins—we want to specify the *functional* requirements of such a computational system so that one day a more technical approach (ideally from computational neuroscience) can provide detailed working blueprints based on the outline we have sketched. We are working toward a theory that would allow humor, as it is experienced—and created—by human beings, to be computed and experienced by a nonhuman agent, a digital machine of some kind that not only can make jokes but that can truly be said to have a "sense of humor" much like the human sense. This is not a straightforward requirement, by any means. At a minimum, it is not sufficient to say that an agent's manifestation of *behavioral expressions* of humor under many or most of the circumstances that elicit such responses in humans indicates a genuine sense of humor in that artificial agent. In order to count as artificial computational humor, the behavioral expression, although necessary as an indicator (how else could it be known that humor was felt?), must also emerge from or be produced by some of the same underlying processing methods and informational contents as natural humor. What aspects of these processes matter? Not the presence of proteins or other biochemical substances, we will argue, but more abstract features of the information-handling processes *and the reasons for their existence*. We will argue that a strict algorithmic approach will be inadequate to imbue an agent with a sense of humor, because the structure of humor is dictated by the riskiness of heuristic processes that have evolved to permit real-time conclusion-leaping, and by the safeguards that have also evolved to protect our minds from these risks. The pivotal causes of genuine amusement and laughter are not simply intrinsic features of the triggering stimuli that are somehow "detected," but *internal* responses that could not be elicited by the triggering stimuli in agents that didn't have a rather specific computational architecture that depends on processes exploited by humorous items.

It will come to light, as we proceed, that computational humor is what we may call an *AI-complete problem*. (In the theory of computation, theorists have developed a classification scheme, in that branch called *complexity theory*, that sorts all computational problems into, roughly, the easy, the hard, and the "impossible." The most difficult set of problems are called *NP-complete problems*—they require nondeterministic polynomial time to solve, in case you wondered—and if you can solve one of them, you should be able to solve them all.) We use the term *AI-complete* to refer to a class of problems that are no less difficult than the problem of *strong AI* (Searle 1980) or general intelligence—if you can solve any one of them, you've done it by making an artificial agent that *really* thinks.[2] Humor, we will argue, depends on *thought*—it is not just a reflexive response to a stimulus that is inherently funny; it requires a certain category of information processing involving most of the faculties of thought, including memory recall, inference, and semantic integration. It follows, then, that our book must sketch a theory of the kind of general intelligence that could support a genuine sense of humor.

Consider, in contrast, some recent attempts at creating computational humor algorithms. These attempts include JAPE and STANDUP (Binsted 1996; Binsted and Ritchie 2001; Ritchie et al. 2006), WISCRAIC (McKay 2000), and HAHAcronym (Stock and Strapparava 2005). All of these models are algorithmic and syntactical in nature—using punning riddles, phonological word substitution, and acronyms, respectively, as a specific grammatical structure of humorous sentence and then making semantic or phonological substitutions out of lexical tables to create the joke. The largest drawbacks of all the models are that they cannot evaluate the humor they have created, nor can they even be said to know in any sense that they are creating humor. In fact, they do not always create humor; rather, at best they have a higher than chance likelihood of creating a stimulus that can evoke a mildly amused response in humans. They have no critical capacity to understand or evaluate the humor created by others, to say nothing of the capacity to be amused by it.[3] Instead of a "sense of

---

2. This complexity class has not been proven to have the property of reducibility that is found in complexity theory; take our comparison metaphorically, for now. We're told that the class of AI-complete problems was first described by Fanya Montalvo. Salvatore Attardo may have been the first to apply the similar term "AI-hard" to humor in his book *Humorous Texts: A Semantic and Pragmatic Analysis* (2001).

3. We are aware of one attempt at computational humor detection: Mihalcea and Strapparava (2005) used Naïve Bayes classifiers and Support Vector Machines to separate "one-liner" jokes from other one-line text snippets with impressive results. However, we must interpret these results carefully; these and other machine classification methods notoriously segment the datasets they are given based on features that are not necessarily apparent to the experimenter. In this case, it is very likely that the superficial content or grammatical structure of these one-liners (rather than their effects on the mind) is enough information to suggest which are jokes and

humor," then, they have a very strict generation algorithm reminiscent of traditional grammar-based natural language processing models. Recent research in sentence comprehension suggests that the grammar-based model of language processing does not describe the human mechanism that performs the same job (Jackendoff 2002). We agree, and we will argue moreover that a nonalgorithmic approach is more suited to the problem of comprehension in general, and to the problem of humor comprehension and appreciation in particular.

As we have said, we do not yet offer any running computational models. Instead, we will show what features a good computational theory should contain, and what subproblems we will have to solve on a path to getting to that theory. Its key novelties are a new evolutionary explanation of the origin of humor; an ecologically motivated theory of the emotional component of mirth; and a cognitive theory of humor and laughter (based on insightful earlier theories, but made more precise here) that lays out some of the informational and procedural requirements for a computational substrate that could support artificial humor. The base capacity for humor, the innate[4] "funny bone" that provides the underlying machinery without which humor could not exist, is described for the first time, but it is only part of the story. We also deal with how the base capacity has been extensively exploited by our highly social species. We show how the intentional stance—the involuntarily adopted perspective that "automatically" attempts to attribute beliefs and desires to every complex moving thing we encounter—has allowed humor purveyors and aficionados to extend the reach of their art. Being funny is not just for fun; humor has been exapted as a tool in mate selection and sexual competition, allegiance

---

which are not—no cognitive processing is being performed whatsoever. Although not an instance of humor detection, such a computational humor indicator is interesting because it points to cues that humans (or machines) can use to determine whether they are being told a joke before they find the humor in it, thus giving them a head start in looking for mirth-inducing content.

4. A note on nativism: We are aware that claims of innateness may immediately offend the sensibilities of many developmentally minded researchers. Those readers will certainly, and correctly, note that many factors about our subject of study—or any biological subject of study—will be determined through environmental interaction during ontogeny. If you are one of these readers, we ask you to withhold your judgment for just a moment, while we explain: There is certainly a complex developmental path from pure genetic information to the behavioral characteristic of humor; however, if environmental regularities ensure that this path is taken in all healthy members of the species so that some fundamental aspect of the trait is shared in us all, then *in a useful manner of speaking*, the trait is innate. In this fairly regular environment, the genes specify the trait.

probing, belief extraction, and the building of social capital, for instance. Our theory is an unabashedly eclectic theory, drawing heavily on existing work on humor while providing a novel unifying framework for that work that accounts both for the patterns already discerned by generations of earlier humor theorists and for their failure to find a satisfactorily deep account of the biological mechanisms that account for those patterns.

Humor is a hard problem. Consider how wildly diverse a collection you can make of funny things:

1. Puns and wordplay
2. The rubber-faced antics of Jim Carrey or the deadpan gestures of Charlie Chaplin
3. Caricatures
4. Situation comedies
5. Musical jokes
6. Cartoons
7. "Real-world" humor, the perhaps uncategorizable *objets trouvés* that occur in daily life, and cause us to laugh, whether or not they get turned into items of comedy

What could these possibly have in common—aside from the fact that they can all be very funny? This baffling diversity (and there's more) tempts everyone to concentrate on a few favored genres that work well for one's theory and set aside the others "for the time being." Moreover, everywhere one looks, one discovers the lack of sharp boundaries or thresholds. For instance, some caricatures are entertaining without being amusing, some provoke a smile or a chuckle, and others are downright hilarious; the spectrum of wordplay runs from intriguing puzzles to laugh-provoking puns, with every intermediate shade well exemplified. To make matters worse, there is tremendous variability in who finds what funny. Humor is heavily dependent on shared background assumptions, moods, and attitudes. Then there are the secondary effects or metaeffects, such as the pleasure that a good joke brings to someone who has heard it before, a pleasure that is less "emotional" than "intellectual"—the appreciation from a critical standpoint of the excellence of design of the particular item. (This is like a chef's pleasure in just thinking about the perfect sauce for some dish.)

Taking the evolutionary perspective seriously is the only way, we think, of finding the unity in this diversity. Before Darwin articulated his theory of evolution by natural selection, life forms were bafflingly diverse— what did they have in common aside from being alive? Darwin drew on a vast repository of excellently observed and codified natural history, a magnificent database waiting to be turned into evidence by a suitably fundamental theory. Following his example, we will canvass the treasury of earlier work on what might be called the natural history of humor, taking advantage of the many insightful analyses and observations to be found there and trying to show how to position them into a theoretical structure that can explain both the patterns and the exceptions.

2 What Is Humor For?

Q: How do you tell the sex of a chromosome?
A: Pull down its genes.

Much of the recent research on humor has been devoted to determining what makes a thing funny (or *how* a particular stimulus makes us laugh). This investigation, while interesting and insightful, is incomplete in that it explores the effects of possible mechanisms of discernment without considering their ultimate purposes. Knowing the purpose of any mechanism can help one understand the operation of that mechanism, while knowing the operation can often make apparent the purpose. Arthur Koestler expressed his own puzzlement about the purpose of humor eloquently:

> What is the survival value of the involuntary, simultaneous contraction of fifteen facial muscles associated with certain noises that are often irrepressible? Laughter is a reflex, but unique in that it serves no apparent biological purpose; one might call it a luxury reflex. Its only utilitarian function, as far as one can see, is to provide temporary relief from utilitarian pressures. On the evolutionary level where laughter arises, an element of frivolity seems to creep into a humorless universe governed by the laws of thermodynamics and the survival of the fittest. (Koestler 1964, p. 31)

Consider the old-fashioned device pictured in figure 2.1. If the purpose is not already known to you, it might take you quite a while to figure out how all the parts interact with gratifying efficiency to peel, core, and slice an apple in one fell swoop. When you know its purpose, its procedures of operation—the affordances it provides within the context of an apple—become obvious, however elusive they were before. A sense of humor is like the apple peeler without any apples around. It is a complex trait, seemingly unique to our species, with some awkward facets that make it look as if it was designed for some very specific purpose that we cannot yet deduce. What could it be for?

Figure 2.1

Sometimes a trait may be something that was an adaptive solution to a problem that now no longer exists. (For example, though effective for our hairier hominid ancestors, goose bumps from a shivering chill, in relatively hairless humans, provide only a futile attempt at trapping an insulating layer of air.) Perhaps humor served a difficult-to-deduce purpose in times past that it no longer is required to serve. (Our sweet tooth no longer serves us well, but it was a fine adaptation in earlier environments. Perhaps our funny bone is like that.) Or perhaps we might discover that evolution did not design the trait at all—it is just a nondebilitating by-product of another trait that *has* enhanced the fitness of the bearer's progenitors. Music appreciation—and the concomitant desire to make music—is a plausible (but contentious) candidate for an example of such a by-product (Patel 2007; Huron 2006; Pinker 1997; Dennett 2006; cf. Levitin 2006).[1] Perhaps humor is like this.

Here is another possibility: If some aspects of our sense of humor were designed, they may have been designed for the benefit of some replicators other than us. The swift, broadband information highway that language

---

1. Though see Minsky 1981 for a conjecture that is quite in line with the current theory of humor in explaining the evolutionary benefit of the joy in music.

provides our species is no doubt a major adaptation, permitting huge amounts of valuable (acquired) information to be transmitted from parents to their offspring, but this highway can also be used by other traffic, such as oblique transmission of possibly maladaptive information by manipulative nonkin (Boyd and Richerson 2005; Richerson and Boyd 2006; Sterelny 2003), and various species of opportunistic *junk*. Just as cold viruses have evolved to exploit the sneezing reflex, the better to broadcast their progeny to infect new hosts, so informational viruses may have evolved to exploit the human dispositions to communicate so as to spread themselves through a population of (amused) hosts. This *meme's eye* perspective (Dawkins 1989, 1993; Dennett 1990, 1991, 1995, 2006; Blackmore 1999) highlights the possibility that our communicative adaptations make available a new kind of niche in which certain kinds of cultural replicators may thrive. Humorous memes seem to be a particularly plausible candidate for fecund cultural replicators that may not be particularly good for us, though they fuel their own replication by providing us with a bounty of pleasure. (It has often been speculated—but not yet proven—that sexually transmitted disease vectors may have adaptations that enhance sexual pleasure or desire and thus promote promiscuity, the better to ensure their own spread to new hosts. Similarly, the pleasure we take in humor may be less a sign that it is good for *us* than that it is good for the replicative prowess of the memes that provoke it, exploiting a susceptibility that evolved for other purposes.)

On the other hand, whether or not humor started out as a neutral or even parasitic cultural symbiont, it may have been appropriated at some point for various fitness-enhancing purposes. An obvious possibility is that human hosts who have a large store of high-quality humor to dispense (and dispense well) are more popular, more likely to influence others, and hence more likely to accumulate the social capital that enhances their reproductive fitness. A more direct link to fitness would be proposed by a sexual selection hypothesis: Females use sense of humor (in males) as a hard-to-fake advertisement of intelligence and power:

> Some theories of humor have proposed that laughter evolved to promote group bonding, discharge nervous tension, or keep us healthy. The more laughter the better. Such theories predict that we should laugh at any joke, however stupid, however many times we have heard it before, yet we do not. A good sense of humor means a discriminating sense of humor, not a hyena-like shriek at every repetitive pratfall. Such discrimination is easy to understand if our sense of humor

evolved in the service of sexual choice, to assess the joke-telling ability of others. (Miller 2000, p. 241)

Since humor is hard to fake, both in the creating and in (the suppression of) appreciation, it is particularly valuable as a litmus test not just for intelligence but for enduring personality traits, hidden loyalties, and socially crucial attitudes and beliefs. A young man who cannot abstain from snickering when presented with a juvenile scatological remark wears his immaturity on his sleeve; people who cannot chuckle at satire when it is deftly on target may betray their political loyalties, just as someone who casually makes a racist quip betrays a cast of mind that might otherwise be concealed. Detecting these signs, and other such practical uses of humor, may well have become established in societies without the (full) appreciation of the individuals who adopt them. Cultural evolution of valuable behaviors such as these does not depend on the behavers' understanding the rationales of their value, any more than cuckoo chicks have to understand the point of their precocious attempts to murder their nestmates in order to get a larger share of the food provided by their foster parents. For instance, people may not have the slightest idea just why they distrust various others who laugh or don't laugh at various moments; these folks just "strike them the wrong way," while others, whose laughter is felt to be genuine and which synchronizes with their own, are sought out and categorized as friends. But before any of these effects can evolve culturally, there has to be a genetically evolved basis with a more fundamental rationale, a proclivity that can be harnessed by these social ends, wittingly or unwittingly.

We think we have identified the core mechanism from which humor indirectly emerges. It is part of our genetic endowment, a design feature that evolved to solve a computational problem faced by our brains that has not heretofore been identified. In short, we have Chevrolet brains running Maserati software, and this strain on our cerebral resources led to the evolution of a brilliant stopgap, a very specific error-elimination capacity that harnessed preexisting "emotional" reward mechanisms and put them to new uses. Using terms that we will explain in due course, here is our theory in a nutshell:

Our brains are engaged full time in real-time (risky) heuristic search, generating presumptions about what will be experienced next in every domain. This time-pressured, unsupervised generation process has necessarily lenient standards and introduces content—not all of which can be properly checked for truth—into our mental spaces. If left unexamined, the inevitable errors in these vestibules of consciousness would ultimately continue on to contaminate our world knowledge store. So there has to be a policy of double-checking these candidate beliefs and surmisings, and the discovery and resolution of these at breakneck speed is maintained by a powerful reward system—the feeling of humor; mirth—that must support this activity in competition with all the other things you could be thinking about.

3 The Phenomenology of Humor

He who laughs last thinks slowest.

In its original meaning, *phenomenology* refers to a reasoned catalog of phenomena—patterns of features or behaviors—in advance of theory. Thus William Gilbert compiled a brilliant phenomenology of magnets— what they do, where they are found, how they can be influenced—in 1600, centuries before there was a good theory of magnetism. Many have tried to produce theories of humor, without much success, but they have left us with the good beginnings of a phenomenology of humor, the set of phenomena—both subjective and objective—that any good theory must account for. We will draw heavily on this work, but none of these writers has yet drawn all the features together in one place, a task which we will attempt to do. We will also draw attention to some features either not mentioned or underappreciated by other theorists, features on the outskirts of humor, or even outside humor altogether, but important, we believe, in understanding the central phenomena.

The dependence of humor on intelligence is made manifest in a variety of English words. *Nonsense* and *absurdity* both play dual roles, alluding to incoherence, contradiction, or ungrammaticality on the one hand—failures of reason in a fairly strict sense—but also being used to characterize amusing anomalies and nonserious wordplay. The absurdity of Albert Camus is not the absurdity of the Marx Brothers, but it takes considerable intelligence to appreciate either of them. The terms *ridiculous* and *ludicrous* remind us that something absurd can be an object of ridicule or mockery. Being a *fool* is being stupid, whereas *playing the fool* can be a demanding exercise of intelligence. When one *feels foolish*, one is embarrassed by one's own display of low intelligence. A quick-*witted* person is smart but not necessarily funny, whereas a *witty* person is endowed with a talent for creating (mainly verbal, intellectual) humor. The witless fool and the witty comedian both have the capacity to make us laugh heartily, one inadvertently and the other intentionally.

A. Humor as a Property of Objects or Events

I wondered why the Frisbee was getting bigger, and then it hit me.

If you tell a joke in the forest, and nobody laughs, was it a joke?
—Steven Wright

As usual, when broaching a puzzling phenomenon about which people have strong convictions and pet theories, we need to say a bit about how we propose to define humor, casting aside some of the misbegotten common conceptions of it. The *Oxford English Dictionary* mirrors common thought when it states that humor is:

a. That quality of action, speech, or writing, which excites amusement; oddity, jocularity, facetiousness, comicality, fun.
b. The faculty of perceiving what is ludicrous or amusing, or of expressing it in speech, writing, or other composition.

The *American Heritage Dictionary* proposes "the quality that makes something laughable or amusing; funniness." There is a tight little circle of definitions that go from *humor* to *funny* and *amusing*, and then to *that which causes laughter*—and when you look up *laughter* you find that it is the expression made when something is funny, amusing, or humorous. From this, and from our daily lives, two apparent truisms emerge: humor causes laughter, and humor is a *quality* of the things that we laugh at. Both truisms are in need of serious adjustment. The first has already been argued against by Provine (2000) and others: Although humor is often followed by laughter, laughter is not always, and is perhaps only seldom, the effect of humor. We will consider these points in due course. Laughter has a variety of causes, and when we look more closely at how (and why) laughter is caused, the idea of humor as a quality of perceived objects and events will also have to be abandoned, or at least transformed into something quite unfamiliar.

The obvious first adjustment to the idea of humor as a quality is to avail ourselves of the familiar distinction, first formulated by Charles Boyle in the seventeenth-century and most famously articulated by John Locke (1690) shortly thereafter, between *primary* qualities like size, shape, and solidity, and *secondary* qualities like color, taste,[1] smell, or warmth, which can be seen to be *dispositions to produce experiences* of certain sorts in organisms of certain kinds. Primary qualities may be thought to be "intrinsic," owing nothing to the idiosyncrasies of any observer, whereas secondary qualities are—and must be—defined and identified by virtue of their common effects on a reference class of (normal) observers. What all red things have in common is just this: They provoke the *red response* (something to be defined in terms of phenomenology, psychology, neurophysiology . . .) in normal human beings, for instance. No matter how similar, chemically or structurally, the surface of B may be to the surface of red object A, if people don't see B as red under normal circumstances, B is not red; and no matter how different the surfaces of A and B may be, if normal human observers can't tell them apart visually and declare them both red, they are both red.

So, is the humor in a joke or cartoon like redness, a Lockean secondary quality? First we should note that humor is definitely not a primary quality of anything, in spite of the conclusion one might uncritically draw from some observations. One of the colloquial views of humor is that it is an intrinsic property of certain things in the world. Jokes have been said to be "context free" in comparison with other speech acts, for instance (Wyer and Collins 1992). But humor is definitely not context free, and it is not a simple intrinsic property of things in the world. We may or may not "see the humor in the situation" depending on the contents of our mind at the time. This is not like failing to appreciate the size or shape of something we see because we are distracted. The joke, rather than being funny intrinsically, can be seen as an object that reliably provokes the sense of humor in a mind.

Humor is like redness in that it is best understood as a product of the way we have been designed by evolution to detect a certain type of information about the world. There is a type of information in the world (information presented to us by what we call red objects) that, because of a cognitive architecture that has evolved for detection of

---

1. The chemical phenylthiocarbamide is often used as a demonstration of this fact: It tastes bitter to the majority of people, but about 30 percent of the population can't taste it at all! Clearly, there is nothing intrinsically bitter about phenylthiocarbamide—it's not that those 30 percent are deficient in being able to taste "phenylthiocarbamide's bitterness." Rather, there is a category of people whose perceptual constitution creates the sensation of bitterness when tasting this chemical, and another category of people, built differently, for whom no bitterness-receptors are activated by this chemical.

exactly this type of information, produces the sense of redness in us. Similarly, there is a type of information in the world (presented by jokes, for instance) that, also because of the architecture that evolved to detect it (among other things), produces the sense of something funny or humorous in us.

In the absence of any object that normally produces redness in us, we can still experience redness. For example, we can experience it while looking at white objects, in a white light that has been filtered by red sunglasses to let only red through. So a red object—an object normally seen as red—is not necessary for the experience of redness. Any object might do. Alternatively, we could trick our minds by closing our eyes and stimulating our optic nerves in the proper manner to make our minds think there is redness somewhere in the world. The only thing that is necessary for an experience (veridical or hallucinatory) of redness is an architecture of sensation and perception designed to detect a certain kind of information, and a history of sensing that kind of information. This history is "practically" necessary because, barring a miracle or cosmic coincidence—of the imaginary sort philosophers are fond of talking out—it is the history of interactions, of use of this kind of information, that shapes the architecture to make it sensitive to just this kind of information.

The same goes for humor. Redness has evolved in plants as a sign to attract pollinators on the one hand or to alert potential grazers to their toxicity on the other, and just as we can't understand what redness has evolved to mean to us and other species by a microscopic examination of the structural details of red surfaces or red pigments, so we will fail to understand humor by a focused and tunnel-visioned examination of the intrinsic or structural features of jokes, funny pictures, and other humorous objects and events.

What does it mean, then, to call something funny? It means that the item in question is a package of information that can reliably be predicted to evoke the humor response in certain people. Likewise, saying that someone is funny means that that person often says or does things that evoke the humor response in people—who have a sense of humor. (Red things don't evoke the red response in those who are color-blind.)

What we are proposing has a kinship with David Hume's account of our experience of causation: We see B following A on many occasions and eventually acquire a disposition to expect B as soon as we encounter A; this feeling of anticipation, which is a habit in us, we tend to misidentify as a direct perception of causation outside us. This foible of externalization or misattribution has many well-known instances, such as when we mislocate our own anger in others. There are even jokes about it: "I think you should stop drinking; your face is getting all blurry." Funny things, we will argue, are like blurry faces—they depend on the subjective state of the audience for their existence. We are going to call this fallacious tendency— to consider the blurriness as a property of the face—*the projection error.*

Consider an example of how the projection error can influence even our scientific inquiries into humor. Provine (1993, 2000) provides some evidence that we laugh at many things that are not humorous. In survey- ing the statements made before laughter during casual settings between friends and strangers at social gatherings, he found that "only about 10 percent to 20 percent of prelaugh comments were estimated by [his] assistants to be even remotely humorous" (2000, p. 40). As it stands, this claim risks serious misunderstanding, since there are at least two distinct kinds of laughter.

B. Duchenne Laughter

> Why do Germans laugh three times when you tell them a joke? First, when you tell it, second, when you explain it, and third, when they get it.

Provine claims that laughter has its own reason for being, and that laughter is neither necessary nor sufficient for humor—and we agree. On the other hand, however, laughter and humor are clearly not disconnected phenom- ena. We want to pursue a somewhat different claim: The relation between humor and laughter has some similarity to the relation between thought and speech. Thoughts "happen in the mind," but their expression in speech acts is usually indirect, monitored, and often censored. There is thought without speech and speech without thought. (As Mose Allison's song puts it, "Your mind is on vacation and your mouth is working over- time.") Laughter and humor also come apart, but in somewhat different ways. Laughter, like speech, must be understood as a social phenomenon, not just a feature of individual psychology or physiology, though its evolved physiological basis is very important.

Let's first review the difference between amused and merely social laughter. Laughter comes in two physiologically distinct varieties: sponta- neous—expressed heartily by smiling and laughing with the brow fur- rowed and the corners of the mouth turned up strongly by pull from the *orbicularis oculi*—and simulated (either consciously or not), in which the orbicular muscle plays little or no part. Guillaume Benjamin Duchenne de Boulogne (1862) first noted this difference in his patients, and so the former variety is now known as *Duchenne laughter*. It has been shown that true enjoyment only occurs with Duchenne laughter, whereas non-Duchenne laughter usually implies some ulterior purpose in laughing other than as an expression of enjoyment. Duchenne's conclusions have been shown to be robust by many studies (Duchenne 1862; Frank, Ekman, and Friesen 1993; Frank and Ekman 1993; Keltner and Bonanno 1997). The Germans in the joke above emit non-Duchenne laughter twice, and Duchenne laughter the third time.

It has been argued that Duchenne laughter may be a reliable indicator of humorous emotion, but (as noted by Gervais and Wilson 2005) Provine doesn't draw the distinction between Duchenne and non-Duchenne laughter, so the possibility that non-Duchenne laughter makes up a portion of his results needs to be investigated. It is also possible, of course, that his data include cases in which non-Duchenne laughter is used to express the detection of humor—for instance, by those who have already heard a joke, or are not particularly amused but wish to support the mood—and this also needs exploration. Answering these questions would require a different and far more difficult methodology from that which Provine has used thus far. Simple observation of when people laugh, and what stimuli preceded the laugh, is a good start, but it will not do for the larger picture. To determine whether there really was humor in the things that subjects laughed at, a researcher would need to interview the people who laughed and ask, one way or another, if they felt that something was funny when they laughed; and, if so, what was funny, and why? (It might not be at all obvious to the researcher, but very obvious to the in-group being studied.) The "what and why" will be a complex tale of semantic integration between speech, memory, gesture, and inference data—not simply a review of the comment made before the laugh. Some of these factors would be very hard, or impossible, to measure experimentally in the natural environment that Provine was collecting his data in. If captured, those data would then need to be further explored experimentally to determine whether the same stimuli, presented in the same order, were objectively funny to other subjects (in various categories, with some level of statistical significance). It would be useful, too, of course, to determine whether the laughter was of the Duchenne variety or not. Although this would not be an easy task, anything less leaves too many important questions unresolved. We think Provine is right that not (quite) *all* of laughter is provoked by humor, but we would expect that much more of laughter would prove to be associated with humor if Provine's experiments were extended in light of these details.

The theory sketched in this book predicts that if someone were to pursue such studies, they would reveal that even non-Duchenne laughter often indicates some level of humor detection by the laugher (according to the definition of humor to be given here). For now let's continue pursuing the hypothesis that we do laugh, at least sometimes, at things that are not humorous. It is difficult to find incontrovertible evidence for this hypothesis, but we will evaluate some prospects here.

The usual anecdote surrounding the behavior of laughing without a proper humor stimulus (often called *inappropriate laughter*) is the idea of laughing at a funeral. However obtrusive or disturbing it is, the "inappropriateness" of this behavior does not imply that there was nothing humorous running through the mind of the laugher. The laugher may be laughing appropriately as the result of any number of humorous thoughts in their internal monologue, or at a bit of public fumbling that is—unfortunately for the solemn occasion—hilarious. What is inappropriate is imposing this reaction on an unreceptive public audience who cannot be expected to share the amusing content.

There is another possible trigger of laughter at funerals—one that arises in other situations as well. We've all experienced laughing in times of nervousness when (apparently) nothing funny has happened. Yet this (anecdotal) evidence is also difficult to distinguish from the humor that may occur internally due to a wandering mind. Among these possible wanderings is laughing at oneself for being inordinately nervous. A different explanation might be that the laughter has been faked (non-Duchenne) for various reasons, including a conscious (or even subconscious) attempt to disarm oneself or one's audience or to mask other perhaps embarrassing emotional expressions.

Further evidence that we have the capacity to laugh in the absence of humor comes from cases of neurological damage as well as studies in neuroscience. Diseases such as Angelman disorder, pseudobulbar palsy, and gelastic epilepsy seem to provide unprovoked laughter, as does Kuru, a prion-based neurodegenerative disease similar to Creutzfeldt–Jakob disease (Provine 2000; Black 1982). Santiago Arroyo and his colleagues report an epileptic patient who presents with frequent seizures that include laughing and crying. The patient self-reports a high level of confusion at her own behavior because she does not feel any level of joy or mirth associated with the laughing (Arroyo et al. 1993). Another patient was observed (Sperli et al. 2006) who would smile and laugh, but reported no sense of mirth whatsoever, when his cingulate cortex was stimulated electrically.

These cases suggest that there is a *functionally* discrete network in the brain that controls laughter and perhaps another that is involved in the feeling of mirth. This is interesting, because although there must be *some* complex causal chain (possibly redundant and replete with recurrent loops[2]) between the discrimination of humor and the normally resulting laughter, absent these indications from neurological irregularity, there would be no strong reason to suppose it was organized into discrete parts that might become dissociated cleanly by pathology. Additionally, the confusion reported by Arroyo's patient indicates a sense that something is wrong when laughter does not accompany mirth, suggesting that even our subconscious understanding is that laughter and mirth are associated.

Lastly, there is research claiming to show that people are prone to laughing in the presence of other laughers even when they are not provided the stimulus that caused the others to laugh. The wide use of television and radio laugh tracks is predicated on research into a related effect, the enhancement of the perception of humor in experienced content by the presence of laughter in others. Provine (2000) removed the confound of associated content by presenting listeners with canned laughter from a laugh-box in the absence of other stimuli. He says that almost half of the student participants in his test, given no humorous content, laughed when they heard the laughter the first time. To be cautious, we should note that it is possible that the idea of someone laughing when nothing seems to be humorous may be found to be humorous itself, and we also need to consider the prospect that this laughter is of the non-Duchenne type. The social demands of the experimental situation may be an additional confound.

All told, there is some evidence, though none is overwhelming, that laughter can occur without humor, but probably not as often as Provine suggests. The question remains whether there is any Duchenne laughter without humor. We are inclined to agree with Gervais and Wilson that

---

2. Parvizi and colleagues (2001) have reported on a patient with pathological laughter and crying disorder who reported that, if his irregularly triggered laughter lasted long enough, he usually began to feel mirth, which indicates the existence of some kind of feedback loop that allows laughter to trigger mirth, even though mirth typically triggers laughter. Researchers have also found evidence that facial expressions including Duchenne smiling and laughing (Laird 1974; Lanzetta, Cartwright-Smith, and Eleck 1976; Soussignan 2002; Strack, Martin, and Stepper 1988) can in fact be *determinants* of emotion. It is not clear why this may be the case, but one idea is that there is a benefit—of commitment—to actually feeling an emotion you may have chosen to fake. It is possible that such reports may someday also help inform an explanation of the mechanism of contagion in laughter.

there is not—except perhaps in neuropathological cases. It is also possible that fabricated, non-Duchenne laughter is frequently conjured intentionally to exhibit appreciation of circumstances that are at least *similar* to humorous ones, or simply very weak forms of humor that don't have the potential to drive us naturally into Duchenne laughter. For instance, you can appreciate the humor in a circumstance—a joke, a line in a comedy, a stereotypic situation—that you find too familiar to evoke genuine mirth in you on this occasion, but you may wish to acknowledge that the occasion really is funny, and join in the laughter. In chapter 12, we will consider whether non-Duchenne laughter may have arisen in an evolutionary arms race: A false display of laughter, if convincing, may help a suitor impress a potential mate.

Nonetheless, the simple existence of volitional (nonspontaneous) non-Duchenne laughter is enough to tell us that not all laughter need be in response to humor. (In Batesian mimicry, a poisonous snake that is brightly marked to warn off predators may be imitated by a nonpoisonous variety that sports the same colors. The warning signal on the nonpoisonous snake is still "about" poison—it is just a false signal. Non-Duchenne laughter can similarly be "about" humor, even when humor is not its direct cause.) On the other hand—we don't need experimental evidence to show us this—we don't always laugh when we do find something funny. For instance, you will encounter jokes in this book that you may find funny to a mild extent and yet they do not make you laugh out loud. (If you want to describe yourself as "laughing on the inside," this is what we call the *feeling* of humor or mirth.) There is apparently something of a continuum: Sometimes we see the humor that others are laughing at but do not find it particularly funny, funny enough to provoke our laughter; other times we find ourselves—for one social reason or another—stifling our urge to laugh, and sometimes this is quite a strain.[3]

Laughter, then, is neither necessary nor sufficient for humor. This double dissociation suggests that laughter exists—or used to exist—for its own purpose aside from humor, that it arose originally to serve other biological, psychological, or social ends and has been exapted into its current normal, but exceptioned, role. Humor cannot be defined simply as what we laugh at, even though—as we all know from our own experience—

---

3. Ekman and Friesen (1971) theorize a similar relationship between all emotions and their expressions, suggesting there is a one-to-one relationship and that although each emotion commonly begets its attendant expression, volitional control can allow us to, at least sometimes, feign or mask these expressions.

laughter consistently accompanies humor. A thorough explanation of humor should give a reason for humor to exist independently of laughter, a separate purpose for laughter, and an explanation of the relationship between the two that describes why laughter normally expresses the detection of humor.

C. The Systematic Ineffability of Humor

Circular definition: *see* Definition, circular.

I don't have to tell you it goes without saying there are some things better left unsaid. I think that speaks for itself. The less said about it the better.
—George Carlin, *Braindroppings* (1997)

We are confronted by a tight circle of interlocking, and hence uninformative, definitions. Humor lies in the recognition—a sense we have in the mind—that something is funny. Funny things provoke the feeling of mirth. Mirth is the response to humor.

Saying, informatively, what humor is proves to be as difficult as saying what redness is. We all know these things well from our own private experience, but something prevents us from engaging in any further analysis of those experiences. It may seem that we are even unable to tell if our own mirth or our subjective experience of red is similar to others'. This is an instance of the notorious philosophical "problem of other minds," and the difficulty defining humor looks suspiciously similar to the particularly frustrating case of the possibility of "inverted qualia" or "inverted spectrum" (see, e.g., Dennett 1988, 1991, pp. 389–398).

The etymology of the term provides an interesting but in the end not very satisfying intuition: The *humors* were, in ancient physiology, the four fluids of the body (blood, phlegm, yellow bile, and black bile). As the proportions of these fluids was thought to determine our temperament, the term *humor* came to be associated with mood—one could be *in good humor*, meaning one's fluids were in balance. Eventually, the word came to be associated primarily with the positive temperament of amusement, as it still is today, but the only insight this chronicle of historical development provides into the nature of the phenomenon is that we use the term to refer to some kind of enjoyment.

We can close in a little on the phenomenology. Mirth—alternatively called amusement or hilarity—is, like most emotions, a graduated phenomenon. It ranges from a gentle tickling of the mind to an intense and overwhelming emotion. It sometimes forces uncontrollable laughter on us, and at other times, when we feel just a mild blush of amusement, we still feel compelled to indicate the feeling with intentional (non-Duchenne) laughter or perhaps just a smile. What is common in all of these conditions is, well, a feeling, the feeling we get about the things we laugh at when we are genuinely entertained. When you "get" a joke, there is enjoyment—including a kind of satisfaction in having figured it out. (We will explore the relation of humor to problem solving and discovery in detail in a later chapter.) Moreover, humor, like beauty, is "in the eye of the beholder." If others say that nothing was funny, one may still be willing to claim that "it was funny *to me*." And if pressed further about why it was funny one may find that one cannot answer, but not be willing to rescind the claim, saying something such as "I'm not sure why it was funny, *it just was*."

Earlier we discussed Arroyo's patient who laughed during seizures without knowing why. Arroyo also reports two patients in whom laughter was elicited through electrical stimulation of the fusiform and parahippocampal gyri. For both of these latter patients, mirth did accompany the elicited laughter, but neither of the patients could specifically attribute the mirth to a particular humorous content. The first made attributions such as "'the meanings of the things changed' in a funny way, and 'things sound really funny,'" whereas the second attributed the mirth to simply a funny feeling, denying any particular thoughts (Arroyo et al. 1993). A similar result was reported many years ago by Wilder Penfield, who, through electrostimulation of the brain in conscious patients, found a region in the frontal lobe that, when stimulated, also caused a patient to laugh (Penfield 1958). Itzhak Fried has duplicated Penfield's findings in a patient undergoing tests for her epileptic seizures. When asked what exactly was making her laugh, the patient invariably announced that it was the particular stimuli she seemed to have been attending to at the moment of the external stimulation (Fried et al. 1998). Electrostimulation can clearly cause spurious or hallucinated feelings of humor, presumably analogous to phantom limb pains, déjà vu experiences (hallucinated feelings of familiarity), and hallucinated odors and auras during epileptic seizures.

The type of feeling we call mirth can be readily enough located in its normal milieu of circumstances and reactions, but we want to know why there should be such a sort of feeling at all—not just what causes the feeling, but *why* those causes provoke such a feeling. Yet, the only access we have to humor is the self-report of its occurrence. Dennett (1991) draws our attention to the inscrutability of the matter with a thought experiment:

There is a species of primate in South America, more gregarious than most other mammals, with a curious behavior. The members of this species often gather in groups, large and small, and in the course of their mutual chattering, under a wide variety of circumstances, they are induced to engage in bouts of involuntary, convulsive respiration, a sort of loud, helpless, mutually reinforcing group panting that sometimes is so severe as to incapacitate them. Far from being aversive, however, these attacks seem to be sought out by most members of the species, some of whom even appear to be addicted to them.

We might be tempted to think that if only we knew what it was like to be them, from the inside, we'd understand this curious addiction of theirs. If we could see it "from their point of view," we would know what it was for. But in this case we can be quite sure that such insight as we might gain would still leave matters mysterious. For we already have the access we seek; the species is *Homo sapiens* (which does indeed inhabit South America, among other places), and the behavior is laughter. (Dennett 1991, p. 62)

What is it like to be a human experiencing humor *"from the inside"*? Attempts to answer for ourselves lead us round and round the circle if we restrict ourselves to what we can "introspect." The question, still conspicuously unanswered, of what all funny things have in common has been called the "central conundrum" of humor research by an anonymous reviewer of our manuscript, and even though there is agreement among many theorists of humor that the answer to this conundrum *must* lie in the internal processes that are provoked in the subject by humorous stimuli, most researchers have simply not been prepared to theorize realistically, and in sufficient detail, about possible cognitive and emotional brain mechanisms churning away behind the veil of conscious access. Faced with the inability to just *see* the internal structure, the decomposition of parts, the way the gears mesh, when people "look inward" at hilarious moments, they often cannot resist the urge to become impromptu theorists. The traditional confound in research that uses this kind of data is that subjects claim to be able to know not only *that* something is funny, but also *why* it is funny. Taking their accounts as authoritative descriptions of humor would oblige us to accept many folk theories, uninformed explanations about what lies behind the invisible wall. An alternative to the traditional phenomenological approach is *heterophenomenology* (Dennett 1991, 2007a), a perspective that accepts people's claims *that* they have a certain phenomenological sense, but reserves judgment about their claims as to *why* they have that sense. Once the claims about how it *seems* to subjects are isolated by the heterophenomenological approach, this opens the path to using other external sources of data (and logical analysis and empirical theory-construction) to explain why in fact people have the phenomenal experiences they do.

The approach this book takes toward explaining what humor is and how it operates will thus not rely on people's reports about how and why they see the humor in jokes. It will be informed by such reports but will not take such data as authoritative or decisive. We will first try to discover the universal features that seem to coincide with the feeling of mirth. Once we have a theory sketch that tells an evolutionarily plausible story about how and why the phenomena might arise, we can begin sketching a blueprint toward engineering an artificial agent that can detect, and respond appropriately to, humor.

D. Funny-Ha-Ha and Funny-Huh

Q: How do you know if the head chef is a clown?
A: When the food tastes funny.

During a lecture the Oxford linguistic philosopher J. L. Austin made the claim that although a double negative in English implies a positive meaning, there is no language in which a double positive implies a negative. To which the philosopher Sidney Morgenbesser responded in a dismissive tone, "Yeah, yeah."

As already mentioned, there is an undeniable similarity between the joy of humor and the joy of problem solving. When we "get" a joke we feel a sense of discovery rather like the sense of triumph when we solve a problem. And when we are unable to solve a problem, there is a sense of confusion or missing knowledge that is reminiscent of the feeling we get when we are unable to get a joke.

The multiple senses of the English word *funny* may help prime an intuition about humor and its relation to these and other feelings. The primary sense is the one we have already been discussing: that synonymous with *humorous*, the provoker of the emotion of mirth. The second sense of the word *funny* is more subtle: We use the word at times when we don't feel like laughing but rather find some event or state of the world to be unusual or strange in a mildly disturbing way. Unexpected discoveries, such as coming home to find the lights on when you know you left them off, can cause this feeling and make us say, "That's funny, I remember turning them off . . ." The joke about the clown chef is a pun that depends on our understanding of both senses of the word. (A third, closely related, sense just means peculiar or atypical, as in a funny [looking] tree or snowdrift or pebble. Whether the anomaly is in any way noteworthy or threatening is another matter.)

Related to this second sense is one of trickiness or deceitfulness. The old lady next door asks the kids, "What kind of funny business are you up to?" when she sees them skulking around, planning something secret. The question implies that she is suspicious, not that she expects to be amused. Another example offers yet another shade of meaning: "Doctor, my head is feeling funny." In this patient's claim, *funny* is used to mean "My head is feeling a way that I am unfamiliar with, a way that I am suspicious of." The adjective *funny* in both senses—"funny-ha-ha" and "funny-huh"—is applied colloquially to the noun *bone* to produce strikingly different meanings: Your *funny bone* is the unprotected part of the ulnar nerve by the elbow; when you hit your funny bone, especially the first time it happens as a child, the feeling is anything but laughable; but you may also speak of your sense of humor as your funny bone (parallel to your sweet tooth).

Are these secondary uses of *funny* just a lexical coincidence, like the fact that *bank* can mean a river's margin or a financial institution, or might there be a deep relation between them? We will argue that, somewhat surprisingly, there is indeed an important clue lurking in this family of meanings, one that is not restricted to English.

An informal survey of linguists and native speakers of a number of languages shows that, although far from universal, it is quite common for there to be a term for funny-ha-ha that carries a second sense that means something along the lines of unusual, strange, unexpected, illogical, or senseless. In Mexican Spanish, although not in other dialects, we find that two words each carry this meaning. The first, *chistoso*, is used in the following ways:

(A) "¡Que chistoso! Pensé que habia cerrado la puerta pero ahora esta abierta," which is translated as "How strange! I thought that I'd closed the door, but now it's open."

(B) "Ayer vi una pelicula muy chistosa," which means "Yesterday I saw a very humorous movie."

The second term is *gracioso*, which can be substituted into the same sentences and offers the same two senses but with a more formal flavor:

(A') "¡Que gracioso! Pensé que habia cerrado la puerta pero ahora esta abierta."

(B') "Ayer vi una pelicula muy graciosa." Or: "Ayer vi una pelicula que me hizo mucha gracia."

In a very regional dialect of Argentine Spanish, we have been told, the word *loco*, which primarily means crazy or insane (a type of senselessness), can be used to describe both things that are found to be out of the ordinary and things that are humorous.

In (Brazilian, if not all) Portuguese, the word *engraçado* does both these jobs. Apparently, it is rather significant—not definitive, but an aid to disambiguation—to alter the intonation and speed of pronunciation of the word to change its sense. Said quickly and lightly, it means funny-ha-ha— "Este filme é mesmo muito engraçado!" ("This movie is really funny")—but spoken slowly and deliberately and intoned with a bit of confusion usually implies the second sense—"En-gra-ça-do, eu achei que tinha deixado a minha chave na bolsa . . ." ("Funny, I thought I had left my keys in my purse . . .").

The French have a number of words with this property too. First, the word *drôle* carries those two senses exactly. The word *marrant* also means humorous, and, although it doesn't conventionally mean "strange," it can be used with that implication in many contexts (e.g., "that's *marrant*, I could have sworn my keys were on the table"). The word *rigolo* has similar usages as well. In German the word is *komisch*, and is used commonly in both senses: A joke can be *komisch*, or one could say "that's *komisch*, I thought I left my keys right here." In Greek, the same term is αστείο (*astio*), while γέλιο (*gelio*), the term for laughter, is clearly tightly related to γελοίος (*gelios*), the word for ridiculous. This is the same in Hungarian, which uses *nevetség* for scornful laughter and *nevetséges* for ridiculous. While *komisch* and αστείο connect "funny" to "strange," the extensions of the multiple senses of *gelios* and *nevetséges* show the link between the senseless or ridiculous and the laughable. It is a short semantic step from the kind of strangeness or sense of unusual/unexpectedness that is carried by the English term funny-huh to the kind of senselessness or sense of irrational/unexpectedness that is carried by *nevetséges* and *gelios* (in their second senses). Hungarian has another word, *vicces*, which commonly means "humorous" or "funny" but can also (though, only occasionally, we are told) be used to mean "puzzling," as in "That's *vicces*, I thought the lights were off when we left."

Other related senses for words that mean funny can be found too. In Bulgarian, the word смешно (*smeshno*), translated directly as "humorous," can also be used to mean stupid or irrational. For instance, "Смешно е да се мисли, че това може да е така" ("*Smeshno* e da se misli, che tova moje da e taka") means "It's stupid/ridiculous to think that this could be so," and "Не мислиш ли, че е смешно да искаш такива неща?" ("Ne mislish li, che e *smeshno* da iskash takiva neshta") translates to "Don't you think it's absurd to want such things?" Смешной (*smeshnoy*) in Russian does the same job, and *derîs* in the Moldovan dialect of Romanian is quite the same. Another Russian word, курьезный (*kurieznii*), reminds us of a related English word, *curious*. In Russian, as well as in English, the term can be used to describe a strange or outlandish incident that may provoke a smile or laugh—one could say "a *kurieznii* thing happened on the way to the forum" and then go on to tell an actually funny story of the incident.

The trend is also found in some Asian languages. The Japanese have a similar word for funny which has a second sense that is subtly related to *gelios* and *nevetséges*. Their word, おかしい (*o-ka-shi-i*), is used in the following two sentences:

(C) 彼はおかしい人ですね 。

(D) 彼の頭はおかしい 。

In the first sentence, the word provides the meaning "He is a humorous person, isn't he?" In the second sentence, the translation, we are told, is more or less like "There's something wrong with his head," implying that he is being irrational in some way. In Korean, the word 웃기다 (*woot ggi da*) also carries both the senses of the English word *funny*. It can be used in the primary sense to say simply, "That's *woot ggi da*," meaning the foregoing situation was humorous. In the secondary sense the usage can be, "That's *woot ggi da*, I thought I left my keys right here on the table," where *woot ggi da* is translated as something akin to "unusual" or "strange."

This collection of terms is the result of an informal survey, not a rigorous linguistic exploration, and we have not even begun the glossogenetic inquiry to determine whether the two senses for these terms in each language emerged in isolation from the other languages. Whether this is convergent cultural evolution with many independent adoptions of meanings, or the result of a few particularly persistent threads of inherited meaning, the sheer volume and variety of responses[4] and the fact that modern speakers of these languages seem eminently comfortable with the relationship should stimulate the intuition that there's something funny about the word "funny."

---

4. The terms reported here reflect about 60 percent of our respondents. We were told (not conclusively, mind you) that there is no term that serves this double meaning in Chinese, Thai, Dutch, European Spanish, or Czech.

E.   The Knowledge-Relativity of Humor

What do Alexander the Great and Winnie the Pooh have in common?
They both have the same middle name.

The humor of a situation is dependent upon knowledge that you may or
may not have.

You can tell a joke in one crowd and be rewarded with laughs, yet in
another group be repaid with anger.[5] Here's a joke that some find funny,
though others might not agree and some may even be offended:

(1)   Q: What has two legs and bleeds?
    A: Half a dog.

Perhaps only those who are able to distance themselves from any emotion
while hearing this joke find it humorous.

Much humor is culturally specific. In the most extreme case it depends
on features of a particular language, including puns, rhymes, grammatical
constructions, or homonymy. This type of humor cannot easily survive
translation. Here is an example:

(2)   A: 昨日鎌倉でおしゃれなタケの箸を売ってる店があったよ。
    B: へ それで? 何か買った?
    A: なんにもタケの箸は5000円もするんだ! これタケ なと思った!

    A: Yesterday in Kamakura there was a shop selling stylish bamboo
    chopsticks.
    B: Did you buy any?
    A: Nope, those bamboo chopsticks cost 5000 yen! Expensive!

The humor from this joke derives from the fact that in Japanese, the words
for *bamboo* and *expensive* are homonyms. Other jokes can be translated
without loss, but depend for their humor on background information that
is restricted to one culture. Consider, for instance, the joke translated
below.

(3)   엄마한테 혼날걸 뻔히 알면서 소금물이랑 맑은 물을 계속 섞어대는
사람이 어딨어?!

---

5. We concentrate on jokes as examples in this book not because all humor is jokes—think of
comedies from Aristophanes to *The Office*—but because jokes are compact, self-contained mirth-
delivery systems that require little or no context, and hence enable us to focus instantly on the
fundamental machinery in action.

Who in their right mind mixes salt water and clean water back and forth knowing his mother will give him a beating?!

We have been told that this can be funny to Koreans of middle- or high-school age because of three pieces of cultural information: First, in Korean schools there is a common type of mathematics word problem that involves mixing salt water and fresh water to calculate proportions. Second, it is obvious to Koreans that you would do this (mix salt and fresh water) in the kitchen. And, third, Korean children wouldn't dare make messes in their mothers' kitchens. Given this background information, an English speaker can understand why the statement is funny to Koreans, but is very unlikely to feel the humor.

This draws attention to another important feature of humor: It is not just dependent on background knowledge; the *way* that background knowledge is exploited is critical. This is why explaining a joke drains it of its humor. It is typically the case that telling a joke in the wrong order ruins it.

(4)   A man walks up to a hot dog vendor and says "make me one with everything." Oh, and the man is a Buddhist.[6]

Dennett (1987, p. 76) notes that many jokes are *enthymematic*. That is, they depend on leaving one or more "premises" tacit or unexpressed. In a successful telling of the joke, the enthymematic expression provokes the audience to "fill in" an implication or assumption, or even a series of assumptions, without which no humor can be detected.

(5)   A man went to visit his friend the Newfie [Newfoundlander, a traditional ethnic slur of Canadians] and found him with both ears bandaged. "What happened?" asked the man, and his friend replied, "I was ironing my shirt and the phone rang."—"That explains one ear, but what about the other?"—"Well, I had to call a doctor!"

This joke would be diminished or ruined by explicit mention of any of the many facts one needs to know in order to get it. Indeed, this joke is fast on its way to extinction, because few telephones these days have a shape and heft similar to an iron, and for that matter many young people today have never seen anyone ironing clothes. You will have to explain it to your

---

6. The standard joke is, of course, "A Buddhist walks up to . . . ." We've recently heard this amusing extension: When the hot dog vendor hands him a hot dog, the Buddhist pays and asks for his change. The vendor smiles and replies, "Change comes from within."

grandchildren: "Well, back in the old days, telephones were hefty, stationary things, with a corded piece you grabbed *like so*, more or less the way you had to grab the handle of an iron, another corded piece of metal of some weight that has a very hot surface when you use it—hot enough to burn flesh." At that point it would be about as funny to them as the Korean joke is to us.

In-group humor among people of the same religion, hobby, or profession is an extreme example of this highly specific knowledge-dependence. For instance, among computer engineers there is the following joke:

(6) There are only 10 kinds of people in the world—those who read binary and those who don't.

If you don't know that "10" is the binary representation of the number 2, you are left wondering what the other eight kinds of people are.[7]

In the limiting case, there are instances of humor that have single individuals as their sole target audience, depending as they do on allusions to or tacit assumptions about particular events in that person's private biography. This accounts for the phenomenon of the lone chuckler who declines to tell an inquirer what they are laughing about; it really was funny *to them*, but they'd have to explain it, and then it wouldn't be funny. One can only laugh about what one can think about *in a particular order and way*. The folk notion that humor is "universal" is actually an artifact of a misunderstanding of statistical samples: since *most* of the people we encounter in contexts where humor might arise do share a massive amount of common knowledge with us, the idea that *everybody* would see the humor in anything that was "really funny" naturally arises and seems to receive confirmation. Then it is puzzling to us—but shouldn't be—when we encounter putative examples of humor that depend on shared knowledge that we don't share. It is not that Koreans have a weird sense of humor; it is simply that they share knowledge with each other that we don't share with them.

Ted Cohen (1999) gives us the joke about Winnie the Pooh, and goes on to observe:

> Of course I want you to like the one about Winnie the Pooh. I want you to like
> it because I like you and I want you to have something you like, and I want you

---

7. This joke is a rarity in that it only works in a written (and silently read!) format. How should one pronounce "10"? If you say "There are only *ten* kinds of people in the world . . ." the joke is destroyed; and if you say "one-zero" the humor of the joke is given away before it can be discovered.

to be grateful to me for supplying it. But I also need you to like it, because in your liking it I receive a confirmation of my own liking. I put this by saying that the joke is *funny*, as if this were an objective matter; like there being damned little sand along the coast of Maine, but what I mean is that I laugh at it, and if everyone laughed at it, then it would really *be* funny (or as good as funny), and I do so want you to laugh at it. (Cohen 1999, pp. 31–32)

His last point is slightly mistaken. He shouldn't mean that if *everyone* laughed at it, then it would *really* be funny; what he means (or ought to mean) is that if everyone *"like us"* laughed at it, then it would really *be* funny—to us, and we're the ones who count right now. The fact that something is *really funny* to a select reference class of appreciators is just as objective as the fact that ripe tomatoes are *really red* (to normal human observers).[8]

F. Mating and Dating

Two behaviorists lie in bed after making love. One of them says to the other, "That was good for you, how was it for me?"

You know "that look" women get when they want sex? Me neither.
—Steve Martin (quoted in Carr and Greaves 2006, p. 140)

Provine (2000) draws attention to one more feature ignored by many earlier theories of humor: gender differences. In his studies of conversational laughter, female listeners laughed far more often than did male listeners, regardless of the gender of the speaker, and male speakers were met with far more laughter than female speakers by either gender of listener. Moreover, in personal ads more than twice as many women as men seek "a sense of humor" or someone who will make them laugh (Smith, Waldorf, and Trembath 1990). Women also tend to seek humor more than offer it, whereas men are more likely to offer a sense of humor than to seek it, in both their ads and natural conversation (Crawford and Gressley

---

8. It is often observed that the large literature on humor is remarkably solemn, and the jokes discussed are typically lame at best. But before we go searching for an explanation of why people with no comedic talent or taste are drawn to humor theory, we should note that, as this chapter explains, humor travels poorly, in both space and time. We have no doubt at all that many of the examples of humor we have included here will fall like bricks outside the rather narrow circle of early twenty-first-century Anglophone academics and other well-informed bookreaders, our primary intended audience.

1991; Provine 2000). Bressler, Martin, and Balshine (2006) found that when further interrogated, men reported that their view of a woman with a good sense of humor is, in effect, a good humor appreciator, whereas women reported that their view of a man with a good sense of humor is a good producer. Provine also reports studies that observe the dating behavior of men and women, showing a positive correlation between the amount of female laughter and the self-reported level of desire of both men and women to meet again.[9]

Other researchers have found a further gender divide in production performance: McGhee (1976) reports that boys (between the ages of 6 and 11) attempt to initiate humor significantly more than girls of the same age group (see also Goldstein and McGhee 1972; McGhee 1979; Chapman, Smith, and Foot 1980; and Ziv 1984). Weisfeld (1993) notes, though, that the early developmental pattern of male humor production coincides rather well with the stabilization of dominance hierarchies in children and thus may simply be an artifact of the latter (see also Omark, Omark, and Edelman 1975). Additionally, Greengross (under review) provides evidence that cartoon captions written by men, as opposed to those written by women, were rated as funnier by independent blind judges of both genders. Of course, this may not indicate natural differences in capacity, but rather that men may have more practice at the skill, or even just that they may try harder at the task.

For humor appreciation, at least, the gender differences are also reflected in brain activity: While engaging in a cartoon-rating task during functional magnet resonance imaging (fMRI), aside from many shared regions of activity, women were shown to have greater activation than men in the left prefrontal cortex (PFC) as well as in mesolimbic structures including the right nucleus accumbens (NAcc) (Azim et al. 2005). The authors suggest that this indicates women use more language and executive processing (as per the PFC activation) during humor comprehension and have less reward prediction (in the NAcc) and thus more predictive error signal at the actual reward. Whether or not these conclusions hold up, the neurophysiological differences they found do indicate some gender disparity.

Taken together, these studies suggest, if nothing more, that being funny is at least a desirable trait for men, and appreciating men's sense of humor is a desirable trait for women. These curious facts will be addressed later in the book.

---

9. These effects may be culture dependent. Most of this work, to date, has been performed in a Western cultural context.

4 A Brief History of Humor Theories

A gentleman entered a pastry-cook's shop and ordered a cake; but he soon brought
it back and asked for a glass of liqueur instead. He drank it and began to leave
without having paid. The proprietor detained him. "You've not paid for the
liqueur." "But I gave you the cake in exchange for it." "You didn't pay for that
either." "But I hadn't eaten it."

—Freud (1905); also cited by Minsky (1984)

Many theories of humor have been offered over the centuries, and each
seems right about some aspect or type of humor while overlooking, or
being just wrong about, the rest. Ideally one would like to combine their
strengths and compose a full theory that can explain all aspects of humor
in a unified way. Although most overviews list three categories of humor
theory (*superiority, release,* and *incongruity*), Patricia Keith-Spiegel (1972)
gives an analysis that arrives at eight primary categories, each of which
treats some aspect of humor capably. Combining and adjusting these
categories, and updating them with an analysis of more recent work, we
can get a bird's-eye view of the terrain. Though the boundaries are rather
fuzzy and the blending together of some cases is common, the primary
categories are: *biological, play, superiority, release, incongruity-resolution,* and
surprise. We'll mention a few other views that resist categorization but
introduce elements that shouldn't be ignored.

A. Biological Theories

Instead of working for the survival of the fittest, we should be working for the
survival of the wittiest—then we can all die laughing.

—Lily Tomlin

Biological theories are motivated by the observation that humor and
laughter are innate. Each notes that laughter appears spontaneously in

early infancy (and even in congenitally blind and deaf children—see, e.g., Thompson 1941; Eibl-Eibesfeldt 1973), and that the existence of humor is universal throughout human cultures (although it varies in its manifestations). The fact that laughter and humor seem to have positive physiological effects is sometimes cited as further grounds for seeing humor as a genetic adaptation, but this claim, tempting as it may be, is unwarranted. Why couldn't people—whole societies—have stumbled upon a practice that had positive physiological effects but did not have an instinctual foundation? It might be passed on for its (apparent) good effects whether or not these were understood or underwritten by an instinct. Suppose it is true that an apple a day keeps the doctor away, and imagine that we all ate apples daily and thrived thereby. We wouldn't need an apple-eating instinct to account for this regularity—culture alone might suffice.

If laughter and humor were selected for, the traits must have had a raison d'être, served an adaptive function, and the blueprint for these "instincts" must have been somehow encoded in our genes. Keith-Spiegel cites some instinct theories that have emotional components, such as the hypothesis that laughter (incited by a sense of the ludicrous) is a corrective for the depressing effects of sympathy. Others, of varying plausibility, propose that "laughter and humor are but *vestiges* of archaic adaptive behaviors" (Goldstein and McGhee 1972, 6), such as the hypotheses that laughter was originally a signal of safety to the group, an expression of unity in group opinion prior to language, or a relic of fighting behavior. These explanations begin to probe the important question of what benefits humor and laughter could have conferred upon our predecessors, but a more detailed analysis of the underlying mechanisms will provide better clues. These biological theories all treat laughter as a communicative expression of the recognition of humor, and each one attempts to build a communication-centered explanation of the benefit of laughter. This idea is in some regards a good one, and we will keep it in mind when we later explain laughter; but as Provine emphasizes—and we agree—humor and laughter are not as coextensive as once believed.

B. Play Theories

> When I was young we were so poor that if I hadn't been a boy, I'd have had nothing to play with.
>
> —Dickie Scruggs, quoted by Peter Boyer in "The Bribe," *New Yorker*, May 19, 2008[1]

---

1. Humor can be touchy. Jokes are not always in good taste. We decided, while writing this book, that avoiding any particular kind of humor—even distasteful and prejudiced

Play theories are an important subcategory of biological theories, and the first of them was proposed by Darwin himself (Darwin 1872), who said that humor was a "tickling of the mind." Ernst Hecker (1873) proposed quite the same thing, and the suggestion that there is a similarity or identity between the underlying mechanisms of tickling and humor has since come to be known as the Darwin–Hecker hypothesis (e.g., Fridlund and Loftis 1990; Harris and Christenfeld 1997).[2] Gervais and Wilson (2005) recently seconded this, arguing that both humor and tickling are causative of Duchenne laughter and that there is an "undeniable relationship" between the laughter that results from jokes, tickling, rough-and-tumble play, and even infant laughter that results from such things as peek-a-boo. Given that some species of apes also produce a kind of repetitive noise similar to laughing when tickled, and that they try to tickle each other sometimes, it is highly likely that laughter due to tickling was phylogenetically prior to other uses of laughter, including modern humor (Provine 2000).

Play theories on the whole tend to focus on the connection between laughter—not humor—and play. More recently, though, theorists have claimed that the laughter from humor is associated with the laughter from tickling (the natural bridging-concept between play and humor) (Ramachandran and Blakeslee 1998; Ramachandran 1998; Provine 2000; Gervais and Wilson 2005). There is no suggestion within these theories that play *is* humor, just that humor evolved out of play and has thus

---

forms—would be, in some way, "biasing the data." That last phrase is in scare-quotes because, of course, we haven't used any advanced data analysis methods with statistical tests here—this is *theoretical*, not experimental, cognitive science (analogous to the same distinction in the discipline of physics). But, nonetheless, in order to avoid biasing our theoretical analysis of the phenomena we wanted ourselves, and our readers, to engage with all humor: racist, sexist, religion-ist; crude and clean alike. In doing so, we ran across some gems in every genre. And, in our writing, we found a number of very relevant, yet crude or sexist, epigraphs for sections of this book, which we eventually (at the suggestion of some reviewers) chose to omit. Some others (see the above, or chapter 5, e.g.) were retained in the main text, perhaps against better judgment, in order to offer a balanced review.

2. The Darwin–Hecker hypothesis has recently found some experimental support. Fridlund and Loftis (1990) found a significant correlation between self-reported susceptibility to tickling and self-reported tendencies to laugh, and Harris and Christenfeld (1997) demonstrated that individuals who are objectively more ticklish, in that they are observed to laugh more, also produce more laughter when viewing comedy. Both studies measured *expression*, not mirth, so they are not conclusive, but they are insightful. Harris and Christenfeld also found evidence against the Darwin–Hecker hypothesis, which they consider stronger. We take this issue up later when we discuss tickling in more detail.

maintained the similar expression. For instance, Gervais and Wilson (2005) suggest that Duchenne laughter promoted social play during early bipedal life and that "a general class of nonserious social incongruity," which indicated times of relative safety, began to be a useful elicitor of this laughter. This nonserious social incongruity has evolved into our modern humor. This is an interesting hypothesis, but it is unclear how detection of a nonserious social incongruity can assure you of safety. One might think that hominids at play—and laughing—expose themselves to attacks from outsiders and predators by being louder and paying reduced attention to possible threats. There should be some benefit to humor and laughter other than simply stating that it "seems relatively safe." Still, the link between play, tickling, and humor pointed out by Gervais and Wilson is undeniable and needs to be accounted for. It is possible that humor developed for another purpose and then appropriated aspects of the apes' play behavior. Perhaps, for instance, as Gervais and Wilson and others (Eastman 1936) suggest, the use of laughter to *express* humor evolved from its use in facilitating nonaggression in play and tickling.

Play theories of humor recognize that we need an explanation of how humor developed evolutionarily, how laughter came to express humor, and what the relationship between tickling and humor is. All of these relationships should be accounted for by a complete theory of humor.

C. Superiority Theories

Texan: "Where are you from?"
Harvard grad: "I come from a place where we do not end our sentences with prepositions."
Texan: "Okay—where are you from, jackass?"

The only thing that sustains one through life is the consciousness of the immense inferiority of everyone else, and this is a feeling that I've always cultivated.
—Oscar Wilde

Superiority theories are presided over by Thomas Hobbes's definition of laughter as a "sudden glory" or triumph that results from the recognition or sense that we have some level of superiority or eminency over some other target, the butt of the joke, as we say, or the protagonist in some humorous episode. Humor's role is to point out problems and mistakes for the purpose of boosting one's current view of oneself in comparison with the disparaged party. Hobbes tells us that the target can even be an earlier version of oneself as long as one has overcome the infirmity at which one is laughing (Hobbes 1840). Aristotle, too, supported a similar theory, saying that humor is the recognition of a failing or a piece of ugliness, resulting from an implied comparison between a noble state of a person or thing and an ignoble state.

Certainly a vast quantity of jokes and social instances of laughter fit well under this rubric. We often laugh *at people*. And the implied superiority is what makes sense of the familiar disclaimer: I'm not laughing *at* you; I'm laughing *with* you (or: I'm laughing at myself, or: at the situation). The pleasure of trouncing an opponent in competition is often expressed with a triumphant laugh. We laugh at the behavior of drunkards or fools, and ignorant and ill-mannered folks are known to laugh at the plight of the disabled (not to mention that the genetically or developmentally deformed were once employed alongside jesters for exactly this purpose). Schoolyard taunting, too, is often if not exclusively derisive in nature. Laughing, especially in social settings, typically does imply membership in an elite group—those who laugh at this matter in some way, in contrast to those whose acts and circumstances are the occasion for the laughter—and this is no doubt often reassuring, and hence pleasurable, to the laughers, but it is still far from clear that humor exists for the purpose of generating such feelings of superiority.

Here are some jokes that exemplify the superiority theories:

(7) Four surgeons were taking a coffee break and were discussing their work. The first said, "I think accountants are the easiest to operate on. You open them up and everything inside is numbered."

The second said, "I think librarians are the easiest to operate on. You open them up and everything inside is in alphabetical order."

The third said, "I like to operate on electricians. You open them up and everything inside is color-coded."

The fourth one said, "I like to operate on lawyers. They're heartless, spineless, gutless, and their heads and their asses are interchangeable."

(8) When asked his opinion, in 2005, about the *Roe v. Wade* decision, President Bush responded that he "didn't care how they got out of New Orleans."

Other jokes are hard to explain under such a model:

(9) Theater sign typo: Ushers will eat latecomers.

Neither the ushers (who don't intend to eat latecomers) nor the latecomers (who don't fear, or deserve, being eaten) are being laughed at. A careful supporter of superiority theory might argue that we are laughing at the incompetence of the person who mis-lettered the sign, but the flaw may not be attributable to a mistake by the sign-maker—we could as easily imagine the letter "s" falling off the sign, or even being removed by a mischievous teenager, and we would still find the sign comical. It seems more reasonable that we are laughing at the disparity between what we recognize that the sign should say and the unexpected meaning found in the actual sign. Such a large effect created by such a small change! Some puns are equally hard to fit into the mold:

(10)   Two goldfish were in their tank.
          One turns to the other and says, "You man the guns, I'll drive."

Eastman (1936) points out one more place where there is clearly no derision in humor. He remarks, "I suspect [superiority theorists] not only of never having seen a baby, but of never having been one." Anyone who recognizes the naïve enjoyment of babies and children or who recollects their own such episodes should carefully reassess their superiority theory to perhaps exclude this category of humans.

Superiority theory has had many proponents over the years, and is perhaps the second most popular explanation for humor, for good reason. It covers a large proportion of instances, enough to motivate some theorists to work hard to shoehorn the awkward remainder (see Bain 1875, for example)—but with diminishing persuasiveness. The claim that a value judgment is implied in all humor may owe much of its plausibility to the fact that judgment is involved in just about every conception one can have. To identify a thing (as an F or a G), perceived or conceived, is always to raise the issue of whether it is a good or bad F, an exemplary G or at least a good G for our purposes. Moreover, the disparagement based on this judgment, so typically found in humor, is not a sufficient requirement for humor. There is derision in many instances of human communication that is not humorous and is not expected to elicit laughter in anyone. Not all comparative value judgments are grounds for ridicule.

The core weakness of superiority theory, however, is that although it provides a generic reason underlying much (if not all) humor, it does not provide a *mechanism* of humor, and thus it also doesn't provide a reason for the reason! It tells us that (in fact) we laugh when something makes us feel superior; but what makes us do that, and why? What benefit do we get from having a strong disposition to express a feeling of superiority? Could the question betray a mistaken assumption? Might humor have never had any purpose at all and simply be a universal glitch in our nervous systems, a "frozen accident," to use Francis Crick's term for something fixed in our genes by historical happenstance, a mutation that survived for no reason at all? This is *logically* possible, of course, but why should this accident have persisted in just one species of mammal, and why hasn't it been selected against?

A thorough superiority theory should at least address the question of what the adaptive significance of our sense of humor might be, but such a theory has never been offered. Such a theory would need to explain (1) how we come to the realization that someone or something is lesser in some way; (2) how we distinguish the humorous instances of these value comparisons from the others; (3) what purpose is served by our normal enjoyment of such discriminations; and (4) what purpose is served by communicating this through laughter. If we have evolved such a discrimination-leading-to-laughter system in our brains, we need to ask what boost to reproductive fitness this system confers on those who have it. To first appearances, such a system would appear to be an extravagant waste of both emotional and communicative energy, and moreover might encourage risky delusions of superiority, luring an agent, too boldly, into danger.

Still, the motivation for the superiority theory is a good one. It reminds us that we do feel pleasure in humor—laughing is not like a reflex knee-jerk, however automatic it may be. And it highlights the fact that humor is used competitively, even if this was not its original or grounding function. Humor points out failures, as Aristotle told us; we use it to point out each others' failures, and perhaps the competitive nature of humans that has always existed for other reasons co-opted humor for this purpose. Finally, and most importantly, it draws our attention to the role of negative value judgments in humor. But what are we judging to be somehow flawed? Superiority theory sees the fault in the butt or target of the humor, but we will argue that the fault lies in ourselves, in our dynamic models of the world and its denizens, and recognizing this, and correcting it, is the occasion for the intense pleasure, the "sudden glory," of humor. Our tendency to perceive humor in the faults and mistakes of others is parasitic on our capacity to detect such flaws in ourselves, and the transfer or externalization highlighted by superiority theories has its own reasons for occurring.

D. Release Theories

> Last night I made a Freudian slip. I was having dinner with my mother, and I
> wanted to say, "Please pass the butter," but it came out as, "You bitch, you ruined
> my life!"

Release theories construe humor as a form of relief from excessive nervous
arousal. Keith-Spiegel separates the psychoanalytic theory of humor from
release theories, but we will discuss them together.[3] In general, release
theories claim that tension from thought can build up, and when this
tension is released by a positive emotion that results from further thought,
the energy is transformed into (or spent by) laughing. Herbert Spencer's
(1860) version of this theory spoke of purposeless nervous energy that
needed an outlet. Freud's version (Freud 1928, as cited in Keith-Spiegel
1972) works on the principle that certain events create repressed sexual
and/or aggressive energy, and when that tension is undone in a dramatic
way (suddenly or surprisingly), rather than gradually, the nervous energy
is released, and relief ensues in the form of humor. This builds on his earlier
(1905) theory of jokes, which indicated that they were one way to overcome our internal mental censors that forbid certain thoughts—the joke,
by fooling the censor, allows the repressed energy to flow, thus creating
the pleasure of mirth and releasing that energy through laughter.

Release theory has lost popularity for a variety of reasons. First, in the
information age, the metaphor of psychic energy, and the tensions and
pressures that build up as this ghostly gasoline accumulates in the imagined plumbing and storage tanks of the mind, seems old-fashioned and
naïve. Why would one build up a special reserve of a strange kind of *energy*,
and where would one save it, instead of simply dissipating it in the first
place? Perhaps, though, with the increased recognition of the importance
of neuromodulator imbalances, and the appreciation of the opponent
processes that work to achieve homeostasis among all the different participant systems, aspects of these quaint theories can be rehabilitated and put
to good use. Relief from what we still call *tension* (in spite of abandoning
the pseudo-physics that underwrote that term) is a salient psychological
phenomenon, and the alternation between tension and relaxation that
strikes many as a hallmark of humor may still prove to be an important

---

3. Keith-Spiegel also provides another category, which she labels ambivalence theories, which
hold that humor arises out of the conflict between two or more incompatible emotions. We see
this as a specialized case of the incongruity theory (see below) where the incongruity is simply
between emotions.

element of the theory we are looking for, but only if we can transform and clarify the constituent notions.[4]

Although humor involving emotionally charged topics fares rather well in release theories, other kinds of humor, such as logical humor, are not well explained by them. For instance, simple puns and grammatical traps such as the following involve neither aggressive tension nor sexual tension:

(11) What, according to Freud, comes between fear and sex? Fünf! (Cohen 1999) (*Eins, zwei, drei, vier, fünf, sechs* . . .)

(12) Email is the happy medium between male and female. (Hofstadter 2007)

(13) Photons have mass? I didn't even know they were Catholic.

(14) The face of a child can say it all, especially the mouth part of the face.

One of the attractions of release theory is that it purports to explain, in a way different from superiority theory, the prominence of sexual and aggressive content in humor. And it gives prominence to the emotional nature of our *response* to humor—after all, it does usually *feel* very relieving to release a hearty laugh. And on a related point, it at least attempts to account for the energy *spent* in laughing (and in seeking out humorous things to laugh at). Unlike most other theories, it recognizes that we need to posit some *reason* for that expenditure, since it is a fundamental fact of biology that such an expenditure of energy needs a purpose, even if that purpose has expired or been directed to new ends.

E. Incongruity and Incongruity-Resolution Theories

Humor is reason gone mad.
—Groucho Marx

Of the current theories of humor, the most strongly championed is the incongruity-resolution (I-R) theory. As its name implies, this theory says humor happens whenever an incongruity occurs that is subsequently resolved. A classic example from Suls (1972) is this:

---

4. Huron (2006) has done just that, in his account of the role of "contrastive valence" in his "ITPRA" model of expectations, which he applies both to music and to humor. We will follow him in several regards and depart from him in others.

(15) O'Riley was on trial for armed robbery. The jury came out and announced, "Not guilty."

"Wonderful," said O'Riley, "does that mean I can keep the money?"

Suls explains the humor of this joke as arising from the fact that O'Riley's response is incongruous with the situation of being not guilty, although on second thought it can be reinterpreted to make sense. The concept is quite effective for a large range of cases, but it has its flaws too. Most notably, I-R theory may be able to tell us that incongruity plays a role in humor, and it may even help point out which stimuli should be humorous; but this does not give any explanatory power to the theory—it is little more than descriptive. If incongruity plays a role, we still need a theory of *how* and *why* it plays a role. What is it about incongruity that is funny? There are many descriptions in the literature that analyze the incongruous pair of elements and how they get resolved, and they may help us categorize stimuli as humorous or not; but that doesn't go far to tell us what humor is or why it exists.

Another trouble with I-R theories is that the theorists do not all use an agreed-upon definition of incongruity. Each author has an intuitive sense that some kind of incongruity is involved when they see humor, but on just what kind of incongruity, or what exactly it means to be incongruous, they do not all agree. Some of the uses of the word invoke ambiguity, or a deviation from the customary, or a pair of simultaneous schemas that just don't logically match (i.e., nonsense). Semantic script theorists claim that, for narratives, the incongruity is between opposing scripts that arise at different points in the narrative (Attardo 2001; Raskin 1985). Even those who agree on what incongruity is differ on what role it plays in humor. Ritchie (1999) points out that Shultz (1976) and Suls (1972)—whose I-R theories are two of the earliest and best regarded models—have fairly different interpretations of how incongruity operates. Shultz claims that the setup is ambiguous and that an incongruity of one interpretation with the punch line forces recognition of the other interpretation. Suls says that the punch line creates an incongruity with respect to the setup, and that logic resolves the incongruity thereafter. Both writers give good examples of their concepts, and although the examples certainly have incongruities, the two models have very different informational requirements. It is hard to find something theorists can all agree on that says anything more than that "some aspect of the incongruous" is involved. Still, we agree with the widespread opinion that I-R theories provide at least a good foundation for a model of how and why humor happens, and we shall try to provide a more rigorous and informative account of incongruity.

Kant gives the first rendition of the basic incongruity theory. In his *Critique of Judgment* (1790), he writes that "In everything that is to excite a lively convulsive laugh there must be something absurd (in which the understanding, therefore, can find no satisfaction). Laughter is an affection arising from the sudden transformation of a strained expectation into nothing." To illustrate this "expectation" Kant tells a joke about an Indian who sees a freshly opened bottle with beer foaming out and expresses his surprise. When asked by an Englishman why he is surprised, the Indian announces that the reason for his surprise is not that it is flowing out, but rather surprise about how they got it in. In Kant's joke, we experience an expectation, the same as the Englishman in the story does, of wondering why this Indian is surprised that the beer comes out of the bottle—it seems natural to us that there is nothing to be surprised about there. The Indian surprises us, though, in showing us that our expectation was wrong: he was never surprised about that—our expectation was false. (Or the Englishman's expectation was false.) The additional information the Indian gives us causes that expectation to disappear instantly—to be suddenly transformed into nothing. We no longer have reason to expect it. There is certainly more to the story, but Kant has given us an excellent starting point.

Kant did not elaborate his model much beyond saying that an expectation disappears, so a lot is left to our interpretation. A more specific version of it may work well. The most influential version of I-R theory started with Schopenhauer (1969), who tells us that Kant's model fails easily under counterexamples of expectations that dissolve but are not humorous. Schopenhauer may be right, and Kant's model may need more details, but there is much merit in his use of the term "expectation."

Schopenhauer's model is the basis for many of the modern theories, although most of the more recent versions neglect some of his details. He starts with a comment that specifies a bit more precisely what incongruity he is talking about. "My theory of the ludicrous," he says, "also depends on the contrast, which I have . . . so forcibly stressed, between *representations of perception and abstract representations*" (Schopenhauer 1969, our emphasis). The incongruity, Schopenhauer makes explicit, must be between a representation in the mind (for which he sometimes uses the word "concept") and a real object (by which he means a perception of an object). The incongruity occurs to the extent that the concept was mistaken and the perception was veridical. It is a very persuasive model. Let us restate it for clarity: Humor occurs when a perception of the world suddenly corrects our mistaken preconception. Schopenhauer adds that the extent of the feeling of mirth and ensuing laughter is proportional to the degree of surprise involved within the correction. Before this suggestive claim can be recast in anything approaching a testable formulation, we must construct a more precise identification of the key categories of concepts and perception, a task we will address in a later section.

Incongruity theory is effective. By most estimates it manages to explain at least as many cases of humor as superiority theory does, and can even be used to explain the laughter that results from tickling (Ramachandran and Blakeslee 1998; Ramachandran 1998—more on this later). Additionally (and quite importantly) it draws our attention in a way that no other theory does to the fact that we have, in humor, a sense of nonsense— that is, it shows the deep relationship between the laughable and the illogical.

The primary argument against the incongruity theory has been given in the form of counterexamples. Alexander Bain, for instance, gives a list of incongruities that he says do not instill in us a sense of the ludicrous. He illustrates:

> A decrepit man under a heavy burden, five loaves and two fishes among a multitude, and all unfitness and gross disproportion; an instrument out of tune, a fly in ointment, snow in May, Archimedes studying geometry in a siege, and all discordant things; a wolf in sheep's clothing, a breach of bargain, and falsehood in general; the multitude taking the law in their own hands, and everything of the nature of disorder; a corpse at a feast, parental cruelty, filial ingratitude, and whatever is unnatural; the entire catalogue of the vanities given by Solomon, are all incongruous, but they cause feelings of pain, anger, sadness, loathing, rather than mirth. (Bain 1875, p. 257)

As Pinker (1997) points out, motion-sickness is another counterexample that makes this case. It occurs when the perception from the vestibular system does not correlate with the perception from the visual system. For instance, when one is below deck on a ship tossing in a storm, the visual system may be provided with input that suggests that one's body is hardly in motion with respect to its surroundings, while the balance system records every bump and sway in a violent vestibular cacophony. The effect of the collision between these two incongruous inputs is hardly amusing. Not laughter but vomiting is the irresistible impulse triggered, probably a by-product of circuitry designed by evolution to expel accidentally ingested neurotoxins from the stomach when dizziness occurs. Reflecting on the example may help remind us that however natural laughter seems to us as the appropriate response to humor, we need to explain *why* it is more appropriate than, say, vomiting. Why should we be wired up to *laugh* when something strikes us as funny, and why should anything strike us as funny in the first place?

Some of Bain's examples could be put in contexts where they would indeed strike us as funny, and some instances of visual-vestibular incongruity may also make us laugh (think of some of the highlights of a carnival funhouse[5]). When an instrument is out of tune, sometimes the sound it makes surprises us with its oddness and forces a laugh. Encountering falling snow in May might well be so incongruous as to provoke laughter along with wide-eyed wonder. The sheer outrageousness of an instance of parental cruelty (as in "sick jokes" and the theater of cruelty) may sometimes cause an urge to laugh, if the behavior is not just mean or vicious, but bizarrely unreasonable, or preposterous.[6] So Bain is no doubt right that not all instances of incongruity cause us to laugh, but there may still be something worth pursuing in incongruity theory. It is telling that we can often if not always devise some kind of context in which an incongruity turns into a humorous circumstance, and reflecting on how this is accomplished may help us in uncovering some further differentiating factor(s) so that we can tighten up, and save, the incongruity theory.

Suls (1972) offered an expansion on incongruity theory requiring that an incongruity must not only be detected, but also *resolved by reason* for there to be humor. According to this incongruity-resolution (I-R) theory, the incongruity exists between the setup of a narrative and the punch line. The resolution happens when the mind, following a logical rule, finds a way to make the punch line follow from the setup, and when this resolution is discovered, we laugh. Wyer and Collins (1992) show, again, that even the resolution of an incongruity does not always produce humor. Here is an example (drawn from a recent conversation): A friend speaks of his ill father, describing his symptoms as *incongruous*. The doctors are baffled about why he has this unusual mix of symptoms, which don't belong together, based on their experience. Suppose a solution presented itself suddenly—for instance, the doctors find an article in a medical

---

5. A particularly memorable example consists of a stable bridge across a space that has a rotating painted tube surrounding it. When walking on this bridge, because of the visual input, one cannot help expecting that the bridge is spinning and that there is a fall impending. The illusion is so strong that one overcompensates and falls in the other direction, against the side of the still stationary bridge. The typical response is laughter, not panic, but that may be a result of the carnival atmosphere more than anything else. Encountering such a phenomenon in, say, a factory or a mine may not produce mirth.

6. In chapter 10, we will walk through one of Bain's counterexamples to show how it can be turned into an occasion for humor according to our model.

journal recounting a rare disease that does exhibit this exact range of symptoms. This resolution would no doubt provoke excitement, and perhaps glee, but not mirth. Problem solving sometimes provides sudden resolutions to incongruities but does not always produce humor in the process. Once again, we could no doubt imagine ways in which this same circumstance *could* be funny—if, for instance, the doctors discovered it was something that they think they *should have* known, something even obvious that they had overlooked. It appears that still further qualification needs to be placed on the incongruity resolution. Wyer and Collins suggest additional requirements for a theory of I-R+, based on a model presented by Michael Apter (1982). Apter's proposal contains two more facets, which Wyer and Collins call *nonreplacement* and *diminishment.* The principle of nonreplacement says that, when a reinterpretation is made, for humor to exist the new interpretation and the old must both be valid rather than the new one forcibly supplanting the older one. The principle of diminishment, reminiscent of superiority theory, says that the new interpretation should be in some way reduced in value relative to the initial interpretation (Wyer and Collins 1992).

By this point the term "incongruity" means something different than it did when proposed by Schopenhauer or alluded to by Kant. It is no longer an incongruity between an expectation and that which dissolves the expectation or between an object of perception and an object of conception. Attardo and Raskin (Attardo 2001; Raskin 1985) offer a more sophisticated version of the incongruity theory in which the stimulus itself is not claimed to be humorous; rather, the scripts that elements of the stimulus activate in the mind are found to be overlapping yet opposing (or incongruous) and therefore excite the sense of humor. So, for instance, in the joke that Attardo and Raskin both use as an example:

(16) "Is the doctor at home?" the patient asked in his bronchial whisper. "No," the doctor's young and pretty wife whispered in reply. "Come right in."

The Doctor script is evoked by the patient's question and confirmed by his bronchial whisper, but the doctor's wife's reply informs us that another script, that of Lovers, could as well describe the situation. These opposing scripts are what make the joke funny because both can't be invoked at the same time. This model is very good for a limited domain of verbal humor, but it fails to offer an actual explanation for humor, not only because it remains purely descriptive (and, at that, descriptive only of *some* verbal humor), but also because until we know how scripts are invoked, we have, at best, description without explanation (more on this in chapter 6). Moreover, to repeat our standard theme, there are cases in which overlapping and opposing scripts are aroused by texts that do not cause humor. Most notably, a joke told in the wrong order, with the punch line first, maintains the overlap of opposing scripts but is typically devoid of humor. And Apter (1982) throws another bit of cold water on any version of I-R theory by reminding us that there are instances of humor that provide incongruity in the stimulus without any specific resolution—for example: "the phrase 'Don't panic,' spoken in a frightened voice." The entire class of humorous non sequitur provides a bounty of further counterexamples, such as these gems from Steven Wright: "OK, so what's the speed of dark?" and "I couldn't repair your brakes, so I made your horn louder." Here's another case of non sequitur:

(17)   A man at the dinner table dipped his hands in the mayonnaise and then ran them through his hair. When his neighbor looked astonished, the man apologized: "I'm so sorry. I thought it was spinach." (Freud 1912, as cited in Minsky 1984)

Minsky (1981), noting that Freud's censor model and release theory could not explain logic-based humor or grammatical humor (such as the puns in examples 12–16), attempted to expand the model. His innovative claim was that aggressive and sexual humor may not be too different from what he designated as nonsense humor: Humans need to learn to avoid irreparable mistakes in reasoning by anticipating and preventing them via something like Freudian censors. These censors, unlike Freud's, prohibit certain types of *logical operations* rather than certain types of *content*. "Intellect and Affect seem less different once we theorize that the 'cognitive unconscious' considers faulty reasoning to be just as 'naughty' as the usual 'Freudian' wishes" (Minsky 1984, 176). Under this model, having a morally wayward thought is treated similarly to having a logically inconsistent thought—both are things that the mind wants to develop filters against.

Minksy operationalized his faulty-logic model using the language and concepts of *frames* and frame-shifting in addition to censors. Frames are similar to Schank and Abelson's (1977) *scripts*, which underlie both Raskin's and Attardo's models: They are general knowledge representation packages that are called to mind and fleshed out during comprehension by binding details of the actual situation to terminals that represent variables of the frame (cf. Minsky 1974, 1975, 1984; Coulson 2001).[7] Thus a normal modern human being in our culture would have a birthday-party frame, a restaurant-meal frame, a getting-money-from-the-ATM frame, a finding-one's-car-in-the-parking-lot frame, a slipping-on-a-banana-peel-frame, but probably not a tiger-wrestling frame or a scythe-sharpening frame, or a deciding-which-demon-to-invoke-while-mixing-a-potion frame. Minsky suggests that what causes the mistake in logic to be discovered in jokes is "an improper assignment-change" (often discovered by a contradiction in the bindings) that causes a frame shift—a reanalysis and replacement of the frame being used to represent the event being comprehended. The newly shifted-to frame should be more consistent with all of the binding details than the original frame.

Although it is related to Freud's understanding of humor, we list Minsky's theory under incongruity resolution because of its more significant reliance upon contradiction-detection (incongruity), frame-reanalysis (resolution), and related cognitive features rather than the emotions, tensions, and psychological censors of release theories. Although the idea of cognitive censors (either Freudian or Minskian) does not persuade us, we think there is something deep and right about Minsky's mention of faulty reasoning, and we will pursue this line of thought later. But we should remember that not all humor is the result of performing faulty reasoning (for instance, slapstick[8]), and not all faulty reasoning is followed by humor (you don't usually laugh when you discover that you forgot to carry the one while solving a cumbersome addition problem).

Coulson and Kutas (Coulson and Kutas 1998, 2001; Coulson 2001) further championed the frame-shifting model—a concept that Coulson (2001) has developed much further than Minsky had taken it—in a series of ERP (event-related potential) experiments, which measure electrical activity from the brain. They pointed out that frame-shifting seems to be operative in a number of jokes but did not go so far as to claim that this was an explanation for all humor. In fact Coulson (2001) gives a thorough treatment of frame-shifting, showing that it is pervasive in much of our semantic construction, yet most of these semantic processes are not humorous.

---

7. See also Bartlett's (1932) notion of *schemata*, made perhaps more popular by Piaget's similar use of the term (e.g., Piaget 1952) for another similar construct. We don't discuss schemata because the concept has seldom been used in historical humor theory and does not play a role in our own theory.

8. Perhaps Minsky would suggest a Freudian aggression censor is in play here, rather than one of his own faulty-reasoning censors.

While semantic reanalysis seems to be present in many jokes, frame-shifting as a model of humor suffers from the same problems as do incompatible overlapping semantic-scripts and other incongruity-resolution theories: Although it may sometimes be associated with humor and can describe humor to some extent, it does not *explain* humor. Why do some frame-shifts produce humor and others not? Is there still humor if the same frame-shift occurs in a different context, or a different frame-shift in the same context? We need to answer the more fundamental question: What is it about frame-shifting that is—can be—*funny*?

F. Surprise Theories

An atheist explorer in the deepest Amazon suddenly finds himself surrounded by a bloodthirsty group of natives. Upon surveying the situation, he says quietly to himself "Oh God, I'm screwed!"

There is a ray of light from heaven and a voice booms out: "No, you are *not* screwed. Pick up that stone at your feet and bash in the head of the chief standing in front of you."

So the explorer picks up the stone and proceeds to bash the living heck out of the chief.

As he stands above the lifeless body, breathing heavily and surrounded by a hundred natives with a look of shock on their faces, God's voice booms out again: "Okay . . . *Now* you're screwed."

Some theories claim that surprise is at least a necessary feature of humor, if not sufficient. Descartes claimed that humor was a mixture of joy and shock. Our release theorists required that the tension be undone "suddenly and surprisingly." Surprise is mentioned by both our incongruity theorists and our superiority theorists: Hobbes, as noted, said laughter is due to a "sudden glory," and Schopenhauer often stressed the occurrence of the element of surprise in the resolution. Aristotle noted, when speaking of riddles and "novelties," that "In these the thought is *startling*, and, as Theodorus puts it, does not fit in with the ideas you already have. . . . The effect is produced even by jokes depending upon changes of the letters of a word; this too is a surprise. You find this in verse as well as in prose. The word which comes is *not what the hearer imagined*" (*Rhetoric*, Book III, ch. 11, our emphasis). Surprise is typically defined as the characteristic emotion caused by something unanticipated, but this way of putting it conceals an error. Not just anything that is unanticipated can cause surprise. The world as we experience it consists largely of activity that we do not have the ability to anticipate: people speaking particular sentences to us, birds flying by, somebody honking their horn in the distance, being dealt two sevens and a nine, a change in the weather. Yet we are not constantly in a state of surprise. What surprises us is not unexpected things—most of the things that happen were not expected to happen just there and then—but rather things we expected *not* to happen—because we expected something else to happen instead. It is the contradiction between an anticipated event or state and a perceived event or state that surprises us.

G.   Bergson's Mechanical Humor Theory

A lawyer was approached by Mephistopheles, who offered him a brilliant career as a defense attorney, leading to a seat on the Supreme Court, and a Hollywood movie biopic—in exchange for the souls of his wife and three children. The lawyer thought and thought, sweat pouring off his brow. Finally he looked up at Mephistopheles and said, "There's a catch, right?"

Bergson (1911) said that "society will be suspicious of an inelasticity of character." A body, a mind, or a society that is inadaptable is given respectively to infirmity, mental deficiency, or misery and crime. So, Bergson suggests, a mechanism that enforces adaptability would be a solution to all of these problems. It is rigidity that causes humor, according to Bergson, or rather: Humor is the solution to rigidity. Laughter acts as a "social corrective." If one's behavior is inelastic, laughter from others reminds one of this and acts as a pressure to cause one to behave more adaptively. Another striking claim from Bergson is that "laughter has no greater foe than emotion." According to him, humorous circumstances appeal strictly to the intellect.

The comedian Mike Myers, in an e-mail to the author of a *New Yorker* article on humor, says "Comedy characters tend to be a _____ machine; i.e., Clouseau was a smug machine, Pepe Le Pew was a love machine, Felix Unger was a clean machine, and Austin Powers is a sex machine" (Friend 2002). This excellently illustrates the Bergsonian theory of humor. The designers of these characters choose a central humorous aspect for the character's personality, and mechanize it—make it a rigid and dominating determinant of the character's responses. Then we can see humor in how that characteristic makes the character behave in nonadaptive ways, performing actions that are not normal (or not expected) for the situation at hand, yet typical and obvious given the way the character has been sketched.

Bergson's model has several strengths worth noting. It provides a beneficial purpose—a raison d'être—for humor. It sketches a more or less mechanical method for detecting or producing humor. And it purports to explain the social significance of humor as well. It shares aspects with superiority theory as well as an aspect of incongruity theory (in that the rigid mechanical behavior is incompatible with the expectedly appropriate adaptability of the human mind) and suggests that these aspects may be smoothly compatible. Still, while his model makes good predictions for certain forms of the comic, such as the comedy resulting from deformity (caricature and the like), physical situations (someone slipping on a banana peel), and "mechanical" behavior, it draws a blank on the sorts of humor found in many jokes and witticisms. Koestler (1964, p. 47) finds a number of counterexamples: "If rigidity contrasted with organic suppleness were laughable in itself, Egyptian statues and Byzantine mosaics would be the best jokes ever invented. If automatic repetitiveness in human behaviour were a necessary and sufficient condition of the comic there would be no more amusing spectacle than an epileptic fit; and if we wanted a good laugh we would merely have to feel a person's pulse or listen to his heart-beat with its monotonous tick-tack. If 'we laugh each time a person gives us the impression of being a thing,' there would be nothing more funny than a corpse."

Lastly, Bergson reminds us that humor is strictly human (Koestler calls us *"homo-ridens,"* the laughing animal). He notes not only that only humans laugh but that "[We] might equally well have defined [humankind] as an animal which is laughed at." We laugh only *at* humans or animals or objects to which we have assigned anthropomorphic characteristics. This suggests that humor is the intellect laughing at the human, or at a failing of the human, and more particularly, at a *mental* failing of a human. Perhaps, then, only humans laugh because only humans have the capacity to be *higher-order intentional systems,* that is, to adopt the intentional stance (Dennett 1987) toward other entities.[9] This will be a feature of our model explained in detail below.

---

9. In the last twenty-five years there has been a vigorous and controversial body of research attempting to demonstrate that nonhuman species, especially great apes and dolphins, are—or are not—higher-order intentional systems, but the results are inconclusive in spite of many ingenious experiments. See, e.g., Premack and Premack 1983; Tomasello and Call 1997; Hauser 2001. Even if some apes do have something like a "theory of mind," it does not ramify as exuberantly as the effortless "folk psychology" of human beings.

5   Twenty Questions for a Cognitive and Evolutionary Theory of Humor

There are two rednecks in a field:

Bobby Joe: "Hey, you wanna play twenty questions?"
Billy Bob: "Sure. Lemme thinka somethin'."
Bobby Joe: "Got it?"
Billy Bob: "Yeah, got it. Ask me."
Bobby Joe: "Is it a thing?"
Billy Bob: "Yeah."
Bobby Joe: "Can you fuck it?"
Billy Bob: "Yeah."
Bobby Joe: "Is it a goat?"
Billy Bob: "Yeah."

This brief summary of the history of humor theory yields a laundry list of the features that would comprise a complete cognitive theory of the subject. The list is presented here in the form of questions. Each question has been raised before, and even, to some degree, answered. Our goal is to synthesize the best points from the existing theories into a unified model that answers all of the questions. A good model should not overlook any recognizable variety of humor and should not identify items as humorous that don't provoke mirth. A very good model should, moreover, make some surprising predictions: It should tell us how to turn a humorous event into a nonhumorous event by making minimal changes, and, ideally, it should give us good recipes for generating humor. It is one thing to be able to account for the favored cases purportedly accounted for by earlier theories; it is another thing to generate new classes of cases, or new taxonomies of existing cases, showing how *and why* they are humorous. In short, a good model should be testable in a variety of ways. We will address general concerns of refutability in more detail in chapter 10.

1. *Is humor an adaptation?* Is there a benefit that is conferred upon the genes by the humor trait and, if so, what is that benefit? What might the trait do to increase the likelihood of reproduction to the genes of its bearer? Humor is innate (see footnote 4, p. 6) and it is pervasive across all human cultures. Laughter shows up in infants ontogenetically early, and appears apparently spontaneously in congenitally blind and deaf children. The humor trait has not genetically drifted out of any population. Why not?

2. *Where did humor come from?* Do other species have humor, or anything like it? We should be able to tell a clear story about the behavioral precursors to humor, and eventually even plot the path of mutation from those precursors to the modern-day phenotype of the trait.

3. *Why do we communicate humor?* Making unnecessary noise draws the attention of predators. Communication also costs the organism in energy expenditure. There ought to have been some adaptive purpose to the early communication of humor. How does the communication differ from humor itself and what, if any, benefit is conferred upon the genes by such behavior?

4. *Why do we feel pleasure in humor?* We not only feel happy when we laugh; there is also a particular quality to that form of pleasure that is unique to humor: mirth. In what ways is mirth qualitatively different from other pleasures, and can we explain why this should be? Is there a benefit to our genes that pays for the energetic costs of the specific phenomenon of mirth?

5. *Why do we feel surprise in humor?* Most, or at least many, humorous stimuli contain an element of surprise, to the point that some have postulated surprise as the root cause of humor. (Others tack on surprise or suddenness as an additional but unmotivated requirement at the end of their theories.) Why is it so pervasive?

6. *Why is judgment a ubiquitous component in the content of humorous stimuli?* Superiority theorists often claim that judgment between a noble state and an ignoble state of a thing causes humor. But judgment exists extensively outside of humor as well. Why is there such value comparison in humor? What would be the purpose of a humor that made such judgments?

7. *Why does humor often get used for disparagement?* To *make fun* of something is to disparage it; when we *make fun* of people we often humiliate them—although there is also the derived practice of light-hearted mocking or roasting, "just for fun," which people are supposed to endure with good humor. Why does this occur? You can insult someone, but you can't *make*

fun of or mock someone, without using humor. Superiority theorists think this is why humor exists. Should this be part of our theory? And is there a reproductive benefit derivable from disparagement or the feeling of superiority?

8. *Why does humor so often point to failures?* Aristotle claimed that humor points out failings. Even in good-hearted humor, there is often an aspect of mistakes made: mistaken identity, misunderstanding, misperception, and so on. Why does this connection exist?

9. *Why, in humor, do we have a sense of nonsense?* There are many models of incongruity—all different. Is there a simplifying view that treats them all as subclasses of a more general base class? (Relatedly, what is the role of expectation as Kant saw it? How can we explain Schopenhauer's model of perception versus conception? Can we explain each of Suls's, Shultz's, Attardo's, and Raskin's models all under one rubric?)

10. *If incongruity causes humor, how does it do it?* We need something more than a descriptive account here. What causal mechanisms are triggered by incongruity and why? (See Ritchie's questions about incongruity in chapter 10.)

11. *Why is it that we laugh only at humans or anthropomorphized objects?* It seems that only things that have minds, or are interacting somehow with things that have minds, can be humorous. Some aspect of the mind, then, might be the source of humor. What is it about humans that make them the topic of humor and not just the perceivers of humor?

12. *What is right about Bergson's claim that mechanical behavior is humorous?* Bergson notes that it is detrimental to act nonadaptively, and a telltale sign of mechanical behavior is its failure to mesh adaptively with subtleties in the environment. Is he right that humor is a way to keep us in check? Is mechanism a marked subclass of humor?

13. *Why can humor be used as a social corrective?* Why do we laugh at someone when they do something inappropriate? What makes us judge that some kinds of inappropriate behavior are laughable while others are not? Why do we feel humiliated when people laugh at us? Does this process make us change our behavior? Does it tend to return us to "normal"?

14. *What unites the broad variety of types of humorous stimuli?* As Socrates never tired of saying when given a collection of examples: That's fine, but what do they all have in common?

15. *How does play relate to humor?* What aspect of play is similar to humor? Both have an aspect of the nonserious in their content and both lead to pleasure. Play often leads to laughter. What common cause may there be for both? What is their relationship to tickling?

16. *What is the relationship between problem solving, discovery, and humor?* We tend to exclaim "Aha!" when we discover something new or solve a problem. Occasionally we even laugh. The same emotion of discovery occurs when we "get the joke." What is the relationship between these phenomena?

17. *Why do we desire humor so intensely?* We are motivated to seek out humor. We lay our credit cards on the counter at the box office for comedies and wait in line to hear standup comedians. Situation comedies and animated cartoons dominate commercial television. Magazines keep their subscribers happy by inserting humorous cartoons every few pages, and every bookstore has a profitable humor section. Billions of dollars are spent annually on the comedy industry. Why is comedy such an attractive commodity?

18. *What is the peculiar specificity often found in humor?* Humorous stimuli often have less than universal appeal. In the limit, an "in-joke" may have a qualified audience of one. What features qualify one for what varieties of humor?

19. *What is the generality in humor?* On the other hand, much humor is universal. Some humor will reliably provoke mirth in almost everyone in the world. And why do we typically desire to spread humor to a wider public? Why is humor so seldom a solitary pleasure?

20. *Why are there gender differences in humor?* Why do men get more laughs and women give more laughs? Why do women, more than men, seek "a sense of humor" when writing personal ads? And why are there overwhelmingly more male comedians than female?

Each of these questions points to an important part of humor, and a theory that doesn't answer to them all satisfactorily will be missing something. Of the many models in the previous chapter, only incongruity-resolution is a serious contender today, although a few theorists (e.g., Alexander 1986; Gruner 1997) and many armchair theorists—interview your friends and you'll find some—are still trying to give the superiority theory a run for its money. However, as we explained in the previous chapter, while on the right track, even current incongruity theories have fallen short of describing all the phenomena in this list. The theory we offer in the next few chapters is, in some ways, simply a new twist on the incongruity theory; but in other ways, it offers something quite different. We claim it answers all twenty questions.

6 Emotion and Computation

A. Finding the Funny Bone

> We have reason to believe that man first walked upright to free his hands for masturbation.
> —Lily Tomlin

The last few chapters, our brief survey of the phenomenology of humor, and our even more cursory survey of the attempts by researchers to explain it all with a single theory, should drive home the following conclusions:

1. It is very hard—verging on impossible—to see what puns, slapstick, classic comedy, and dirty jokes have in common aside from being (potentially) funny. As legions of partial theories attest, if there is something that unites these very different species of humor it is far from obvious.

2. Humor is dependent on (or sensitive to) both content restrictions and the dynamics of presentation. A hilarious joke lamely told, out of order or with poor timing, will have *almost* all mirth drained out of it, and a good comic actor can milk a laugh out of *almost* any line chosen at random from a book. The key word is "almost." There is excellent humor that exists in written (or drawn) form, with little or no discernible help from the dynamics of presentation—for example, variation in font, type size, lighting, or the speed of reading by the audience. And some physical humor seems to be almost entirely dynamics: the juxtaposition of disparate sights and sounds at just the right tempo and volume to trigger a guffaw.

3. Since there is no *topic* that is intrinsically comic, the content requirement must be something to do with how the content (on whatever topic) is derived, obscured, used, or misused. That is, it must be a function of the *cognitive processing* of the content.

4. Since dynamics is so important, there must be conditions of humor that depend (somehow) on the actual physical, "mechanical" parameters of

operation of this cognitive processing: the variable speed of processing, the variable rate of increasing arousal, the variable intensity and duration of phases in the processing, and so forth. Whatever the details of this neurophysiological story, they will be completely inscrutable to the subject, and no more "intuitive" than the details of the operation of digestion or blood clotting. (Thus we can imagine that there could be a drug that turned off or disrupted or heightened one's sense of humor "simply" by preventing the buildup of some neuromodulator, or changing the relative speed of two semi-independent processes, mechanical disruptions that would *make no sense* in a theory attempting to explain *humor*, independently of a very specific model of the machinery underlying humor detection.)

5. This innate neural system for cognitive processing—the "funny bone"[1]— must be for something. What is it for? Here we turn to elementary evolutionary considerations. It must have been designed by evolution to perform some substantially important cognitive task, since it is ubiquitous in human beings, and its activity is powerfully rewarding. This task should be at least uniquely well-developed in human beings, since there is nothing that looks much like our humor in other species. "What do we do better than we otherwise would do, thanks to the mechanisms that carry with them, as a price worth paying, our susceptibility to—our near addiction to—laughter?" (Dennett 1991, 63).

6. Whatever pressing need was met by wiring us up this way may not show much resemblance to the roles humor now plays in our lives. For instance, the humor system might have compensated for some strain that human beings once put on their brains, but which no longer has much if any adaptive significance. Consider a parallel: We know that *ensuring reproduction* is the important project that pays, in evolutionary terms, for the existence of libido in human beings. Getting the gametes united is nature's

---

1. The neural "funny bone" should not be imagined to be a single brain region. It is actually a very complex, temporally and structurally distributed system that requires a coordinated network of responses involved in generating expectations and associations, perceived incongruities, revision and coherence, and of course the affective and expressive responses. Mobbs et al. (2003) found mesolimbic "reward" activation, including the ventral tegmental area, nucleus accumbens/ventral striatum, and amygdala; as well as activation in a variety of cognitive and semantic regions including the inferior frontal gyrus (involved in generating initial expectations), the temporo-occipital junction (involved in detection of contradiction), and Broca's area and the temporal pole (involved in establishing coherence or resolution). Other regions likely related to the expression of humor, including supplementary motor area and dorsal anterior cingulate gyrus, were also activated.

highest imperative, more important even than staying alive in many species, and yet in our species this project is very often systematically thwarted, leaving the underlying machinery with a host of derived roles to play that do not contribute at all to anybody's genetic fitness, such as providing the reward system that underwrites pornography and the use of sexual imagery in advertising. At a conference on the evolution of religion in 2007, Dennett was challenged to give even a single example of a ubiquitous human phenomenon, genetically based but culturally evolved and transmitted, that didn't have positive adaptive significance as an enhancer of genetic fitness. His answer: masturbation. To his amazement, several of the interlocutors went on to try to argue that masturbation *had* to be "good for something" if it survived; perhaps it was rehearsal designed to improve one's techniques of impregnation, for instance! We must guard against this naïve understanding of evolution when we canvass the legitimate possibilities for humor. Enthusiasm outruns rigor among the fans of evolutionary explanations of psychological phenomena, and we recognize that this has led some skeptics to choose the simplistic path of dismissing all of it, but that is just as unscientific a position as that of the silliest evolutionary psychologists. A good evolutionary theory will account for a wide variety of independently observed phenomena that have heretofore defied any unified explanation, and will offer the prospect of clear empirical tests that could falsify the theory.

This is the set of inferences that led us to the model we develop in the coming chapters. It is *one* hypothesis that fits all the requirements quite handily; there may well be another, better hypothesis, but we can't think of one, so we're making the case for this one, the best candidate for the task we have been able to construct, and using it to illuminate how a theory of humor might be a particularly effective bridge for uniting our evolutionary, neurocomputational, cognitive, and social understanding of ourselves. Before we present our model, however, we need to clear the decks. There are several common misapprehensions about brains and computers, emotions and logic, that we need to expose and expel, replacing them with foundations on which our model can be built.

B.   Does Logic or Emotion Organize Our Brains?

There can be no knowledge without emotion. We may be aware of a truth, yet until we have felt its force, it is not ours. To the cognition of the brain must be added the experience of the soul.
—Arnold Bennett

The intellect without the emotions is like the jockey without the horse.
—Laurence Gonzales (2003)

In a long tradition going back to Aristotle and his syllogism, logicians have defined proper reasoning according to a set of rules that originally come from *intuitions*. The intuitions of everyday reasoning once were the only source, the only judge, of what was rational or illogical. Aristotle presented his syllogistic logic in a book called the *Organon*, a Greek word for *tool*; he had devised a thinking tool, a prosthetic device that was meant to sharpen and systematize the intuitions one encountered when thinking "with the bare hands," in effect. These rules were formalized and, subsequently, in the nineteenth century they were developed further into symbolic logic, a *technology*—memetically evolved, and "formal" in Haugeland's (1985) sense. This symbolic, or mathematical, logic nowadays pervades philosophy, computer science, and engineering and is even sometimes applied, when special care needs to be taken (writing contracts and insurance policies, for instance), in everyday reasoning and argument. The internal consistency of mathematical logic is so convincing that it usually evades questioning. Although logicians occasionally make forays into the realm of alternative internally consistent systems, thereby questioning whether all these intuitions are appropriate, here instead we question not their soundness but their origin: What makes it *seem* right—to any person on earth—that you *cannot* have p and not-p both be true?[2] Or that either p or not-p *must* be true? Whence do such beliefs originate? It is often said that a few basic rules such as these are "a priori" or "self-evident logical principles" (e.g., Russell 1912), but even if this verdict is sustained, it remains to be seen how the psychological and neurophysiological constitution of our brains guarantees that such a principle will be judged self-evident. For instance, infants, without training, discover such logical constructs as object permanence apparently on their own (Piaget 1936/1952, 1937/1954).[3]

---

2. Certain philosophers and logicians who take various "paraconsistent" logics to be valid disagree with the fundamental nature of the law of noncontradiction. Under such views, some contradictions may in fact be valid. We are agnostic on all this; our point here is that the subjective sense of validity in a particular *kind* of mind—the kind of mind that we humans typically have—is the source, historically, and the (defeasible) testbed against which all logics—logical tools—are judged.

3. Experimenters looking for evidence of infants' appreciation of object permanence have proposed—and used—indicators from which they attempt to infer a child's level of surprise or lack thereof. These indicators include such measurables as preferential looking, emotional

It is tempting to interpret their startle reaction when confronted with trick cases of object *im*permanence as indicating their innate allegiance to the law of noncontradiction—manifesting an instance of their belief that *not* (*p and not-p*), but articulating the precise content of *p* in such an instance is not a task for the fainthearted. In any event, there seems to be something innate—or at least innately learnable sans supervision—about such self-evident principles of reasoning.

Although this self-evidential nature was certainly a boon in getting formal logic off the ground (one needs axioms before one can derive theorems), it has been the source of endless trouble for another group of researchers: the architects of reasoning systems. Many of those who would endeavor to sire an artificial intelligence (e.g., GPS—the General Problem Solver—as reported in Newell and Simon 1972) have imported the formal system of reasoning into their designs directly—often including, for their brainchildren to employ, as many of the theorems that have fallen out from these axioms as possible—with very limited success. These early architects and those following in the tradition after them can be forgiven: Logic is the basis of programming in modern computing substrates—it is only natural to want to extend its ambit into the minds of their intellectual progeny when delivering them into life upon those very same substrates. Yet, it may be more suitable, we suggest, to endow these models only with a sense, similar to ours, of the self-evident axioms, and then to allow the employment of these endowments to help those agents engage in nonformal reasoning (much like ours) as necessary to solve the problems they come to face in their ecological niche, and perhaps to eventually discover the theorems of formal logic. It is well accepted, by now, that humans are not normatively rational thinkers, yet are often, under the right conditions, capable of rational thinking (Samuels, Stich, and Bishop 2002). The heuristics and biases that characterize our thinking may be the result of a certain kind of cognitive apparatus, yet to be fully described, which reasons informally based on some approximations to the axioms of logic, but which also provides the cognitive scaffolding (Clark 1997; Clark and Chalmers 1998) and tools necessary to learn technologies such as formal systems that allow for more effective nonheuristic truly rational reasoning.

---

expressions, and pulse rate. The attribution of actual belief in "object permanence" is a theoretical extension of these measurements, but what any of these experiments shows in any case is that infants show what we *take to be* the emotion of surprise.

The field of artificial intelligence was founded on the presumption that with the advent of computers, formal reasoning could be straightforwardly mechanized and automated, creating "inference engines" that could churn away on large sets of "axioms" to deduce all the propositions needed to inform and guide the behavior of an intelligent agent, whether a robot lumbering around in the real world or a bedridden agent playing chess and answering typed questions on all manner of topics. Tremendous progress has in fact ensued, creating large systems packed with real-world data presided over by inference engines that, like reference librarians, are adept at finding the right stored items and putting them together to infer the answers to many questions (e.g., Lenat and Guha 1990). But the idea that a human being's brain is basically a computer with a large database in memory and a superb inference engine to update and exploit it (what Dennett 1984 calls the "walking encyclopedia" model of the mind) has fallen on hard times. It has long been recognized that, in one way or another, such a hyperrational agent would almost certainly flounder in the real world, unable to direct its cognitive resources in a timely and appropriate fashion.

Some cognitive scientists have taken the moral of the story to be that logic *is not enough*. To get a behaviorally adroit and resourceful agent, you have to supplement your *cognitive* system, with its perceptual subsystems and memory subsystems and inference subsystems and the like, with an *emotional* subsystem (or two or three or more). But we—along with others (e.g., Damasio 1994; de Sousa 1987; Elster 1996; Frank 1988)—want to draw an even more radical conclusion: Emotions are not a set of important subsystems sitting alongside the cognitive subsystems; in the brain, emotions *rule*. We mean this literally. *All* control in the brain, all prioritizing, all organizing, all demoting and promoting, starting and stopping, enhancing and squelching *within* cognitive processes, is done by what we refer to as the *cognitive emotions* or, more precisely, the *epistemic emotions*.[4] These

---

4. While it may be the more profitable taxonomic label for our category, the term "cognitive emotions" is apt to be misconstrued owing to the broad usage of the term "cognition," which often refers to all the results of mental processing, both epistemic and pragmatic (Kirsh and Maglio 1994). Also, some (e.g., Griffiths 1997) have already used the term "higher cognitive emotions" to refer to emotions that require cognitive appraisal in their triggering mechanisms. Such a taxonomy is not at odds with, but runs orthogonal to ours, which carves up emotions according to which kinds of behaviors are motivated by each rather than which mechanisms are involved in the transduction of their objectives.

are a set of emotions that, together, have the effect of encouraging the mental behaviors that constitute a certain form of reasoning and epistemic assurance. This is not the first time this idea has been explored. In "Explanation as Orgasm," Alison Gopnik (1998, 109) described insight, or the sense of discovery, in similar terms: she remarks, "We not only know an explanation when we have one, we want explanations, and we are satisfied when we get them." There is a motivation toward explaining things. We *want* the world to make sense. Insight is not the only emotion in the set. Before we look at *mirth*, the motivation for a mind to search out subtle oversights made in reasoning that could infect the integrity of our knowledge, we should briefly survey other members, each of which seems to have a different purpose, but all of which are important in organizing the particular kind of reasoning that humans perform.

C. Emotions

I've read that the brain is the most amazing thing in the universe (but look what's *telling* us that).

—Emo Philips

We know why we are born curious: We are, as George Miller once said, *informavores*. Our hunger for novelty drives us to fill our heads with facts we might need some day, and this is a feature we share with vertebrates in general, and at least some of the other clever locomotors—cephalopods most strikingly. Some of our innate experiential hungers are tuned to specific topics (Dennett 2006). For instance, we know what *libido* is for, even if we don't know the details of its evolutionary history. It evolved to ensure that mating opportunities would be seized more often than not, by installing a nearly irresistible urge (not as irresistible as the urge to breathe, but able to hold its own against the urge to eat, to stay safe and sound, to sleep, to go fishing . . .). We also know what our *sweet tooth* is for: We evolved with a hard-wired preference for high-energy food. And we know why we are also suckers for *cuteness*; our perceptual-motivational systems have a bias for infant faces that serves those infants well when they depend on our willingness to give their care and protection a higher priority than they otherwise would have. In each case, the deeper, evolutionary explanation almost inverts our everyday wisdom: We don't like sugar because it's intrinsically sweet (whatever that would mean!), it's sweet because we're wired up to like it; guys don't go for girls (or guys, for that matter) who are intrinsically sexy, we go for those who are perceived by us to be sexy;[5] the cuteness of babies is an effect derived from the triggering of our nurturing instincts, not the cause of our nurturing.[6] These three built-in "flavors" of experiential hunger are now exploited by culturally evolved systems of artifacts designed to tickle our fancies for many ulterior purposes. We have pornographers and confectioners; we have cartoonists who know how to make a cute mouse, bear, alligator, or ogre; and we have advertisers who know how to exploit any or all these tastes to sell things that can't be mated with, eaten, or nurtured. (We will eventually show how comedy similarly exploits the mirth-instinct.)

All emotions are anchored in our neurophysiology, but they also have physiological effects outside the brain. Various emotions cause us to sweat, salivate, cry, modulate our breathing, pulse, and/or blood pressure, dilate or constrict our pupils, blush or pale, tighten or relax various muscles. These effects are mediated by internal diffusion of hormones and neuromodulators whose distinct identities, in ebb and flood, we can discern both "directly" (by discerning some of their internal effects—such as an adrenaline rush, or a blissful bath of oxytocin) and indirectly (by observing their external effects, in ourselves and others).[7]

William James's well-known theory of emotion (James 1884; see also Lange 1885; James 1890) maintains that the physiological effects of the emotions are created in response to certain perceptual and cognitive events, and the ensuing sensory detection of these physiological effects is what gives the emotions their phenomenological qualities—the qualities that allow us to feel a consistency in them from episode to episode. If we did not blush, what would embarrassment feel like? James and Lange would claim that it wouldn't feel like anything at all. This position is another inversion of everyday wisdom: We don't cry because we're sad, we're sad because we cry! This is perhaps an oversimplifying tagline, but

5. Likewise, the inverse holds as well. The natural wiring *inside a perceiver* that detects various gender-specific traits is what makes people with those traits sexy.

6. Somewhat more circumspectly: The spatial properties we perceive as cuteness would not be so perceived independently of our evolved disposition to nurture infants that *looked like that*. The cuteness we perceive is as much an *effect* of our evolved way of responding as an independently existing perceptible property.

7. Notice that the phenomenal sensations available to us from our bodies are far from exhausted by those senses we can enumerate with the words in our languages. There is a plethora of internal sensory transducers that provide distinct "feels" for various physiological events (e.g., interoceptors for carbon dioxide in the bloodstream, or, as noted above, for oxytocin or epinephrine).

it gets the idea across. Some (e.g., Griffiths 1997; Solomon 1976) have argued against this position, insisting that certain emotions (e.g., envy, guilt, jealousy) can occur without physiological responses. Others have challenged the James–Lange view, underscoring that severing the viscera from the spinal cord does not seem to alter emotional behavior (e.g., Cannon 1927; see also Chwalisz, Diener, and Gallagher 1988) and that identical physiological changes can lead to different emotions (Cannon 1927; Marañon 1924; Schachter and Singer 1962). In our view, Prinz successfully defends a version of the James–Lange theory, discounting the Cannon and the Schachter and Singer results as inconclusive and multiply interpretable (see Prinz 2004 for details). He also says that the jealousy that Griffiths has in mind is a disposition to be jealous, rather than an occurrent instance of jealousy. Such dispositions may make us hope our lover comes home on time every evening; but occurrences, which only happen when that lover actually is late, do have physiological effects.

Extensions of the James–Lange model (by, e.g., Damasio 1994, and Prinz 2004, who calls emotions "embodied appraisals"; see also Niedenthal 2007, for a concise review of the ways in which emotional information is embodied) argue that emotions are a type of informational feedback loop that takes place not just in the brain but in the rest of the body—some stimulus causes a cognitive event, which releases hormones into the body, which in turn create the physiological changes that are then perceived through proprioceptive senses and become an integrated sensorial element of that event. These loops have properties that a purely cerebral processing system would not—could not—have. The first important property is temporal: Emotions are extended over time as the physiological effects that are initiated and the signaling chemicals that are released by the sympathetic and parasympathetic nervous systems to induce those effects both require significantly more time than purely cognitive events—the firing of neurons—to run their course.

Second, emotions always have *valence*; they are positive or negative.[8] Valence means that events that we sense through these kinds of feedback

---

8. The physiological effects of the emotions and the perception of those effects are involuntary—if the emotion occurs, you will feel it. But, the behaviors that are associated with those emotions are at least semivoluntary. That is to say, different kinds of pains (and pleasures) of varying intensities are an impetus to act, but inasmuch as they are sensory input, they can then be cognitively modulated with respect to other goals, given other simultaneous emotions or pragmatic information—pains can be disregarded and pleasures resisted, if necessary. We are setting aside, for present purposes, a host of interesting questions on the interaction of

loops are not just things that we recognize can benefit or injure us, but things that we perceive as *good or bad* for those reasons.[9] With valenced feedback of this sort, a "merely cognitive" event (e.g., witnessing a death or watching your child win a spelling bee) can become painful or pleasurable *in the same way* that more "bodily" events (e.g., orgasm, weariness, and satiation) are painful or pleasurable—that is, the value of the event is known because there are valence-coupled physiological repercussions played out through the body.[10] In the more visceral conditions the pleasure or pain is directly (physically directly) caused in the body (by, e.g., sexual activity, hard work, or eating), and in the emotional feedback loop it requires the quick (automatic) assessment of factual or implicit content to impact the emotional system and instigate it to then signal the bodily response. In this way, the intangible quite literally becomes tangible—a thing that could only be cognitively assessed before now has substantial material value, and we can say without metaphor that watching the opening scene of *Saving Private Ryan*, for instance, is a truly *visceral* experience.

It is well known that crude but effective danger-transducing sensory circuits can swiftly trigger orientation responses before the cause of the danger is identified by a slower cognitive process that can declare a false alarm and cancel the incipient adrenaline rush, if there is probably no danger (see, e.g., LeDoux 1998, 2002). This can result in *almost imperceptible* and vanishingly brief emotional twinges, which can still have potent ongoing motivational effects. Emotions, in general, must be *felt*, but we shouldn't make this true by definition, since there are fundamentally similar processes that lurk just beneath the threshold of noticeability.

This rather broad definition of emotion is quite contrary to some more specific categorizations (e.g., Descartes 1649/1988; Ekman 1992, 1999; Tomkins 1962; Izard 1971; Oatley and Johnson-Laird 1987),[11] but it has

---

cognition and emotions, such as appraisal theories and their critics. See Arnold 1960, Zajonc 1984, and Lazarus 1984.

9. A pain without valence is a qualitatively similar sensation that we just don't see as problematic—as attested by patients on morphine (Melzack and Casey 1968). For a detailed account of anomalous pain, see Grahek 2007.

10. For arguments considering pains to be a subclass of emotions, see Craig 2003, Gustafson 2006, and Vogt 2005.

11. Though Prinz (2004) does not offer a categorization of emotions, he might theoretically disagree with our broad definition. He considers pains, desires, and hungers to be affective

had several recent excellent defenses, among them those by Damasio (1994, 1999) and Huron (2006).

When classifying the emotions, it is often noted that the time scale of emotional episodes is widely variable, sometimes operating only on a scale of seconds, and other times, as in the emotion of love, over a span of years. This perception is a mistake. The love that lasts years is not an uninterrupted stream of loving, but rather a strong tendency, over those years, to repeatedly feel discrete instances of the emotion of love (see, e.g., Solomon 1976). So, the love that a person has for their spouse is not a continuous activity, but rather a disposition to experience a protracted series of relatively brief emotional episodes that may be experienced over the course of many years. These episodes may occur multiple times per day, and one may be well aware of them. Such episodes may in fact interrupt (deliciously) whatever train of thought one is engaged in, but they do (normally) soon end, at which point one's attention is free to return to other topics, other projects. They may nevertheless have cumulative effects far beyond the introspective reach of the person, solidifying bonds of loyalty, trust, and sympathy, creating a long-term relational state that is also known as love, but is not itself an emotional state.

In contrast, a number of emotions such as anger, giddiness, or guilt often seem to last uninterruptedly for at least hours, if not days, without apparent episodic interruption over those time scales. But this kind of consistency can be explained as a series of overlapping episodes. There is either a constant stimulus or a feedback loop that is reinitiating the emotion regularly. If the stimulus that causes an emotion is consistently present, then the emotion may be continually triggered. More interestingly, if the event that triggered an emotion is dwelled upon owing to the intensity of the emotion, then the ensuing thought can, as a surrogate for the initial stimulus, consistently retrigger the emotion. If you keep thinking about what made you dejected in the first place, you'll become more miserable. These feedback loops, as we all know well, can be difficult to escape.

---

motivational states, but not emotions. We think this is just a disagreement in terms. Prinz admits the same category of valenced motivators that we label as emotions and finds it very important that they all form a category; he just prefers to reserve the word "emotion" for one subset of these—those that are instigated by cognitively transduced feedback—while calling the others, variously, pains and hungers. We are content to coclassify the valenced motivations under the name emotions, as we think the differentiating factor (the complexity of the transduction process) is less of a defining characteristic than the motivational function.

This triggering of an emotion from conception rather than perception plays another significant role in the minds of thinking agents like humans. Most animals apparently have emotions associated with expectations and memories—a dog viewing a bowl of food will most likely have a "thought" of eating that drives an emotional desire. So it is with us, too; in this way, not just our experiences, but our memories and expectations, can have valence. Coupling this with our perhaps unique ability to dream up hypothetical futures and counterfactual pasts not only allows us to live out those imaginary events, but also to *evaluate* them. Damasio (1994) termed this notion the *somatic marker hypothesis* and suggested that because of the availability of these evaluations we have the capability to choose between alternative futures by comparison of the emotional values of potential events as measured by their similarity to past events. (See also Huron 2006 on anticipation-driven emotions.)

In sum, an emotion is an internally induced pleasure or pain—a valenced perception—caused by a variety of processes of transduction of information in the world. In being valenced, they provide value—a sort of default motivation—to their associated stimuli. We are not *indifferent* to emotionally valenced perceptions. In being perceptual, they are capable of taking part in informational processing in the mind much like other perceptual data. This allows cocategorization of emotionally similar events, but perhaps more importantly it allows for emotional priming, in which a memory or a thought may awaken a feeling, or a feeling may reference a memory.[12] Such priming may underlie the operation of somatic markers providing the ability to make informed decisions by evaluating potential futures. Generally, emotions occur on the time scale of the physiological changes in the body that are caused by neuromodulator and hormonal floods and their reabsorption or diffusion refractory period—seconds to minutes. But briefer, less noticeable effects—indeed, subliminal emotional effects—are not ruled out, and may play important roles in the dynamics of experience (Booth 1969; Huron 2006). In any event, when they and their effects are gone, you no longer *feel* the emotion, though effects way beyond this may occur as a result of the way the cognitive system or the world interacts with the triggering content for that emotion.

---

12. Bower (1981) showed that inducing emotional states that are congruent with those occurring during an event facilitates recall of the event.

D. The Rationality of Emotions

> We really need to change that historic dichotomy of cognition on the one hand,
> emotions on the other hand, and realize that our emotions are the fuel that gives
> rise to social behavior but also to different levels of intelligence.
>
> —Stanley Greenspan

Both the English words *emotion* and *motivation* derive from the same
Latin root, *movere* (meaning "to move"), indicating that, early on, it was
recognized that the emotions are motivations to action. A number of
modern theories of emotions also conclude that the purpose is to motivate:
Zajonc (1980) saw that a number of emotions seemed to characterize their
attendant stimuli as things that we like or dislike and induce in us a tendency to approach or avoid those kinds of phenomena; Frijda (1986) used
the term "action tendency" to describe an emotion as something that
increased the likelihood of particular behaviors; and, Prinz (2004) argues
for a similar position that assigns motivation not to the appraisal quality
of the emotion but to the valence. It should be clear that our view of the
emotions (as pleasures and pains not different from hunger and satiety) is
aligned with these theories (see also Damasio 1999).

Now that we have framed the higher emotions as corporeal feedback
systems that provide valenced assessment of contents which do not have
direct sensory transducers (see above, p. 68), we can see that their effect
on behavior can be much the same as external rewards[13] and punishments;
though content-mediated, they still have the power to reward or punish a
reinforcement learning system in the same ways that resident corporeal
pains and pleasures can. Thorndike's (1911) "law of effect"—the idea that
punishment or reward will increase or decrease the likelihood of recurrence
of the associated behavior—applies equally to these mediated sensations
as to direct sensations, and behavioral tendencies are thus equally modified
by emotional feedback as by rewards such as food, sugar squirts, or cocaine.
It is, in fact, unnecessary to posit any motivations beyond those that fit

---

13. External rewards such as food are of course "directly" valuable to organisms, as means to
their survival, but they serve as rewards *by way of* causing physical stimuli ("pleasures") which
trigger internal rewards in the limbic system (Olds and Milner 1954). Since physical pains and
pleasures are registered in the limbic system as are emotional pains and pleasures, there is a
kind of central system for reward regardless of whether the distal mechanism is an emotional
content or an "external" reward such as food.

the law of effect when the full range of emotions is seen as identical with the other corporeal, valenced sensations. In some instances, when the behavior at issue is external and writ large, this is obvious. Hunger pangs, gustatory pleasure, nausea, and satiation (and even the dull ache of having an overstuffed belly) orchestrate our schedule of eating behaviors. Less readily discernible emotional modulations, with several emotions working in concert, or in opponent processes, provide the net motivation for further sorts of behaviors, including covert, internal behaviors: whatever the behaviors are that are likely to be effective at reducing the pains or achieving the pleasures.

Thorndike argued that, if the learning curve was smooth (which he found to be the case), then we needn't posit a rich internal mental life to explain an animal's behavior. Reinforcement learning alone would explain such learning as long as the reward increased the behavioral likelihood in a regular fashion—something that Herrnstein (1970) later formulated mathematically. The contingencies in the environment—regularities of rewards and punishments—will structure the behavioral tendencies of the animal, *modulo* its inherent sensitivities to each particular reward as well as interaction effects between types of rewards and punishments. Under this formulation, the emotions as motivators provide a *kind* of rationality. They direct our behaviors, and they had better direct them in a reasonable manner, or evolution will punish them with extinction. For such "visceral" urges as hunger, thirst, disgust, and libido, the benefit to our genes' replicative imperative is obvious. Thanks to these kinds of peremptory sensations, we know when to eat, sleep, and mate; we know to avoid sharp or too-hot or too-cold objects; we know to avoid bumping into hard objects; when our muscles are overworked; when to hold our breaths, and when to gasp for more. These behaviors are most often performed at precisely the right— the most reasonable—moments. But it is not quite as clear what roles the more sophisticated emotions play. Why should we well up with pleasure when seeing cute children (or animals), fall into romantic love, blush with embarrassment, or behave in destructive ways (even to ourselves or our own families) when enraged?

Frank (1988) clarifies these cases and others. His evolutionary account takes an economic stance on the passions, arguing that the emotions were each naturally selected for as a way of creating behavioral benefits to the (genes of the) individual that the individual would not have chosen on their own given a purely rational outlook. For instance, love and guilt, he says, are solutions to the *commitment problem*. A commitment problem "arises when it is in a person's interest to make a binding commitment to behave in a way that will later seem contrary to self-interest" (1988, p. 47). The belief that one's prospective mate might shop around and try to find a better mate than oneself can leave two rational—overly rational—agents in the mating marketplace unwilling to settle for a deal that may be the best they can ever get. Exhibiting the exaggerated and moonstruck behaviors of "falling in love" can be a fine guarantor of one's steadfastness, but only because it is not (apparently) within the rational control of the agent.[14] Moreover, without these emotions, cuckolding and philandering would run rampant in the population. People who otherwise might stray instead feel a compulsory commitment not to do so as a result of the physiological effects of the gratifying sense of attachment and the agonizing sense of loss furnished by love, as well as the deeply anguished sense of wrongdoing provided by guilt. The benefits, to our genes, of causing us to feel these emotions are that we do make commitments to family unions—a type of implicit economic agreement that raises the likelihood of offspring survival.[15]

Another example, elaborating on Trivers's (1971) account of reciprocal altruism, is that of the emotion of guilt, which, as Frank's hypothesis asserts, is meant to discourage social cheating and/or encourage redress—a set of behavioral patterns that create a future social-capital surplus that exceeds the spurious short-term benefit of the social cheating episode. You don't steal your neighbor's dinner when he's not looking, because collaborating with him gains you more than just a dinner in the long run. *But,* on Frank's account, *you* don't need to know that's the benefit—you only need to know that you feel guilty about the thought of stealing his dinner. Evolution, which has learned the larger

---

14. There will be more on Frank's account of the *expression* of emotions in chapter 12.

15. Konner (1982) provides an account of romantic love that suggests its purpose is for the passionate start to new relationships as opposed to relationship maintenance and instead motivates behaviors such as mate *desertion*. Griffiths (2003) claims that this position opposes Frank's. We have two notes to make on this: First, it seems that the two emotions that Konner and Frank are describing are different ones. The new, passionate love of an affair is of a very different nature and quality than the familial love of a long-term partner. Each has its own purpose but, like many emotions, they may sometimes come into conflict with each other. Moreover, if only one of these stories is right it harms neither Frank's overall thesis that the emotion helps us give a well-backed signal of our commitment nor the additional thesis that the emotions are evolution's way of directing behaviors we would not otherwise choose.

social calculus for you, simply takes care of making you feel guilty, and you, unwittingly, do the rest.

Each emotion begets a related set of behaviors that generate a lasting, durable advantage, which sometimes, perhaps, is immeasurable to the organism's sensors but which evolution has found usually outweighs a smaller short-term benefit that may be more directly obvious to the organism. Each emotion is, in this way, tied to *particular* behaviors for the simple reason that those are precisely the behaviors that have been learned to have a causal effect on inducing the pleasure or relieving the pain that is that emotion.[16] The reinforcement learning system that is intertwined with this emotional motivation model, using the kind of learning curve that Thorndike described, will learn how to balance (roughly) all of these pleasures and pains to optimize the behaviors it stumbles upon in achieving the goals it has evolved for. All together, the system of emotions interacting with one another drives a kind of behavioral decision making that, for the most part, makes reasonable choices (although see the next section for ways in which this system fails).[17]

This kind of rationality conferred upon us by these kinds of emotions is useful for a great many tasks. It is the kind of rationality that helps all animals navigate the physical world—and even some aspects of the social world—and choose reasonable paths of behavior most of the time. But there is a kind of rationality that distinguishes humans from other animals: the kind of methodical, logical reasoning founded (supposedly) on axioms such as the law of noncontradiction. This is the kind that helps us solve riddles, for instance. For that kind of rationality, a different set of emotions are necessary, different not in operation (for they are emotions, after all), but in the kind of content that can trigger or relieve them. Said another way, the difference is only in the kinds of behaviors they induce—only in the kinds of things that we approach and avoid as a result of these epistemic emotions. Much of our epistemic behavior consists of covert behaviors occurring in the brain; but they are, nonetheless, *behaviors*, with most of the other features of overt behaviors, including that they are often

---

16. In direct transduction motivators, the short-term cost to be overcome is not as complicated as something like social cheating. It is often as simple as the expenditure of energy to act, rather than to not act.

17. The prediction made here is that, with an extremely similar general mental architecture, most of the diverse behavioral differences seen in the denizens of the animal kingdom can be explained primarily by differences in bodily structure and differences in emotional structure.

deliberate activities that tend to require attention, are usually instigated by perceived events, and can even be conditioned.

It is both customary and intuitive to draw a distinction between thinking and doing. But to take this distinction strictly and nonmetaphorically—assigning thinking as a process that is not something that "is done"—would be dualist, indeed. The claim made here is that it is not only a physical process, but a motivated and deliberate physical process. We view the distinction between thinking and doing simply as whether or not the neural process that is occurring terminates on motoneurons or on other internal neurons that don't excite motor activity, but that perhaps correspond to concepts involved in the thought. In the case of dancing, the motoneurons must be activated such that the body actually glides about in the world; but it is likely that, in the case of simply thinking about dancing, most of the rest of the neurological process is the same except that the motoneurons are inhibited from causing actual movement.[18]

Then, broadly, a cognitive behavior is a mental function—an intentional (in the casual sense of the term) change of intentional (in the philosopher's sense of the term) states. They effect some change of state in the brain, which restricts the possible future states of the neural dynamics. Some examples of regularized cognitive behaviors may make the point clearer: certain kinds of data collection (e.g., the direction of attention—the search through perceptual space—in order to detect some necessary piece of information to support ongoing semantic processing), various parts of the act of problem solving (which often consists of the selective insertion or deletion of information from a mental space [a term, borrowed from Fauconnier 1985, that we lay out in more detail in the next chapter] in order to see if the consistency of the new sum total can reduce the path

---

18. It is not unlikely, given the research on mirror neurons (e.g., Gallese et al. 1996; Rizzolatti et al. 1996) showing identity between neurons involved in activity and perception of the same activity as well as recent work suggesting identity between the neural machinery involved in both perception and conception (see Goldstone and Barsalou 1998 or Kosslyn, Ganis, and Thompson 2001 for reviews), that the neurons active in Popper's simulated worlds are the same ones that move muscles in real activity, but that other simultaneous circuits are inhibiting the actual motion of the muscles in the real world. Proponents of the ideomotor theory of perception and action (James 1890) and its successor, the common code theory (e.g., Hommel et al. 2001), also support the notion that perception and action share common representations and are thus functionally intertwined. See also Chalmers, French, and Hofstadter 1995 for arguments that conceptual processes cannot exist without perceptual components.

to a conclusion or suggest something about the validity of the inserted or deleted premise), and creative acts of semantic recombination.

Just as overt behaviors require emotional motivation—social behaviors are directed by social emotions and survival behaviors are directed by survival emotions—so too do covert behaviors such as cognitive behaviors require incentive to drive an actor to perform them. Dennis Proffitt recently began an essay saying "Perception is effortless. It just happens. Unlike perception, acts of thinking, remembering, speaking, and reasoning often require some effort and planning" (Proffitt 1999). Not only do we have to be coaxed into doing the tasks of thinking, but we also have to be shown just *how* to do it. We are not natural-born thinkers—*we have to be taught* both when and how to think. Of course, this requires supervision, but the supervision need not come from other humans—parents and teachers—as we might expect. Instead, it is a kind of *auto-supervision* performed within the system, by the epistemic emotions, which tell us—just as pain tells us when to withdraw a hand from a heat source—when to question, when to imagine, and when to laugh.

Gopnik and colleagues noticed that problem solving in children is associated with a positive affective response (and often a concomitant expression of joy), which she aptly named the "theory drive" (Gopnik 1998). The idea is that the positive emotion (which she calls "explanation" but we will refer to as "insight" or "discovery") that is associated with the successful accomplishment of creating an explanation—the sense of "Aha!" that comes with the piecing together of a consistent theory of the situation at hand or a string of related events—is a prime motivational factor for performing the kinds of covert cognitive behaviors of theory development that lead to those kinds of theories/explanations. We are innately endowed with a desire to work on building theories. Gopnik continues to explain that theory-construction in both infants and scientists is the same behavior, lying on an unbroken continuum, where the scientists' version of theorization is simply a socially organized extension of the child's (really, everyone's) basic theory-construction device (Gopnik and Wellman 1994; Gopnik and Meltzoff 1997; Gopnik 1998). In fact, children discover and verify their theories in quite the same way as scientists do: through experimentation. They manipulate the world and discover regularities of causation from those manipulations. Why do they do it? The discovery of regularities comes with a pleasurable burst of insight, which all of us, but especially children and scientists, continuously long for like bonbons or opium. Gopnik takes Frank's (1988) argument seriously when she says,

"Again, the analogy to sexual drives should be obvious. Nature ensures that we do something that will be good for us (or at least our genes) in the long run, by making it fun (or at least compelling) in the short-run" (Gopnik 1998, p. 107).

Insight does not stand alone in performing this job, and theory development is not the only cognitive job that needs to be motivated. A series of other epistemic emotions are involved in driving us to construct a stable and faithful "representation" of the world. If insight is like orgasm as Gopnik's metaphor declares, then, likewise, curiosity might be the analogue of lust. The epistemic hunger of curiosity—a burning desire to find reason and order—prompts us to fervently advance upon situations that require explanatory exertion (often to exhaustion) that ultimately leads to that religiously adored moment of insight. And just as lust suddenly dissolves into triviality with orgasm, so does the hungry feeling of curiosity hastily retreat upon the achievement of insight. Though it may have killed the cat, curiosity more than compensates for its cost: Without it we mightn't seek answers or theories at all.

Not all of the epistemic emotions fit so aptly to the sexual metaphor; cognition is probably not as simple as sex. Boredom has its place in driving us out from cognitive malaise. Though curiosity inspires our cognitive apparatus into detailed exertion surrounding particular as-of-yet-unexplained regularities, we would scarcely commence toil at all without the dull pain of boredom to keep us from the simple irresponsibility of just doing nothing. If there is no pressing topic to think about, we still bother to think, and incessantly so, because it hurts not to.

While curiosity and boredom oppose insight in the same way that hungers oppose satiation, there is another kind of counterpart to discovery. More of a pain than a hunger (and certainly not a pleasurable feeling such as the wonder of discovery), this converse is the emotion of confusion. One version of confusion is that *nagging* sort of anxiety when you sense that something is funny-huh. Rather than rewarding one for achieving a consistent theory, this negative signal punishes one for inconsistency and encourages the rapid resolution of contradiction. When things make sense we feel great (insight); but, on the contrary, when sense is lost we feel a distinct pain in the mind: a deep, and sometimes desperate, confusion.[19]

---

19. Let us not neglect the close cousin of confusion, doubt, an also negative but less strong sensation which indicates not quite a full contradiction but a partial inconsistency.

Epistemic uncertainty—the lack of a persuasive answer to a pressing question—has its own emotional accompaniment, also called uncertainty, and this is the negative emotion that accompanies and drives cautious probing, heightened sensitivity to alarm, putting orientation-responses on a hair-trigger. There are likely to be more epistemic emotions than those described here, or more refined subdivisions among these.[20] What we have given is a start at analyzing cognitive/epistemic behaviors in terms of the emotions that motivate and direct them. Much more can be said about the mechanics of thought and how simple pleasures and pains administered at just the right moments can direct those mechanisms in meaningfully rational ways, but that is a much more extensive work for another time.

E. The Irrationality of Emotions

Love is like pi—natural, irrational, and very important.

—Lisa Hoffman

Nothing defines humans better than their willingness to do irrational things in the pursuit of phenomenally unlikely payoffs. This is the principle behind lotteries, dating, and religion.

—Scott Adams

How did reason come into the world? As is fitting, in an irrational manner, by accident. One will have to guess at it as at a riddle.

—Friedrich Nietzsche

---

20. E.g., recent findings (Reber, Brun, and Mitterndorfer 2008) have linked truth and beauty. Things that incite our sense of aesthetics are more likely to be believed as true regardless of their actual truth value. Perhaps this aesthetic sense is one of the epistemic emotions. Also, current theories about play (Fagen 1993; Byers and Walker 1995; Spinka, Newberry, and Bekoff 2001) indicate that it may be for the purpose of honing skills—physical, mental, and social. A useful trait, indeed, but only if one performs it. The emotion of "fun" or "playfulness" is what encourages us to spend the energy on the games that constitute play. However, it is not yet clear to us whether this notion of fun is a separate emotion in its own right, or whether it is a catch-all term used to refer to any of a number of other positive emotions including various kinds of social enjoyment, insight, and the like. The joy of carving a good corner on a waterski or a snowboard may be the reward of sustaining a delicate vestibular perceptual balance, along with making a proper prediction and perhaps conjoint with a bit of social ego-stroking from looking good in front of onlookers.

In the previous section we argued that the emotions, broadly construed, are rational motivators that encourage us to do the right things at the right times in order to balance all the survival and reproductive needs we face, assuming we live in roughly the same (physical and social) environment in which our genes underwent selection. Thanks to the emotions of physical fatigue and mental weariness, we know when to spend energy and when to save it. Moving beyond that, hunger tells us when to forage for more energy; thirst, when to hydrate; and fear, when to run for our lives. An agent that can manage the coordinated timing of just these behaviors already will have solved a number of important environmental challenges. Augmenting this view with Frank's explanation, we realize that superficially irrational emotions, such as romantic love, solve even more complicated natural quandaries such as the commitment problem, allowing us to engage successfully in even more complicated social environments. Lastly, we suggested that the most complex problems—problems that require open-ended thinking—are also solved by a certain set of emotions: curiosity, boredom, doubt, confusion, insight, mirth, and the like.

In spite of all this well-planned behavioral control handed down to us by evolution, we are still quite unreasonable people. Some emotions make us behave in ways that seem to be overreactions, with costs that seem to outweigh their benefits: extreme outbursts of violence due to either jealousy or rage, or suicide in the wake of heartbreak, for instance. Ending up in jail for murdering the fellow who made you a cuckold may seem beyond reason, but recall that for much of the history of our species, until quite recently, there were no systems of law with such a consequence. So, one explanation for this apparent irrationality might be that the environment in which these emotions evolved was not the one we live in today. The better answer, we think, is that these emotions may occasionally have had the cost of overreaction, but the sum benefit these emotions provide over a lifetime, in their usual circumstances, simply outweighed such infrequent costs. Overreaction is one kind of irrationality, but there is an even more pervasive—and thus more important—way that we act unreasonably.

We helplessly procrastinate when we have important jobs; we smoke cigarettes from packages printed with images of lung cancer; we become addicted to liquor and drugs and then watch them destroy our careers, families, and social lives; we cheat on our diets; we cheat on our spouses; we fail to save for the future; and we gamble away our hard-earned cash when we know the odds are against us. Why didn't evolution provide us with the right emotional constitution to restrain us from engaging in these damaging behaviors? Though some of them, such as cocaine and diets, are relatively new environmental challenges, this is not the primary reason. Cheating and procrastination are age-old problems. And, though we might just chalk it up to evolutionary oversights, problems yet to be solved but which aren't markedly injurious to reproductive success, there is another more convincing answer: Because it can't.

Each of the above examples is due to a runaway—but necessary—desire that participates in a heuristic system that chooses behaviors by balancing and time-sharing control of resources between various necessary goals. These are all forms of addiction. Drugs, alcohol, and gambling are all well known as addictive activities. Procrastination is an addiction to laziness— an effective energy-conservative strategy; diet cheating is an addiction to the joys provided by the flavors of sugars and fats; spousal cheating is an addiction to various social and sexual emotions; and wasting your savings may be a result of an addiction to any number of things. The key point here is that each of these behaviors is one that we should be motivated to do—in moderation (except drugs, which hijack our reward systems at a chemical level)—but when the balance is thrown off by improper valuations we behave irrationally.

Choosing how to behave under uncertainty requires a heuristic choice process. Good heuristics give excellent approximations much of the time. But, in the (restricted-by-design) areas where they fail, they give predictably—even pathologically—poor results. The emotions are rational, but the system is a heuristic driver of behavior that operates on incomplete information; so we must accept that the emotions will fail us in some ways, such as overreactions and addictions, that are irresolvable.

Ainslie's (2001) discussion of hyperbolic discounting is a brilliant account of just where the system we have fails, but he also shows how over the centuries we have cobbled together layers of corrective ploys that—when they work—can smooth out some of the awkward bulges in our emotional control systems. Many moves familiar from personal experiences and hundreds of films and dramas emerge from his analysis, such as Ulysses' encounter with the Sirens, where he tied himself to the mast and plugged his crews' ears with wax so that he could resist temptation. These ploys are also favorite targets of humor. Raising the stakes for ourselves changes the task of self-control we confront, for instance:

(18) As the old-time Maine farmer began to hitch up his overalls after using the outhouse, a quarter rolled out of his pocket and fell down the hole. "Dang!" he said, and pulled a five-dollar bill out of his wallet and

threw it down the hole after the quarter. "Why on earth did you do that?" he was asked. "You don't think I'm going down there for a quarter, do you?" he replied.

F. Emotional Algorithms

Figure 6.1
© Tribune Media Services, Inc. All rights reserved. Reprinted with permission.

The mind has often been viewed as a tripartite organ, comprised of distinct, but interacting, processes for cognition, emotion, and conation or will (Hilgard 1980). Cognitive science has consistently focused well on the first of these—the information processing that allows for perception, categorization, and rational decision making—but has mostly left the studies of emotion and motivation to psychologists and even, recently, economists. Joseph LeDoux, for one, sees this as shortsighted:

> The kind of mind modeled by cognitive science can, for example, play chess very well, and can even be programmed to cheat. But it is not plagued with guilt when it cheats, or distracted by love, anger, or fear. Neither is it self-motivated by a competitive streak, or by envy or compassion. If we are to understand how the mind, through the brain, makes us who we are, we need to consider the *whole* mind, not just the parts that subserve thinking. (LeDoux 2002, p. 24)

Modeling cognition, emotion, and motivation together is difficult; so cognitive scientists have decided to *modularize* their work, and focus first on what seems the more important part—the thinking—while leaving emotions and motivation for separate studies. The problem with modularizing the work is that it has the tendency also to modularize the models of the mind produced from such work in ways that may not reflect natural divisions. This book suggests, instead, that what was once seen as pure rationality may itself be intricately bound up with emotions and motivations.

LeDoux makes an excellent point: A science of the mind does need to account for all of the aspects of mind, not just an idealized cognitive rationality; not just perception and reason. And, it must not only account for all of the aspects, but they must be accounted for *together, in the same mind.* This issue has been partially addressed. More and more, these days, the emotions and motivations are being welded together to form a unifying notion in which behavior is driven principally by a reward system that, while perhaps neurologically complicated, is phenomenologically comprised simply of the passions (Frank 1988; Ainslie 2001; Damasio 1994, 1999, 2003). On Ainslie's account (see ch. 4 of Ainslie 2001) pleasures and pains, as well as itches, hungers, addictions, compulsions, and desires—and our various proclivities for giving in to each by executing the behaviors associated with them—are all results of the same hyperbolic discount function being applied, on different time scales, to emotional valences derived either from direct experience or from expectations.

This would still leave us with a dichotomy between cognition and the passions. But, we think our sketch of an account of the epistemic emotions is another step in unifying the trichotomy. By seeing thought as consisting of behaviors, albeit largely internal *mental* behaviors, and as fully motivated by a subset of the passions in the same way that overt behaviors are, we can classify higher cognition—reasoning, puzzling, and decision making—as simply a resultant component of the emotional mind.

High human cognition depends on a large range of these emotions—without them there would be no curiosity, no discoveries, no problem solving, no creativity, and no humor. One might presume that those joys and skills are *luxuries* that are afforded only after the basics of rational thought have been acquired—add-ons that piggyback atop standard rationality—but we submit that the epistemic emotions do not simply encourage us to use our reasoning; *they control it.*

For instance, without a sense of confusion, we claim, you would not know what a contradiction is—it is *only* the inclusion in your biology (and thus in your phenomenology) of this exceptionally strange pain that allows you to notice contradictions. This is not a quantitative matter; it is not that confusion helps you to use a rationality, which already knows how to see contradiction, just to see more of them. Rather, what we are suggesting is that, without confusion, there would be no underlying sense that contradiction exists (and is bad!) *at all*. (Jackendoff 1987, chs. 15 and 16, and 2007, ch. 3, develops a pioneering version of this claim.) An explanation of rationality that assumed a skill at contradiction detection, rather than positing a mechanism for it, would be no explanation. Confusion (together with its neural-level trigger) *is* the detection mechanism and the fundamental basis for our innate appreciation of the law of noncontradiction. (To be clear, while pain tells us when our skin has been cut or bruised, it requires a special kind of nerve—nociceptors—to do so; likewise, confusion will require some kind of neural level "absurdiceptor" to trigger it. There are connectionist toy models for this [e.g., Shastri and Grannes 1996], but we currently have no idea what kind of homology such models have with actual neural structures.)

The same can be said for each of the epistemic emotions. And, collectively, they provide a much more complicated and nuanced kind of rationality: a kind that detects contradictions and abhors them as if they were hangnails; a kind that looks for and longs to solve problems even when there is no problem to solve; a kind that thrills with excitement when it finds a missing puzzle piece; and, as we will show in the next chapter, a kind that is mirthfully delighted with itself when it suddenly discovers that it has made a bold mistake. Higher cognition in its many forms—what it means to think like a human—is simply the chasing of the pleasures and the avoidance of the pains that are supplied by this eclectic group of cognitive, but of course ultimately neurobiological, emotions.

Saying that "cognition is simply X," no matter what X you are touting, is bound to be an oversimplification. Human cognition consists of analogy, metaphor, and conceptual blending (Hofstadter and the Fluid Analogies Research Group 1995; Lakoff and Johnson 1980, 1999; Fauconnier and Turner 2002), and happens in a rich embodied context with distributed extension and much scaffolding (Hutchins 1995a; Clark 1997; Clark and Chalmers 1998). And it is based on innate and automatic skills of perception, categorization, attention, and memory that we share with animals (though they don't show humor, complex logic, and human-like creativity). But at the outset we are going to embrace this simplifying imprecision for its rhetorical value, to push back against the traditional view. Our point is that our higher intelligence largely consists in the use of these basic faculties *in the service of* the epistemic emotions. We are using the same metonymy here as people do when they credit the directors of a company for the whole company's achievements—we are crediting the epistemic emotions for the work that they direct, though it is performed by the whole mind.

Our focus on the epistemic emotions has another implication for cognitive science: It suggests a radical revision of some fairly standard assumptions of computational modeling. We endorse the challenge of designing what we will call *emotional algorithms*.[21] It will not be an easy job. Emotional architectures, of the kind we envision, will be of a fundamentally different nature than today's machine-learning algorithms and integrated AGI models (such as SOAR [Laird, Rosenbloom, and Newell 1987], ACT-R [Anderson 1976], OSCAR [Pollock 2008], and LIDA [Franklin and Patterson 2006; Franklin 2007]).[22] These existing architectures don't account for emotion in any way at all—but to revise them would not consist of adding an "emotion module" alongside the working memory modules and the symbol-manipulating "inference engines." Our notion of emotional algorithms implies a control structure that relies on emotional states in competition and collaboration for inducing state changes in the system to drive both its bodily *and cognitive* behavior, not algorithms that compute emotional content as if it were simply an output. Emotional algorithms, in our sense, are not algorithms that have a state variable, for instance, called "anger" that gets adjusted up or down by events, and can then be read off by an observer who would subsequently compare it to a threshold value to determine whether the system is or is not angry, or which would be read by another subroutine that then perhaps "decides to initiate anger behaviors," as in robotic architectures such as those discussed by Mochida et al. (1995), Shibata, Ohkawa, and Tanie (1996), and Yamamoto (1993) (but see Kismet [Breazeal 2000] for some early baby steps in the right direction). Rather, we envisage an architecture for cognition in which the functional implementations of emotions are the computational substrate from which reason emerges by way of *motivating* the manipulation of data

---

21. This endorsement applies generally to the modeling of decision making that is mediated by emotions. However, we are especially interested in the epistemic emotions.

22. AGI (artificial *general* intelligence) is the recent term for the field of research that distinguishes its goals from those of the more common field of machine learning AI. These used to be known, respectively, as strong AI and weak AI.

in various ways that engender, among other activities, data-gathering (curiosity, boredom), recombinant thought (discovery), contradiction avoidance (confusion), and—we're getting to this soon, we promise—mistake recovery (mirth). Here we would distinguish the underlying "logical" competence that automatically generates implications from the *reasoning* that must emerge from, and be guided by, the interplay of epistemic emotional algorithms.

The contrast we are proposing can perhaps best be appreciated by considering the layperson's contrasting stereotypes of computation and human mentality. People understand that computers have been designed to keep needs and job performance almost entirely independent. Down in the hardware, the electric power is doled out evenhandedly and abundantly; no circuit risks starving. At the software level, a benevolent scheduler doles out machine cycles to whatever process has highest priority, and although there may be a bidding mechanism of one sort or another that determines which processes get priority, this is an orderly queue, not a struggle for life. (As Marx would have it, "From each according to his abilities, to each according to his needs.") It is a dim appreciation of this fact that probably underlies the common folk intuition that a computer could never "care" about anything. Not because it is made out of the wrong materials—why should silicon be any less suitable a substrate for caring than organic molecules?—but because its internal economy has no built-in risks or opportunities, so it doesn't have to care.[23]

Computational models in cognitive science have adopted the hierarchical control and ruthless efficiency of traditional software development for the obvious reason: There is a lot of number crunching to be done as swiftly as possible, so profligacy is to be avoided. But the result has been models that could not afford to be emotion driven, and, as a result, have left out the *underlying* level of processes we propose as necessary to explain higher human cognition—and, of course, humor. These processes are "wasteful,"[24] often seriously at cross purposes, and under no higher level of control (unlike the benign opponent processes that are *called up* by

---

23. This paragraph is drawn, with revisions, from Dennett 2007d.

24. The scare-quotes are here to indicate our disagreement with this term, *wasteful*. These processes are simply inefficient *on this measure*. Any architecture that utilizes resources to accomplish a goal necessarily embodies a variety of trade-offs—to optimize for one factor means to be inefficient on another front. This so-called wastefulness is the cost—in fact a small cost, and a necessary trade-off—paid in order to reap the benefit of a very different computational result.

higher-level controls in traditional computational systems, given a task to do, and then dismissed when the task is done). Such processes are still computational in the sense that they are ultimately information-driven and information-modifying processes whose only product is the induction and control of various behaviors. (In the same extended sense, what happens on the trading floor of the New York Stock Exchange is also a computational process, however unruly and competitive; its only products are the exchange of ownership of shares; today its by-products include exhaled CO_2, ulcers, and body odors, but the components that yield these by-products could be, and are on the verge of being, replaced by computational machines that are just as competitive, just as acquisitive, just as information-hungry.)

It may seem disconcertingly inhibitive that we think AGI researchers should attempt to replicate the mechanisms of human thought instead of trying any of a number of different methods to solve the problems they face. As one of our anonymous reviewers put it: "If you can make an emotionless machine that can play chess better than humans (such as Deep Blue), why could you not do this for a host of other skills?" The answer is that you *can* for many skills, but whether you can or not is very much contingent upon the demands of the particular skill or problem being solved. The emotionless machine that plays chess better than humans does so in a very different way than humans do. Hofstadter and colleagues (1995) argue convincingly that, although Deep Blue can beat us, the existence of such a machine says more about the domain of chess than it does about intelligence: Chess is the kind of problem that does not necessarily require full human intelligence in the same way that other domains do. It is not an AI-complete problem.[25] So, in many domains, AI researchers certainly can and should do as the reviewer suggests—a system for playing chess, or doing limited-domain household chores, or recommending books you might be interested in (cf. Amazon.com) will not require an emotional architecture. On the other hand, we think *AGI* researchers, who intend to create general-purpose thinking machines, should carefully consider the epistemic challenges their agents are facing and ask themselves whether the architecture they are building has a heuristic decision-making process to choose, under time-pressure, which behaviors to perform at which

---

25. The game of Go, on the other hand, has proven much more resistant to AI; while it may or may not be AI-complete, it surely requires much deeper modeling of human spatial thinking than chess does. See Müller 2002.

times, often blending multiple drives into singular actions; and, further-more, whether it has some embodiment of epistemic drives that competes with those other drives in order to perform the covert epistemic behaviors that an open-ended thinker inevitably must perform.

Our call for emotional algorithms is not necessarily a call for a wholly alternative cognitive modeling architecture (though it might come to that). Each of the currently competing paradigms of cognitive model captures some important features of cognition (perhaps like the blind folks captur-ing various important features of the elephant).[26] We are eager to adopt and adapt as much of this insightful work as possible. While we have argued against the weak form of augmentation which would implement a separate "emotion module," we expect the epistemic emotions may be implementable as more fundamental and pervasive augmentations of one or more of the existing paradigms that do account well for some aspects of memory, learning, and comprehension. For the time being, we want to avoid premature commitment to any operational suggestions that might limit the breadth of exploration.

G.   A Few Implications

A rope walks in to a bar. He calls the bartender and says "Barkeep, gimme a beer." The bartender says, "I'm sorry, we don't serve ropes in here."

Frustrated, the rope walks out. But this is the only bar in town, so he thinks about it a little. Then, in a spark of insight, he gets himself into a bind and frizzles his ends and walks back into the bar, and says, "Barkeep, gimme a beer."

The barkeep says, "Aren't you the same rope that came in here earlier?" The rope answers, "Nope, I'm a frayed knot."

Implications for the Axioms of Logic

The axioms from which we derive logic are not coded in us at birth as propositional knowledge, though the intuition to believe this is partially

---

26. We have in mind symbolic architectures (as argued for by Fodor and Pylyshyn 1988; Fodor 2004a,b); connectionist models (McClelland, Rumelhart, and the PDP Research Group 1986; Rumelhart, McClelland, and the PDP Research Group 1986; Elman 1991; Elman et al. 1996); dynamical systems models (see, e.g., Thelen and Smith 1994; van Gelder and Port 1995); the integrated AGI systems mentioned above; or some sui generis or hybrid designs such as Leabra (O'Reilly 1998; O'Reilly, Munakata, and McClelland 2000), or the "active symbol" model in parallel terraced scan architectures (Hofstadter and the FARG 1995; French 1995). See also Marcus 2001 for a theoretical description of a connectionist-symbolic hybrid.

correct—they are, in some way, innate, as Socrates demonstrated in the *Meno* with the example of the slave boy and his first geometry lesson. A learning process *of sorts* can bring the axioms into awareness, but they are not a part of the natural environment (outer *or inner*) to which a learning system would have direct access. The self-evident logical principles that Russell (1912) took for granted as the foundation of reason are brought to our attention via a feedback loop of *auto-supervision*. They are embodied not as principal propositions in a database of knowledge, but as covert generators of emotional reactions to certain structures of content perceived in the world. Evolution has learned that by simply enticing us with properly balanced rewards and punishments, by building in the proper auto-contingencies, she can make us behave as coherent and (somewhat) rational thinkers. Reflection on our native talents and habits of thought led Plato and Aristotle, and others, to formulate good rules for thinking, laying the foundations for formal logic and other technologies for extending and improving the cogency of our thinking.

Such a system could not replace the long-established form of cognition that exists in animals; it can only supplement it. Indeed, it is just one part of the emotional motivation-and-decision-making system that controls all behavior. Human behavior and decision making are based, like the behavior of other animals, on the outcome of interplay among the full array of emotions. It is only knowledge maintenance and higher-level thought that are managed by the cognitive-emotional subsystem. The choice to breathe is made prerationally. You do so because it hurts not to. The choice to eat is also made prerationally, driven by the "emotion" of hunger, just as it is in chimpanzees and other animals. But in people, unlike other animals, these brute passions have been partially supplanted by the ever more flexible and nuanced behavioral control provided by the epistemic emotions. No matter how hungry we are, we can choose not to eat food that we reason may likely have been poisoned by our enemies. We can choose not to stay and breathe in a garage deemed likely to be full of carbon monoxide—without *detecting* that the air is unbreathable, we can *reason* to that conclusion. Complex thoughts like these require the logical construction of mental spaces—and doing so requires the emotions that can produce such logic.

If rational thinking is an emotional process, it is clearly in competition with other emotion-driven processes. Emotional episodes must compete for time, energy, and functional real estate in the landscape of temporal embodiment where their existence is played out; and they must compete, just as other senses must, for attention from the perceptual system. This makes clear why humans are apt to have their reason overcome by such emotions as panic, distress, or rage. It outlines why, although we have an innate competence for rational thinking, we often lapse into performance that is less than reasonable. Reason is just as liable to succumb to cognitive temptations, to be forgone because of hyperbolic discounting (Ainslie 2001), as any other drive. Nonetheless, it is our ability to reason, at least occasionally, that allows us to build a complicated understanding of our world, and that differentiates *Homo sapiens* from apes.

Implications for Epistemology

If the methods of reason that we use to create inferences are a result of emotional processing, then belief itself is dependent on these emotions. Even the most unmodulated, basic beliefs—the beliefs about the layout of the world most directly anchored to current perception—depend on the play of emotions to the extent that they can be disrupted or distorted by strongly unbalanced emotions. The effects of wishful thinking begin right in the optic and auditory nerves (see McKay and Dennett 2009 for an analysis of putative cases of adaptive misbelief). To say that you believe something is to say that that information successfully passed through your mind without triggering the emotions of confusion or humor, but quite possibly having triggered the sense of insight. We will make this much clearer in the coming chapters, but, in short, human epistemic capacities are emotional capacities.

Implications for Embodiment

Descartes thought that all abstract conscious thought occurred in an immaterial system, a *res cogitans* (thinking thing) that had no corporeal properties; but although materialism has now become the default presumption in all of cognitive science, as it is in the rest of the natural sciences, residual images and connotations of reasoning and comprehension as *disembodied* phenomena still persist. These have been combated by the new traditions of distributed, situated, and embodied cognition, and we concur: We see knowledge maintenance, reasoning processes, and comprehension as richly embodied processes that cannot be disengaged from the emotions that play out in varieties of bodily sensation. Not only are the concepts that make up our thoughts derived from embodied interaction with the world (as per, e.g., Lakoff and Johnson 1980, 1999; Lakoff and Nuñez

2000), but the methods for manipulating these concepts, rather than being somehow purely abstract and disinterested rule-following, are also richly entangled with bodily feedback. We *feel* whether something makes sense or whether something *strikes* us as "true"; and we *feel* our way through problem-solving episodes—in the same way that we feel a stomachache or a cool breeze. The most abstract thought and the most abstruse and rarefied logic can only come to be because of bodily sensation.

7   A Mind That Can Sustain Humor

A.   Fast Thinking: The Costs and Benefits of Quick-Wittedness

Stick-up robber: Your money or your life!
Jack Benny: . . . . . .
Stick-up robber: Your money or your life!
Jack Benny: I'm thinking, I'm thinking![1]

Why should speed matter? For the same reason that it matters in a "Star Wars" system designed to detect the lift-off of enemy missiles. No matter how reliable the sensors and software are, if they cannot deliver their accurate verdict in time to trigger an appropriate response before the deadline for action is past, the system is of no use. All brains, from the simplest nervous systems of invertebrates to our own magnificent organs, are anticipation-generators. Their primary function is to extract information on the fly from the world around them and generate expectations that will serve the organism well in its odyssey through an uncertain and often hostile world. There is nothing mysterious or alchemical about this power that brains have, and there is quite a variety of proven techniques in machine learning for deriving predictions from experience through both supervised error-driven methods as well as unsupervised associative methods.

The brain confronts an unrelenting risk of combinatorial explosion, in which every detail of every unfolding situation could be explored literally *ad infinitum* for relevant threats and opportunities, a game of speed chess

---

1. The radio and early television comedian Jack Benny contrived a lot of humor from his supposed miserliness. This was his best line, and although it has been endlessly recalled since his death, it will probably nevertheless soon go extinct. A joke that needs a footnote is not long for this world, as we noted in the discussion of the Newfie joke in chapter 3.

Figure 7.1
Reprinted by permission of United Feature Syndicate, Inc., doing business as United Media ("UM").

with thousands of pieces and millions of legal moves. Unlike chess, the games we play against time—and specifically against other agents acting in time—are ultimately a matter of life and death. Whether or not the world we inhabit is as saturated with purpose as we tend to assume, our brains are designed to impute purpose whenever and wherever possible. Purpose is like the air we breathe; we don't think about it or notice it until it is absent, and then we panic. One of our purposes is not falling down and hurting ourselves—by slipping on a banana peel, for instance. Another is simply staying alive. In this time-pressured behavioral environment, the brain's task of producing real-time anticipations on all important topics is accomplished by processes that have been engineered by evolution to take many, many risks in the interests of timeliness.

The development of heuristic search mechanisms meant to take these "calculated" shortcuts is an unavoidable task in the process of designing a mind. The structure of any architecture of thought necessarily embodies a strategy—or set of strategies—both for taking these risks and for either accepting or recovering from the failures that inhere within them. These strategies are not calculated by the agent acting in real-time; they are calculated by the designer who deploys a metric of fitness, external to the mind of the agent, used to measure the success of those strategies. The risks of the heuristics we are talking about are built-in *architectural* risks; although an agent may use *learned* heuristics to calculate the risks of certain behaviors, the agent does not have a sense of the functional qualities of the kind of brain it has.

Evolution faced this problem when designing us, and human engineers will need to face the same problem when laying out the blueprints for an artificial cognition. There may be a number of different solutions to the problem—a number of different ways to make an efficient heuristic search tool—but we are interested in the one that Mother Nature has stumbled upon primarily because it is a known working variety that interfaces successfully with the solutions to the rest of the problems of open-ended cognition (i.e., perception, attention, categorization, etc.). Our quick wittedness as humans is a result of a series of evolutionary kluges stacked one upon another—one of which is the humor trait. This chapter lays out the features of thought that create a niche for humor.

A brief disclaimer is necessary: A good theory of thought would explain not only how we think—how we recombine information into new beliefs and anticipations—but how we think *validly* about just the right things— and not too much else—in order to perform just the tasks we need to. At this point in our science, it would be excessively bold for anyone to commit to a full model of thought. Nonetheless, something along those lines will be necessary in order to buoy up what we are trying to offer: a full model of the cognitive trait called humor. As we said in the introduction, humor is an AI-complete problem and requires most of the still-unexplained faculties of cognition. In order to present our model clearly within this broader context, we are going to begin by drawing an impressionistic sketch of a particular model of thought. This sketch is not meant to provide a novel account of all cognition; it is meant only to provide the assumptions underlying our work and will consist primarily of extensions and regroupings of pieces already on offer by other theorists. As the sketch is drafted, we will employ just the *interfaces* it provides to frame and constrain our model of humor. Keep in mind as we proceed that the commitment to this model of cognition is very open—we are allowing space for further discoveries in the understanding of cognition to refine the model over time. What we expect to remain of our account, as cognitive science proceeds to shed further light on the human mind, is exactly these interfaces—the ways in which humor *relates* to thought (whatever the details of the latter turn out to be) and how it interacts with the rest of cognition and emotion.

B. The Construction of Mental Spaces

Perceptions do not remain in the mind, as would be suggested by the trite simile of the seal and the wax, passive and changeless, until time wears off their rough edges and makes them fade. No, perceptions fall into the brain rather as seeds into a furrowed field or even as sparks into a keg of gunpowder. Each image breeds a hundred more, sometimes slowly and subterraneously, sometimes (as when a passionate train is started) with a sudden burst of fancy.

—George Santayana

Figure 7.2
Comic by Randall Munroe, <http://xkcd.com/248>.

The key problems, again, are the relevance and validity of our thoughts. Our minds must be designed to think—and think well—about primarily the things that matter. Although it seems logically possible that we might think about penguins while frying eggs, it doesn't ever happen (except maybe the next time you are frying eggs after reading this) because there is no relevant reason to do so in the ongoing situation or in your experiential past.[2] Thought just doesn't work like that. We are designed with minds that think relevantly and validly, most of the time.

This sets the brain an extremely difficult task, first clearly articulated by McCarthy and Hayes (1969) and called by them the *frame problem* (for an introduction, see Dennett 1984, reprinted in Dennett 1998). How is the brain to do a passable job of thrifty search without lapsing into combinatorial explosion on the one hand or failing to represent key elements on the other? It is important that we neither squander all our precious time and energy in an exhaustive consideration of the prospects (which we might call *Hamlet's problem*[3]) nor let ourselves be blindsided a dozen times a day.

---

2. Although penguins do lay eggs, it is entirely irrelevant because most of us never think of penguin eggs as food—it's not part of our culture or experience.

3. Or *Elliot's problem*: Damasio (1994, pp. 46–50) reports on a patient named Elliot whose emotional impairment, Damasio hypothesizes, causes him to do just this with respect to social decisions, quite to his own detriment—he can be sidetracked for hours contemplating the possibilities, and as a result, he literally never decides.

One way to conceptualize the frame problem is to note that a perfect solution to the frame problem would be an essentially unsurprisable agent. There would be many things the agent couldn't predict, of course, but it would have neither positive nor negative expectations about these matters (like coin flips—neither heads nor tails is a surprise). The expectations it actually generated would all be fulfilled. It would be a virtuoso anticipator/ extrapolator who managed to do this without combinatorial explosion. Very probably the perfect solution to the frame problem is like a perpetual motion machine: strictly impossible. The furniture of the world is just too loosely tied down to admit of being perfectly anticipated on the basis of a finite examination. So any solution will have to be an approximation, a workaday bag of tricks that does a pretty good job keeping us *au courant* and unfazed.

A crucial move made by evolution in addressing this design problem has been endowing the mind with a skill for the on-demand creation of *mental spaces* via a process of *spreading activation*. Theorists of cognition have long postulated various mental structures—frames, scripts, schemas— designed to render learning and comprehension more efficient and tame the frame problem. We will consider these in due course once we have described a more fundamental design feature: *mental spaces*. Gilles Fauconnier's analyses of the complex cognitive powers of the adult human mind led him to propose a role in the process of information absorption and manipulation for what he calls a *mental space* (Fauconnier 1985; Fauconnier and Turner 2002; see also Ritchie 2006). A mental space is a region of working memory where activated concepts and percepts are semantically connected into a holistic situational comprehension model. (It should go without saying that these are functional places—logical spaces—not anatomical regions of the brain!) They are built incrementally and revised constantly. Unlike frames, scripts, and schemas or other *idealized cognitive models* (ICMs) (Lakoff 1987; Fauconnier and Turner 2002), which can be thought of as data structures resident in long-term memory and ready to use when needed, mental spaces are *constructed* during comprehension tasks as well as during abstract and creative thought. Fauconnier proposed mental spaces as a foundation to support a theory of reference, which later evolved into a theory of *conceptual blending* (Fauconnier and Turner 2002), in which spaces are combined through mappings to provide creative, comprehensible combinations in thought maintaining separate referents in multiple spaces. We are persuaded by the general notion of their account, though we have reservations about their incorporation of ICMs as the raw materials of construction. We will return to that shortly.

Whereas a simple mind might contain only the one mental space that corresponds to present first-person reality (in which case the concept might well be superfluous), in a more complex mind, such as a modern, noninfantile human mind, these mental spaces act as containers that delineate regions of thought. This is what enables us to have a daydream while watching a movie and keep both separate from each other, as well as separate from our ongoing sense of reality. When you hear Hamlet tell Ophelia, "Get thee to a nunnery," you can put this into the mental space that you created to contain that story and thereby avoid coming to believe that Hamlet was telling you where to go. Studies of attention indicate that perhaps only one mental space can be active at a time (Broadbent 1958; Treisman 1960), but that we may quickly, and with little effort, slip back and forth between them (Lachter, Forster, and Ruthruff 2004).

New spaces are promptly constructed with ease in a variety of ways: Space-building expressions such as prepositional phrases (*in this picture*) or connectives (*if___then___*) are among the many ways in which new spaces may be initialized, and numerous methods for the further elaboration of these spaces have been enumerated (Fauconnier 1985). Whenever a new *topic* is confronted, whether introduced by the direct perception of a novel circumstance, or by hearing a speech act, or by an endogenous "reminding" of one sort or another, if this topic cannot be routinely or seamlessly incorporated into the currently constructed and active space, a new space is created to host that information. A sort of *unconscious triage* generates new spaces as needed. In particular, whenever details become salient that contradict a current space so that that space becomes unusable for the new information, a new space needs to be constructed to accommodate it (Coulson 2001). Fictional worlds, in fact, can be conjured up in their own mental spaces, having their own local consistency. The demand for local coherence (within each mental space) is part of what drives the generation of new mental spaces, and as Ritchie (2006) notes, the same search for coherence is what yields the discoveries that mark the recognition of humor.

Sentence comprehension has recently been shown to be both incremental and predictive (Kamide, Altmann, and Haywood 2003; Spivey 2007). Garden-path sentences are a much-studied variety of sentences that lure hearers into false expectations, because of misleading syntactic—or sometimes just semantic—features.

(19) The horse raced past the barn fell. (A famous example discussed by Chomsky)

(20) That deer ate the cabbage in my garden surprised me.

(21) She told me a little white lie will come back to haunt me.

(22) Uncle Henry finally found his glasses, on the mantelpiece, filled with sherry

(23) Bundy beats latest date with chair. (An actual headline when the serial sex-murderer, Ted Bundy, representing himself, won a reprieve in his attempt to avoid the electric chair)

Many garden-path sentences are often found to be funny. They have a lot in common with, and sometimes simply are themselves, puns.

Experimental studies of comprehension show that humans regularly predict the meaning of an ambiguous sentence fragment and then readjust their mental space as disambiguating information arrives (Spivey et al. 2002; Chambers et al. 2002; Kamide, Altmann, and Haywood 2003; Chambers, Tanenhaus, and Magnuson 2004; Spivey 2007). This means that a mental space is built incrementally: As each word of the sentence arrives, the space is augmented to model the full set of data then available. Data from these studies also show that pragmatic, conceptual, and perceptual information is added to the space-building task as soon as it becomes available, suggesting that not just sentence comprehension but also situation and event comprehension operate incrementally in a unified continuous system. Altogether, these results (and others—e.g., Marinkovic 2004) strongly favor the view that comprehension is always accomplished by a "holistic" attempt to integrate the information, from all sources, that has arrived in the brain up until that point, and that when further information (from any semantic source) arrives that can disambiguate an earlier piece of information, the model is adjusted accordingly. During the process of comprehension, the mind does not wait passively until it has "enough" information in a buffer to complete the disambiguation of what it has so far received but rather attempts to disambiguate by assumption until proven otherwise. These predictions may be "educated" assumptions due to quite explicit *noticing* of a telling feature, local priming that makes one possibility appear more likely than another, or they may be due to a subliminally learned statistical regularity that suggests the likelihood of one meaning rather than another.[4]

---

4. Psycholinguists have shown that, to a first approximation, *all* meanings of a term are accessed simultaneously in the course of sentence comprehension until disambiguating information arises (see, e.g., Swinney 1979 and Tanenhaus, Leiman, and Seidenberg 1979). This is normally beneath notice, but it has clearly discernible downstream effects that have been tested.

In the past, the reassessment process in disambiguation has been called *frame-shifting* and has been implicated as a mainstay of ordinary comprehension, not just a feature in joke-comprehension (Minsky 1984; Coulson 2001). Frame-shifting is the process of jettisoning a frame that was previously invoked and rebinding the information from it into another frame that fits the whole of the data more completely. Minsky (1984) notes that frame-shifting "is done very swiftly because the 'corresponding' terminals of related frames are already pre-connected to one another. This makes it easy to change a *faltering interpretation or a frustrated expectation*" (p. 183, emphasis ours). Minsky's theory of humor involves frame-shifts being initiated by the contradiction of bindings. The semantic script theories of humor (cf. Raskin 1985 and Attardo 2001, or see above, pp. 50–51) similarly use the notion of scripts to describe humor as arising from the incompatibility of two scripts, each evoked by some overlapping parts of the humorous context. Given the historical reliance in humor theory on these kinds of representations, we need to pause for a moment and neutralize the charm of such a representational scheme. Although Minsky and Schank certainly saw a salient pattern in cognition, they made a mistake in treating it as a core theoretical entity—a basic kind of "data structure" in the brain. In fact, scripts and frames are more like clouds. They're real enough, quite visible, but *not basic meteorological entities* (Hofstadter and the FARG 1995, p. 125). Here's why:

It is difficult to say what should constitute a frame or script for a particular type of event. Let's take, for example, the classic *going to a restaurant* script. Details for going to a restaurant vary considerably across cultures and levels of affluence. It would be as difficult to put bounds on the set of necessary terminals for this frame as it would be to give necessary and sufficient conditions for being a game (Wittgenstein 1968). Yet, having a separate frame for every ethnic variation of restaurant-goings is the first step down the slippery slope toward having a separate frame for every individual possible restaurant-going at all. This is a slope that ends in a heap of frames that no longer have any of the generality for which they were originally proposed. If, in order to salvage the theory, it is proposed that in addition to a set of very general frames (with some completely arbitrary threshold for what constitutes generality) there are additional, more meticulous tools for adjusting each to the idiosyncratic semantic contents of individual situations, then it seems obvious to wonder next why these more flexible and adroit tools for detailing don't simply do all the work of semantic construction. The latter is exactly what we think happens.

In place of whole categorically delineable structures, such as frames, scripts, or ICMs, we are going to lean on a model of *just-in-time spreading activation* (JITSA)—a process that can account for Minsky's and Schank's intuitions and approximate the structure of frames without requiring their existence as fundamental entities. The term "spreading activation" has been used somewhat loosely among modelers in cognitive science (e.g., Collins and Loftus 1975; Bower 1981; Anderson 1983; Hofstadter and the FARG 1995) because the notion can be applied to many kinds of models. Activation may spread between concepts in either active concept models or semantic nets, or it may spread between nodes in either localist or distributed representation neural networks. Since, as we said, we're giving a high-level view of just the interfaces of cognition, we don't need to commit to either a neural or superneural implementational model here. It's the general notion that counts: Initial semantic contents are activated by sensation in working memory mental spaces, and the process of perception and any deeper thought ensue from the diffusive triggering of related semantic contents and interference patterns therein.

We must acknowledge at the outset that we don't know—nobody yet knows—how to implement in neural structures a system of JITSA that can detect contradictions or even maintain enough consistency to be a reliable updatable store of world knowledge. There are small, "proof of concept" models (Collins and Loftus 1975; French 1995; Shastri and Grannes 1996) that show how in principle some such competences could be achieved by networks, but there are doubts about how these models would scale up, so we are just helping ourselves to the assumption, at this point, that the brain's functional architecture will prove to bear a useful resemblance to such models. This is the weak spot in our theory: Taking inspiration from a wide variety of exploratory work in cognitive science (see references cited above), we are supposing that the brain can be modeled as a JITSA system with the information-handling capacities we describe, and then looking at how humor could emerge from such a system.

It is also important to specify that the model, borrowing the term from data provision models in software engineering, uses "just-in-time (JIT) processing" (see also Milner and Goodale 2006 for a discussion of psychological experiments indicating JIT processing in the brain). JIT processing is an economic model of processing (or *thought*, in our case) in which computation is not performed until the moment it needs to be, on demand, as it were. This is, of course, not just biologically likely (whenever there is a choice, organisms are energy-conservative) but also realistic with respect to how thought works phenomenologically. It may not always seem well directed, but on reflection we realize that thought is never random. There is always some link back to pertinent recent perception, desire, or emotion. To clarify this issue: If processing were not done only on demand, then there would be a very deep quandary as to just how much (and which) forethought a mind need perform. Remember, speed matters. Needlessly computing all manner of thought is not a rapid strategy, not to mention that it also violates the economic principle.

We want to head off a complaint that might arise here. It might seem that JIT processing implies a lack of foresight, whereas earlier in this chapter, we characterized humans as the ultimate anticipation generators. There is no contradiction. People do generate—ceaselessly—a bounty of pertinent anticipations about the world, but such anticipations are not created through effortful enumeration of all possibilities followed by the comparisons of individual assessments of likelihoods for each possible future. Rather, the expectations we have at hand each are the result of current situation-pertinent thought or recollections of other pertinent-at-the-time thoughts each of which are the result of JITSA. We expect future events to fall in line with our experiences and with such inferential anticipations as we have had occasion to create now or during historical comprehension of events. This adds up to quite a number of expectations, though it is not nearly as many as an enumeration-machine might create. It is our good luck (thanks to evolution by natural selection) that the expectations created by JITSA happen to be, on the whole, the most *relevant* anticipations, out of an infinite space of logically possible thoughts. This relevance follows for the simple reason that these anticipations are most applicable to precisely the environment from which they are drawn.

Just-in-time processing can be performed piecemeal, in keeping with the comprehension data mentioned earlier. Instead of thinking of a set of carpentered frames that get looked up and installed in mental spaces wholesale, we prefer to think of the *functional near-equivalents* of frames being *grown* by JITSA in a large network of meaningful nodes. Thanks to probabilities and associations already incorporated into the strengths and proximities in the network, this spreading activation has the capacity to take on the functional structure of a particular instantiation of a frame, with chains of nested conditional probabilities.[5] The speed, alone, created

---

5. Thus the probability of MENU given RESTAURANT is higher than MENU given DENTIST, and then, given MENU, the probability of the FIRST COURSE meaning of "starter" is higher than the GUY WITH THE STARTER PISTOL or ELECTRIC MOTOR TO CRANK THE ENGINE meanings.

by the parallel processing of spreading JIT activations in the brain causes an illusion of cognitive completeness in working memory, or a *frame-illusion*, as we might call it. The frame-illusion is due to the simple fact that comprehension, thought, and recall (as opposed to the more effortful problem solving described in a later section) happen so fast that we seem to have instantaneous access to a number of elements about any situation or thought *as if* all these details are already actively loaded into working memory.[6] In reality, some details will be strongly activated, some will be on the fringe (there may be wine glasses in your current restaurant model, but you haven't specified whether they are glasses for red or for white), and some details will not be activated at all. Yet, all of these things are instantly accessible upon the slightest inquiry because of the capacity for JIT activation.

Thus, when you learn of a fictional character entering a restaurant, spreading activation may turn on nodes for tables and chairs, waiters and menus, and other customers, with some of the links *appearing* obligatory (part of the "very definition" of a restaurant) and others appearing as likely options, perhaps with highly favored "default" values included in the frame, and demanding to be accepted without checking or else bumped out by experience. We think that such dynamic structures of activation can account for the frequency of spurious "filling in" of the sort that is one of the main contributors to falsehood in mental spaces. For example, when you are told that Tom and Bill are playing catch on the beach, there are several different constructions you may make, unbidden, in your mental space that will show up if you are then asked what kind of ball it was. The JITSA model would suggest that you *may* have already thought of some statistical default—a baseball, football, or beach ball—and inserted it thoughtlessly (without notice) in your mental space. On the other hand, you may not have thought of any kind of ball at all, but upon interrogation, your exceedingly nimble just-in-time activation allows you to supply one so quickly that it may seem *to you*—not just to your questioner—as if it had been there from the start, much like a frame-terminal

---

6. Ironically, this speed of access was one of the impetuses for the advancement of frame theory in the first place (Minsky 1974, 1984). We're not sure why the JIT possibility didn't seem better at the time. The opposite of JIT is just-in-case, the representation-heavy kind of *full* data model processing that was widely in practice when frame and script theories were proposed some years ago. We suspect that the frame-illusion, coupled with this engineering practice, may have led earlier theorists to posit these unwieldy and unsustainable models of cognitive mechanisms.

default.[7] Yet another possibility is that you may not have thought of any ball to begin with, nor are you ready to commit to a particular kind upon interrogation. There just may never have been a ball in your mental space at all. The answer "I don't know" is a perfectly reasonable one, though perhaps less likely, empirically, given the social pressure to provide an answer when confronted with an interrogation. You might "explain" your answer by noting that no ball seems any more likely to you than any other, or you might say that it is *probably* a beach ball but might be something else.

This invocation of probability raises the issue of variable levels of epistemic *commitment*. If you entered an *uncommitted* default—you "filled in" with a baseball, let's say—and later it emerges that it was a beach ball, you may hardly notice the revision. On the other hand, if it turns out that Tom and Bill were playing catch with a live fish, this is bound to interrupt your complacency since you were at least committed, in your mental space, to the default (but generic) *ball*. We will discuss epistemic commitment in more detail in an upcoming section.

The JITSA model provides a foundation for the interfaces of cognition that are necessary for humor. Building on that foundation, we can now give the rest of those interfaces.

C. Active Beliefs

Q: What is alive, green, lives all over the world, and has seventeen legs?
A: Grass. I lied about the legs.

A belief is a commitment to a fact about the world. You probably believe that the sun rises every day. You may believe that Neil Armstrong stepped onto the surface of the moon on July 20, 1969. You certainly believe that you are reading a book right now. Such commitments allow us to act in the world, with some assurance that our actions will have their intended

---

7. As we shall see in the discussion of Huron (2006) below, one of the most liberating ideas in cognitive science is the recognition that subthreshold or even deeply unconscious (and unrecoverable) versions of conscious cognitive actions and processes are often implicated by the phenomena, once a good model is posited that requires them. Transformational linguists long ago got fearless in positing unintrospectible *moves*, some of which have proven bogus in due course, but the idea that we are not, in general, authoritative about what we have and haven't been thinking is now widely recognized.

consequences. This bland and uncontroversial generalization obscures the fact that there are different *kinds* of commitments. In this section and the next we distinguish between various kinds of belief that are necessary for describing the mechanism of humor.

Working-memory beliefs are, for our purposes, the most important beliefs—these are the contents of mental spaces. They occur as both causes and effects of dawning comprehension and during problem solving, and they may have any of a number of semantic sources. All of the following are ways of coming to a working-memory belief: Someone may tell you that the liquid in a cup is coffee (and you believe her). Or you might taste it and find out it is coffee. Or you might infer what it is from its color and the fact that it's in a coffee cup. Or you might have left it there from yesterday morning's coffee break, and simply recall the fact. Linguistic comprehension, quite "direct" sensory perception—tasting—or inference— "looks like coffee to me"—or long-term memory can all provide working memory beliefs.[8] While such sources themselves are only *potential* contents of thoughts, once information becomes a working-memory belief, it participates in a thought. Let's call the participating contents of working memory *active* beliefs.

Long-term memory beliefs, on the other hand, are better seen as *acquired dispositions* to have particular active working-memory beliefs. We have learned things in our lives that dispose us to a likelihood of activating certain beliefs in working memory under certain circumstances of spreading activation. Consider long-term memory as a sort of surrogate world; just as the external world is a vast source of information (about itself) that, thanks to our sensory systems, triggers active beliefs when attended to, so long-term memory is a source of additional information, not currently perceivable in the external world but readily available on demand. So, unless you have some reason—some cue from the environment or from spreading activation—to be thinking about the Falkland Islands War, you do not have an *active* belief about the conflict, however much you may

---

8. *Caution:* These illustrations are, perforce, *articulated* (as if they were more or less spoken to oneself) so that they can be easily distinguished by the reader, but no judicious inference ("Hmm, I believe her") or *salient* conscious act of recollection ("Ah, yes! From the coffee break!") need mark the transition to active belief. If retrospectively queried about which path was followed we may even be quite uncertain, or our ready answer ("I tasted it"—"No, you didn't; you just looked at the cup") may be confabulatory guesswork. We have less "privileged access" to the workings of our minds than some philosophical traditions suppose.

know—and hence believe in the long-term sense—about it. The fact that dispositions to believe are only potential thoughts contrasts with the active status of working-memory beliefs. While we each have billions of long-term memory beliefs, at any particular moment we have only a few active beliefs.

There is an all too common vision of this distinction that we must vigorously oppose here: the idea that long-term memory is a storehouse of sentence-like things (propositions expressed in the "language of thought") that can be *retrieved* and *moved* (or copied) to a special place, *working memory*, rather the way data are copied from your disk drive to RAM or from RAM to the accumulator, where all the work happens. First of all, as already hinted in footnote 7, the individuation of content into isolated beliefs (billions of them!) is an artifact of our need, in exposition, to draw attention to focal aspects of the information in long-term memory, and should not be taken to imply a GOFAI processing model (Dennett 1987, 1998). More important, in this context, is the mistaken image of working memory as a *place where things are sent*. The antidote to this vision is to remind yourself that we are developing a spreading activation model: Working memory is simply that distributed portion of the vast neural network that is current *working*, awakened, not dormant. (Nothing is *moved* anywhere.) This is a difference that naturally comes in degrees. For instance, as noted above, the work of Swinney and others shows that *all* the meanings of an ambiguous word are *activated* when it is perceived, but typically only one will be so much more strongly activated as to be noticeable. (It took subtle experiments to show that the introspectively dormant meanings were actually awakened, if not wide awake.) When we speak of active beliefs we will typically mean the most strongly activated beliefs, but as we shall soon see, many effects in humor depend crucially on there *not* being a sharp threshold between what we might call wide-awake beliefs and drowsy beliefs.

A good way to see the bearing of this is to consider in more detail the phenomenon of surprise. To be surprised by something, it must have been *unexpected*—and this does *not* mean just not expected. Suppose you are expecting us, and we arrive at your house driving a blue car. That it is blue will not surprise you (you weren't expecting it to be any particular color), but if it is a Kandy-Kolored Tangerine-Flake Streamlined Baby (Wolfe 1965) you will be surprised (unless you already know or have surmised that we are the sort who would have such a car). Suppose we glue the coffee cup to the kitchen table and you manifest surprise when you can't pick it up.

If the belief that coffee cups are typically movable, not glued to tables, were not *somewhat* active (in our sense), there would be no expectation violated by your failure to raise the cup, and you wouldn't exhibit surprise. The level of activity may be low, but it is just the sort of activation that the JITSA voluminously and swiftly produces in rolling response to the flow of stimulation arriving from your senses. In reaction to your unfolding experience it has "confidently" placed you in a normal kitchen situation (constructing, on the fly, the normal-kitchen frame or script, in effect, as contrasted with the funhouse frame or script), which is why you are genuinely surprised when you can't raise the cup. Likewise you would be surprised if the hot water faucet *did* detach itself when you grabbed it. In an unfamiliar environment—a biochemistry lab, say, or an assembly line in a factory—you would altogether *lack* expectations about many such things, and hence would be informed, but not surprised, by whatever you discovered.

How far does such automatic expectation-generation go? This is an empirical matter, depending sensitively on the individual and varying circumstances. Each of us embodies an approximate solution to the frame problem, and we share a lot of common strategy while also having our differences. To anticipate our humor theory a bit, if Tom and Dick get a joke and Harry doesn't, it is likely because Harry's solution to the frame problem (in this setting) doesn't make the same heuristic prunings that Tom and Dick have made.

The opportunistic and individualistic heuristic paths taken by each person's JITSA seem to be governed by two different kinds of "forces" that limit and modulate the spread of activation:

1. *Friction:* The activation racing down one path or another just "runs out of steam" of its own accord, petering out without making even a crude contribution of specific content. Whatever the energy limitations on spreading activation are, the energy budget for this activation avenue is exhausted and it ceases operation wherever it is.

2. *Closure:* Something about the content in some avenue actively *closes off* further exploration: "Nothing down these alleys! Save your time and energy!" This kind of heuristic search terminator is necessarily risky and crude, *not* involving further analysis of the path. When a chess player riskily *ignores* his opponent's surviving bishop (tacitly asking: How could that bishop possibly play an interesting role in this part of the game?), this is distinct from simply not having found time to consider the bishop at all.

All the cognitive power of an individual person's JITSA system lies in the use of closure, since friction is as good as content-blind, stopping the search *for no reason at all* other than running out of time or energy. Closure, in contrast, is teachable, adjustable by experience. We can think of it as a thrifty triage system, helping not-quite-blindly to allocate resources, by "selfishly looking for excuses" to terminate its own activation any time its local hunch is that the current task is unlikely to engage its talents productively and so it should conserve its resources for a better occasion to shine.[9]

Long-term beliefs that remain dormant on an occasion because of friction are simply not assigned any probability at all in the circumstances, and generate no expectations. Long-term beliefs that remain dormant because of closure are different; the closure generates some kind of signal that does create an active—but typically "drowsy" and generic—expectation. When you imagine an office, for instance, the belief that there are no hyenas there does not, typically, become active. There are also no baboons or wildebeests in your imagined office, but your brain doesn't deal with each of these possibilities in turn as an active belief, because closure has weakly activated the catch-all belief that (of course) there are no wild animals whatsoever in the office. That is why the presence of a hyena (or a wildebeest or a baboon or . . .) would genuinely surprise you, violating an expectation. If asked (by somebody else *or by yourself*) whether there are baboons in the office, you might "instantaneously" respond that of course there are not, but this very question alters the cognitive situation, provoking your JITSA to generate and activate the belief you express in response. Contrast this with the question of whether there are any potted plants in the office, or lawyers. Here, perhaps, friction has set in, and your JITSA never got around to opening, or closing, this search avenue.

The issue of what to include and what to exclude in such a setting has been called, by John McCarthy, the *qualification problem*, vividly illustrated via the famous puzzle of the missionaries and the cannibals:

---

9. It is instructive to compare this view of heuristic search with the problem facing the US intelligence community in its massive attempt to keep terrorists from blindsiding the nation. Every agency has a budget and must make a risky attempt at thrift, expending resources only when its personnel believe they can make a significant contribution to the immediate situation.

Three missionaries and three cannibals come to a river. A rowboat that seats two is available. If the cannibals ever outnumber the missionaries on either bank of the river, the missionaries will be eaten. How shall they cross the river? Obviously the puzzler is expected to devise a strategy of rowing the boat back and forth that gets them all across and avoids disaster. . . . Imagine giving someone the problem, and after he puzzles for a while, he suggests going upstream half a mile and crossing on a bridge. "What bridge?" you say. "No bridge is mentioned in the statement of the problem." And this dunce replies, "Well, they don't say there isn't a bridge." You look at the English and even at the translation of the English into first order logic, and you must admit that "they don't say" there is no bridge. So you modify the problem to exclude bridges and pose it again, and the dunce proposes a helicopter, and after you exclude that, he proposes a winged horse or that the others hang onto the outside of the boat while two row. You now see that while a dunce, he is an inventive dunce. Despairing of getting him to accept the problem in the proper puzzler's spirit, you tell him the solution. To your further annoyance, he attacks your solution on the grounds that the boat might have a leak or lack oars. (McCarthy 1980, pp. 29–30)

Getting "on the same page" with this puzzler requires sharing enough of a JITSA with him so that the two of you can share a setting of the puzzle without articulating it (an endless task, apparently) precisely. A similar convergence is required, as we shall see, for effective humor.

D. Epistemic Caution and Commitment

What gets us into trouble is not what we don't know; it's what we know for sure that just ain't so.
—Mark Twain

Another distinction between kinds of beliefs is necessary for humor. You might think that a particular restaurant downtown is open this afternoon, but suppose you are also aware that there is some likelihood it is not. If you drive down for lunch, you might be disappointed but you won't be *surprised* to find the shop closed between lunch and dinner or for renovation or holiday. This kind of common, uncommitted belief can be contrasted with what we'll call *committed* active belief.

When you go bungee jumping or skydiving you are betting your life on the integrity of the apparatus—whether through direct knowledge and checking of the equipment or via the proxy beliefs of trusting the knowledge and intentions of the adventure sport operator you've paid. Beliefs you would bet your life on are some of the many committed beliefs we have.

Consider another example: When you go to anchor your boat and throw the anchor overboard, you have a variety of beliefs. You have a rather general belief that it will land somewhere below the bow, but you aren't committed to exactly where. If it hits bottom a few feet to the left of where you expected it to, there is no surprise or confusion. On the other hand, you are likely to be committed to the belief that the bitter end of the anchor line was fastened to a cleat on the deck, and when you watch the tail end of the rope run into the water behind the anchor, you will be shocked. In certain circumstances (which we'll explain later), you may even find it funny. Another person, watching you, almost certainly will.

Committed active beliefs like this are beliefs that we act boldly on. Epistemic caution is the foretaste of behavioral caution, and epistemic commitment engenders behavioral audacity. This holds generally, apart from whether the cautious or audacious behaviors are overt or covert. If you are uncertain whether the running tap water is hot, you will carefully test it. But if you are certain it is not scalding, you won't hesitate to stick a hand right in. And if it's something you "know for sure that just ain't so," you will burn yourself. Likewise, for the covert behaviors of semantic comprehension: Upon hearing the sentence fragment, "they were in a tank . . .," if you are uncertain what "tank" means, you will be cautious about whether to infer things about fish tanks, gas tanks, tanks of molasses, or military tanks. But if someone tells you they "went to the pet store and brought home a tank of fish," you won't hesitate to conclude that the tank at their house is transparent, full of water, and smaller than a Buick. The goldfish pun takes advantage of just this—tricking us into thinking we know something for sure that just ain't so by giving just enough information (the context of fish, and the use of the word "tank") to make us prematurely commit to a fish-tank belief when the word "tank" still isn't completely unambiguous.

The level of commitment to a belief is entirely orthogonal to the level of activity. Your readiness to plunge your hand into the tap water does not at all depend on how "consciously" you have deemed the water to be safe; indeed, the weakness, the peripherality, of your *strong* conviction that the water is safe probably explains why your belief hasn't been tempered by doubts—you haven't got around to wondering whether your default commitment is justified in this instance.

Belief commitment is an integral part of the traffic on the two-way street between the long-term and working-memory systems. The level of commitment of a belief in working memory accompanies the belief as it turns into long-term memory and, when recalled, returns again to new working memory spaces. If you watch a raccoon, with its masked face, cleverly try to open your trash can, you will remember the fact and be committed to the belief that there is a raccoon in the neighborhood. If you catch a glimpse of a raccoon (well, wasn't it a raccoon—what else could it be, and it moved so fast?) darting into your garage you'll approach the belief that there is a raccoon in the neighborhood with some reservation and epistemic caution. We expect that the degree of certainty of such a belief is embodied somehow—perhaps by something like Damasio's somatic markers—in differences in the way the spreading activation modifies the neural network. Such markers on beliefs indicate how much we can trust the belief and thus how much we can trust the inferences drawn from those beliefs when they become active.

This reveals its importance when the system goes wrong. A committed belief in working memory is likely to become a committed belief in long-term memory, and a committed belief in long-term memory is a disposition to construct future active beliefs and use those contents in acts of reasoning. Allowing this ballooning process to continue unchecked when one of our committed beliefs just ain't so can generate a cascade of false beliefs resulting in a substantially faulty world representation. This problem can be enormous. The information we ultimately remember from an experience is not a high-resolution copy of the experience, however vivid it may have been, but rather a low-resolution transformation of the experience in which much of the originating context has been lost to compression. If recall leaves out the contextual information, debugging an error later discovered in a descendant belief becomes difficult. The solution is to nip it in the bud—to try to catch false beliefs as often as possible before they become compressively encoded, while we still have the context to work on them, and before we end up with a disposition to reactivate that false belief.

Evolution has provided us with a couple of solutions, exploiting our epistemic emotions. First, confusion, as described in the last chapter, helps us detect conflicts in working memory, thus casting doubt upon the conflicting beliefs and allowing them to be expeditiously reviewed for repair. Better, detecting an improper commitment before it has a chance to create a long-term memory belief can protect us from the whole string of faulty inferences. This is what we will propose, in the next chapter, is the original purpose of humor—the very important task that pays for its expensive reward system by protecting us from epistemic catastrophe.

E. Conflict; and Resolution

I celebrated Thanksgiving the old-fashioned way. I invited everyone in my neighborhood to my house and we had an enormous feast, and then I killed them and
took their land.

—Jon Stewart

The King of Poland and a retinue of dukes and earls went out for a royal elk hunt.
Just as they approached the woods, a serf came running out from behind a tree,
waving his arms excitedly and yelling, "I am not an elk!"
    The king took aim and shot the serf through the heart, killing him instantly.
    "Good sire," a duke said, "why did you do that? He said he was not an elk."
    "Dear me," the king replied, "I thought he said he was an elk."

—Cathcart and Klein (2007)

We feel epistemic conflict when there is a contradiction between active
belief elements in working memory. Conflicts between beliefs in long-term
memory can lie dormant side by side, unrecognized. It is only when they
are both brought into the same working-memory space—awakened, not
transported—that two beliefs can participate in an epistemic conflict.

There are three possible outcomes to an epistemic conflict. In *unresolved
conflicts* we find ourselves confused and both pieces of information are
stored with the conflict between them noted (perhaps by something
like a somatic marker of the emotion of confusion) such that recollecting
one of the beliefs will rather easily (via JITSA) often bring its uncertainty
and the other conflicting belief to mind. In *cooperative resolution* we may
find a way to accept the truth of both beliefs through a creative insight
that dissolves an apparent contradiction into a compatibility. And in
uncooperative resolution, one of the beliefs will survive while the other is
destroyed.

Any two beliefs, no matter how they were originally derived, may participate in a conflict, but *getting them* to participate in a conflict is often
the outcome of hard work—or luck! A whole society can be blissfully ignorant of the contradictions harbored in their "common knowledge" until
some reflective and industrious thinker rubs their noses in the quandary—
or some chance event draws everyone's attention to the problem. Science
and literature are among the focal sets of processes that have gradually
uncovered and resolved a host of conflicts for everybody, and we each have
our own scientific agenda: rooting out and fixing the residual conflicts in
our personal world knowledge. (It is amusing to realize that a comedian
can be seen to be a sort of informal—but expert—scientist, leading the way,

helping us expose and resolve heretofore unnoticed glitches in our common knowledge.)[10] Simple temporal juxtaposition—getting both beliefs active at the same time—is the necessary first step, kindling the confusion that sets in motion (motivates) the frantic search for resolution. And just as scientists often use thought experiments—readily comprehended, simplified fictions—to help resolve their theoretical difficulties, we have all come to appreciate that fiction is as good as true narrative in drawing out the conflicts in our everyday understanding. When a conflict is resolved by discarding the "false" belief, it is as often as not false only in the local context of a fiction we are considering, not false objectively.

At this point our model begins to differ from Schopenhauer's, which invoked a distinction between perceptions and conceptions. Recent work suggests that any distinction between these two categories may be artificial or, at least, drawn too sharply—perception and conception in fact recruit much of the same circuitry (for a review, see Goldstone and Barsalou 1998; and also Kosslyn, Ganis, and Thompson 2001). The important factor in Schopenhauer's attempt to differentiate between perception and conception is not in how they are or might be neurologically instantiated, but simply in their temporal relationship to each other: "Conceptions" are already in the mind when "perceptions" arrive to conflict with them. Since "conceptions" themselves may be very recent arrivals (from "perception," typically) this temporal distinction is a treacherously slippery slope. How soon after information arrives in a mind via perception can it settle in and acquire the status of knowledge or presumption? There is no obvious way to draw such a line, nor need we insist that there be a bright line. Schopenhauer presumably saw humor as a perception that defeats a conception because it is *frequently* the case that incoming perceptual information modifies existing conceptions by affirming, buttressing, challenging, or integrating with them. Yet this common case is not the only possibility. An endogenously arising "conception" may just as readily disrupt or challenge an ongoing "perception" or two perceptual features may conflict, as in the figures from Roger Shepard where the hips and the feet of the elephant indicate contradictory legs or the intersections of the spokes both with the hub and with the rim indicate different orientations for the wheel.

---

10. It is also amusing to us to notice that we science-minded theorists keep finding deep parallels between humor and scientific investigation. We wonder: Would bankers come up with a theory of humor as really all a matter of risky investments, and plumbers see humor as all a matter of pressure and leaks?

(a)

Figure 7.3
Reprinted by permission of Roger Shepard.

Alternatively, a "conception" may defeat another "conception"—as when a daydream interrupts a mental calculation and then is challenged in turn by a conscientious self-admonition to get back to work. We will consider all forms of information that are involved in the construction and modulation of a mental space as equals for our purposes without distinguishing between conception and perception. What matters, instead, is degree of epistemic commitment. Schopenhauer's conception/perception distinction closely aligns with two ends of this spectrum.

In comprehension that proceeds incrementally, activated beliefs are somewhat serially entered into mental spaces, and upon entry they are immediately subjected to a process of bidirectional epistemic reconciliation with the current contents of that space. Figure 7.4 shows a coarse schematic version of the reconciliation chart that shows approximately what occurs when two active beliefs (not dispositional beliefs!) come into conflict. The top axis of the chart indexes the epistemic status of one belief and the left axis does the same for the other belief. The shading of the square at the intersection of each row and column indicates what occurs when these two kinds of belief contradict each other. As you can see at a

(b)

Figure 7.3
(continued)

glance (the darker gray areas), a number of these are "no-brainers" that dissolve without a fight: When a committed belief encounters an uncommitted belief (or a stronger uncommitted belief encounters a weaker one), the latter (always uncommitted) typically extinguishes itself ("I give up. Never mind"). No battle ensues (and *since* no battle ensues, you "hardly notice"—not enough "fame in the brain" [see Dennett 2005] to "rise to consciousness"). But when two equally powerful beliefs clash, something has to give, and the battle is joined. Confusion arises and they duke it out, enlisting allies, becoming (however briefly) famous in the brain, and eventually there may be some resolution. Resolution is not guaranteed, of course: It depends on how strong the allies on either side are. But, when it occurs, one of the beliefs falls into a more committed category, and the position of the conflict on the reconciliation chart shifts off from the black line into either a light gray or a dark gray area. When it doesn't occur— when a conflict is irresolvable—we call this *epistemic undecidability*. Cases of this kind are examined in detail in chapter 10.

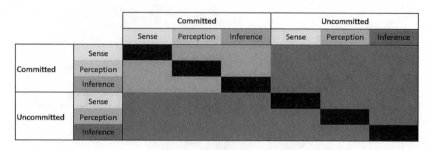

Figure 7.4

As the chart in figure 7.4 indicates, we consider information from our senses to be more reliable than information from later in perception, the latter being modified (by both integration with other senses and top-down cognitive pressures) and compressed relative to the former. Our senses may be fallible, but they are typically more reliable than our perception; and inferences take us still further from the originating sensory information, as they are further modified and compressed versions of things we have perceived from the environment.

(24)   Who are you going to believe? Me? Or your lying eyes?

The light gray regions of the chart are areas where humor can happen. Like the darker gray regions, one belief has more epistemic power than the other and this causes the weaker to forfeit the conflict, but only in the light gray regions are those weaker beliefs also ones that a person was *committed* to. Those are the beliefs that would have been stored in long-term memory, the beliefs that we are prepared to act unreservedly upon; they are the beliefs that can have lasting impact on us. So this little corner of the reconciliation chart, where committed beliefs clash, is importantly different from the rest of the chart; only here can humor happen.

8 Humor and Mirth

A witty fellow being asked by a chatting barber, "How shall I cut it?" replied, "In silence."

—Bubb (1920)

Our sketch of the computational architecture of cognition and the dynamic role of emotions in controlling the processes that can occur in that architecture gives us a map of sorts, in which we can, finally, locate the *basic* or *primitive* phenomena of humor and mirth. (As we shall see, human ingenuity and cultural evolution have combined to elaborate the ways of exploiting the underlying mechanism prodigiously. Before there could be high comedy, cunningly designed by experts to tickle our funny bones, there had to be a sort of low comedy, relatively simple and low-powered moments of cognitively driven pleasure, not jokes or witticisms but the ancestors of jokes and witticisms.)

In short, (basic) mirth is the pleasure in unearthing a particular variety of mistake in active belief structures. And (basic) humor is any semantic circumstance (any convergence of contentful elements at a particular time)—exogenous or endogenous—in which we make such a mistake and succeed in discovering it.

A. The Contamination of Mental Spaces

Look out for number 1, and don't step in number 2, either.

The phenomenon of *automatic heuristic search* has the effect that lots of information gets incorporated into our current representations on a probabilistic basis without thorough examination.[1] The oversimplifications and

---

1. This phenomenon of automatic heuristic search is to be distinguished from the conscious (and often but not always deliberate) use of specific heuristics—such as the "fluency"

biases that thereby accumulate in this background machinery are normally harmless—indeed highly useful—approximations of the truth, but they are always potential weaknesses, dormant sources of potentially fatal errors. Winkling them out of hiding—debugging our heuristic reasoning machinery—is a time-consuming process that must compete with all other cognitive activities for its appropriate share of "machine cycles," time and energy in the brain devoted to it.

This category of relatively hidden or tacit assumptions contrasts with the deliberately articulated, noticed, accounted-for assumptions of serious problem-solving, whose contributions to current mental spaces are more or less manifest. The construction of mental spaces is one of those activities that spans the large space between clearly voluntary or deliberate actions on the one hand and unconscious reactions on the other. For the most part, the incessant generation of mental spaces in the course of our daily lives appears to us to be effortless and automatic and, indeed, involuntary. "We" delegate this task to the unconscious triage mechanism that carries on without further supervision, admonition, or notice by "us." For instance, JITSA constructs frame-like structures on the fly, with all their accumulated baggage, and these temporary data structures contribute efficiently to our sense of what is happening, and, more importantly, our sense of what is *about* to happen. But we can also go into problem-solving mode and attempt to marshal our construction activities. Sometimes we introduce some item of information into a mental space in this deliberate and *uncommitted* fashion in order to see what it leads to, and discover that it leads to a contradiction; on such occasions we may feel surprise, and even pleasure, but not mirthful surprise. We can see the difference in slow motion when a bad joke-teller explicitly informs his audience of the key presumption before telling the story. It is only the information that gets *introduced covertly*—without drawing attention to itself on arrival— into the mental space whose discovery elicits mirth; typically making a presumption too overtly, too explicitly, will draw attention to the possible mistake, thus helping us to approach it with caution and then avoiding it.

In the time-course of comprehension, an element that was covertly entered into a mental space by the JITSA process may, if unchallenged, immediately become an overt element of the space. Although the

---

heuristic (Schooler and Hertwig 2005), "take the best" (Gigerenzer and Goldstein 1996), or "imitate the majority" (Boyd and Richerson 2005)—to solve problems or make important decisions. See Gigerenzer 2008 for an overview.

coactivation of *fish* and *tank* covertly and automatically bring to mind a fish-tank, shortly thereafter we have a fairly overt fish-tank in our mind. This change of status in blatancy, rather than canceling the opportunity for mirth, is the guarantor of it—for a covertly entered element to become an unquestioned overt element, we must make an epistemic commitment to it; such a commitment is always made if no other elements from JITSA successfully challenge the epistemic status of the element in question.

When we distinguish conscious from unconscious or covert cognitive processes, we don't at all mean that the latter are not being "watched" by some central executive, the ego or self. We mean only that they are occurring in a functionally local and hence resource-stingy manner, sending as few waves through the whole system as is consistent with activating them at all. And when we compare different elements that are active—in a mental space, for instance—and note that some are covert or tacit (but still active), we do not mean that all the others are fully articulated in thoughts (though some of them, at any time, surely are); we mean only that they are more global, more resource-hungry, more influential (Dennett [1996, 2005; Dennett and Akins 2008] calls this "fame in the brain"), and hence capable of laying down more lasting and ramifying effects ("memories" in short).

Such surreptitious entry into a current mental space is thus a necessary condition for a humor-inducing bug, but it is not sufficient. Mirth requires this stealth, but it also requires eventual comprehension—not necessarily in the sense of comprehending everything (cf. nonsensical non-sequitur humor and irresolvable visual illusions—see pp. 114–115) but only in the sense that you comprehend the error that had been made. To "get the joke" you have to know what's going on, at least to some degree. As Dolitsky (1992, p. 35) observes, "The humorous effect comes from the listener's realization and acceptance that s/he has been led down the garden path. . . . In humour, listeners are lured into accepting presuppositions that are later disclosed as unfounded." So far, so good; this is an insightful observation about the phenomenology of humor. But why does the process of discovery unfold as it does? Why should our brains provide a playground for this variety of pleasure, and why should it be so much fun? Our answer identifies a *problem*, which creates a *need*, and this need is met most ingeniously and thriftily by a *solution* that exploits the available resources in the brain.

The problem is that the accumulation of "world knowledge" is an opportunistic process that includes plenty of unnoticed inclusions—that is, items that are not consciously considered and accepted. We all know that giraffes in the wild do not wear galoshes, but we've never considered the matter until now, for instance. Our store of world knowledge is only intermittently accompanied by metaknowledge about these contents. The result is that its weaknesses are essentially "invisible" *until they are teased to the surface during the construction of a mental space.* What works 99 percent of the time may fail on occasion, with disastrous results—unless it is brought to the surface in a fictional setting, or in a real-world setting that happens to be a forgiving environment.

The need, then, is for a timely and reliable system to protect us from the risks entailed by our own cleverness. Discerning and locating these mistakes would have the immediate payoff of allowing current reasoning to progress without an error (before we act on such errors), but would also provide a legacy for the future, keeping a fallacious conclusion from becoming registered as verity in long-term memory. A mechanism for consistency checking is indispensable for a system that depends crucially on data-intensive knowledge structures that are built by processes that have been designed to take chances under time pressure. Undersupervised and of variable reliability, their contributions need to be subjected to frequent "reality checks" if the organism that relies on them is to maintain its sanity.

The solution is the activity of building mental spaces, one of the brilliant innovations of human cognition. Attending to the flotsam and jetsam that thereby float to the surface is a practical necessity for the maintenance of epistemic integrity—and this is a task that competes with the pressing demands of the occasion, so in order to compete successfully, its deliverances must be independently *rewarding*—and the reward is mirth. This janitorial work cannot be accomplished by unconscious background processes simply because the weaknesses in question only exhibit themselves in specific, resource-hungry contexts—in mental spaces that bring them into direct conflict with other currently active contents. The mental spaces we construct are, in effect, test beds for elements in our world knowledge, where we get to observe how these elements perform in a variety of settings. The reward provides the motivation for what otherwise would be a low-frequency chore.

Our brains are for "producing future" (as the poet Valéry once put it) both swiftly and reliably, and it is the trade-off between speed and integrity that creates the risks that are patrolled by these bug-seeking mechanisms. The creation of mental spaces permits the relatively safe off-line testing of hypothetical extensions of our lightning-fast anticipation-generators and this activity has to compete with other activities for time and resources in the brain. Unconscious debugging is simply not possible. Debugging requires activating specific contents and *keeping* them activated against all competition for enough time to explore their implications and presuppositions, a process that of necessity involves monopolizing, however briefly, large cortical resources.[2]

The picture that emerges is a time-pressured, involuntary heuristic search for valid expectations, which generates mental spaces in which elements are constantly being tested. According to this model, then, basic humor occurs when

1. an *active* element in a *mental space* that has
2. *covertly* entered that space (for one reason or another), and is
3. taken to be true (i.e., *epistemically committed*) within that space,
4. is diagnosed to be false in that space—simply in the sense that it is the loser in an epistemic reconciliation process;
5. and (trivially) the discovery is not accompanied by any (strong) negative emotional valence.[3]

More simply put: Humor happens when an *assumption* is *epistemically committed* to in a mental space and then discovered to have been a *mistake*. These five conditions are the necessary and sufficient setup for the pleasurable experience of humor. Notice that these conditions are not the kinds of conditions that can be applied directly to a stimulus such as a joke. They are conditions regarding mental behaviors—behaviors that can sometimes, but not always, be well predicted by a joke or other stimulus. This model of humor, then, avoids the projection error categorically.

---

2. At first glance, it seems possible to imagine a computational architecture for an artificial intelligence in which debugging of this sort could go on automatically and intermittently "in the background," the way Google Desktop updates its indexes whenever higher-priority tasks are idle. Such an artificial intelligence—if it is indeed possible—would have no need for the system of rewards that boosts our debugging processes into action, and hence would be constitutionally ill equipped for appreciating humor. It might be capable of understanding the phenomenon of human humor, in the same way it could understand the phenomena of thirst or hunger or lust, and it might even use that understanding to create humor, and exploit it in devising its interactions with us. But aside from scientific curiosity, it could have no appetite for humor. We return to this topic in more detail in chapter 13.

3. Discovering an *immediately* harmful mistake is of course the occasion for strongly negatively valenced emotion, and this will almost always wipe out humor. Only *currently innocuous* errors can be enjoyed as sources of humor—if they are your own errors. The errors of others are another thing altogether, as we will explain.

Let's review what we've done so far. We have sketched the phenomenon of creating mental spaces, during the incremental comprehension of events and sentences, and described a particular sort of incongruity resolution (inspired by the sketches of Schopenhauer, Kant, Minsky, and Coulson) that captures the way humor comprehension fits into the mental space model. Evolutionary theory gives us a powerful hint about why this kind of comprehension is important, and recent theories of emotion explain how we are motivated to engage in it. This gives us a basic explanation of what *primitive* humor is and why it operates as it does. Before we go on to show how cultural magnification has created additional cognitive tools that make higher-order humor possible, we need to give our sketchy model more detail and answer a host of questions.

B. Mirth among the Epistemic Emotions: The Microdynamics

Right now I'm having amnesia and déja vù at the same time.
—Steven Wright

The epistemic emotions all share a similar ineffable quality of being mental feelings—but mirth and discovery are particularly similar, in being the two most familiar *positively valenced* members of this class of emotions. In addition, these two often arrive (especially in well-tailored jokes) with such rapid coincidence as to *almost* evade differentiation. We are certainly not the first to notice the relationship between humor and discovery. Earlier authors found a deep connection there as well. For instance, Terrence Deacon:

> Consider the intensity with which contemporary humans pursue mysteries, scientific discoveries, puzzles, and humor, and the elation that a solution provides. The apocryphal story of Archimedes running naked through the street yelling "Eureka!" captures this experience well. The positive emotions associated with such insights implicate more than just a cognitive act. The reinforcement that is intrinsic to achieve such a recoding of the familiar may be an important part of the adaptation that biases our thinking to pursue this result. A call that may primarily have been selected for its role as a symptom of "recoding" potential aggressive actions as friendly social play seems to have been "captured" by the similar recoding process implicit in humor and discovery. In both conditions, insight, surprise, and removal of uncertainty are critical components. (Deacon 1997, p. 421)

Also, Arthur Koestler:

> The dual manifestation of emotions at the moment of discovery is reflected on a minor and trivial scale in our reactions to a clever joke. The pleasant after-glow

of admiration and intellectual satisfaction, gradually fading, reflects the cathartic reaction; while the self-congratulatory impulse—a faint echo of the Eureka cry—supplies added voltage to the original charge detonated as laughter: that "sudden glory" (as Hobbes has it) "arising out of our own eminency." (Koestler 1964, p. 90)

And again:

> Primitive jokes arouse crude, aggressive, or sexual emotions by means of a minimum of ingenuity. But even the coarse laughter in which these emotions are exploded often contains an additional element of admiration for the cleverness of the joke—and also of satisfaction with one's own cleverness in seeing the joke. Let us call this additional element of admiration plus self-congratulation the intellectual gratification offered by the joke. (Ibid., p. 88)

If we are to distinguish mirth from other pleasurable emotions, especially the joy of discovery, we need to look closely at the details of the cognitive events that can make the difference between a Eureka! moment, a rib-tickler, and a lead balloon. What could it be that generates the insight in one instance, mirth in another, and merely the microsatisfaction of comprehension (mixed, perhaps, with annoyance) in the third? Introspection—or "pure" phenomenology—draws a blank, yielding nothing but the vacuously circular explanation: Well, if the timing is *right* the episode is really *funny* (or *revelatory*)![4] The notorious ineffability of the "qualia" of consciousness confronts us. What is the difference between the sound of an oboe and the sound of a clarinet? One sounds . . . like an oboe, and the other like a clarinet! We need to look backstage to find answers to such questions (Dennett 1991, 1996c).

The *basic* pleasure of discovery is probably shared widely in the animal kingdom. Bison, one can plausibly suppose, are pleased to find new—heretofore unanticipated—patches of edible grass, birds are pleased to discover a new bird-feeder or source of good nest materials, and so forth. We human beings can also enjoy a more *advanced* sort of discovery—*insight*—when elements we have been puzzling over suddenly fall into place, like the pieces of a jigsaw puzzle. It is not clear that any other species has such puzzling experiences. The differently "flavored" pleasure of mirth gets its particular zest, we propose, from the specific conditions of our definition, above (p. 121), which the special cognitive architecture of humans also makes possible.

Different flavors of rewards allow a learning mechanism to distinguish their different sources. Each reward is tuned to a different state of the world

---

4. We explain timing and subtlety in terms of the microdynamics *of delivery* in a later section.

and trains behaviors that achieve that state: "Sweet" makes us eat sweet things, and "salty" makes us eat salty things. Both are behaviors we need to perform, and if they weren't distinct—if both were simply "tasty"—then we would be prone to making mistakes such as eating only salty things and thus missing out on biologically necessary sugars. On the other hand, if sweet and salty were both needs we had but they always came together in the world (e.g., all fruits contained both sugar and salt in the same relative proportions), we would only need one reward to obtain both needs—two separate rewards for these things would be truly indistinguishable in consciousness as they would always co-occur. So, there is a one-to-one mapping between the qualia[5] of a reward and the distinctive triggering circumstance that identify it—once such a mapping exists an agent is then free to discover a variety of ways to obtain that circumstance and achieve the reward with no fear of being drastically misled (into avoiding sugar in favor of salt, for example). This fact tells us why discovery and mirth feel different: They are tied to distinct and discriminable cognitive circumstances. We already gave the precise conditions for mirth—the discovery of an overcommitment to a covertly entered belief.[6] What are the conditions for insight? How do they differ? And how are they the same?

Despite first appearances, insight is not the solution of a contradiction and reduction of confusion, though it can lead to that. Neither is it identical with the discovery of a false belief in humor, though it can lead to that too. Insight is simply the emotion that we feel whenever semantic contents fit together in the mind to produce a novel conceptualization. It is the joy of figuring anything out. Before the cohesion occurred, one might have been facing a contradiction that caused intense puzzling (Q: How could a cowboy ride into town on Monday, stay two days, and ride out on Monday?[7]), or one might have had a *question*, but not a contradiction (The man who makes it does not need it. The man who buys it does not use it. The man who uses it doesn't know that he is. What is it?[8]), or one might have been just *playing* with some object (even abstract objects) and discover

---

5. We are, resignedly, using the term *qualia* to refer to subjective properties of conscious experience despite the fact that philosophers—whose "technical" term it is—have burdened it with much misbegotten conceptual and ideological baggage (see Dennett 1988, 1991, 2005), which is not being endorsed by us.

6. We also discuss some conjectural ideas about the microstructure of the qualia of mirth more in chapter 11.

7. His horse is named Monday.

8. A coffin.

a new piece of information, a new rule that excites the mind. As a child you may have discovered some natural law, such as that if you spin a hard-boiled egg quickly enough it stands up on its own. You weren't puzzling over anything at all, and you probably don't even have a theory of how or why this law holds, but the new piece of information still may have sparked a flash of insight.

It just so happens that many situations, especially many well-constructed jokes, can engender both insight and mirth at almost the same time. An insight can be the necessary trigger to allow us to discover a mistaken belief. But it doesn't have to be—often we can just be shown that the belief is mistaken. This frequent co-occurrence is the reason for Koestler's and Deacon's observations. The contrast between mirth and *Aha!* is quite sharp in many instances, but the boundary is porous between humor and such problem-solving artifacts as puzzles and riddles. After all, many jokes *are* riddles in form, and many puzzles exploit the denial of rather well-hidden assumptions in their solution, and when they do, solving them—or giving up and being told the solution—is often accompanied by laughter.

But why do we alone enjoy mirth and insight to such a great degree? The rudiments of the system would probably have been found in most or all hominid lineages, since there are suggestive analogues in the apes, and possibly in other mammals.[9] It is when our ancestors added innovations to the basic *cognitive architecture* we share with chimps and other apes that a new emotional phenomenon came into existence, a close cousin of the pleasure of discovery that, as Koestler notes, frequently occurs alongside it.

It has recently been shown that, contrary to a longstanding assumption in much of experimental neuroscience, there is a variety of striking differences between human neuroanatomy and chimpanzee neuroanatomy (Kaas and Preuss 2007; Gazzaniga 2008). We do not doubt that these differences were driven, evolutionarily, by behavioral innovations—and remember: thinking is a species of inner behavior!—but nobody has yet devised any very specific hypotheses about how and when this happened, so we will postpone consideration of how much of the difference between us and chimpanzees is hardware (neuroanatomically discernible differences in the "hard wiring") and how much is software (acquired

---

9. See work by Panksepp and Burgdorf (1999, 2003) for data suggesting the existence of rat "laughter," though not necessarily humor.

dispositions to use the hardware we were born with in novel ways). As in computer technology, software innovation typically drives hardware innovation; and, to put our hypothesis metaphorically, we are born with Chevrolet brains on which we must now run Maserati software, and something has to give![10]

The behavioral innovations in our species were first, the kind of reflective self-consciousness that begins to notice not just changes in the external world but changes in one's responses to the external world and one's responses to those responses and so on, recursively, and second, of course, language. These yield the capacity to construct—"without even trying"—multiple counterfactual and hypothetical mental spaces. (In the evolution of language and self-consciousness, with its penchant for constructing mental spaces, which came first? As so often, this chicken-and-egg question should be replaced with subtler questions that acknowledge that coevolution is the norm, with proto-phenomena providing the basis for further boot-strapping, and with neither phenomenon miraculously bursting full-blown onto the scene like Venus being born from the sea foam. The role of language in enabling mental space construction—and vice versa—is an important topic already being explored in detail by others—e.g., Fauconnier 1985; Fauconnier and Turner 2002; Coulson 2001. Suffice it to say on this occasion that we humans differ from chimpanzees in having two capacities: language and reflective self-consciousness. The chimpanzee's thinking is governed by JITSA just as ours is, and this helps them anticipate the world around them, but they don't, apparently, make the recursive step that becomes a great leap.[11] Similarly, a chimpanzee may self-medicate

---

10. The Baldwin effect (for an introduction, see, e.g., Dennett 1991, 1995, 2003) is the coevolutionary mechanism in which learned behaviors (which of course cannot be taken up directly into the germ line) can nevertheless change the competitive environment enough to create selection pressure favoring any genetic innovations that enhance the ability to learn the new behavior, even turning it, in the long run, into a genetically transmitted "instinct"—a nonmiraculous way that natural selection can move innovations from software into the hardware.

11. "Well, it seemed like a good idea at the time!" In many jokes and stories, this phrase has come to epitomize the rueful apology of a dunce, a sign of stupidity, but in fact we should appreciate it as the pillar of wisdom that it is. Any being who can truly say (and mean), "Well, it seemed like a good idea at the time!" is standing on the threshold of brilliance. We human beings can not only think, but *remember our previous thinking*, and reflect on it—on how it seemed, on why it was tempting in the first place, and then on what went wrong. We know of no evidence to suggest that any other species on the planet can think this thought.

with herbs it discovers in its environment, but it can't become a doctor or shaman, even for itself.) These human cognitive capacities give rise to a heightened sensitivity to—and use for—the pleasures of discovery and mirth.

C. Rewards for a Dirty Job Well Done

I got into a fight with a really big guy and he said "I'm going to mop the floor with your face." I said "You'll be sorry" and he said "Oh yeah? Why?" I said "Well, you won't be able to get into the corners very well."

—Emo Phillips

We have at last reached our full definition of the basic humor mechanism, and explained why, and how, it came to exist. To review, the very important business of our epistemic emotions is to produce anticipation, as swiftly and accurately as possible, and to maintain data-integrity in our personal systems of knowledge representation, a task made more difficult by the very profligacy and ingenuity of our anticipation-generation machinery. This custodial task is an expensive, resource-hungry task that would not have a sufficiently high priority in our waking life if it weren't for the reward system wired in by natural selection. This reward system, a descendant or by-product of our reward-for-discovery system, is enhanced by the happy circumstance that our species has invented the involuntary habit of constructing *mental spaces* that can expose (by activating in temporal juxtaposition) conflicting candidates for permanent residence in our knowledge bases. Assumptions *covertly* entered into our mental spaces carry with them an automatic pleasure-amplifier that kicks in when our ongoing quest for anticipation discovers conflicts in those assumptions. This reward, which (probably) only human beings experience, has then become an autonomous target, attracting efforts to design ever more potent and effective stimuli to obtain the reward. Humor, then, is an integral part of the evolved processes for maintaining data-integrity in our world-knowledge representations.[12]

This conclusion may well seem to be an anticlimax, a disappointment. We dig down into the core of the humor machine and find a

---

12. For an earlier version of the hypothesis that mirth is a reward for maintaining epistemic data-integrity, see Hurley 2006; and for a more recent converging view, see Clarke in press.

highly utilitarian clerical task being executed, and the only reason it is a humor machine is that it happens to exploit reward systems that have been opportunistically tweaked, first by natural selection and then by cultural evolution. But reflect: The same is true, oddly enough, about sexual reproduction. The task is the safe delivery of a male gamete into proximity with an ovum so that fertilization can occur. In some species—fish, for instance—the parents may not even touch each other, and in many others they never meet, but just broadcast their gametes into the environment, "hoping for the best." That such a mundane, mechanical task could come to support the elaborate systems of sexual attraction and competition found in us—and in other mammals, birds, and even insects, for instance—can seem like a bizarre extravagance. If it weren't for the reward systems, however, why on earth would we ever procreate? It's a dirty job but somebody's got to do it! One might even venture the maxim: The more arduous and even dangerous the job, the more intense the reward system must be to ensure its completion. Maintaining the security system on our conscious thought is costly, but worth it. So the rewards have to be commensurate.

This evolutionary and mechanistic perspective on humor carries with it an important message: There is no doubt that the intrinsic *dynamics* of the mechanism play a crucial role in the generation of humorous experience; if the experiences come in too slow, or too obvious, or too difficult or too . . . mirth will not arise, or very little mirth will arise. Here is where the arts and humanities must join forces with neuroscience or forever wallow in the mysteries and circularities of pure phenomenology. Only neuroscience could explain the effects of laughing gas (nitrous oxide), the Penfield findings regarding brain stimulation (see above, p. 25), and the well-known but still unaccounted-for effects of alcohol and drugs on humor perception. Anyone who has watched, unmoved, the guffawing of drunks immensely titillated by banal remarks, or the giddy paroxysms of contagious laughter spreading through a room full of pot smokers, appreciates that just as there are people with underdeveloped senses of humor, there are also people who, when intoxicated, overendow their experiences with hilarity, and find wit in the most obvious comments. Surely a large part of the explanation of these phenomena will be in terms of the chemical mismodulation of normal neural responses.

At this point, we expect that half of our readers are thinking: "Well get on with it, then, and gives us the neuroscientific details of how it works!"

while the other half are thinking: "Oh no, spare us the neuroscientific details!" The humor theorists in the arts and humanities suspect, with some justice, that most of the neuroscientific details that emerge,[13] whatever they are, will seldom be in terms that can be tied in any recognizable or "appropriate" way to the social and contentful aspects of humor. Relative to such traditional topics of analysis it will be just a *brute fact* that, given the biological machinery we have, *these* are the dynamic features that matter, these are the differences between successful and unsuccessful jokes, and so on. That will be doubly disappointing, they think, since *their* questions about humor—just what *is it* about the content, from an introspectively accessible perspective, that makes this and that so funny?—will be not only left unanswered, but forcibly replaced with questions and answers that are simply beside the point. This is not so. Huron's pioneering work on music shows how *explanatory* correlations between "qualia" and neural machinery can be devised and tested. But we are not quite ready to be as explicit in our humor theory as Huron is in his work on music.

We must risk disappointing everyone by splitting the difference, for the time being, and providing only a sketch of how such a unification might run for humor. Although we are encouraged by recent proposals and discoveries on these topics, and have our favorites, it would be premature for us to take sides in the ongoing controversies. Our intended contribution is a clarification of the functional specs of the computational architecture, not its technical implementation. This postpones the sort of dramatically testable predictions any theory must eventually generate if it is to be taken seriously, but we think it is more prudent to keep our theory alive for further refinement and improvement than to risk its demise from a failure

---

13. Quite a number of researchers have already begun to probe the neuroscientific correlates of humor (e.g., Mobbs et al. 2003; Mobbs et al. 2005; Moran et al. 2004; Samson, Zysset, and Huber 2008, 2009; Shammi and Stuss 1999; Watson, Matthews, and Allman 2007; Wild et al. 2006; for reviews, see Uekermann, Daum and Channon 2007 or Wild et al. 2003), but what they have found so far is only that reward centers, language and semantics regions, and error-processing networks are all involved. None of this is very surprising and, though interesting, the work has not yet shed much light on the clerical nature of debugging in humor. Samson et al. (2008) do conclude that various logical mechanisms appear to utilize different networks in the brain, and this is very much in line with our expectation that there is no single humor-network—no *centralized* funny bone—in the brain. Hopefully our work will give neuroscientists new directions in which to look; and in chapter 10 we make some suggestions regarding the difficulties they will face in finding neural correlates of commitment.

due to reliance on an overspecific instantiation.[14] Still, we can say quite a lot indirectly about the specs for this machinery by looking at the patterns that earlier theorists have highlighted, inspired by the exploratory successes and failures of would-be comedians. Comedians are in the position of people who know quite a lot about how to drive race cars, how hard they can be pushed under which conditions, but haven't any clear idea of what is under the hood. Earlier theorists, studying the productions of comedians and trying to parse out what works and what doesn't, have not gone into the specs at all, noting only that somehow minds reliably distinguish and react to various patterns in the material fed to them. Nevertheless, they have acquired many telling facts about the profiles of response of the machinery they drive with such expertise, and we are building on their discoveries.

D.   *"Getting It"*: Basic Humor in Slow Motion

> The correct explanation of a joke not only does not sound funny, but it does not sound like a correct explanation.
> —Eastman (1936)

Eastman is right. When we describe an instance of humor and explain just how the mechanism for epistemic integrity has operated in some particular case, the mirth and delight vanish. One cannot help wondering if in exposing the steps of the process we have somehow inadvertently discarded whatever it was that made the joke hilarious. "Certainly it couldn't be *that*—that's not funny!" But consider: It is also true that a recording of ordinary speech, slowed down by a factor of ten, becomes incomprehensible groaning. How could that *possibly* be a witty remark? Showing how our theory explains the process by which a number of jokes provoke mirth, and how minimal variations in them would fail to provoke mirth, will not itself be amusing; but this is the only way to demonstrate that the theory is unified and powerful enough to account for a wide range of humor. In later sections, we will examine more complicated data, but here, we start with basic humor.

---

14. In the same spirit, Fauconnier posits his mental spaces and describes the sort of operations that can and cannot occur in them without saying much of anything about how to implement them in a brain. This places our work in the same tradition as Minsky (2006), Hofstadter (2007), and Humphrey (2006); see Dennett 2007b,c, for reviews of these efforts, and Dennett 1991, for another instance of this strategy.

Basic humor is rather simple-minded humor (it couldn't be any other way). It happens in the first-person perspective, and this strictly limits the kinds of contents that it may operate on. Basic humor happens when you get a jolt of mirth because a belief that you, yourself, are committed to—without realizing it—becomes invalidated. Much of basic humor is nonverbal, and some may not even be elevated to consciousness. The first-person status of basic humor makes it the kind of event that doesn't need social communication—these are private thoughts that you have all the time, yet seldom laugh out loud about and typically don't even con-template converting to language to share because no one else is having quite the same first-person experience with the same idiosyncratic JITSA values. It is also the kind of humor that we expect to exist in infants, apes, and perhaps other animals too. The following examples should spark some recognition in you or at least remind you of some other instances of first person humor in your life.

A. Recall moments when you have been looking frantically for the sun-glasses that are on top of your head or the keys that are in your pocket. The eventual breakthrough in these episodes can be circumstances for mirth.

B. Have you ever hollered to someone in the other room only to discover they must have left the house a few minutes before? Or continued to talk to someone who had already hung up the other end of the phone line? You might feel a little ridiculous when you figure out there's no one there.

C. Imagine standing in an elevator, the door has closed, and you are dis-tractedly typing a text message on your phone. Suddenly (when the door opens and someone gets in, or you just feel like you've been in the elevator quite a while), you realize you've forgotten to press any button for a floor and the elevator hasn't moved at all. You ought to feel mirth for having assumed that you were already on your way. *Silly me . . .*

Sometimes dissecting these cases can be tricky. First, let's see why these can be funny, and how we can vary the circumstances to drain the humor from them. With regard to (A), if you've lost your glasses, and looked all over the house for them, even two or three times in some likely places, you will soon commit to the belief that they are not in the house (since you've looked in all possible places) and you will move on to wonder or even commit to the belief that you left them at, say, the grocery store where you last remember thinking about them. Or, you may commit to the belief that they are just gone forever and you don't know where you lost them. Then, when you find them on your head you realize that the misstep of not looking in one of the *most* common places you put them led you to overcommit to the belief that they are gone. In example (B), you presumed that the person was there in the other room to hear what you hollered. Without entertaining the possibility that they might have gone out, you guessed they were there—and you committed to that guess. We can remove the possibility of this mistake being amusing by adding a condition that in one way or another drew your attention to the possibility that this had happened. You hear a door slam and go on talking, for instance, or there is a noticeable click on the phone in the middle of your utterance. The event becomes annoying, maybe, but not amusing. In example (C), the covert assumption needs to be that you were already moving toward your destination floor. Notice that if you didn't presume this—if you were just standing there thoughtlessly—and you discovered you weren't moving, your response would be more like lackluster recognition—"*oh*"—than any kind of amusement.

These examples are mildly mirthful, but here's an example of basic humor that is a bit stronger:

D. Imagine discovering that you were waiting for the instant replay . . . at a live game.

That twinge of ridiculousness that you feel when you've made a mental blunder like this is the core of basic humor. There is no epistemically strong basis for the belief that an instant replay would occur. One of the funniest moments in Peter Sellars's last film, *Being There*, is when he, in the character of the dim-witted and sheltered Chauncey Gardner, is confronted by some threatening hoodlums and, finding his current experience highly unpleasant, attempts to "change the channel" by pressing on a remote control box he has absentmindedly carried with him. To his dismay this does not make the hoodlums disappear. The next example, which happens once in a while to those who spend too much time using computers, is similar:

E. After knocking over a drink at the desk, you might find yourself clicking on the edit menu to find the "undo" command.

The analogical transfer made here, from the computer interface domain to the real world, sets up a false belief. You might realize with a laugh, "I really thought, for a moment, that that would work!"

A sort of real-world inversion of the Peter Sellars effect emerges in an interesting result obtained by Ravaja et al. (2008). In experiments measuring psychophysiological responses (using facial electromyography) to "first-person shooter" video-game events, they found an increase in *orbicularis oculi* activity (the tell-tale sign of genuine, Duchenne laughter[15]) as well as increased arousal (as measured by skin conductance) when a player's own character was wounded or killed as contrasted with the event of killing or wounding an enemy. The authors found this counterintuitive and suggested that the apparent positive emotion of losing may be related to transient relief (from the stress of the game) or, owing to recognition of the fiction of the game, a positive appraisal of the challenge of the game. On the other hand, we think the positive emotion may just be related to the discovery of an overly committed first-person belief. Although Ravaja et al. only reported averaged measures, we would expect between-subject differences as well as event-by-event differences within their data, but we suspect some of their subjects are humorously surprised when, thinking they were in control of their situation, they suddenly got shot.

These examples are all "jokes" without tellers—endogenously created funny moments when we may laugh out loud, even in private; occasions in which an individual delights in debugging a personal mental space by identifying and repairing an error; instances of proto-humor or quasi-humor from which we can derive hints, because of their similarities to florid humor, about the underlying mechanisms and their purposes.

This first-person phenomenon is the fundamental source of humor, on our model. It is the genus for all the species of humor that are *apparent* exceptions to the rule that there can be no humor without human or anthropomorphized subjects (see Question 11 of our Twenty Questions, p. 59 above). They are not exceptions simply because the human subject *in* the joke is the human subject *getting* the joke! The (first) person both makes the mistake and discovers it. Laughing *at others* is a more sophisticated development of the funny bone, and will be discussed later.

Self-made mistakes can be communicated to others—or more precisely, provoked in others, in jokes that involve linguistic misinterpretations, either *lexical* word meaning misinterpretation (puns), *grammatical* misinterpretation (e.g., garden-path sentences), or *pragmatic* or contextual misinterpretation.

The cliché "no pun intended" nicely draws attention to the fact that puns can be generated quite independently of any authorial intentions,

---

15. We should note that the *orbicularis oculi* is also active during *wincing* (Ashraf et al. 2009; Harris and Alvarado 2005; Kunz, Prkachin, and Lautenbacher 2009; Prkachin 1992), which might also be a resultant expression of being shot in a video game. However, in future experiments this might easily be controlled for via facial action coding (FAC) (Ekman and Friesen 1978) of event-related video data, which could separate winces from Duchenne smiles based on their nonshared attributes.

typically depending on syntactic or semantic rather than situational or pragmatic features of comprehension for their humor.[16] Puns are a notoriously weak form of humor. Occasionally we find a shockingly good one, but it is usually shockingly good because it is a pun and the expectation is that puns are weak. It is just this weakness, however, that makes them a good place for an initial analysis of basic humor; the bells and whistles—the adornments and embellishments of more attractive humor—are typically left out of them. It is a minimal kind of humor.

(25) The butcher backed up into the meat grinder and got a little behind in his work.

(26) A hole has been found in the nudist camp wall. The police are looking into it.

(27) Did you hear about the fellow whose whole left side was cut off? He's all right now.

In each one of the above puns, the reader commits a semantic misinterpretation which is then rethought. In all three, either interpretation could have come first and then been reevaluated by the second, because the text doesn't *really* say one thing or the other—it says both. Whereas in many jokes or unidirectional puns (such as the four puns on p. 45, in chap. 4) an earlier belief is actually "falsified" given the full information of the joke, here neither interpretation is quite "wrong" (in fact the two interpretations may settle into an attractor state in which they are both semantically active); it is the premature commitment to one or the other that is wrong—such a commitment we come to realize, eventually, is unwarranted. (And notice that any of these already pretty lame puns can be ruined by drawing attention to the ambiguity at the outset, e.g., "The butcher patted his behind, and then backed. . . .") Elevating to notice an assumption that would otherwise enter the current mental space covertly ruins the prospects of mirth for a pun as for any other form of humor. We can see this in some deliberately constructed *failed* puns. These are weak because they telegraph their punch lines to some degree:

---

16. Inveterate punsters, however, engage in deeply intentional, indeed almost obsessive, reflective examination of the words they are either hearing or saying, prospecting for possible punning opportunities. The linguist Pim Levelt, a virtuoso punster, acknowledges that he automatically monitors most speech for such windfalls, discarding unsaid the vast majority of the candidates he unearths. The psychologist Richard Gregory did the same. The difference between a brilliant punster and a groan-inducing punster is mostly a matter of how high the threshold is set for public utterance.

(28) As I have no checkbook, the Left Bank is where I kept all my money.

(29) Dr. Jones was very inexperienced, so we all hoped that his medical practice would make perfect.

These are lame because they don't typically succeed in *catching* the audience with a committed (and covertly entered) belief:

(30) "I like your dog."
"Not really, you're more like a cow, I'd say."

(31) Sign on the wall in a bar: IN CASE OF BEER LIFT BOTTLE

A pun that is past its use-by date is this sign, on the bumper of a truck:

(32) CAUTION: HAIR BREAKS

(In the early days of air brakes on trucks, the sign CAUTION: AIR BRAKES was ubiquitous; motorists were overfamiliar with it, making its recognition an ideal microhabit to exploit in a pun.)

And, finally, the following puns are not amusing—to one who hears them as speech acts directed to oneself—because they are instances of would-be first-person humor with strongly negatively valenced dénouements:

(33) Your cancer is improving remarkably; it is now able to resist all known treatments.

(34) The prisoner is free to go . . . to the bathroom before execution.

Similar to puns are these funny advertisements:

(35) For sale: antique desk suitable for lady with thick legs and large drawers.

(36) Dinner Special—Steak $7.65; Lasagna or Meatloaf $6.50; Children $4.00.

(37) Dog for sale: Eats anything and is fond of children.

(38) Used cars: Why go elsewhere to be cheated? Come here first!

Here there is a misinterpretation of meaning; but in these cases, it is not a word-sense misidentification, but a broader semantic misinterpretation often brought about by syntactic ambiguity or imprecise or inappropriate punctuation. When you make one interpretation of the line, you've taken a risk, and when you discover another interpretation is possible, you can see that you may have committed too soon to the first comprehension model. Garden-path sentences are other examples. Many kinds of syntactic ambiguities can bring about humor, for instance a dangling pronoun:

(39) "I'll hold the nail, and when I nod my head you hit it with the hammer, ok?"

Hit what, the nail or your head? Without knowing what "it" refers to there are two interpretations of the sentence—one of which comes first and the other of which may then cause a revision.[17] One who hears this sentence may extract humor from several sources: first, the interpretive ambiguity, but also (since imaginative anticipation never stops churning) an image of the speaker's surprise if he were actually hit in the head by a hammer, and, further, his embarrassed recognition that his command was ambiguous. Such unspoken implications are a rich source of additional humor, both first person and third person. In particularly elegant cases of expressive economy, the punch line is omitted, allowing the audience to carry on to the discovery unaided by the jokester.

(40) Some people are afraid of heights. Not me, I'm afraid of widths. (Steven Wright)

This joke plays more subtly with semantics. Wright, with breathtaking efficiency, draws our attention to an unnoticed asymmetry in our directional concepts; the three dimensions of height, length, and width are all "the same" and interchangeable, aren't they? No. Gravity makes a big difference.[18] (Now aren't you happy that we went to all

---

17. In the early days of natural language processing by computer, researchers were amazed to discover how many sentences were actually, officially, ambiguous. Computers proved to be comically good at finding unintended, unimagined, but grammatically licensed parsings of apparently innocent and univocal sentences. This highlighted, for the first time, just how much unconscious computational work a normal speaker has to engage in to carry on a normal conversation. All that unconscious inference provides a hotbed for humor.

18. Geoffrey Hinton has devised an elegant puzzle that further enlightens us about the asymmetry: Throw a large batch of toothpicks randomly into the air and freeze them (photograph them, perhaps) in an instant, catching them pointing in *all* directions. Will there be approximately as many *horizontal* as *vertical* toothpicks (choosing whatever tolerance you like for strict horizontality and verticality? Or will there be more horizontal than vertical, or vice versa? Amazingly, the answer is: *many* more horizontal, because there is an infinity of ways for a toothpick to be horizontal—facing N, S, E, W, NE, . . .—but only one way of being vertical. Now throw a large batch of *plates* (or CDs) in the air; the answer is reversed. This is a delicious insight, but probably too complex to be compressed into a one-liner, even by Steven Wright. But perhaps not; George Carlin has observed that baseball is the only sport that looks backward in a mirror.

the trouble to explain the joke to you? Part of the expository difficulty of writing about humor is that authors either risk insulting the readers by overexplaining, or risk failing to persuade by underexplaining. You can't reach everybody with one policy.) Let's dismantle another simple joke:

(41) Question: How do you get a philosopher off your porch?

Answer: Pay for the pizza.

Jung (2003), who also offers a kind of false-belief theory (see chapter 9 for a discussion), suggests that "a belief of the reader (e.g., that there is a professor-like philosopher on the porch), is falsified by the reader, as he realizes the philosopher is a pizza deliverer" (p. 222). It is the audience of this joke who comes to the committed assumption that a thinker is sitting on their porch swing, contemplating metaphysics. That (first-person) belief is annihilated when the insulting answer is laid down and is the source of the humor. Ridiculing philosophers creates an additional delight; it is not the cause of the mirth, but it nonetheless adds to the joy. But let us reiterate that not all humor has such further delights. When it occurs, it supplements enjoyment of humor, but does not create *mirthful* enjoyment, the latter only being caused by the epistemic conditions. (We say more on this in chapter 11.)

Another pragmatic assumption is made by the audience in hearing this Irish joke:

(42) An Englishman walks into a pub in Ireland with a small green toad on his head. "Well now," says the bartender, "that's quite amazin'. And where did you get it?"

A tiny voice answers, "well, it all started as a wart on me arse . . ."

Until the frog responds, the audience has jumped to the conclusion that the bartender is talking to the English fellow. As in the previous joke, the mirth is supplemented by the joy of insulting an outgroup member; but the mirth itself is only caused by discovering one's own improper commitment to knowing the recipient of the bartender's inquiry. (The moral is: If you want to insult somebody, you could just say awful things about them, and that wouldn't be funny. Or you can find some comic hook—any of the mechanisms that generate humor—to hang your derision on, and, if you do it well, get a hearty laugh.)

(43) Two muffins are in the oven. The first one says, "Boy is it hot in here!" and the second one responds, "Wow, a talking muffin!"

The logical mechanism here makes humor of the fact that we suspend disbelief when we create a fictional mental space. By the end of the second sentence, the listener has built a mental space of two muffins talking about being in an oven, and then one of the muffins in that space points out that it is kind of ridiculous to have such a mental space. The muffin's words draw our attention suddenly to the fact that we're OK with—that we have been tricked into committing to—the idea of a talking muffin.

(44)   A priest, a rabbi and a nun walk into a bar, and the bartender asks them, "What is this, a joke?"

This one has quite a similar mechanism as the previous one. In realizing it's a joke, we suspend disbelief and accept that it's expectable for a priest, a rabbi, and a nun to walk into a bar together. We accept, in this fictional world, that this is how things are. Then the punch line steps outside the joke, and asks the audience, "What are you doing? You can't believe that— that doesn't usually happen in the real world!" Here is another way to play with our suspension of disbelief:

(45)   A forlorn man is about to throw himself off a bridge into the river when an old hag dressed in black approaches. "Hang on, there, honey! Why would you want to kill yourself?" He replies: "My wife has left me, I found out today I have inoperable cancer, and my embezzlement is about to be discovered when the auditor arrives tomorrow." "Not to worry! I'm a witch, and I can cast a few spells and make everything right. If you will just make love to me tonight, I will restore the funds, put your cancer into remission, and bring your loving wife back to your arms!" It sounds like a good deal, so the man climbs down, takes her to a cheap hotel, and does the deed. The old hag gets dressed, and as she exits through the door, she turns and says. "Say, sonny, aren't you pretty old to be believing in witches?"

There are other varieties of strictly first-person humor, including musical humor and visual humor such as caricature, paradoxical pictures, and even "physical humor" that involves violations of the audience's expectations independently of any specifically third-person interpretation (e.g., in a trick movie shot, a tower of blocks falls with a crash, and then the blocks "bounce" back into place—by reversing the film). These will be analyzed in some detail in chapter 11.

E. Interfering Emotions

A husband and wife were sitting watching a TV program about psychology explaining the phenomenon of mixed emotions. The husband turned to his wife and said, "Honey that's a bunch of crap. I bet you can't tell me anything that will make me both happy and sad at the same time." She replied, "Out of all your friends, you have the biggest penis."

Humor is tragedy plus time.

—Mark Twain

Oddly enough, while mirth is a joy, contents that are funny are, much of the time, negatively valenced. After all, an experience of first-person mirth means our model of the world has let us down, and whenever our beliefs fail us there is a heightened likelihood that some disaster will befall us. Once again, comedy and tragedy have long been seen as two sides of the same coin, and this is why. Taking a third-person perspective on this kind of tragedy in humor is also what ties comedy so closely to *Schadenfreude*— the joy in other people's losses—and what makes the idea of superiority in humor so enticing to some theorists.

We sometimes say a joke is made "at his *expense.*" Since it didn't cost the butt any money, why is the word "expense" licensed in that common phrase? Some prizes are worth more than money, such as "social capital," the sort of standing that money can't buy but that bankrolls our every social interaction. Typically, when a joke is at somebody's (social) expense, they feel it immediately, and the cost is reckoned in emotional pain of one sort or another (such as embarrassment or humiliation), though this is not necessary. (Contrary to superiority theory, the *intent* to "put down" the butt of the joke is also not a necessary condition. It can just happen to be the case that, for the event in question to be expressed humorously at all, the butt of the joke needs to lose face at the same time. It also quite often happens that there is no "author" of the joke at all, and thus no intention to put someone down. An old man discovers himself doing a typically dumb old-man-type thing, and laughs heartily, looking forward to telling his friends what he did. When he does, he is not putting down his fellow oldsters.)

The butt of a joke may sometimes laugh the most, and in such cases we can be quite sure the laughter is *designed* to minimize the social cost, to extract some kind of victory from the loss, by siding with the critics or at least disarming them with a buoyant attitude that expresses confidence. Note that the laughing butt need not realize that this is why he is laughing, and the laughter may even be genuine, Duchenne laughter; the "designer" of this proclivity may be natural selection or unconscious conditioning. At the same time, we can appreciate that the amusement expressed is not unalloyed with displeasure (cf. public roasts). Whereas similarly valenced emotions usually enhance each other, oppositely valenced emotions appear to compete and inhibit one another (e.g., Solomon and Corbit 1974; Fredrickson and Levenson 1998; Fredrickson et al. 2000). If a negative passion is monopolizing the system, then positive passions are momentarily blocked from access. If the butt's embarrassment is strong enough, then he cannot feel mirth, nor can one who feels empathy for the butt, and any laughter manifested will be non-Duchenne laughter.

Theorists working on the role of the passions in behavior often speak of a "currency of reward," supposedly a globally recognized resource for brokering the competition between the passions. Though "currency" is an imperfect metaphor (who gets paid? what do they want to buy with their money? and can they trade it for any other goods?), the idea of competition between the passions is astute—at any moment our behavior can only be directed by a few goals at a time, and our constant intrapersonal conflicts bear witness to this. (Should I eat the cheesecake or stay committed to my diet?) Mirth, as a passion in its own right that is part of that motivational system, competes in the marketplace of reward just as every emotion does.

The common retrospective remark, "Well, it's funny now, but at the time . . ." reminds us that one's perspective on a situation can modulate the detection of humor. In fact, we are, or can be, expert self-manipulators of our perspectives, seeking and finding the humorous way of recasting our memories, for instance, in order to salve our emotional injuries (see Greenspan 2000 for thoughts on similar emotional strategies).

Our personal techniques of perspective-shifting have been mirrored and amplified in the narrative arts. The filmmaker and filmwriter Jon Boorstin has identified three principal perspectives that have been discovered by Hollywood writers for the telling of stories through film—he calls them the *voyeur's eye*, the *vicarious eye*, and the *visceral eye*. Each of these perspectives in filmmaking, we think, is drawn from a natural perspective of the mind when viewing the world; and each has its effect on the perception of humor (cf. Ritchie 2006).

The voyeuristic perspective is the disengaged rational third-person point of view. From here no emotion is felt that could interfere with humor:

> The voyeur's eye is the mind's eye, not the heart's, the dispassionate observer, watching out of a kind of generic human curiosity. It is not only skeptical, it is easily bored. . . . I'm not talking about plumbing depths of character or living through the thrills of a lifetime but something simpler: watching events steadily unfold in rational, explainable sequence, an engrossing story that never violates our sense of logic. This is the armature on which a Hollywood movie hangs. (Boorstin 1990, p. 13)

This is the perspective taken when you watch *The Three Stooges* or *Mr. Bean* on television. You have no empathy for these characters—they are not your friends, and you do not feel their embarrassments, fears, or losses. This emotional disconnection is exactly why you can laugh at their antics and experiences—their mistakes do not matter to you.

(46)   Tragedy is when I cut my finger. Comedy is when you walk into an open sewer and die. (Mel Brooks)

The vicarious perspective, on the other hand, is the third-person perspective in which you do have empathies and sympathies with the subject of the event. Boorstin says, "The vicarious eye puts our heart in the actor's body: we feel what the actor feels, but we judge it for ourselves. . . . there is more at stake in the vicarious transaction than the voyeuristic one. We have invested part of ourselves" (Boorstin 1990, p. 67). When a friend or loved one or a protagonist in a story with whom you identify makes a tremendously embarrassing blunder, the crowd may laugh, but far from joining the cruel audience, you only want to usher your loved one off the stage into protection. Imagine a good friend taking a public stumble: The situation may evoke humor for some onlookers, but your empathic position puts you in the shoes of your friend, and you are overwhelmed with compassion, not mirth. When an antagonist in a televised skit slips on a banana peel, you are compelled to laugh, but when it is your own child, humor is the least prominent feeling. If the harm is not too big, this can sometimes be overcome and you feel compassion and mirth at the same time ("Oh, honey! Look what you did!"). This, Bergson says, requires "a momentary anaesthesia of the heart."[19]

---

19. There is a category of puns that we call *groaners*. Why do we groan instead of laughing? Well, sometimes we do both in a blended expression that might be described as a staccato sigh. The groan, on our view, is simply a response to the disappointment felt at the punster's weak

Boorstin's visceral perspective is the only first-person point of view, and it is much closer to the vicarious than it is to the voyeur's perspective: One can never (save through dissociative drugs and rare neuropathology) have a lack of emotional involvement with one's self: "The point here is not to feel what the character feels but to feel your own emotions, to have the experience yourself, directly" (Boorstin 1990, p. 110).

When experiencing an event in person you are bound up in the effects of the situation, and evaluative emotions are very likely to result. It is only when you can divorce yourself from negative emotions in a situation that you can whole-heartedly laugh (Duchenne-style) at yourself—at your own mistake—in that situation. The most common method for such detachment is through recollection: We laugh at ourselves in the situation only when we later recall it. That's why "it's funny now, but it wasn't funny at the time." What was it at the time? More often than not, it was embarrassing, humiliating, concerning, unnecessarily costly (in time or another resource), terrifying, or tragic.[20] But, now, in reminiscing, the reality of the situation is gone; it is no longer the visceral perspective that you are taking but, instead, a third-person voyeur's perspective, even on an event that was part of your own life.

(47) An Australian man won the 26th Annual Empire State Building Run-up Tuesday taking just 9 and a half minutes to run up the 86 floors to the observation deck. Nobody was more surprised than the handyman caught masturbating on the 73rd floor stairwell. (Jimmy Fallon, *Saturday Night Live*, February 8, 2003, as cited in Jung 2003).

While the empathetic asymmetry of these three perspectives accounts for some of the difference between first- and third-person humor, much more of the difference is accounted for by cognitive asymmetry, discussed in the next chapter.

---

level of creativity or disappointment with their use of some disagreeable content in the creation of the pun. Such disappointment can be simultaneous with the mirth—it may not have been tasteful or particularly creative, but it did lead us down a brief garden path. There may also simply be no mirth, in which case there is just a groan or perhaps a groan mixed with non-Duchenne laughter.

20. Occasionally mirth may even be derailed by an overwhelmingly more powerful *positive* emotion—if the recognition of the mistake you made brings to light a truth that is of extreme importance, your delight at that may overrun your humor.

9 Higher-Order Humor

A. The Intentional Stance

A man tells his doctor that his wife hasn't had sex with him for six months. The doctor asks the man to send his wife in so he can talk to her. So the wife comes into the doctor's office and the doc asks her why she doesn't want to have sex with her husband anymore.

The wife tells him, "For the past six months, every morning I take a cab to work. I don't have any money so the cab driver asks me, 'So are you going to pay today or what?' so I take a 'or what.' When I get to work I'm late so the boss asks me, 'So are we going to write this down in the book or what?' so I take a 'or what.' Back home again I take the cab and again I don't have any money so the cab driver asks me again, 'So are you going to pay this time or what?' so again I take a 'or what.' So you see doc when I get home I'm all tired out, and I don't want it anymore."

The doctor thinks for a second and then turns to the wife and says, "So are we going to tell your husband or what?"

After the birth of first-person humor, the most populous and important kingdom to evolve in the tree of humor is the wide variety of specimens that invoke the *intentional stance* (Dennett 1971, 1987), the tactic of attributing beliefs, desires, and other mental states and actions to *other* minds—the minds of other people, but also animals, computers, magic lamps, talking choochoo trains and the like. This kingdom so dominates our standard vision of humor that for some theorists, the varieties that lie outside it get ignored altogether, or are deemed not really humor at all. This is reminiscent of the obliviousness to bacterial life—the original form of life, after all—by many natural historians and biologists until quite recent times. As recently as 1942 the prominent biologist Julian Huxley could opine that bacteria had no genes![1] Living things that are visible to the naked eye are no doubt more interesting, at least to the lay person, than mere bacteria, and jokes that involve other people and their minds are no doubt more interesting to most consumers of humor than puns; but it is important to recognize these species as offspring, dependent on basic humor for their very existence.

Adoption of the intentional stance gives us robust predictive power over otherwise unfathomably complex entities. When we confront phenomena that cannot readily be understood in terms of their conformity to physical law or simple regularity (predicting from the physical stance) or by making assumptions about their design (adopting the design stance), the intentional stance is an option that can provide dramatic predictive leverage, by hypothesizing (or imagining) the beliefs and desires of these entities considered as rational agents, thereby allowing us to predict their behavior. The intentional stance is also known in the literature of psychology as "theory of mind," a term that is misleading, but usually harmlessly so. (It is misleading since it invites us to see the intentional stance as invoking myriads of theorems or generalizations inductively gleaned from experience, a cognitively sophisticated activity that need not be imputed to those who are adept at this normal kind of mind-reading via the interpretation of behavior. It doesn't take much of a "theory" to deduce that the dog whining at the door wants to go outside to relieve itself and believes that by whining it is alerting a cooperative door-opener to this fact.)

Using the intentional stance is how we manage our social lives, by modeling what other people believe. We assume other minds use processes similar to our own, and we automatically attempt to build a model of the knowledge that they embody. Doing so in a separate mental space allows us to keep that model distinct from our own knowledge. So, at any time, we may have a number of active mental spaces, corresponding not just to our model of our own perceptual world, but also to recursive models of other people's models of the world, and their models of our model of the world.[2] The doctor, in the joke above, could only have thought to say

---

1. In *Evolution: The Modern Synthesis*: "They have no genes in the sense of accurately quantized portions of hereditary substances; and therefore they have no need for accurate division of the genetic system which is accomplished by mitosis" (Huxley 1942, p. 131).

2. The recursive nature does not open us up to the need for possibly infinite mental spaces to be created. There is certainly a (fairly shallow) depth limit to the recursion. You can discover this for yourself by constructing longer and longer sentences of the form "I thought that you thought that I thought that you . . ." until the point (which occurs after only a few layers)

"so are we going to tell your husband, or what?" if he'd had a well-structured recursive model of both the husband's and wife's beliefs and their beliefs about each other's beliefs. None of us could survive the modern social world without using the intentional stance to make predictions.

So, how does this apply to humor? The use of the intentional stance to see situations from more than one perspective allows us to have more than one mental space relevant to each situation. The more mental spaces we create, the more places there are for humor to happen. We may find things funny either if they are invalidated mental spaces in our own knowledge representations or if we recognize that they are invalidated mental spaces for another entity's knowledge representation. This model supports the amusement we feel when we deceive someone in play, for instance, a particularly primitive form of deliberate humor; examples would be hiding around a corner to scare a person, or moving something and watching them look for it. Some foreshadowings of this primitive form of humor can be discerned in the play behavior of chimpanzees, but it is not easy to distinguish observation from anthropomorphic overinterpretation here. Behaviors that we would unhesitatingly interpret as higher-order intentional stance explorations if observed in human children, and find confirmed in their verbal responses to questions, may get demoted to less elaborate forms of interaction in the case of chimpanzees. The literature on higher-order intentional states in chimpanzees and other primates has more controversy and dashed hopes than confirmation. And, though there recently have been some partial reassurances for chimpanzee intentionality (e.g., Call and Tomasello 2008), it is still notable that many of the pratfalls taken by caged chimps—episodes that precipitate intense laughter from human onlookers—don't appear to provoke any marked interest whatsoever in their conspecifics (Daniel Povinelli, personal communication, 2010).

---

at which the sentence's actual meaning is incomprehensible without resort to the sort of analysis that requires paper and pencil. The bafflement induced by such sentences is not an accurate measure of our prowess, however, since it is to some degree an artifact of the effort to render our basic understanding *explicit*. Watching a subtle comedy of manners, we may break into effortless laughter, and we wouldn't laugh if we didn't tacitly appreciate that, for instance, she didn't expect him to realize that her familiarity with the facts betrayed her intention to discover the secret behind his reticence regarding his whereabouts on the aforesaid evening! But it might take us quite an effort to explain all this to an outsider.

We can find anticipatory humor in that knowing another person has an incongruity, and will soon resolve it. We are caused to laugh when an arrogant or pompous person slips on a banana peel because we see that his models of both physical and social reality were just corrected (harshly) by a new perception. We create a mental space in this case, which we may call the person's personal perspective, in which his excessive overconfidence (which we perceive as pompousness) may be central and an expectation of having control over the physical world is also active. The fall provides simultaneous information to the man that his erstwhile sense of dignity is false as well as his understanding of the immediate physical world. These data together destroy a larger set of expectations in the mental space than either would have alone—making it funnier than if either one or the other was presented on its own. And notice how the humor would wax or wane as we alter these elements in his perspective. If he is manifestly forlorn or self-deprecating, or walking fearfully and vigilantly, his tumble will not evoke mirth.[3] Charlie Chaplin recognized that with the right timing and emphasis we might be made to laugh even harder at a film in which the pompous person does *not* slip on the banana peel when we had been expecting him to do so—an instance of metahumor in which it is a mistaken anticipation in our own mental space that makes us laugh.

> It starts with the guy walking, cuts to the peel, cuts to a wide shot of the guy approaching the peel, back to the peel, and then, when his foot is about to hit the peel, he steps over it—only to fall in an open manhole. (Bloom 2010, p. 197)

A gullible, "clueless" person gliding through the world can be hilarious without any mishaps befalling them if we anticipators have all our expectations about *their* soon-to-be-dashed expectations elegantly dashed. The classic and most extreme example of this is the nearsighted Mr. Magoo,

---

3. Ramachandran and Blakeslee (1998) give an explanation of this example under the "false alarm" theory (a derivative of I-R theory) indicating that we laugh because we want to indicate that while it looks at first like something bad has occurred, it's actually OK (in the case that the man is not hurt). They say that if we knew the man were hurt, we would not laugh because the false alarm is actually a real alarm and we are concerned. We think that the absence of laughter in the case when he is hurt has a different explanation. The humor remains, but if the man is hurt, we have conflicting emotions, and the sympathy or empathy in us overwhelms the humor. This explains the occasional instance when something like this happens and we find ourselves having to say *"I shouldn't be laughing, but . . ."*. In this case it is the humor that overwhelms the sympathy. See more on conflicting emotions in the next section.

where the ongoing joke is that Magoo is radically misinformed about his surroundings but manages, by preposterous series of coincidences, to avoid calamity. It is no accident that Magoo has the habit of muttering, talking out loud to himself as he blunders through life; since we adopt the intentional stance, as always, we would never attribute to him these wildly false beliefs if we hadn't heard them from his own lips, since his nonverbal behavior fits the environmental facts quite felicitously. A similar comic character, with a broader array of comic styles than Mr. Magoo, is Rowan Atkinson's character Mr. Bean.

The evolution of third-person humor out of basic, first-person humor creates a new emotional dimension for mirth. It is here—and only here—that the superiority theory finds its application, for instance. As we have seen, anticipation-generation is a risky business, and the discovery and repair of our slips is the task for which we are rewarded in basic humor. Each episode adds a smidgen to our self-knowledge, so we are only too aware of our own proclivities to err in these ways. This creates a mild anxiety or insecurity, which third-person humor evolved to alleviate: Others, we see, are in the same boat, just as vulnerable to betrayal by covert entry inferences as we are, *but we are better at it than they are!* The involuntary habit of comparing oneself to others, sizing up the competition, is a deeply engrained disposition that we share with animals as distant on the phylogenetic tree as fish, and the outcome of any such comparison is a valenced emotion, somewhere on the scale between anxiety or fear—*uh-oh, time to retreat!*—through the reassuring— *I'm OK; you're OK*—to the triumphant—*sucker!* The self-congratulatory flavor of all third-person humor is due to the addition of the positive emotional valence generated by comparing self to other and coming out ahead. And the greater the disparity, on at least two dimensions, the greater the pleasure: not just on the idiocy scale—how stupid can you be?—but also on the scale of the severity or intensity of the consequences—now look what you've done! When consequences are negligible, the humor is faint to nonexistent. Here we see a huge difference between first-person humor and third-person humor: A dire immediate consequence always squelches first-person humor entirely, but can enhance third-person humor.

Mental spaces spawn mental spaces which spawn further mental spaces. Though not all of these spaces are related to each other, they all reside in a context of background knowledge and perception from the world. Because of this semihierarchical structure, our own knowledge can dash a character's beliefs *without* the character being aware of it. That is, global information that the audience knows or learns or somehow activates may be applied to any mental spaces—even those used to model others' beliefs. In this way, something the audience knows, but that a character does not know, can still invalidate something that the character believes. Here's a simple example of this kind of humor in a joke:

(48) She's so blonde she spent an hour looking at a can of orange juice because it said "concentrate."

We set up a mental space that mimics the reality for the character in the narrative. The space contains her beliefs and inferences, including her conclusion that she should be concentrating on the can. Our own recollection that juice cans say "concentrate" not as a command but as a description of contents is the premise that invalidates the space and engenders the humor (note that if the audience didn't know this they couldn't find the joke funny). She need never get this information—and, indeed, does not—but we're already laughing. Our own knowledge, not our expectation of her knowledge, invalidates the belief in the mental space we constructed to contain her thoughts. This kind of asymmetry is explored in more detail in the next section.

B. The Difference between the First Person and the Third Person

> I don't have a girlfriend. But I do know a woman who'd be mad at me for saying that.
> —Mitch Hedberg

Perspective matters. The model we gave of humor in chapters 7 and 8 was egocentric but *heterophenomenological* (Dennett 1991). It focused on the reasoning processes of comprehension inside the mind of a subject *from the subject's first-person perspective*, the kinds of thoughts one could have and the kinds of mistakes one could make from that perspective, and to do so it had to assume, as a primary source of data, subjects' first-person access to the contents of their own conscious minds, which is "direct" and voluminous, however problematic.

While the intentional stance allows us to conceive of things that others believe, we must realize that such conceptions are simulative, not completely faithful representations of the contents of another mind. We do our best to represent the thoughts of our fellow humans, but without access to their experiential histories we can only approximate their beliefs based on our own historical knowledge and a number of heuristics. Understanding the cognitive basis of our model helps us understand how this asymmetry plays out in a divergence between these kinds of humor. In the first person, recall, humor requires a leap in an active mental space that leads to a committed false belief, which is then detected. In the simulated third person, these requirements all still exist, but they are, perforce, relaxed. The belief must *appear* to be active, committed, and false, and we must *guess* that it was heuristic-inferentially derived. Since we can't know whether the belief actually exists in the other person's mind, nor do we have access to the knowledge context of their semantic construction processes, we can never fully ascertain whether there was a faulty heuristic leap. We can only assume there was and deduce that the belief is not true within the context of our own knowledge.

Let's see a bit of the internal workings of a third-person joke to show how these differ from the earlier examples:

(49)   An Aggie saw a classified ad for a cheap Caribbean cruise. He signed up and got on the boat, noticing that most of the other passengers were Aggies as well. As soon as the boat left the dock, the passengers were turned into prisoners and made to row. They were chained to the oars, and whipped by the master. The Aggie said "This guy seems unnecessarily cruel," and another Aggie replied, "He's bad but he's ten times nicer than the one we had last time."

Notice that the humor is not in the facts of the punch line—that the Aggie thinks the whip-master is ten times nicer this time. It lies in a further thought that the text doesn't make explicit—a chain of reasoning leading to a belief, which we attribute to the responding Aggie. In particular, when the punch line refers to the previous experience we realize that after one bad experience, the Aggie either somehow assumed it wouldn't happen a second time or thinks that this is what a cruise is supposed to be like. Either seems like an unreasonable thing to assume, but no other possible reason comes to the audience's mind for his going a second time—so we simultaneously attribute one of these beliefs to him and realize it is false. (And note in passing that if we vary the joke to diminish the severity of the consequences, it loses most of its mirth: Suppose our Aggie discovers merely that the waiter in the dining room is shockingly imperious and rude to the passengers. Almost no humor would remain in the second Aggie's response.) Compare this with first-person humor in which the belief that is false is not attributed but discovered in one's own mind:

(50)   I want to die peacefully in my sleep like my father, not screaming
in terror like his passengers. (Bob Monkhouse, as cited in Carr and
Greaves 2006, p. 265)

Here, like the examples in the previous chapter, we ourselves are carefully
led to the presumption that the grandfather is in his bed dying of old age,
before the scene suddenly becomes one of a highway accident. With the
difference in perspectival mechanisms in mind, let's have a look at some
situations where only perspective makes for humor differences.

We may laugh at someone for what appears to be a slip of reasoning
only to learn from her that we underestimated the situation. What we
found humorous, she found rational. We may, in fact, laugh again when
we discover that the actual fault was in our own mental space. These are
cases where the asymmetry of access plays a decisive role in creating the
humor. Such an episode, amusing to the participants, may then be further
recounted, as a joke:

Jane and Joe have pulled over to the side of a country road with a flat
tire in her car. Joe glances at the spare tire as he grabs the tire iron and
jack from the trunk. They get the popped tire off the car, and Jane says,
"Come on, let's go!" as she starts rolling it down the road. Joe laughs
and says, "Hey, where are you going? We have a spare!" to which Jane
responds, "No we don't. That one's flat too!"

In this rather mundane little story, Joe laughed at Jane because when she
started rolling the tire down the road, he attributed to her the belief that
there was no spare. In fact that was the belief that she had, yet it was not
funny from her perspective because it was true. Why did Joe laugh?
Because, *in his intentional model*, the Jane character had mistakenly
reasoned that they needed to go to a shop.

In general, third-person humor may happen "in the wild" (in contrast
to being contrived in a composed joke) more often than first-person humor
because the process of "finding" a false belief is easier in the third person:
We may simply *assume* a belief in the other person whether they believed
it or not.[4] The same humor won't happen in the purely first-person case
because of our own more intimate access to what we are actually thinking.

---

4. You might expect the fact that there are more third persons (billions) out there than selves
(1) would contribute to why there is more third-person than first-person humor. We suspect
this is not the reason—though there are more perspectives to be taken, and we do commonly
take them, the majority of our thoughts are from our own perspective.

In third-person cases, again, it is the inherent risk of adopting the intentional stance and *projecting* beliefs that creates the scope for amusing errors to arise.

For instance, if you are carefully wading across a river and suddenly slip and fall, you probably won't find it funny. But if I am wading across the same river, you have no knowledge of just how careful I was being when I slip and fall. So, even if I was being *more* cautious than you, if you don't assume that caution (because you cannot detect it), you may still laugh at me, attributing my fall to overzealousness or overconfidence in which I hubristically assumed the task was easier than it proved to be.

In both first- and third-person humor, a simplifying assumption provides a false belief which we then discover, but there are many ways in which the perspectival asymmetry can manifest. There are cases of *bipersonal* humor in which an agent in the situation and the humor comprehender are led down simultaneous garden paths. In these cases, the third-person humor takes the same form as the first-person humor, but only because it stands alongside the first-person humor. In the following story we comprehenders are in the same position as the deceptive little girl's mother:

(51)   A little girl asked her mother for a dollar to give to an old lady in the park. Her mother was touched by the child's kindness and gave her the money.

"There you are, my dear," said the mother. "But, tell me, isn't the lady able to work anymore?"

"Oh yes," came the reply. "She sells candy."

Bipersonal humor is to be distinguished from *dual-perspective* (or multiperspective, multipersonal) humor in which the two or more perspectives fail on different beliefs, albeit at the same time. For example:

(52)   Taking his seat in his chamber, the judge faced the opposing lawyers. "I have been presented by both of you with a bribe," the judge began. Both lawyers squirmed uncomfortably. "You, Attorney Leoni, gave me $15,000. And you, Attorney Campos, gave me $10,000."

The judge reached in his pocket and pulled out a check, which he handed to Leoni. "Now, then, I'm returning $5,000, and we are going to decide this case solely on its merits."

Once again trying our readers' patience, let us take the trouble to explain the joke. The first-person belief set up at first is that the judge is reprimanding the lawyers for engaging in bribery at all. From the way he begins the conversation and the way the lawyers squirm, we expect the judge to be morally immune to this corruption. This belief is proven unwarranted, however, when the judge states the punch line. At the same time, both of the lawyers' beliefs that their payments to the judge would garner them some advantage in the case are destroyed by the judge's equalization of the situation.

Another effect of this asymmetry is that it allows us to turn the base metal of our own misfortunes or near-misses into the gold of humor, in *practical jokes*. When we endure some rather uncomical mishap, the experience may inspire us to realize that a reprise of the incident, with somebody else as the victim, might be pretty amusing to watch. Although we may not have had a mistaken commitment ourselves, we can try to arrange for the same event to happen entertainingly to someone else; our newfound knowledge will help us attribute to them a false inferential belief, with potentially delicious—to us—results. A prankster who discovers that there is wet paint on a handrail may not find his own painted hand humorous, but removing the wet-paint signs, he might happily anticipate his victims making the same mistake. When a child playing chase slips in a patch of mud, she may, with sly intention, then lead her chaser across the same path in the next round, laughing this time because her own knowledge allows the attribution of a false commitment, even if the false commitment did not really happen (if the chaser exercised exemplary epistemic caution about traction and ground conditions but slipped nevertheless).[5]

One more example of asymmetrical humor worth mentioning is the curious delight people take in watching serious mishaps. Week after week, the television program *America's Funniest Home Videos* shows a parade of people getting hit in the crotch by errant baseballs, golf balls, and other flying objects, kicking mules, and—most excruciating of all—by their own bicycle crossbars as they crash after attempting some lunatic stunt. Ouch! We wince and guffaw at the same time. Why? Why are these painful vignettes—and dozens of others showing people felled by collapsing furniture and buildings—amusing? Is it Schadenfreude, plain and simple?

---

5. In Jacques Tati's masterpiece, *Mister Hulot's Holiday*, some boys hiding at the top of a bluff overlooking the town watch pedestrians walking along the sidewalk. Every now and then one of them whistles sharply, and the pedestrians look around, involuntarily and automatically seeking to locate the whistler. What's going on? Eventually, on about the fourth try, a whistle succeeds in luring a man to look up—and crash headlong into the lamppost. Bong! Victory for the boy whose whistle was so perfectly timed.

No, it is more interesting than that, even though the violence we laugh at can be appalling. One example that comes to mind is a video of a toddler who wanders into a break-dancing circle and gets kicked in the head by a dancer who never saw the child. Another example is a video in which a man walks out of a pizza restaurant, begins to cross the street and gets hit by a speeding car that apparently kills him. (The pizza man video is a safety advertisement, achieved by special effects—we fervently hope—but it certainly looks realistic and that's what counts here.) Getting hit by a car or a dancer is definitely not funny in the first person. And while we'd all *like* to say that it's not even funny in the third person, the phenomenon of many people laughing at these videos is undeniable. We would argue that these laughers are not necessarily cruel or sadistic people, but that they laugh because they attribute mistaken assumptions to the participants portrayed—and note that the dancer who kicks the child is as much a victim as the child, for she must confront the guilt of what she has done, thanks to her too-casual assumption that the dance floor was cleared for action. We can dial down the humor potential by adjusting these variables: If the child is not a toddler but a crawling baby, too young to have *any* sense of caution, or if the man is pushed into the path of the speeding car, the humor disappears. Perhaps the Boorstinian voyeuristic perspective is in play here, so that empathy is close to zero, but the winces and groans that accompany the laughter suggest otherwise. Part of the framing that contributes to the potential for laughter when watching *America's Funniest Home Videos* is the very fact that what we are watching is a home video. This implies that the people in the scene are almost always self-consciously performing—even *showing off*, especially in the failed stunt videos—and hence are ripe candidates for the attribution of foolhardy assumptions.

In third-person humor, we make an attribution of an overcommitted belief in another's mind. Having made such an attribution in the past doesn't stop us from making it again when we see the character behave the same way. That is, in repeating the joke, we can reexperience the humor. This differs from first-person humor in which we *may* learn from our own mistakes and predict them to avoid making them again. Notice that bipersonal or multiperspective humor can have both effects during a repeat hearing—the first-person humor may be drained by prediction, while the third-person attribution still occurs—and in these cases the joke is still funny, but not quite *as* funny as the first time we heard it. In general, this consequence of our model offers a fine explanation of why puns (typically first person) are not very funny on repeat occurrences and why *Monty*

Python and the Holy Grail, watched twelve times in a weekend, can still be (almost) as funny the last time as it was the first.

Finally, the perspectival asymmetry leaves us with a new question: If first-person humor encourages the maintenance of epistemic integrity, what benefit, if any, does third-person humor confer? One answer may be that it does not confer any benefit at all. It could be an evolutionary spandrel, an accidental by-product of the fact that both first-person humor and the intentional stance are useful traits in their own rights, which, in combination, happen to produce third-person humor. But even if this is the original source of third-person humor, it might still be opportunistically exapted for various purposes, and there are several good candidates. The first, and most obvious, is that third-person humor appreciation evolved to enhance cultural transmission of valuable information. At the minimum, helping your compatriots discover mistakes in their mental models can be used as currency in a kind of reciprocal altruism (Trivers 1971). That is, by doing so you may be able to count on them doing the same for you in the future, creating an implicit cognitive collusion that forms a kind of distributed or extended cognition (Hutchins 1995a; Clark and Chalmers 1998) in which we literally help each other to think. Not to mention that pointing out your colleagues' mental missteps before they behave on them may also save the whole party, including yourself, from possible injurious consequences. Think of the classic "wait don't!" situation in which you see a friend about to light a cigarette at the gas station, swiftly imagine the consequence and interrupt him. Such an automatic and involuntary expectation can be humorous . . . and lifesaving.

A more extended version of this is the transmission of myths and tales for pedagogy. Stories, whether sad, shocking, funny, or just bland, and whether truth or fiction, convey much valuable information to use in enlarging and updating our world knowledge, our JITSA dispositions. Even before Aesop composed or compiled his fables, people appreciated that an unforgettable tale, with a "moral," is an excellent vehicle for passing on acquired wisdom (Dennett 1996a). The reason we so seldom paint ourselves into the corner or saw off the limb we are sitting on is because we have (often) heard tales of these mishaps, and their traces lie dormant but easily awakened in our long-term memory. A treasury of tales is salted away in long-term memory, in neural structures hungry for action ("Me, me! I want to 'happen' now!" yells the Boy who Cried Wolf, in competition with Complacent Frog in the pot of slowly heating water, and the Grasshopper and the Ant and a host of others). These are valuable prosthetic devices, worthy (and more realistic and natural) versions of Minsky's frames and Schank's scripts.[6] A tale that provokes mirth—or fright, or some other strong emotion—is more unforgettable than a bland tale, and hence a more robust transmission vehicle. If a disposition to share stories has evolved, it is most likely by cultural evolution, not genetic evolution, though there might be Baldwin effects that somehow focused or otherwise enhanced our neural machinery for sending, receiving, composing, and comprehending narratives, as well as whetting our appetite for them.

C. Anthropomorphism and Anthropocentrism

The chicken and the egg are lying in bed and the chicken is smiling and smoking a cigarette and the egg is upset. The egg mutters to herself, "Well, I guess we answered THAT question. . . ."

Man is the only animal that chews its ice cubes.

—Oring (2003)

We have already mentioned Bergson's observation that more important than the fact that only people find things funny is the fact that the only things found to be funny are people. He gave the following example: "You may laugh at a hat, but what you are making fun of, in this case, is not the piece of felt or straw, but the shape that men have given it, the human caprice whose mold it has assumed" (Bergson 1911, p. 3). What, then, about the human is funny?

As our model tells us, what is central to all instances of humor is the discovery of a locally inconsistent commitment in a mental space, and this phenomenon occurs only in minds like ours, so far as we know. There must be an intentional agent whose perspective is required for the humor to exist. An informal review of the jokes we know discovers no exceptions, and we challenge the reader to supply amusing counterexamples. Jokes or witticisms that do not contain either familiar intelligent entities—people or Martians or anthropomorphized agents (such as a talking egg or chicken), always involve the direct perception of the obliteration of a mental space created within the audience's frame of reference. Try to compose a joke involving two oysters and see that there is absolutely nowhere to go unless you can get the oysters talking to each other, or trying to deceive each

---

6. In Schank's later work, *Tell Me a Story: A New Look at Real and Artificial Intelligence* (1991), he develops the idea that the principal role of stories is as constant reminders of the lessons of experience, one's own and others'.

other nonverbally, or otherwise acting like two tiny people dressed up in hard shells. With inanimate entities it is even more obvious: "Did you hear the one about the daisy growing next to a rock, when a cloud floated by. . . ." Now what?

This fruitless exercise suggests strongly that any joke about any subject must necessarily anthropomorphize: There can only be a ridiculous rock, a hilarious daisy, or a preposterous cloud if these objects are imaginatively endowed with human characteristics such as vanity or laziness and some capacity to perceive their circumstances—or else perhaps if they belong to somebody (Mount Olympus, home of the gods, portrayed as a molehill, for instance). Thus "impersonal" humor—such as puns and other word-play—is actually *first*-personal humor: The audience's own mind is the arena in which the mental-space error is encountered. It is we ourselves whose anticipations, whose jumps to conclusions, are subsequently falsi-fied. So in first-person (impersonal) humor, in which the audience is also tacitly the subject, the subject must "get it" for humor to occur. Not so when audience and subject are distinct.

Now we have a basic model that reveals the underlying structure of all humor. And we have shown how this structure can serve as the launching platform for the human capacity to create additional mental spaces allow-ing for models of fictions as well as models of intentional agents' minds. These extensions to our cognitive capabilities create, in both cases, a much broader range of circumstances for us to find humorous. These higher-order varieties of humorous stimuli are the forms that attract most of the attention in the modern humor environment, probably because as we adults grow more sophisticated, we become too habituated to the more primitive forms of humor—childish humor—to take pleasure in them.[7] There are also forms of humor that don't readily fall under the descriptions we've given so far, and we will deal with them in due course. The variety of humorous contents mirrors the variety of thought, and the model is open-ended in one sense: As new topics or new modes (habits, techniques) of thought arise, they may extend both the domain and the processes of humor construction and appreciation. Some of these potential mecha-nisms are explored in the next chapter by way of example, though it would be misguided to try to classify them all exhaustively. We know that our

---

7. One can see a similar arms race, and subsequent habituation curve, in pornography. What will arouse the relatively innocent pubescent teenager will be too bland by far for the jaundiced tastes of the aging Lothario, whose persistent seeking after ever spicier fare supports whole industries producing exotic erotica.

creative minds, especially those of our comedians (and our children, who are always restless pioneers), are constantly trying to find novel ways of provoking the sense of humor in each other. Just as with genres of music, it is possible that entirely new types of humor may be invented at any time. While humans will use whatever cognitive tools they can get their hands on to engineer situations that will make each other laugh, those engineered situations are always sophisticated logical mechanisms that somehow cause a concealed false belief to become apparent.

D. Intentional Stance Jokes

> I can analyze any joke you bring me, if you will leave it overnight—for the task requires reflection—and give you in the morning the chemical formula upon which it is composed.
> —Eastman (1936)

Eastman was bold, but at the same time he was careful when he said that a single joke may take all night to reflect upon. The fact that gifted "intuitive" comedians create jokes apparently effortlessly, even on the fly in witty ripostes, conceals the fact that many conditions must be met, many constraints satisfied. The sometimes tedious processes of deconstructing a joke, and providing an inventory of its working parts, is not simply the inverse of the process of constructing the joke in the first place, so it would be a mistake to imagine that comedians diligently follow some recipe involving these ingredients when creating humor, just as it would be a mistake to imagine that jazz musicians compose their solos by deliberately invoking the structures and patterns that retrospective analysis reveals. We see some traces of an analytic mode of construction in the deliberate *editing* of jokes, making them more streamlined, punching up the punchline by changing the word order, adding a beat here, a sly misdirecting digression there; but this is, in effect, "postproduction" refinement—arrangement, not composition, to continue the musical parallel. Depending on whether the humor is from the first- or third-person point of view, or both, an analysis must assure:

• that long-term memory beliefs are distinguished from working-memory beliefs;
• that, even if something is a working-memory belief, it still is active, or has been reactivated before the moment of dénouement;
• that the belief was not simply the result of misperception, misremembering, or just plain forgetting, but rather the result of a faulty heuristic leap;

• that there is an epistemic commitment to the belief, which is not simply assumed to be probable;
• that this is all done within the framework of the intentional stance—that is, that the analyses are all done from the audience's point of view as well as from the points of view of the audience's recursively[8] constructed intentional-stance models of other agents. These analyses may also need to account for varying expectations or estimations by agents of other agents' degree of epistemic caution. And,
• finally (remembering that we don't all find the same things funny), that we have an accurate inventory of the shared world knowledge that must be available to activate the assumptions that generate the covert errors, both by the audience and by any agents depicted in the episode.

It sounds complicated, but remember: A joke has a very demanding job: it must enter the brain and gently trigger just the right activations, in the right order, with the right timing, and the right relative emphasis, and it must find in that brain all and *only*[9] the content resources it needs to do its job. As you'll see in the next chapter, these factors play a much more detailed role in the analysis of nonjoke humor (and episodes of nonhumor that seem at first to meet the conditions). Jokes are, comparatively, rather easy to analyze. Though they are just a small subset of humorous stimuli and events, they make for compact, relatively "portable" objects of analysis. A joke is a carefully engineered humor-elicitation package, but credit for the R&D may not be assignable to any intelligent designer; it may have evolved by differential replication of variations on a story, with only the most unforgettable and enjoyable variants being reliably transmitted.

Ecologists have discovered that many instinctual behaviors in animals are elicited by particular salient stimuli they are hard-wired to respond to.

---

8. Yes, recursive. For the simplest example of recursive intentional-stance humor (that is, second-order intentional-stance humor), imagine: An audience member may see that one character in a story or joke has a fully rational viewpoint, but they may also see that another character's perception of that first character's viewpoint contains humor because of having been informed, in some way, that the second character thinks the first character has a mistaken belief. The complexity is only limited by the span of attention and size of working memory of the audience.

9. Just as *not enough* world knowledge can render an audience immune to humor, so *too much* knowledge can also destroy humor. In the most obvious case, reminding a person of a key item prematurely—telegraphing the punch line—is a killer, and some too-clever, too-knowledgeable audiences may not need reminding; they may be way ahead of the would-be comedian; he won't kill, he will die.

Gull chicks, when they see the bright orange spot on their parent's beak, peck at it, and this initiates regurgitation in the parent and eating by the chick. Niko Tinbergen famously showed that the chicks would peck even more vigorously at exaggerated orange spots, brighter and larger than any in nature (Tinbergen 1951, 1953). He experimented with other species and found that they often responded more vigorously, and preferentially, to *supernormal stimuli* than to the real thing. Inspired by Tinbergen's work, various theorists have suggested that some human artifacts—paintings and sculptures, and pornography, but also music and even aspects of religion (Boyer 2001)—have been devised as supernormal stimuli that (over) stimulate our instinctual systems, producing more intense reactions than they were designed (by natural selection) to deliver. We think this is often a plausible conjecture, and jokes are prime examples of super-normal stimuli that take advantage of our natural propensity for humor-detection in much the same way that perfumes, makeup, artificial sweeteners, music, and art give us exaggerated experiences with respect to the natural world.[10] Thanks to their refined designs, they tend to have the power to induce in us a far stronger and richer sense of the ludicrous than everyday "found" stimuli, however humorous. Few events in real life are so funny, on their own, as to be unimprovable into still funnier episodes with a few fictional touches.

Now, in order to demonstrate our theory in action, we have to break one of the golden rules of comedy: Never explain a joke! But such is the price of explanation: A theory of humor that didn't *reduce* the joke-getting process to a relatively stupid, mechanical, cognitive process would be a theory that still appealed at some point to an unexplained "sense of humor"—and that would be no explanation at all. So, with due warning that each joke will be followed by a dogged description of the mechanisms on which it depends, we are almost ready to get into the "data." (The scare quotes are because we must take the word "data" loosely here. All, or almost all, previous theorists have taken jokes as a primary data source for measuring the success of their theory. So, for fair comparison, we must do some of the same, and we think that doing so can be very convincing. Still, jokes and humorous situations are not the only kind of data to use for a theory of humor elicitation, and we will discuss the problems with them in more detail and then provide some alternatives in the next chapter.)

---

10. Alexander Chislenko (1998) may have been the first to describe jokes in terms of super-normal stimuli.

We can streamline our task somewhat by taking advantage of some quite regular patterns, molecular structures, you might say, composable from our atomic elements, just listed. These are the heuristics of folk psychology, highly reliable but fallible shortcuts of the intentional stance. For instance, a *secret* is not just something the agent A *knows* (or believes) and agent B does not; A must *know* (or believe) that B does not *know* it, and moreover must *believe* that it is somewhat in A's power to maintain that state of *ignorance* in B. (If A knows that B's pants are on fire, and B doesn't [yet], and A knows that B doesn't [yet], this is not much of a secret—but there is still a brief window of opportunity for A to do something with his fleeting asymmetry of knowledge. But if A is not sure—committed to the belief—that B is still ignorant of this, A will not be motivated to attempt some actions, which would likely be futile if A were wrong.)

(53) "Hey, did you know you have a banana in your ear?"
"Speak up! I have a banana in my ear!"

You can see how an *atomic* analysis of even simple situations like this could get quite tedious without the molecular level of description and explanation to speed things along. For instance, there is all the difference in the world between *telling* somebody something you believe and saying something to somebody that *betrays* the fact that you believe it. In the former case, you *intend* your audience to *recognize* your *intention* to cause them to *believe* what you *express* by your words (Grice 1957, 1969, but see, e.g., Sperber and Wilson 1986 and Millikan 2004 for important refinements). In the latter case you may have no idea what you have inadvertently conveyed by your utterance; you may indeed *assume* that your *secret* (which we won't bother to spell out again) is safe when it isn't: You don't *realize* that he now *knows* and *knows that you don't know he knows* that you have divulged what you *know and think he still doesn't know*—but he does! All sorts of opportunities are created by such complexities, and it is entirely possible, of course, that you deliberately *pretended* to betray a belief you didn't hold, and so on. Consider the complexities of this story, adapted from Close (2007):

(54)   A man wakes up from his terrible hangover, and finds his wife has prepared a beautiful breakfast in bed for him. What has he done to deserve this? He came home stinking drunk, vomiting all over everything, after a night on the town. He was too far gone even to get himself into bed, and his angry wife had to half-carry him to the bedroom. When she tried to pull the puke-drenched clothes off his almost inert form, he yelled out "Stop, bitch! Get your hands off me! I'm a married man!"

A stroke of genius!—*or*, was he as out of it as he seemed, and just plumb lucky? We'll never know, and it's funny either way, but notice that the ploy, deliberate or not, could not have worked if his wife didn't believe he was too drunk to recognize her, but not so drunk as not to realize it was a woman who was undressing him. Apparently she never even considered the hypothesis that he's played this trick on her—she is *committed* to taking it at face value. His speech act, an imperative, said one thing; what she derived from it was something else, and the *last* thing he would want is for her to suss out his intention in saying it! What she derives depends on committed assumptions she makes, covertly and automatically generated from both her current perception and her world knowledge—about what happens in bars when there are loose women around, about the perceptual limitations of drunkenness, about marriage vows. Change any of the details regarding this, and the story falls apart, humorless.

This story makes essential use of the *commitment indicator* (via action): Actions speak louder than words. This is the most important heuristic tool helping to indicate where humor in a third-person situation occurs. It explains why Mr. Magoo's soliloquys are obligatory; if we couldn't *overhear* his mutterings—he's not talking to us or to anyone else—we'd be unable to fathom the depths of his false beliefs. The intentional stance is a tool within our own thought processes subject to its own epistemic failings. Epistemic commitment in others is often difficult to assess via the intentional stance, and attribution errors are the pivotal sources of much humor, even when there is *apparent* confirmation. (Maybe his wife is on to his little trick and has poisoned his soft-boiled egg!) For the most part, we do a good job, and among the most reliable tools we use to guess with high likelihood that there was an epistemic commitment is seeing how the agent acts. Because of the costly repercussions of mistaken acts in the world—the problem that anticipation machinery evolved to solve—an action taken by a person, unless seen to be taken with caution and vigilance, is usually an indication of a set of committed beliefs (and desires). A person firmly kicking a ball manifests a commitment to its being filled with air, rather than lead. In contrast, a person who carefully and slowly feels their way through a dark room shows no commitment to the presence or absence of obstacles they might run into, and each little accidental bump discovered along the way cannot be a source of humor—unless the person is so familiar with the room that they might say "D'oh! I *knew* that corner was there!"

The very tight evidential relationship between action and commitment is relaxed only in cases where epistemic caution is not obvious to the observer. When the actor is uncommitted to a belief but nonetheless acting on it, the commitment indicator will typically yield a false positive. For instance, when the actor decides (seldom self-consciously!) that the cost of further information-gathering is higher than the cost of the probable loss if one is proved wrong—the observer, ignorant of this private fact, may falsely attribute commitment based on how the actor acts. The actor isn't throwing caution to the wind, perhaps, but, not being sure, and not caring much, acting anyway. A comeuppance here is not humorous *to the agent* but can be to the observer who has made the false positive attribution.

Another heavily used heuristic in humor is the *deception indicator*. In some cases we, the knowing audience, are explicitly shown the process by which the butt of the humor is induced into contaminating his mental space. In other words, we are shown, in slow motion, as it were, the very entry into the mental space that is the source of humor in the first place. In other cases, such as joke (62) below, we are equally deceived along with a character, and we later learn how we were deceived.

Deception humor at its simplest is being tricked by a friend into behaving in some mildly nonconstructive way—the old pull-out-the-chair trick, for instance. Hilarious in childhood and not very funny thereafter. More subtle and admirable practical jokes exploit more subtle commitments on the part of the butt. A man is annoying his neighbor by bragging about the fuel-economy of his new car. "*Forty* miles per gallon! *Forty* miles per gallon!" The neighbor retaliates: Every night he sneaks over and pours a few extra gallons of gas into the new car's tank. "*Fifty* miles per gallon! Now I'm getting *fifty!*" Then later, "*Sixty!* Can you believe it, I'm getting *sixty* miles per gallon!" Then the neighbor abruptly stops. The bragging stops, and the man starts making anxious phone calls to the perplexed car dealer. The covert assumption on which the joke depends is that nobody would secretly donate fuel to somebody else's car, a pretty good assumption under normal circumstances.

Another practical joke with a similar structure: A somewhat foppish businessman shows up in the office one day sporting a preposterously ostentatious homburg hat (this was perpetrated back in the 1950s, when men wore fedoras), which he displays to all and places lovingly on the shelf in the communal closet. After a few days of this, it gets tiresome, so the secretaries, during their lunch hour, pool their resources and buy a duplicate hat in the same expensive shop, one size too large and substitute it on the shelf. The man goes home with his prize hat resting down on his ears. The next day he returns, hat looking just fine on his head. During the morning the secretaries investigate and find a carefully folded lining of newspaper inside the hat. They fit this newspaper carefully inside the original hat and replace it on the shelf. The man goes home with his hat perched precariously on his head . . . And so it goes, with the foppish man increasingly worried about the periodic swelling and shrinking of his head. Like the other practical joke, this one depends on the default assumption that people will not go to considerable expense to play a joke, but also on the entirely reasonable assumption that hats don't change their size spontaneously. (One presumes that the size-labels had to be doctored or removed to protect the assumption that there is just one hat involved.) Some narrative deception jokes are just practical jokes recounted or otherwise depicted—as in the long-running and often hilarious television program *Candid Camera*—but most deception jokes invoke the deception indicator in other ways, as we shall see.

The *compression* tool takes advantage of widely shared general knowledge. The exploitation of stereotypes in jokes and witticisms has a deservedly negative reputation, not so much for the politically incorrect content typically exhibited (some of the funniest humor is outrageously prejudiced and all but unspeakable), as for the crudeness of the logical mechanisms that they employ. A stereotype functions as a data-compression device that instantly references a huge library of exaggerated or oversimplified information. Just mentioning the stereotyped class is a blatant invitation to the audience to create a mental space that is bound to have contaminating errors in it—as almost everyone already knows—so the best use of stereotypes in humor involves metaeffects, and meta-metaeffects, in which the audience, already braced for a lame attempt to extract mirth from a tired old cliché, is ambushed by one reversal or another. (It is worth noting just how extensive the genus of metahumor is; so populous are the humor lineages in our ken that we are well endowed with expectations that arise from our (fallible) recognition of humor types.

(55)   There was a young lady named Tuck,
        Who had the most terrible luck:
        She went out in a punt,
        And fell over the front,
        And was bit on the leg by a duck.

There is obviously nothing funny about this little story, unless you were expecting something else.

Similarly, there is a large class of jokes that exploit variations on cultur-ally embedded stories. Shared stories are excellent data-compression devices. (Recall the discussion of the role of remembered stories in alleviat-ing the frame problem, in chapter 8.) They serve almost literally to "get everyone on the same page," and this creates opportunities for exploita-tion. The more of a story you can tell with few words, the more efficient your joke or witticism will be. Stand-up comedy avails itself of this immense compression. Comedians often relate a short story about their lives that is analogous to something in your own, and you are thus induced to bring in a large amount of compressed inference to complete the picture that they briefly sketched, making it easier for them to apply a *pointer mecha-nism* and demonstrate the humor in the situation. A line such as "Only in America do sick people have to walk to the back of the drugstore to get their prescriptions while healthy people can buy cigarettes at the front" points to something we "all" know but never saw the humor in before—and it would be utterly ineffective in another culture. One of the most efficient pointers is the pained exclamation. For instance, when Homer Simpson says "D'oh!" we laugh. A wordless gesture or facial expression, by a good comic actor (for instance, a double-take performed in slow motion) can accomplish a similar communicative effect.

(56) A couple of New Jersey hunters are out in the woods when one of them falls to the ground. He doesn't seem to be breathing, his eyes are rolled back in his head. The other guy whips out his cell phone and calls the emergency services. He gasps to the operator: "My friend is dead! What can I do?" The operator, in a calm soothing voice says: "Just take it easy. I can help. First, let's make sure he's dead." There is a silence, then a shot is heard. The guy's voice comes back on the line. He says: "OK, now what?"

The LaughLab was an Internet-based social experiment run in 2000 and 2001 by UK researcher Richard Wiseman. The experiment was meant to discover general statistics about appreciation of jokes in various (Internet-connected) cultures. The world's funniest joke according to his survey was the one above. An incomplete inventory of the "working parts" of this joke includes the following: At the outset we don't *know* how *committed* the hunter is to the *belief* that his friend is dead, though that is what he *says*. The operator shares our uncertainty, and *wants* (for good reason) to resolve it; she *wants* to help (it's her job, for one thing), and taking a time-pressured stab (in a more leisurely conversation she would no doubt choose her words more carefully), she adopts the well-worn "supportive" second-person-plural diction—the nursely "we" of "how are we feeling today?"—and makes a "helpful" suggestion, utterly ignoring the possibility of ambiguity in her words. That covert ambiguity leads the hunter to mistake the meaning of the operator's advice (just the way a dumb computer might) and *commits* him to a *belief* that he should act in a certain way, a commitment he probably wouldn't make if he didn't *believe* he was talking to somebody with expertise and authority who *wanted* to give him the best possible advice. He is distraught—and stupid, of course—but would he as mindlessly *obey* the same command if he *believed* he was talking on the phone to one of his other hunting buddies? We know he *commits* because of the drastic thing he does, which we infer from the elegantly compressed conclusion of the story. The shot being heard is somewhat ambiguous, though we begin to think we know what happened, a guess that is confirmed when he says "OK, now what?" (Notice that much of the humor would be drained from the story if all this were explained, instead of left to the reader's imagination. Here the basic mirth is enhanced by the pride of lightning-fast problem-solving, the appreciation of how much smarter we are than those dunces—for the operator is certainly complicit in the homicide.[11]) And needless to say, the characters are facing far too serious a situation to laugh, but for the reader or hearer it is a fiction, and thus emotions of pity, horror, or despair do not interfere with our humor.

(57) One Sunday morning, the priest noticed Little Johnny was staring up at the large plaque that hung in the foyer of the church. It was covered with names, and small American flags were mounted on either side of it. The seven-year-old had been staring at the plaque for some time, so the priest walked up, stood beside the boy, and said quietly, "Good morning, Little Johnny."

"Good morning, Father," replied the boy, still focused on the plaque. "Father Scott, what is this?" Little Johnny asked. "Well, son, it's a memorial to all the young men and women who died in the service." Soberly, they stood together, staring at the large plaque. Little Johnny's voice was barely audible when he asked, "Which service, the 9:45 or the 11:15?"

---

11. It is also possible, we have learned, for somebody to experience first-person humor directly; one who did told us that he didn't notice the ambiguity in the operator's advice until he learned of the shot, whereupon his own committed expectation to the hunter feeling for a pulse was dashed.

Johnny's question at the end of the joke should set off an analyst's commitment indicator. His use of language is a speech act, and betrays (but does not express) his commitment to the belief that "service" here means church service rather than military service. Had Johnny been on a tennis court or in a restaurant, he would no doubt have made a different *commitment* about the meaning on that occasion of this multiply ambiguous term. Probably he doesn't yet *know* the intended meaning of the term—he's only seven—and in any event it doesn't *occur* to the priest that Johnny might not *know* this meaning. We in the audience infer all this and more, utilizing our knowledge of churches and priests and little boys, and having already constructed a mental space for Johnny's beliefs, we have no difficulty diagnosing Johnny's mistake. We may go on, anticipation-generators that we are, and imagine the priest explaining the mistake to Johnny, but that is not a necessary part of the joke, the way such implied sequels often are.

(58)   If you step onto a plane and recognize a friend of yours named Jack don't yell out "Hi, Jack!"

This is not just a simple pun, since it is higher-order humor, making use of the intentional stance. Interestingly, the necessary perspective is not of any explicitly introduced character in the joke. The root of the humor is the point of view of other passengers, flight attendants, pilots—the default population of your airport "script." We automatically assume that you and Jack are not the only people within earshot. If Jack finds humor in your call, it is only because he, unlike you, already recognizes the ambiguity in it and, then, in his own use of the intentional stance (like ours in understanding the joke), anticipates the problems it can pose. We involuntarily imagine the passengers constructing mental spaces in which they incorrectly believe the word "Hijack!" to have been uttered. When they see you waving at your friend, they may realize their mistake and collapse those mental spaces in deference to the one where they figure out your friend is named Jack, but it is not necessary that those (imaginary) passengers comprehend the actual situation; we need only imagine their construction of this mental space and then use our own world knowledge to provide the necessary information to invalidate it (as we did in the previous joke about Little Johnny). But that is not enough; until you go on to create a further mental space containing something like air marshals and their mental spaces, and (hence) their likely committed actions, and the dire effects of this on the mental space of Jack's friend, and so forth, the intensity of the consequences of the advice offered in the speech act which *is* expressed in the joke would be missing. To see this, compare (58) with this unfunny variation:

(59) If you step into a bar and recognize a friend of yours named Ball, don't yell out "Hi, Ball!"

Or even lamer:

(60) If you are in the dairy section of the supermarket and see a friend of yours named Gert, don't yell out "Yo, Gert!"

The role of unmentioned but irresistibly imagined consequences is even stronger in the following (true) story:

(61) Great Britain is a land of pet-owners who often take their pets very seriously. Dennett was once the house guest of a distinguished—indeed knighted—professor who greeted him at breakfast with "Good morning, Dan. Did you sleep well? I wonder if you would like to see some photographs of our daughter's prize-winning pussy!"

This is not just an inadvertent pun, of course. The humor lies in our immediate and irresistible re-creation in our own minds of much of the emotional roller-coaster that beset Dennett in that brief moment: Did I hear Sir Cecil correctly? Could he *possibly* mean what he seems to be saying? They have *contests* like that here in England? His *daughter?* At *breakfast?* And then the recognition that British English and American English must have some subtle usage differences, confirmed by the photos of a rare and beautiful Siamese cat. Sudden relief—and let it be known that Dennett somehow managed to stifle the urge to guffaw that shook his body (which is yet another humor-enhancing element of the implied scenario: Was Dennett going to be trapped into revealing what a smutty-minded chap he was?). Notice, by the way, the narrative problem encountered by anyone telling this story. This is not, strictly speaking, a joke, but rather an anecdote, and it could more naturally be told in conversation without the preamble sentence about pets, ending with an explicit account of the very next thing that happened: the showing of the cat pictures. Still funny, but awkward in its timing. It is better to take a page from the joke-engineer's book and provide a hint in the early going. The hint should be as delicate and remote as possible. "Great Britain is a land of cat-fanciers who often take them very seriously" riskily sets the covert entry threshold a little higher, and "The British do love their doggies and pussycats" almost gives the game away. And note that the details count for a lot. This is a distinguished professor talking, not a Hollywood producer or a bartender or a sailor, and the fact that it takes place in Great Britain plays an important role in permitting us *expect* a somewhat higher level of decorum (compression by stereotype) in a British gentleman, and then to *tumble* to the correct interpretation and not just consider it as a tentative surmise.

(62)   A man and a woman who have never met before find themselves in the same sleeping carriage of a train. After the initial embarrassment they both go to sleep, the woman on the top bunk, the man on the lower.

In the middle of the night the woman leans over, wakes the man and says, "I'm sorry to bother you, but I'm awfully cold and I was wondering if you could possibly get me another blanket."

The man leans out and, with a glint in his eye, says, "I've got a better idea . . . just for tonight, let's pretend we're married."

The woman thinks for a moment. "Why not," she giggles.

"Great," he replies, "Get your own damn blanket!"

This is a classically deceptive bipersonal joke. The man's speech act, "just for tonight, let's pretend we're married," provokes the inference that he means they should sleep in the same bunk to stay warm. When she giggles "Why not," we see that the woman interpreted it the same way we did, and by her speech act we feel confident that she has committed to this interpretation of his sentence—and in fact we too may have been tricked into committing to it. His final statement reveals the deception, as we discover that the belief we shared with the woman in the story was based on a faulty assumption.

Another example of bipersonal humor is the following:

(63)   "Do you mind telling me why you ran away from the operating room?" the hospital administrator asked the patient.

"Because the nurse said, 'Don't be afraid! An appendectomy is quite simple.'"

"So . . ."

"So?" exclaimed the man, "She was talking to the surgeon!"

The administrator is really just a prop, a straight man, to enable the conversation to unfold. We and the administrator make the same mistake, but it is our mistake that creates the humor: We infer—without noticing—from the content of the patient's speech act, that the nurse was talking to the patient. (We tacitly go back and insert "to me" after "the nurse said," but only because of the content that follows. Had the patient said that the nurse said "Isn't that mayonnaise on your scalpel?" a different insertion, "to the surgeon," would have been tacitly and automatically made, and a different inference train would have been set in motion.) When our error is revealed, the puzzling situation is resolved, but only because we all share world knowledge about surgeons, their training, and their legendary *sang-froid*. The patient had good reason to run. (Exercise for the reader: Vary the participants and the circumstances and see how the humor evaporates.)

(64)   A young ventriloquist is touring the clubs, and one night he's doing a show in a club in a small town in Arkansas. With his dummy on his knee, he's going through his usual dumb blonde jokes when a blonde woman in the fourth row stands on her chair and starts shouting: "I've heard enough of your stupid blonde jokes. What makes you think you can stereotype women that way? What does the color of a person's hair have to do with her worth as a human being? It's guys like you who keep women like me from being respected at work and in the community and from reaching our full potential as a person, because you and your kind continue to perpetuate discrimination against, not only blondes, but women in general . . . and all in the name of humor!"

The young ventriloquist is embarrassed and begins to apologize, when the blonde yells, "You stay out of this, mister! I'm talking to that little jerk on your knee!"

This is another example of dual-perspective humor with a nice reversal thrown in. The setup creates a mental space in which there is a member of a stereotypically unintelligent party (*compression*) who seems to have something valuable to say (our covert stereotype assumption is shattered or challenged). In our mental space representing the blonde's own model of the world we infer from her initial speech act (*commitment indicator*) that she intends to berate the ventriloquist. Her punch line collapses both of our covert assumptions at once: our recently acquired belief that she was above the stereotype, and our mistaken belief about what is in her model of the ventriloquist and his dummy.

(65)   A member of the United States Senate, known for his hot temper and acid tongue, exploded one day in mid-session and shouted, "Half of this Senate is made up of dunces!"

All the other Senators demanded that the angry member withdraw his statement, or be removed from the chamber.

After a long pause, the angry member acquiesced. "OK," he said, "I withdraw what I said. Half of this Senate are *not* dunces!"

The backbone of this joke is the simple logical observation that negation cannot always be expressed with the same surface word forms. Although the negation of "Tom is tall" is "Tom is not tall," the negation of "Half the eggs are fresh" is not "Half the eggs are not fresh." Our senator has exploited this fact, appearing at first to deny what he earlier said. We appreciate that he thus doesn't deliver what he promises. The joke would be funnier if a mollified senator then said "That's more like it! Apology accepted!" betraying by this act that he still doesn't get it, and that the senator's estimate is probably accurate. It does not matter whether the first senator believes what he says, but only what his audience takes him to have asserted. Absent a commitment (as in the variation suggested) the joke is funny but just barely so, an example of first-person humor (like a pun) that gets a bit of extra zing by the derogation of a species people love to derogate: politicians. The variation, by catching us underestimating the duncehood (we don't expect the senators to fall for this transparent move), gives us a better moment of mirthful surprise, and demonstrating—not merely insinuating—senatorial stupidity.

A similar joke, on the borderline between first-person and third-person humor, is this one reported by Koestler (1964):

(66)   P1: "Tell me comrade, what is capitalism?"
           P2: "The exploitation of man by man."
           P1: "And what is communism?"
           P2: "The reverse."

Only the word "comrade" gives us the third-person setting, inviting us to infer that the questioner is some sort of communist authority figure, and making the response slyly subversive.

(67)   A senior citizen is driving on the highway. His wife calls him on his cell phone and in a worried voice says, "Herman, be careful! I just heard on the radio that there was a madman driving the wrong way on Route 280!"
           Herman says, "Not just one, there are hundreds!"

The role of the wife is negligible in this joke, and indeed a variant version has an Irishman in a rental car on a US freeway listening to the car radio and hearing the broadcaster break in with the bulletin that a madman is driving the wrong way. Since the narration *doesn't say* that the driver is going the wrong way, we make the default assumption that he's on the right side of the road; this is the covert insertion that creates the opportunity for humor. In a setting where transatlantic driving habits have been under discussion, the joke will lose most or all of its humor by telegraphing the punch line. But in either case, the lion's share of the humor comes from our recognition that this fellow, senior citizen or Irishman, is obtuse in his complacency. His commitment is apt to have dire consequences, and he is nevertheless oblivious. Similar incaution in a less dangerous setting would not be as funny.

(68) Once there was a little boy in church. He had to go to the bathroom so he told his mother, "Mommy, I have to piss."

The mother said, "Son, don't say 'piss' in church. Next time you have to piss, say, 'whisper' because it is more polite."

The next Sunday, the little boy was sitting next to his father this time, and once again, he had to go to the bathroom.

He told his father, "Daddy, I have to whisper."

The father said, "OK. Here, whisper in my ear."

The only interesting feature of this juvenile bathroom humor is that the humorous event occurs only in our imagination, not in the narrative, in a mental space that is temporally posterior to the events in the narrative. The listener must extrapolate an anticipation of what the boy would next attempt to do. Were this drastic event to occur, we realize that many mental models would have committed beliefs invalidated: the father's reasonable belief that his son needs to whisper something (thanks to the *commitment* tool at work in the father); the boy's expectation that doing what Dad says is (as always) a good policy, even if you don't understand why; and the mother's broken expectation, along with that of the other churchgoers, that such events will not occur anywhere, and certainly not in church. We wouldn't expect any of the three principals in the story to find the outcome humorous at first, though other members of the church may be able to laugh—if they, like us, are using Boorstin's "voyeur's eye."

Earlier I-R theories, especially semantic script theories, might assign the humor in this joke to the opposition between the behavior of urination and being in church, and perhaps additionally between urination on somebody versus not (and, on that, superiority theory would agree). Our model suggests that these factors are merely content that surrounds the discovery of a faulty belief, though such contents add spice to the mix and may thus increase the pleasure of the joke through misattribution and transfer of arousal, as we'll describe in the next chapter.

(69) One time Dennett and the Stanford AI pioneer John McCarthy were at an academic conference, and shortly after the speaker began his talk somebody from the back of the room called out "Louder!" The speaker duly obliged and continued his talk in a more robust voice, and a few seconds later McCarthy yelled "Funnier!"

Timing is crucial in this case: The disruption causes by the first yeller has to settle down, so that everyone is "back to normal," but not too much time must pass since they have to have the echo of the first yell "in the back of their minds" to recognize, instantly, the utterly unexpected sequel as a reasonable enlargement of the set of interests an audience has when it commits its attention to a speaker. The faulty tacit assumption was that the speaker had "fixed" the situation and no more improvements were in the offing.

(70)   An Asian man walked into the currency exchange in New York with 2,000 Japanese yen and walked out with $72.

The following week, he walked in with 2,000 yen, and was handed $66. He asked the teller why he got less money than the previous week.

The teller said, "Fluctuations."

The Asian man stormed out, and just before slamming the door, turned around and shouted, "Fluc you Amelicans, too!"

This joke nicely illustrates how our spurious automatic filling-in during spreading activation can contribute to a falsehood in a mental space (see p. 103). At "stormed out" and "slamming the door," the joke causes the audience to fill in a reason for the man's anger; we attribute it to the now-unfavorable exchange rate for yen and perhaps his lack of expectation that these things fluctuate. Our filled-in reason is false, however; spreading activation and default pragmatic assumptions have led us astray. The man's real reason for anger turns out, at the punch line, to be his mishearing of the teller's response. This is a multipersonal/dual-perspective (not bipersonal, as the beliefs in the two perspectives are different) joke because we recognize both that his reason for anger (in our first-person model) is not what we had committed to, and that he himself thinks he has been insulted, though we know he hasn't. This latter point, the man's own mistaken belief, comes to light through his speech act, which indicates his commitment via his action.

(71)   A young Catholic priest is walking through town when he is accosted by a prostitute. "How about a quickie for twenty dollars?" she asks.

The priest, puzzled, shakes her off and continues on his way, only to be stopped by another prostitute. "Twenty dollars for a quickie," she offers. Again, he breaks free and goes on up the street.

Later, as he is nearing his home in the country, he meets a nun. "Pardon me, sister," he asks, "but what's a quickie?" "Twenty dollars," she says, "same as it is in town."

This joke is used by Wyer and Collins (1992) to exemplify their model. In their explanation of it, there is a semantic shift in the meaning of "what's a quickie?" which could mean either 'what is the price of a quickie?' or 'what is the meaning of 'a quickie'?' and a second shift from the nun being a nun to being a prostitute. They use this analysis to support the diminishment and nonreplacement requirements, which we have already argued are insufficient (see chapter 4). Using our model, our analysis is similar to their standard I-R analysis, but goes a bit deeper into the mechanisms involved: The joke is funny because beliefs occurring in three mental spaces are collapsed simultaneously. First, at the punch line we realize that the nun believed the priest was asking for a price—we know that's not true given the setup and we invalidate her committed (via speech act) belief. Second, we know from the setup that the priest truly expects the nun will give a description, not a price: The priest's expectation is broken by the punch line. These two broken expectations are a classic mark of misunderstanding humor in which two people each expect each other to understand the same things—causing each to have mistaken expectations in their models of the world. Third, our own mental space is populated by a default nun, who is, by stereotype, nonsexual, or at least outwardly so. The punch line explodes this belief with a quick jab. (The joke would be crippled by a longer conversation between priest and nun.) These three simultaneously invalidated mental spaces make this joke a strong case of humor (for any listener whose world knowledge silently generates all three).

(72)   The young man and his date are sitting at a table in a Las Vegas casino lounge, and the young man notices that Frank Sinatra is sitting at the corner table with some friends. When his date goes to the ladies room, he dashes over to Sinatra's table and says, "Excuse me, Mr. Sinatra, I apologize for intruding on your evening, but my girlfriend, who just went to the ladies room, is the biggest Sinatra fan ever, and if you were to come over to our table when she gets back and say something like 'Hi, Johnny! Who's the beautiful chick? You've been holding out on us!' it would mean the world to her, and I'd be forever in your debt." Sinatra shrugs, and the young man goes back to the table. After his girlfriend returns, Sinatra approaches the table and says "Hi, Johnny—who's the beautiful chick, you've . . ." but the young man interrupts: "Frankie, Frankie—where's your manners? Can't you see I'm *occupied?*"

This is an exemplary trickster joke, where we admire the hero's virtuoso exploitation of the intentional stance. The deference with which Johnny approaches Sinatra's table (enhanced by our world knowledge of how celebrities are treated by their fans) sets us up for Johnny's completely unanticipated act, but that is just the surface layer. We have a mental space of the mind of Sinatra, the star, being moved by the appeal of the callow young fellow to an act of amused generosity, inspired, perhaps, by the fellow's pluck, and perhaps even more by being invited to join in an innocent deception of a young lady. This might be fun! And vanity, a sense of noblesse oblige, may enter as well. Sinatra is a big enough guy to help out the little guy. And we have a mental space for Johnny's mind that, we soon discover, seriously underestimates his deviousness. This is particularly potent because the very structure of the joke, obviously a trickster joke, invites the listener to anticipate a clever move, to expect the unexpected, and to try to figure it out before the punch line. Presumably this joke will lose its moxie as the reputation of Sinatra as a mob-connected tough guy recedes into the history books, but even without that world knowledge, the audacity of the young man is evident. And if we can't help imagining the beating that Johnny is probably going to get in the back alley for all his efforts, we may, on reflection, decide that Sinatra might appreciate Johnny as a kindred spirit and congratulate him instead.

(73) Two mathematicians were having dinner in a restaurant, arguing about the average mathematical knowledge of the American public. One mathematician claimed that this average was woefully inadequate, the other maintained that it was surprisingly high.

"I'll tell you what," said the cynic, "ask that waitress a simple math question. If she gets it right, I'll pick up dinner. If not, you do." He then excused himself to visit the men's room, and the other called the waitress over.

"When my friend comes back," he told her, "I'm going to ask you a question, and I want you to respond 'one-third x cubed.' There's twenty bucks in it for you." She agreed.

The cynic returned from the bathroom and called the waitress over. "The food was wonderful, thank you," and the other mathematician started: "Incidentally, do you know what the integral of x squared is?"

The waitress looked pensive; almost pained. She looked around the room, at her feet, made gurgling noises, and finally said, "Um, one-third x cubed?"

So the cynic paid the check. The waitress wheeled around, walked a few paces away, looked back at the two men, and muttered under her breath, ". . . plus a constant."

As most of our readers can no doubt attest, the deliciousness of this in-group joke can actually be appreciated by someone with no calculus background. At first the story seems to be just like its predecessor, the recounting of a practical joke. (Many other jokes have a similar structure, complete with the convenient trip to the rest room to enable the setup.) The beauty of the punch line lies in the fact that, contrary to our stereotype as well as that of the mathematicians, the waitress knows more than we ever imagined; it is she who has been concealing her knowledge, for she knows a more precise answer than either mathematician had in mind. It is interesting that her actually quite obscure addendum is so readily identified, even by nonmathematicians, for what it is. We who have forgotten whatever calculus we ever learned effortlessly infer from the situation that what she has said is the truth! When we suddenly adjust our mental space, a curious thing happens: Even if we don't at all understand what she said, we label it "true mathematics" in our mental space and infer that she is one smart cookie. The pleasure is heightened, of course, by our recognition that the mathematicians are none the wiser; *we* know, and they don't, that they have hugely underestimated her, thanks to their stereotypes. This is a knockout feminist joke, exploiting our stereotypes while exposing them—the opposite, in this regard, of the blonde-and-ventriloquist joke—but no funnier for being politically correct.

(74)   Ad in a newspaper: "Illiterate? Write today for free help."

This supposedly real ad derives its drollness from the reader realizing that the advertiser is *committed* (via action) to the self-contradictory belief that illiterate people might find and read the ad.

(75)   Recall the joke from the beginning of this chapter in which the doctor asks the woman, "So are we going to tell your husband, or what?"

Though comprehension of this joke is thickly laden with the intentional stance, the main humor is actually from the first person. We, the audience, assume the doctor's role to be that of the good guy who should be solving the marital troubles of this couple. Then the punch line explodes that tacit assumption, showing him to have become just a continuation of the problem. The mistake was ours. But, there are elements of third-person humor too: We see the poor husband's default belief that the doctor would help him dashed—so the fact that it was the husband who sent his wife to the doctor contributes to the humor. Also, as the woman tells her story, the falsity in the husband's belief that she has just become cold to him emerges, giving us mild twinges of humor along the way. Then there is Bergson's point about mechanicity: We are amused at this woman's somewhat ridiculous and repetitive behavior of trading sex for such little favors as a cab ride or the freedom to come in late to work. There are multiple sources of enjoyment in this joke, as in many: The final punch line is strengthened by the wit of the doctor—he's rather clever to find this self-serving solution. And the enjoyment of the entire thing is heightened by the arousal of the sexual theme. These kinds of pleasurable content augmentations are the subject of the last section in the next chapter.

We have now completed a first-pass application of our model to a broad range of jokes. Like Eastman, we claim that our theory can explain "any joke you bring us." We also acknowledge that, while jokes are a good starting point to help us get our footing in the subject matter, they are actually the easiest variety of humor to explain. Other kinds of humor need to be explained too, and, just as important for our theory, we must show why various ordinary serious and sober events are not humorous, in spite of seeming, at first, to meet our conditions for humor.

10 Objections Considered

Man is the only animal that laughs, or needs to.
—Mark Twain

We hope our readers are beginning to be persuaded by our model, but they should not be impressed yet; they should instead be ransacking their imaginations for counterexamples, either funny items that don't fit the model or unfunny items that do. Both types must be canvassed before we can rest any confidence in our model. It is important that an empirical theory—which we aspire to present—should be refutable, but not too *easily* refutable! By looking at a variety of apparent counterexamples to the model, we can illuminate and refine its articulation, and sharpen the challenge for those who think they can find a fatal flaw in our account. In the next two chapters we will "turn all the knobs" of our model, reviewing— and defending against—every kind of purported counterexample we have been able to find, to see how it behaves with altered parameters and conditions. As you will see, there are relatively few knobs to turn, so almost all of the cases we will examine will turn on the notions of whether a belief is *active* and *committed*, though once in a while, an apparent counterexample turns on whether the belief is actually false or whether it is attained by a heuristic leap. First, however, we must explore a digression on methods of falsifiability.

A. Falsifiability

Two men are making breakfast. As one is buttering the toast, he says, "Did you ever notice that if you drop a piece of toast, it always lands butter-side down?"

The second guy says, "No, I bet it just seems that way because it's so unpleasant to clean up the mess when it lands butter-side down. I bet it lands butter-side up just as often."

The first guy says, "Oh yeah? Watch this." He drops the toast to the floor where it lands butter-side up.

The second guy says, "See? I told you."

The first guy says, "Oh, I see what happened. I buttered the wrong side!"

—Cathcart and Klein (2007)

The process of twiddling the knobs on a humorous event—"Now it's funny . . . now it's not"—is one way to test our model, as you will see when we consider a number of variations on examples in the coming sections. These analyses, together with our analyses of jokes in the previous chapter, allow us to catalog both hits and correct rejections, and to show that, in a rather extensive array of examples, we have not yet stumbled upon any clear false positives or false negatives. While such a result is compelling, the astute reader will have noticed that our analysis requires the intervention of *interpretation*. For any theory of mirth elicitation to explain a joke, an attributive interpretation of the intentional states evoked by the joke is necessary to bridge the theoretical gap between objects in the world and their semantic impact on the mind. An analyst has no choice but to suggest that an audience has, for instance, activated, to degree A, belief B, with commitment level C, and then disproved and debugged it by event E. Such an interpretation introduces one more complicating level of indirection and possibility of analytical error than we would have if *jokes* were the object of study, rather than humor and mirth. Our results, then, have to be taken with the proper caution that, ultimately, if no more objective method can be found, at least we should look for converging evidence or methods for assuring intersubjective agreement.

The most promising alternative—one that has a chance, at least eventually, of actually probing for the relevant entities and events in the mind and brain—may be a neuroscientific approach. Be that as it may, what should a neuroscientist look for? What kind of dependent variables can be used, and what are the independent measures that we should look at?

The dependent variable may be easier to locate. As Duchenne pointed out, laughter is not well-enough correlated with mirth to be a reliable indicator. The only alternative is to use mirth itself. But how can we measure it? In time, we might find that it is correlated with some very specific temporal fingerprint of activity in mesolimbic structures, but until then, as is the case with colors, flavors, and other qualia, felt mirth can only be determined by self-report of amused subjects or coding of Duchenne laughter, which is hard to fake. These kinds of measures, taken across subjects, can be a reliable method (called "heterophenomenology" by Dennett 1991) for producing objective measures (or at least statistically significant intersubjective measures) of subjective phenomena, as long as, in the case of self-report, subjects are introspecting purely for the qualitative aspects of an experience, rather than (folk-)theoretical causes for those sensations. When the object of interest is a subjective quality, like mirth, then we have few alternatives—even the mesolimbic fingerprint that we just hypothesized as a possible neuroscientific eventuality could only be established by firstly correlating patterns of activity with such measures of mirth. Any later use of such a fingerprint as a gauge would ultimately rely on the validity of those initial self-reports or Duchenne laughter.

While perhaps sometimes difficult to work with, and somewhat methodologically restrictive, the dependent variable can at least be found. The independent variable may be a bit more complicated. Our theory posits that the elicitors of mirth are the commitment of an active belief; the discovery that that commitment was made in error, covertly, by a heuristic leap; and the lack of interference from other overpowering emotions. Though no doubt there is a neural difference between those active states of working memory that contain committed beliefs and those states of belief that are activated but uncommitted, nobody can say today how such a difference would present itself in a brain scan. As theory in cognitive neuroscience matures, such features may become detectable in the near future, and if the correlation we postulate is not found to hold, our model is wrong.

Characterizing our model in terms of JITSA belief activation and commitment as well as the emotional response of mirth brings us closer to knowing what kinds of events to look for in the brain when subjects experience mirth. We won't attempt (prematurely) to provide a precise independent criterion now for commitment of belief or these other conditions. But in the meantime the importance of these conditions can be seen by varying the inputs—revising jokes and experiences—and noting that *commitment* is a good provisional term for the crucial internal response: When it is missing, no mirth results. For centuries people knew that *conception* was the triggering cause of pregnancy, and knew that not all intercourse led to conception, without having any good physiological account of just what internal event conception was, but they knew *what to look for*; and today we have an essentially complete theory of conception, which would not exist if people hadn't first isolated the target condition, conception, to inquire about.

Until the proper neuroscientific tools can be developed, there are several other methods that may be used to test our theory. Of course, the first method is to review humorous circumstances and look for counterexamples, as we do here. Suppose, however, a rival model were offered that appeared to do just as well as ours on all the examples considered. How could we arbitrate between them? First, look at our twenty questions about the phenomenology of humor. If the model can answer these questions more cleanly and convincingly than ours, it should be provisionally accepted until falsified. Such a theory would correctly explain—better than ours—not just which things are humorous, and which are not, but also why they are and how they have various social and behavioral effects on us.

Our theory, with its sketch of the underlying mechanism of humor perception, also makes a number of specific behavioral predictions unavailable to earlier theories. Just to name a few: We predict differential levels of intensity in mirth-elicitation during repeated exposure to first-person versus third-person humor (see pp. 153–154); we also predict that intentional-stance-dependent humor[1] (perhaps, like the Jake Cress sculpture on p. 237) should not be as readily or as often appreciated by those without a well-developed theory of mind, including young children and severely autistic persons. Similarly, children who are just learning the difference between first-order and higher-order interpretations of the word "why" should be the ones who find the staple chicken-crossing-the-road joke funny. Our theory predicts that children before this point won't find it funny while children who are sophisticated enough to have the ambiguity—who realize that there is a proximate why and a distal why to goals—are led down the garden path: They are enticed to wonder for what (distal) goal the chicken is crossing, before learning that the joking questioner was asking for the proximal goal. Adults, as we all know, have learned heuristics over their lifetimes of experience with this kind of ambiguity (of the word "why," for instance) which tend to keep them from committing to these garden paths and help them recognize that there may be multiple things possibly being asked.

Many experiments in cognitive psychology exploit interference effects: Give subjects one task while distracting them with another, for instance. Other experiments look for enhancement effects, such as masked priming

---

1. Notice that much humor *uses* the intentional stance, but only a certain subclass is highly *dependent* on it. Part of this distinction is made clear by avoiding multipersonal humor.

(see, e.g., the description in Dennett 2005, pp. 39–40). So what could an experimenter do to modulate the key variables in our model: activity-in-a-space, commitment, covert entry, and no interfering emotion? We've given examples of variations of all of these, but we haven't shoehorned the discussion into the form of "rigorous" experiments, for good reasons. First, controlling for differences in background knowledge and taste would be laborious. We would need to give subjects lengthy questionnaires about their general knowledge and interests, and then tailor the stimulus set (the jokes) to fit a number of different profiles. We would test the prediction that particular subject pools with the same profile would tend to find the same set of jokes funny, and unfunny. But we would still risk being swamped by an untold number of unrecognized (and irrelevant) variables in the conditions. Recall that even the funniest comedians turn on only a sizable fraction of their own fans on any one joke. Another problem: How do you screen for prior familiarity with (good) jokes? "Stop me if you've heard this one" cannot, alas, play a rigorous role in a controlled experiment. Moreover, can watching videotapes of (good) joke-tellers (while in a scanner, or while having some secondary task to perform, or . . .) really be natural enough to yield good data?[2] Probably many subjects will glaze over. Without a good way of measuring mirth directly (yet), we're stuck with self-report, augmented by facial expressions and laughter, which can be videotaped and scored by "blind" observers (who don't get to see the stimulus that provoked the reaction they are scoring). So-called *catch trials* could help calibrate the thresholds: Mix a few deliberately constructed nonjokes (like the infamous joke with the utterly meaningless punch line "no soap radio"[3]). That could help establish a baseline for using facial behavior and laughing as a dependent variable of some reliability, along with self-report. Then we could start testing. Take a set of (good) jokes. For each one, create a priming context that should "ruin" the joke—by making the covert leap too overt, for instance, or canceling the default obviousness that would entice the leap in the first place. Then compose control priming contexts for each of them, so that each joke is delivered to half the subjects with a ruining prime and the other half of the subjects get a neutral prime. Prediction: There is a detectable decrease in amusement for the ruining prime cases.

---

2. Many experiments in psychology and cognitive neuroscience are rightly criticized for not being "ecologically valid"—for putting subjects in extremely artificial circumstances that are (almost) bound to distort their performance in significant ways (Neisser 1976; Brewer 2000).

3. See <http://en.wikipedia.org/wiki/No_soap_radio>.

Quite a few other specific predictions emerge from our theory, and we hope that scientists begin to pull out for testing those that dovetail with their own interests.[4] Behavioral experiments based on these predictions may have new methodological avenues opened to them by our theory as well. We expect the results of such attempts at refutation will help refine our model over time.

With this digression aside, we can now get into the counterexamples.

B. Epistemic Undecidability

> The settler was lying in a bloody heap next to his burning Conestoga wagon, an arrow protruding from his chest. A cavalry officer rode up and called to him: "Does it hurt?" "Only when I laugh."[5]

Our first set of potential counterexamples consists of things that are found to be funny in the second sense that we discussed in chapter 3—funny-huh. They may appear to fit the model, but on closer inspection, we find that they do not. Funny-huh events all seem to have an incongruity between a sensory pattern that is anticipated and another that is experienced—that is to say, they are events or states of the world that are found in some way to be different from what one expected. In considering all these examples, you need to adhere strictly to a first-person point of view: would *you* find these events amusing if they happened *to you?*

A. You come home and find the lights on. You expected they would be off because you remember leaving them so, and no one else has keys to your house . . . You may think, "*That's funny*, I could swear I turned them off this morning."

B. You may get an unusual feeling inside your body that you can only describe as a *funny feeling*; perhaps a phantom pain, or the sensation—called *paresthesia*—of the thousand tingling needles of a foot fallen asleep

---

4. If you are such a researcher, feel free to ask us to collaborate on refining the articulation of hypotheses, methods, and protocols. We will be eager to help.

5. This archetypal joke has many variations, involving a World War II pilot lying in the wreckage of his plane, or a Vietnam veteran scarred by napalm, or maybe—who knows?— a wounded Gaul responding to Julius Caesar. Its punch line has been used as the title of several novels, plays, films, songs, and a British situation comedy. Apparently the anomalous juxtaposition of pain and mirth appeals to people of all times and places, ages and tastes.

Figure 10.1
Mother Goose & Grimm, © 2008 Grimmy Inc. King Features Syndicate, Inc.
Reprinted with permission from Susan White-King Features.

due to pinching the neurovascular bundle. It is also common for someone
who gets drunk for the first time or someone who is having a stroke to say
"I *feel funny*." This announcement refers to the unusual way their conscious
experience feels: not as typical.
C. You are driving your car, and you hear an unfamiliar noise. You ask
your children to quiet down so you can listen to the engine, and when
they ask why, you say "because the car *sounds funny*."
D. You are about to drink three-week-old milk (that you may have thought
was fresh), and upon sniffing it say to yourself, or someone else, "This
smells funny."

The incongruity in these examples is clear: In each case the thing that
is funny is something that differs from your ordinary expectation—and in
fact each could be said to have a perception that threatens a conception,
as Schopenhauer put it. You probably expect the lights to still be off, your
foot to feel normal, milk to smell fresh, and the engine to turn with a
smooth regular rhythm. Let's call these beliefs *challenged expectations*. The
incongruities here are not simply in the stimulus; they are incongruities
between a belief and perception.

It is no mere coincidence, we claim, that our language has a word with
two such contrasting senses. Our examples (A) through (D) of things that
are funny-huh are all on the edge of being funny-ha-ha. We have to answer
two questions about these examples. The first thing we want to know is:
What is the same about all four of these examples that makes them

funny-huh? And the second is: What differentiates them from funny-ha-ha—why don't we laugh at things that are funny-huh?

The answer to the first question is that funny-huh is a form of confusion about something that matters.[6] The factor that makes these four events in some way the same as each other (all instances of funny-huh), yet not humorous, is that they all provide an epistemic incompatibility in which neither belief has the power to dislodge the other. That's what confusion is—an unresolved epistemic *concern*. Yes, a perception threatens a conception, but you cannot resolve it on the spot by invalidating one of the beliefs. And with no invalidated belief there can be no humor.

There are different ways this can happen, but all of them come down to epistemic undecidability. In the first case, beliefs with equal epistemic capacity go head to head. When neither can trump the other, the situation is potently undecidable and both beliefs, though conflicting, may remain living side by side. You may go to your grave carrying both beliefs from some potently undecidable contradictions with you, along with a sense of confusion that will invariably arise if such beliefs are ever recalled into working memory again. An example of potent undecidability would be this:

You are looking for your keys. You carefully look on the bare kitchen table. They are certainly not there. Then, after searching the rest of the house for awhile, you find them . . . on the kitchen table. It is potently undecidable whether they were on the table earlier or not. You can't tell, and you probably never will. The belief that they weren't there earlier since you didn't see them there and the belief that they must have been there since that's where you found them are both unwavering. You can't disprove either. You may suspect that someone has tricked you or that your earlier search was seriously imperfect, that you looked right at them but somehow didn't see them (this can happen), but you won't know. You will think: "*that's funny!* I just looked here earlier . . ." and then the matter will quickly be left behind because the keys are in hand, and you are ready to go out. If you are still bothered—as you may well be—it is

---

6. If it was about something that didn't matter, the brain wouldn't bother dealing with it at all; as you look out the window at the winter woods, the hundreds or thousands of tree branches make an indecipherable tangle against the sky, but this confusion doesn't register until, for some reason, it matters—or seems to matter. William James's "blooming, buzzing confusion" in the infant's mind is soon sorted out into the confusions that matter—and bother—and the confusions that are happily neglected.

because of your capacity to extrapolate, to generalize to an ominous but tentative conclusion: Either I am going mad or somebody is playing tricks on me.

Case A above is an example of potent undecidability. Here you may be so certain that you left the lights off that the solid data that they are now on still cannot cause you to revise your previous belief. You can have strong grounds for this certainty, or not. Suppose you don't: When you left home you didn't much think about the status of the lights—you were distracted; in this case, when you discover them on upon coming back, you would be unconcerned and conclude, correctly, that you weren't paying attention, and rather than think *"that's funny"* you would just accept it. Suppose you do: You remember that you assured that they were off in a rather direct way—by looking at them. Looking at the lights off is not a case in which a false inferential belief comes to be. Perception of this sort is hardly inferential at all; it is certainly not a risky heuristic leap. They were off when you looked at them! In this case, since both beliefs are properly committed, you have a potent undecidability, and neither belief is going to be revised— the most likely thing in this circumstance is to realize or at least expect that something serious changed (e.g., someone entered your house) and this is no cause for humor.

In our other three cases, one belief has an uncertainty to it that causes an asymmetric undecidability. We'll call them *weakly undecidable*, to indicate that while the more uncertain belief does not have the power to dislodge the belief that it conflicts with, it cannot itself be removed because its status *as* uncertain already reflects the full assessment of all other beliefs upon it—it hasn't been deemed wrong, just uncertain.

Let's look at the examples more closely: You certainly believe that you smell an odor, hear a noise, and feel a feeling. Call these *unchallenged perceptual beliefs*: These are active sensory data just recently (within the "specious present") detected. But now look at their *implications*—inferential beliefs driven by these sensations—that take part in a conflict. In these examples, none of these inferential beliefs—the *challengers* of the original expectations—is committed. You are not sure if this smell is a sign of bad milk (otherwise you would have said it smells bad instead of funny), you are not sure what the funny feeling in your body is or what it means (because it is novel. If you are sure of it, you'll no longer say it's funny, you'll say what you feel: "I feel drunk"; "I feel like my foot has fallen asleep"), and neither are you sure what the sound that you suspect *might* come from the engine is caused by (you haven't yet stopped the car, you've only asked the kids to be quiet so you can listen closer). The uncommitted status of these new inferential beliefs (i.e., that the milk *might* be bad, there *may* be something wrong with my foot, and the engine *may* be making an unusual noise—the challengers themselves) means that none of them has the epistemic capacity to dislodge any other committed or uncommitted belief that it might conflict with.

So, in all three cases, there is an asymmetric or weak undecidability: The more solid beliefs in the set of challenged assumptions (i.e., the beliefs that your foot should feel normal, the milk would smell fresh, and the engine should be fine) cannot be dislodged by the new perceptually derived beliefs, the challengers, because of the uncertainty in the latter. At the same time, the hunches—or hypotheses—that make up the challengers are also unyielding, as they are based on the solid sensory information provided by the unchallenged perceptual beliefs. So, there is certainly a conflict, but only one that causes funny-huh. The answer to our second question—what differentiates funny-huh from funny-ha-ha?—is that, in humor, the undecidability is resolved by a committed belief being deposed and in funny-huh the undecidability is unresolved. (We will also raise some skepticism below about the *active* status of challenged expectations with regard to humor, though it is not important for funny-huh because there is no unseating of any beliefs in those cases.)

Of course, neither kind of undecidability is permanent. With new information, the commitment status of either conflicting belief can change and break an undecidable circumstance. A hunch can be confirmed, a hypothesis disconfirmed, and a presumption can even be overwhelmed—converting an undecidable case into a humorous case. However, with no new information (either we don't seek it or we just don't get it) undecidabilities may last indefinitely.

One may ask, then, shouldn't we be able to edit these funny-huh stories, without changing the central conflict, to make them funny? Yes, but only if the necessary edits are pragmatically possible. In our strongly undecidable case, you would have to make one of the beliefs be an inferential assumption yet still epistemically committed. That is, you'd have to weaken it. This is possible. Suppose, for instance, the lights—unbeknownst to you—are on a timer that automatically shuts them down at 9:00 AM and turns them on again at 5:30 PM, and suppose you have always returned before 5:00 PM and had to turn on the lights (preempting the timer). Today, you happened to turn off the lights just at the instant that the timer turned off the lights, and arrived home a little later than usual, in time to find the lights already turned on. Discovering the timer solves the mystery (*whew!*), and depending on the timing of your discovery of this solution, it could indeed be a provoker of mirth. In the evening, you may say to yourself, "the lights are on now, but I *definitely* flipped the switch this morning." That's all true, but definitely flipping the switch is not incontrovertible grounds for believing you definitely turned the lights off. That can be the false inferential belief, discovery of which can lead to humor.

In the weakly undecidable cases, we would first have to strengthen the weak premise—that is, give more epistemic commitment to the uncertain challenger belief in order to empower it to have a meaningful conflict. If we don't strengthen it, neither can it oust the challenged assumptions humorously, nor will it have the committed status it needs if it is itself the belief that is to be ousted humorously. We'd also have to ensure, of course, that the rest of our formula for humor holds: that one of the beliefs was active and inferential and committed, yet false. The three cases before us are not promising candidates for such revision, for boring reasons. Consider the case of the funny-tasting milk. Suppose we strengthen the premise by saying you don't just sniff but take a sip and find the milk tastes as bad as it smells. Now you no longer wonder if the milk is bad—but we've gone too far: When we assure that the belief about the status of the milk is not in doubt, we no longer have a *spurious* epistemic commitment to this more powerful version of the challenger. So we might overcorrect in the other direction by introducing some sleight-of-hand that persuades you (the victim of a practical joke) that the milk in *this* glass is not the milk you sniffed and tasted, but "good" milk instead, and you confidently gulp it—ha-ha! Not very funny, and especially not very funny to you, but at least recognizable as a practical joke, in which you committed to an expectation that was then suddenly falsified. Remember, not only does the belief need to have been invalid, but you need to have come to believe it actively (you have to have spent a thought on this topic) and with commitment (without recalling that milk freshness is usually an uncertainty, which would turn off commitment), but heuristically, by a guess. Note how much easier it is for a third person to laugh at you drinking soured milk; the conditions are relaxed when the intentional stance is invoked.

C. Apparent Counterexamples

A man at the airline check-in counter tells the representative, "I'd like this bag to go to Berlin, this one to California, and this one to London." The rep says, "I'm sorry sir. We can't do that." The man replied, "Nonsense. That is what you did last time I flew with you."

"In a riddle whose answer is chess, what is the only prohibited word?"
  "*The word* chess."
—Jorge Luis Borges (1944)

There are situations that may seem to meet all our requirements for creating a humorous climax, but in fact are not at all funny—not even funny-huh. Some of these hinge on types of mistakes in thought that differ in subtle ways from the type that leads to first-person humor. Some of the most obvious candidates are instances of *forgetting*. Here are two examples, drawn from life, which may look, at first blush, as if they fulfill the requirements of our model: Dan shows up for lunch in the cafeteria, as usual, forgetting that he had promised to play tennis with his friend Paul at lunch hour. He finds a few of his friends and joins them for a congenial lunch, but then, twenty minutes later, Paul walks in, in tennis gear and looking peeved. Dan didn't laugh, of course. This was not funny at the time, even if it can be fashioned into a good self-deprecating story later. But didn't Dan just discover a flaw in his mental space, a surreptitiously incorporated simplifying assumption that has just been shown to contradict something else therein?

To see why this wasn't funny we need to look at the spectrum of possibilities:

1. Dan has so completely forgotten his tennis date that he looks at Paul and asks "Why are you in your tennis gear?" and when Paul explains, Dan doubts Paul's word. He really doesn't remember any such promise. This reveals that Dan has an appallingly bad memory, but this isn't funny to Dan. This could be funny to *somebody else* present, along the lines of the joke:

a. Doctor: I have some bad news: You have AIDS and Alzheimer's disease.

b. Well, at least I don't have AIDS.

Does Dan have a false active committed belief in this case? It's hard to say. Should we say that anybody who is going about his business without any nagging concerns *believes* (actively) that all is well with the world? Does a good model of everyday self-control include a not-quite-noticeable periodic check to make sure everything is in order? If so, then any case of a false-positive "All's well" that lets one get on with life is an active false belief, however evanescent. And if—if—Dan had just had such a complacent thought, Paul's arrival could be funny *to him* (setting aside his chagrin). Individual differences in sensitivity to such gaffes would permit some people to laugh while others, in the same predicament, would be mortified.

2. Dan has *almost* completely forgotten his tennis date. When Paul explains, Dan ruefully acknowledges that now he does recall having made the date. The revelation is too slow and laborious to permit humor.

3. Dan tumbles immediately to what has gone wrong, and is filled with dismay and embarrassment, which overpower (at the moment) any mirth that might result. (This violates our nonnegative valence condition.) We can suppose John, who heard Paul and Dan make the date the day before, and instantly recognizes what has happened, breaks out laughing. He, like Dan, had not noticed any conflict in Dan's casual presence at lunch until Paul showed up, whereupon he discovers that he and Dan have made the same mistake; to him, as an onlooker, it is funny. John experiences classic third-person humor, while Dan is too dismayed to feel any mirth.

4. Just before Paul showed up, Dan commented to all on how nice it was to have lunch with friends, with no nagging obligations. In this case the contradiction is perhaps too blatant, too obvious, a real-world case of telegraphing the punch line. When Paul shows up and the situation becomes clear, nobody is amused. This is just a bad screwup. (Compare: Jones, the operator of the nuclear reactor, says, carefully and explicitly, "I now push button A" and reaches over and, looking intently at the buttons, pushes button B by mistake. This would probably be more terrifying—to Jones as well as to observers—than amusing. We don't know whether he has made a slip of the tongue or a slip of the finger, but he has made too obvious a mistake for it to be funny—though we can certainly imagine expanding this event into a hilarious episode in a comedy.)

5. Dan has just said "I'm playing tennis with Paul tomorrow" and he has his dates wrong. Today is Wednesday not Tuesday. Here Dan's false belief is *too* active—he's baffled by Paul's presence, and though he may soon unravel the error and see it, retrospectively, as amusing, at the moment it is just perplexing, a case of funny-huh.

6. Another variation: Paul is playing a practical joke on Dan: the tennis date *is* tomorrow, but Paul, knowing Dan's absentmindedness, thinks—correctly—that he can provoke a sinking feeling in Dan by showing up today. Humor is the eventual result, even for Dan, but it takes some reflection for Dan. What is amusing to Dan is the mistake he made initially when he saw Paul and jumped to the conclusion that his absentmindedness had struck again.

Our second example concerns Lindsay, who was planning to stop at the ATM before going to the supermarket, but it slipped her mind, and when she arrived at the checkout, she discovered she had no money in her wallet. Annoying or embarrassing, not funny. It is not sad, as it would be if Lindsay was so poor she couldn't afford groceries; her predicament is just the result of a trivial foible. But it is not funny—especially not to her.

In instances of forgetting one has mistakenly structured one's mental space, but this mistake is one of *under*activation, not misactivation. Like the activation of all the meanings of a word when you hear it (Swinney 1979), there may be traces of activation of a misbelief to the effect that she has gone to the ATM (because she meant to, because that was part of her plan), but any such traces are not strong enough to trip over in an instance of humor. Once again, we can bring this out by looking at variations:

The simplest adjustment that could turn the event into something amusing to Lindsay would be if she discovers her lapse just before entering the checkout lane. She abandons her full cart in the aisle, dashes outside to the ATM, and returns to the checkout, perhaps chuckling to herself at her own absentmindedness. But here it makes a difference how she discovers her mistake. We'll look at two of many possible variations:

a. A friend she encounters in the supermarket happens to ask her: "Do you know where an ATM is?" and when she hears this, it reminds her that she forgot to go. Not funny.

b. She sees an expensive frying pan that she covets and wonders if she has enough in the bank to purchase it, and starts to hunt in her purse for the transaction receipt from the ATM machine to look at the balance, when it hits her—D'oh!—that she forgot to go. In this case, her search exposes her momentary active commitment to a false belief. Potentially funny, to her, a case of straightforward first-person humor.

There is another possibility, a case of private, but *third-person*, humor: She is looking at her own foolishness from the outside, just as she would look at somebody else's similar lapse. Because she has saved herself the embarrassment and inconvenience of holding up the checkout line, there is no strong negatively valenced emotion to *interfere* with her ability to do this, and hence, on reflection, to find mirth in her error—though she may still not be amused, if she is, for instance, either more than normally self-conscious about her reputation as a scatterbrain, or is currently anxious about other matters.

Perhaps the most important conclusion to draw from the examination of these two cases is that mere forgetting, on its own, is not the sort of mistake that generates humor. But having forgotten something can often lay the foundation for other mistakes that are sources of humor.

The use of hypotheticals and counterfactuals in problem solving yields another kind of counterexample we need to rebut. In cases of deliberate problem-solving, planning, and reasoning, we often create temporary mental spaces that contain an inconsistency. When we recognize the inconsistency and repair it one way or another, the accompanying emotion may be satisfaction but not mirth. When we are working deliberately (however informally), we may *intentionally* insert an uncertain—uncommitted—premise, using hypothetical reasoning to see where it leads: "what if . . . ?" We are already tracking the inclusion of this premise, so if it is a bug, it is not a hidden bug; we use it, but we haven't made an epistemic commitment to it. If, on the other hand, a knotty problem resists all such solution until we discover a tacit assumption that we never realized we were making, the discovery is apt to be met with laughter. We will discuss such problems and their pleasures in the next chapter.

When Hurley presented this theory at a colloquium at the Santa Fe Institute in 2010, David Krakauer asked why making some varieties of mistake—such as a losing move at chess or a tactical error in football—is not funny. As with the discussion of problem solving we just gave, these kinds of errors exemplify the epistemic commitment feature of our model. A chess player—or a football player—goes into each move with the same caution as someone solving a problem. Like the insertion of an uncertain premise into a chain of reasoning, a chess move is the insertion of *a guess* into a process of search in board-space, and the player is well aware of the uncertainty involved in such a guess. Kirsh and Maglio (1994) distinguished between epistemic and pragmatic actions: Hitting a wall with a hammer in order to make a hole is a pragmatic action used to accomplish a goal; but, hitting it to look for a stud is an epistemic action used to gain information. The distinction is a graded, but useful, one that aligns with our notion of degrees of epistemic caution. In the most pragmatic of actions, no caution is exercised and we act boldly, but further along the continuum we find highly cautious, *epistemic* actions. A chess move or a football play lies somewhere in the middle. In being required to do *something* (by the rules of the game), plays in both are pragmatic, but because of the nature of complex games with opponents, a player usually moves with epistemic caution—expecting to gain feedback from the world. Without having made a commitment to the "correctness" of a move, when it turns out to be a mistake, a player won't find humor. There are, of course, some situations, in the endgame of chess, where the combinatorics of possible board-space is greatly reduced and when a player may become cocky or overconfident. In these cases, sometimes a move may actually reflect an overcommitment, in which case a defeat could engender a humor that is simultaneous with the disappointment of loss. In these circumstances—as we gently turn one knob on our model—the typically nonfunny situation of losing at chess can be made to be funny precisely by returning the missing ingredient of epistemic commitment back into the situation.

What about fictions not used in problem solving? People tell each other stories for entertainment all the time, but fantasy worlds or illustrative narratives aren't real. It seems that one of the following should be the case:

1. every fiction should have at least a touch of humor because, although we entertain them seriously, reality should, at least occasionally if not continually, disconfirm the illusion; or
2. fictions cannot have funny moments in them because, if we realize they are fiction, then we don't ever commit to the events within as being true, so no epistemic commitment can be broken.

As you know, neither proposition is true. Fictional dramas are far from humorous, and yet the lion's share of jokes is composed of fictions. Why doesn't either hold? The first one is not true because, in hearing a fiction, we enjoy it for its storytelling value, but we never commit to it as being reality and subsequently discover that it is not (except perhaps in cases where we are being lied to—another important case, which we will examine shortly). We know, all along, that it is not real.

This strengthens the challenge of the second proposition, then. If we are uncommitted to the events in fictions because of our recognition of their fictional status, then how can there be any humor at all in those events? The answer has two parts. First, set aside all the fictions with only third-person humor, since they invoke "false" beliefs in agents in the narratives (false relative to the fictional world implied in the narrative). That leaves the cases in which the audience of a humorous fiction is committed to a falsehood of some sort. Remember, from chapter 7, our claim that fictional worlds are excellent devices for rooting out contradictions (in science as well as in "everyday life"); but this is always a matter of *local* contradiction, within the fictional world, and it leaks out into our store of real-world knowledge only to the extent necessary to make sense of the fictional world. (It is true in the world of Sherlock Holmes that he was born of human parents and wore underwear—even though Conan Doyle never explicitly asserts or implies these propositions—but not true that he had an iPhone or even a hot air balloon—even though Conan Doyle never denies these propositions either explicitly or by implication—and it is indeterminate [neither true nor false in the fictional world] that he had a large mole on his left shoulder blade or was a distant cousin of Oliver Wendell Holmes.)[7] Use of the terms "false belief" or "falsified belief" is not to be taken as relative to some ideal objective truth but rather as shorthand for the claim of local inconsistency with what is taken as true in activated contents. In other words, when entertaining a fiction, we commit to assumptions as true-in-the-fiction, and this is commitment enough to lay the groundwork for humor, as in the joke about believing in witches. The humor in fictions is the humor of a logic internal to the story, constructed from the elements of the story and from nearby spreading activation. In that space, disbelief can be suspended in isolation from our knowledge about reality, unless of course attention is drawn to this fact explicitly. This is the case in much metahumor, such as the muffin joke, or this one:

So this guy dies, right? . . . and he goes up to Heaven . . . and, when he's at the pearly gates, he . . . oh, wait, never mind, I forgot—he just rots in the ground.

Then, what about fabrications we don't recognize as fictions—what about lies? Whenever someone has constructed a story that we take to be about reality, we are committing to a first-person belief, are we not? Bald lies aren't funny, whether the surprise outcome is positive or negative, simply because there is no covert entry of a conclusion jumped to. I tell you I didn't get you anything for your birthday and you discover I was fibbing: There it is, nicely wrapped, on the breakfast table. A pleasant surprise, but not funny. If instead I somehow subtly "betray" the prospect that I've forgotten your birthday (for instance, by whispering into a dead phone so that you overhear me, "I feel rotten! I forgot what day it is") so that you conclude, with a sinking heart, that there will be no present, and then you discover it on the table, this is different, and potentially a funny practical joke. Not so funny if you then open the nicely wrapped box and find it empty—that is negative affect dumping cold water on the joke. If you then find a gift certificate under the tissue paper in the bottom of the box, it's funny again. Such a series of reversals would work better on some people than others, of course; if you've been tricked in the past by the old

---

7. The semantics of fiction is an interesting and delicate topic in philosophy of language. See, e.g., Lewis 1978, Currie 1986, Byrne 1993, and Levinstein 2007.

gift-certificate-in-the-bottom stunt, you won't make the commitment necessary to be amused by the result.

In a footnote in chapter 4 we promised to return to Alexander Bain's (1875) counterexamples of nonhumorous incongruities, which he used to defend superiority theory over incongruity theory. On older versions of the incongruity theory, he is right; but, on our account, Bain's examples all make the *projection error* (see chapter 3)—that is, they each assume that the humor is in the stimulus rather than in the dynamics of the mind during the contextualized processing of these stimuli.

All of Bain's examples, while unfunny on a basic interpretation, have the capacity to be humorous with slight alterations to the situation— notably to the contents of the perceiver's mind.

For instance, under what we assume to be Bain's interpretation of "an instrument out of tune," a person has, without expectation, just picked up a guitar or sat down at a piano and begun to play, and found that most of the strings were out of tune. Typically, when a musician picks up a guitar, or sits down at a new piano (either not their own, or one they haven't touched in a long while), they are *wary*; they wonder how it sounds, how well tuned it is. This lack of epistemic commitment is what keeps them from finding humor in an instrument out of tune. However, small variations to these expectations can make for mirthful circumstances:

a. Imagine the person had just played the instrument half an hour before, and their expectation upon returning to it was (reasonably) that it was still in tune. Within just a few notes, a mirthful confusion may occur.
b. Imagine the third horn in the "Eroica" Symphony arriving ignomini- ously out of tune. The audience—whose expectations have been built up by the setting of the concert hall and their knowledge of the symphony— may find themselves thrust into fits of laughter. Comedic musicians (notably, Peter Schickele) have pressed this idea further by creating songs with just this type of effect in them.

Either such variation, while allowing an out-of-tune instrument to be a source of humor, does so not by simply being an incongruity (inherent out-of-tune-ness) but by using the fact that an instrument is out of tune to break a committed active belief (the *expectation* that it will be in tune) in the mind.

We have four more counterexamples, from early discussions of the model, which we'd like to share along with our discussion of them. The first is a riddle:

(R1)   A man and his son are in a car accident. The man dies and his son is taken to the hospital. "I can't operate on this boy," the surgeon says, "He is my son."

What's going on in this story?

Naturally, the answer to this widespread riddle is that the surgeon is the boy's mother. The riddle, in this form, is not funny (at least we think it's not) but it appears to cause a mistake in reasoning: the prejudiced assumption that a surgeon is a man, before the realization that it is the mother. In fact, its status as a riddle seems to *depend* on the audience making this mistake. Why is such a faulty belief not funny?

The subtlety here is that, although the mistake *seems as if* it is there to be made, we don't actually make it. Ever. When the surgeon says "I can't operate on this boy," confusion begins in the mind. We wonder why not, "Is he inoperable? Is the surgeon's shift over? . . ." then the surgeon quickly continues, "He is my son." And we know just why the surgeon cannot operate. But, note, we did not wrongly take the surgeon to be the father here. Let's dissect the cases:

If we take her to be the mother immediately, there is no problem. That much is obvious. On the other hand, if we try to take it to be the father (a likely attempt because surgeons are stereotypically men—or at least were so decades ago when this little riddle started circulating), we must realize that we do not *commit* to such a belief—there is already information clearly in mind that the father is dead which immediately conflicts with this. No mistaken commitment is made. Here's what we suggest happens instead. Before the line, "he is my son," we may have a *noncommitted*, though more likely than not (i.e., greater than 50% likely), belief that the surgeon is male. We haven't made a mistake—although we have a prejudice, we didn't allow it to convince us completely. But, when we learn that the boy is the surgeon's son, we cannot commit to it being the father, given the strict contradiction with the father's death. We are just hit with the conflict that either causes confusion or directs us to determining the correct answer, or usually both, in that order.

In order to convert this riddle into something more like a joke, one needs to alter the information in order to encourage the listener more toward a commitment of that—or some—belief. For some listeners, another common rendering of the riddle may do just that.

(R2)   A boy is in a terrible bicycle accident. His father picks him up, calls 911, and rides in the ambulance to the hospital with him. He helps wheel the gurney into the emergency room, whereupon the surgeon looks at the boy and says, "I can't operate on this boy. He is my son."

Versions like this, where the father is both alive and meets the surgeon, deepen and significantly reshape the listener's confusion. For one thing, we are made to believe that the surgeon is not the father (because they seem to interact with each other, though this is not explicit). For another, neither does the surgeon seem to be the mother—not just because of the surgeon-as-male prejudice, though. We also realize that if she knew the father (as a boy's mother surely must, no?) then her sentences would not imply that they are strangers (the father would already know that "he is her son" and would not need to be told so). These two changes make a world of difference in the activation in the mind.

In (R1), any inkling that it might be the mother, once sparked, can find no contradiction, while any thought that it might be the father is instantly contradicted by the knowledge of the father's death. Thus, the answer presents itself, at least eventually when one overcomes the surgeon-as-male prejudice, and no overcommitment is made in the meantime. On the other hand, in (R2), entertaining the surgeon-as-mother hypothesis is usually turned back by the original gender-prejudice and the pragmatic circumstances of the interaction—"No—she and the father didn't recognize each other"[8]—and entertaining the surgeon-as-father hypothesis does not result in the strong contradiction we see in (R1); only a bit of confusion, due to weaker epistemic undecidability, occurs—"how can the surgeon also be the father?" The next stage of thought is where one *might* make the mistake that could lead to humor. It happens *if* one commits more certainly to the belief that the surgeon is not the mother, and that he is probably the father, and that one must now find a way to resolve the father coming in to the ER and being the surgeon. Likely, in such an attempt at resolution, one entertains the idea that the father comes in as father, but being recognized by his colleagues takes on the role of surgeon and speaks from that role. It seems awkward, however, and because of the uncertainty one may not be willing to speak it out as an answer, but we think, "surely it must be *something* along these lines?" Upon hearing the

---

8. Of course, different minds may go different ways. Some, when dealing with the fact that the parents didn't recognize each other, may start to ask and wonder about ways that they might have had a child without knowing each other—in vitro fertilization and gamete donation may come to mind, though they may not capture much interest. Our theory would predict (though it is admittedly difficult to test) that those who think this way do not commit to the father hypothesis and won't find it funny.

answer that it is the mother and realizing that they excised that path of logic too soon, such an epistemically liberal person should feel first-person humor. Other more epistemically conservative listeners may be more cautious, not committing to a search for the father playing two roles and thus not being concerned when they hear that it is the mother. And, of course, those witty few who are not misled at all, who search more thoroughly in the space of surgeon-as-mother, will likely find the answer and for that reason find no humor at all.

The subjective interpretations we've made in these claims are subject to falsification. First, by counterexample, our account could be shown to be faulty or incomplete if somebody can produce a (funny) joke that depends on the gender stereotype mistake with no grounds for judging that it depended on a greater epistemic commitment. Second, a carefully designed verbalization paradigm might make it possible to investigate our claims here, on a variety of similar riddle structures, by indicating which beliefs subjects are entertaining before arriving at mirthful, confused, or insightful conclusions. If participants say, as they muse, "well it's definitely not the mother," and then explore the surgeon-as-father hypothesis, we predict more laughter and self-reported mirth than if they say "it's probably not the mother" and decide to search that space later.

The next counterexample was provided by a reviewer of an early draft who asked us to sharpen our model based on examples like this one: "When walking down a staircase, I slip and almost fall: fortunately, I catch myself—and then I laugh. I don't see how 'almost falling' is a contradiction." The early draft, we admit, was not clear enough to let this reviewer understand our answer to his example. But, also, this is a tricky example worth reviewing, which shows that one must be careful when applying the theory:

First off, the reviewer is right: Simply thinking "I almost fell" is certainly not a contradiction. It is a fully coherent thought and a valid one—it may be active and committed, but it doesn't consist of a false belief. That's why the humor doesn't lie in that thought.

Then where does it reside? The example was simple: I almost fell, and then I caught myself. While a description of a situation contains a series of concepts that refer to, or imply, possible beliefs in the situation, events translated into language are always a vast underspecification of reality, and some of the relevant issues are not made obvious from the surface form. The humor here occurs in a thought that the example did not explicitly describe: It is the moment that you almost fall that makes you come to a false belief. In particular, you become pretty certain that you are going to fall and get hurt, and you prepare yourself for the impact. And then you don't hit the ground, like in a trust fall (see p. 221) where the person who catches you is yourself. Therein lays the false belief, which you committed to, though apparently (as reality showed you) unnecessarily.

The same reviewer gave one more counterexample that we'd like to share, which brings up the interesting point of belief asymmetry: "If I suspect my wife is cheating on me, then the realization that I have misinterpreted the evidence (and that she is not cheating) may be cause for laughter. But if I believe my wife not to be cheating, and infer that she is, in fact, cheating on me—this is not cause for laughter."

We agree with both assessments about whether we would laugh or not. At first it seems that the cases are simply mirror images of each other, yet one is funny and the other not. The reviewer's contrast is not, however, as straightforward and symmetrical as it first appears, and fails as a counterexample on two counts, activity of belief and negative affect. One might at first think that this is a simple matter: The nonnegative affect condition explains why one is potentially funny and the other isn't. But this masks a deeper issue—and also jumps to a conclusion that has exceptions. In general, no doubt, learning that your spouse hasn't been faithful to you is a cause for anger, gloom, sadness, and other negative emotions, but if, for instance, you have been contemplating divorce for other reasons, such a discovery might be a positive joy. (Have you heard about the "Divorce Barbie" doll? It comes with all of Ken's stuff.) The nonnegative affect condition certainly has a role to play in such cases. For instance, a practical joke whose consequences are deeply harmful is no joke at all, especially to the victim. We may admire the cleverness of the trickster who defrauds the little old lady, but any laughter his ploy occasions is caused by wonder at the ingenuity, not amusement (see chapter 12 on the difference between wit and humor). But there is also an unnoted asymmetry, in almost all imaginable circumstances, between believing (suspecting) your spouse is unfaithful and believing—notice we wouldn't say "suspecting"—your spouse is faithful. The former is bound to be a (more) *active* belief.

Activity is a precondition for surprise. Gravity is expected to hold everywhere, stones are expected to be hard, snow is expected to be cold, dogs are expected to be mammals, and birds are expected to fly. These and countless others are the default beliefs that we all somehow register or store dormant in long-term memory. They are activated routinely and "instantaneously" by our ongoing perceptual experience. If somebody throws a foam-rubber brick at your head, you expect the worst because you know that bricks are heavy and hard and believe the looming projectile is a brick. You don't have to think the thoughts "out loud" in your head for them to be activated. Your ducking and cringing betray your active beliefs in this instance. Are the same beliefs about bricks *active* when you just walk by a pile of bricks and recognize them as bricks? No, although they might be activated *as soon as* you contemplate needing a projectile to throw, or a doorstop. Similarly, when you recognize your wife as the person in the kitchen, you don't *activate* the long-term default belief that she is faithful, unless, for one reason or another, it comes up. (Magicians know that if they are wielding a fake brick, they have to be very careful not to betray their belief—their knowledge—that it is fake, a belief which is active for them in a way that their belief that the egg on the table is *not* fake is not active.)

So in the case in which one believes one's wife not to be cheating, and then suddenly acquires the contrary belief, the discovery is what activates one's prior belief, so the order is wrong for humor. You weren't actively believing—even in the minimal sense of believing the incoming brick to be hard—that your wife was not cheating on you until your dormant belief was shattered. This is like learning that that looming thing was a brick after it hits you.

To show that the asymmetry in *activity* by itself can account for the difference between an amusing discovery and one that is perhaps surprising but not amusing, consider the following variation: If I suspect that the mailman has been riding a bicycle to deliver mail, then my realization that I have misinterpreted the evidence—the bicycle you saw him parking on the sidewalk was not his, but a child's that he had just retrieved from the street—may be cause for laughter. But if I don't believe the mailman rides a bicycle to deliver the mail, and discover that he is in fact riding a bicycle—this is not cause for laughter.

Dennett presented an early version of our model at a conference on music, language, and the mind at Tufts University in July of 2008, which led to a useful challenge. In the discussion, Marc Hauser observed: "Let's say I come here expecting you to talk about consciousness. Lo and behold, you're talking about humor. That's a violation, there's a debugging. I have no idea why this happened. But not funny. So it seems to me, I've got all the ingredients [of your model] there but not funny." Isn't this a clear counterexample, and if not, why not? Dennett did not think of a good response at the time, but reflection has clarified the situation.

Hauser's mental space includes an expectation that is not fulfilled, as he discovers. Why isn't this at all amusing to him? We must ask how he came to his misexpectation. He didn't say, so let's look at the possibilities. Suppose he just had a hunch, even a fairly confident hunch, that Dennett would be speaking about consciousness, one of his main research interests. A hunch isn't enough; it isn't a *committed* belief, even if Hauser would be prepared to bet on it. Contrast this with expectations that in all likelihood Hauser would be committed to, assumptions included in the mental space with no noticeable evaluation or mental effort at all, such as the expectation that Dennett would be wearing (men's) clothes, and speaking in English. Or that the talk would not be given by somebody else named Dan Dennett. It is not that a violation of any of these would *have* to provoke mirth on our model, but just that it *might well*, if the timing of the revelation was right, and there were no interfering effects. In contrast, it is hard to imagine framing the (sudden? dawning?) realization that Dennett wasn't speaking about consciousness so that it would provoke mirth. The line between a presumption—paradigmatically, a hastily included item thrown into the mental space by the unsupervised triage system—and a hunch (or a surmise, or a guess, or a conclusion ventured) is not a sharp one, and it is easy enough to see that some humor might in fact be provoked by recognition of error in one of the latter cases, when everything else was just right, but not *striking* humor, not the potent brew. The polarity is between what might be called *headlong* commitments and *wary* commitments, and if we understand the polarity we can postpone or finesse entirely the need for a criterion, a threshold that is the necessary and sufficient condition for a mirth-inviting presumption. Here we can see the domain of humor interpenetrating with the domain of riddles and puzzles, the solutions to which may on occasion provoke not just admiration and delight but mirth. Recall the riddle about the surgeon and the car accident victim.

Then there is the covert entry condition. Did Hauser reflect to himself, on his short trip to Tufts from Harvard Square, that he was soon going to hear Dennett's latest line on consciousness? If so, then this ruins any prospect for humor since the false expectation is overtly introduced into his mental space. It would be like the following (ruined) joke:

(76)   Before you criticize someone, you should (as we say
metaphorically) walk a mile in their shoes. That way, when you criticize
them, you've got a mile head start, and they're barefoot.

To which the response is: Oh, so you've suddenly switched from metaphorical to literal; I wasn't expecting that. Not funny.

Epistemic caution and commitment and the epistemic status of various sources of information are all rather subtle matters, as is the working-memory status of any belief. Since there is room for penumbral cases, a good counterexample to our theory would be one in which the belief or beliefs involved are (i) active, (ii) heuristically created, (iii) committed, and (iv) contradicted—and yet the discovery does not yield mirth. Or, of course, something truly funny that doesn't fit this scheme in one way or another. We will discuss the nuances of a number of dimensions of the penumbra in detail in the next chapter.

D. A Brief Glance at Others' Models

What did the 0 say to the 8?
"Nice belt."

We have commented, from time to time, on the family resemblance that our theory holds with earlier incongruity resolution models of humor. The similarities are pretty clear, but we will acknowledge them explicitly in order to highlight our innovations. We quickly review some models which should be familiar from chapter 4, and then look in more detail at a couple of incongruity-resolution models that are the closest kin to our epistemological theory.

The surface similarity between our model and incongruity resolution derives from the dependence of both on logical mechanism. Unlike superiority theory, release theory, mechanical theory, play theory, and other evolutionary theories, incongruity resolution paved the way for our work by noticing that nonsense and logic were *somehow* central notions. But, as it turns out, it is neither incongruity nor resolution that causes humor. Instead, these devices are simply mechanisms that *commonly assist* in the discovery of a mistaken commitment. Discovering an incongruity creates a contradiction. The ensuing confusion causes covert-behavioral review of the situation, and that review is *one particularly effective way* that we might stumble upon a mistaken commitment. And, if it happens this way, then it appears as if we have a resolved incongruity causing humor; but it is only the discovery of the mistaken commitment that caused the humor. We can be sure of this because other kinds of resolved incongruity don't cause humor (e.g., thinking the lights were off, finding them on, and then discovering you've been burglarized), and, further, unresolved incongruities can in fact be humorous.

A magician holds up a piece of rope, with a long loop dangling out the bottom of his hand, and *three* (!) ends poking up out of the top of his fist. He says to the crowd, "How can a rope have three ends?" A rhetorical question with which we all implicitly agree. It's not possible, and so we assume the fourth end of a second rope *must* be hidden inside his closed fist. With the other hand, he then slowly pulls the loop of rope down until the three ends disappear into his hand, and then continues pulling until two ends pop loose and hang down toward the floor, at which point he opens the hand that originally held the three ends—and it is empty.

This kind of trick is often met not just with awe, but with laughter. You might say there is an incongruity between the two ends and the three ends, but there certainly is no resolution. On our theory, the laughers committed to there being two ropes in the magician's hand and then were shown that there were not. They don't actually know quite what happened, but they certainly know that their presumption of there being two ropes there was mistaken. This is just one example of hundreds of magician's illusions that create these kinds of beliefs in us and, without resolving the incongruity, can still create mirth.

Notice, too, that there was an earlier incongruity in this situation: the incongruity between three ends and one loop in the rope. It was this incongruity that caused us *to make* a mistaken commitment by leading us to choose an option from a false dichotomy—this is another mechanism by which an incongruity can lead to humor, but it is very different from the incongruity that causes us *to discover* a mistaken commitment. As you can see, the only thing that is consistently present is precisely the mistaken commitment.

It is easy to see how Schopenhauer's and Kant's versions of the incongruity-resolution theory of humor are subsumed and strengthened by our model. Since these earlier models made no attempt at all to supply a cognitive or neural mechanism for humor, even sketchily, they had no way of "running in slow motion," taking apart the processes to see what steps had to be involved. Our proposed mechanism gives us a new perspective on more recent models. In Suls's (1972) conception of the theory, the incongruity is between the setup and the punch line. In our terms, both a setup and a jab or a punch contribute information that, along with existing knowledge, allows the incremental construction of a mental space in which various beliefs and metabeliefs are committed to with varying epistemic intensities. Somewhere along the way, further logical inference determines that a mistake has been made in inferences used to integrate the setup and the punch line within the mental space. Although resolution commonly occurs, it is not the resolution of the incongruity but rather the identification of (not just the presence of) the mistake that we find funny.

Suls's model is accurate for a certain class of textual jokes in which the setup provides the information for an overcommitted belief which is later found to be inconsistent as a result of information provided by the punch (or by inferences drawn from that information); however, this case does not hold for all instances of humor, as evidenced by a competing model from around the same time: Shultz's (1976) model, which exploits the mechanism of a different class of jokes. In these jokes the hearer conceives of two ambiguous meanings in the setup, only one of which is consistent with the punch line. In our terms, the "first" interpretation contributes to the construction of a mental space—again, including existing knowledge and inferential conclusions. But the mistake—the miscommitment—is already made before one hears the punch line. It is the punch line, in fact, that helps one recognize that some false assumption of inference was made while building the model.

The Wyer and Collins (1992) extensions to Suls's model require incongruity between the setup and the punch line to be resolved with two caveats: First, resolution must happen in such a way that the original interpretation still makes sense without the added information that caused the reinterpretation (this they call *non-replacement*), and second, the resolution must occur such that the new interpretation is diminished in importance compared with the initial interpretation. They give an example of a situation that they say cannot easily be explained by incongruity resolution alone without this condition. The example is from a study done by Nerhardt (1976) in which blindfolded subjects were asked to estimate the relative weights of objects placed in each hand. After a few similar weights, the experimenters gave subjects objects that differed substantially from the first few. The result: usually smiling or laughter. Wyer and Collins suggest that the subjects receiving the deviant weights infer that the experiment is not a serious study of weight judgment at all—they decide that the situation is less important than they had originally interpreted and the reinterpretation causes amusement due to the diminishment. We doubt that this is the only thought one could have had in that situation. One might wonder, for instance, whether the experimenters were trying to prime the participants with the initially similar weights to see if their judgment was affected by a distant cognitive anchor—such a musing would be incompatible with deciding that the experiment is not a serious study of weight judgment, but laughter might still occur. We offer a different explanation: The subjects in the experiment simply expect a weight similar to the first few by extrapolation (a kind of automatic abductive inference) from the early experiences. When the deviant weight is handed to them, they have their active inferential expectation broken. The humor is caused by this only, although thoughts about why the experimenter chose to arrange the weights in that order might well follow on afterward. We do not see a need for a diminishment requirement.

Wyer and Collins's requirement of non-replacement is an interesting anticipation of an aspect of our model: Their requirement says that in humor the first interpretation, before there is incongruity, remains coherent in the absence of the punch line, which shows the second interpretation to be correct. We think this observation is also why the traditional I-R model focused not on mistakes, but on interpretations. In our model, this corresponds to the notion that when one discovers an improper belief commitment, many times the reasoning that led to that commitment is solid (in that it still consists of facts and *most likely* assumptions) in the absence of information provided that supports a second more consistent comprehension model. The humor is, as we've said a number of times, in the detection of the improper belief, not in the comparison of the new interpretation.[9]

Though Minsky (1984) claims that "it is probably futile to ask precisely what humor is" and compares the subject to Wittgenstein's (1953) dilemma of defining a "game," he also gives a couple of notions which he asserts contribute significantly to an approximate definition. The first of these is frame shifting, which we've discussed already, and the second is his idea of "cognitive censors." We will look at both of these, in that order, to see how they compare with our theory. The humor described by Minsky as arising from frame shifting is also a subclass of the humor treated in the model we have described here (although, as spelled out earlier, we are skeptical about the nature of frames in general). Frame shifting is a logical mechanism—not the only one—which in certain circumstances will reliably collapse an inferential belief that was taken to be true. Not all frame shifting is humorous; Coulson (2001) convincingly describes frame shifting as operative in almost all thought, and not all humor is attributable to frame shifts. For example, the weight-estimation experiment of

---

9. Wyer and Collins also discuss a principle of *cognitive elaboration*, which they claim occurs in the comprehension of an incongruity resolution. This seems trivial to us in that cognitive elaboration occurs in the comprehension of any situation, humorous or otherwise. The incessant spreading of activation in JITSA implies that we are cognitively elaborating at every moment, and while it is in some way required for mirth and certainly contributes to both the formation of and elimination of mistaken commitments, it is not a defining factor of mirth-elicitation.

Nerhardt discussed above shows a kind of humor in which there may not be a frame shift. Although the participants laughed, it is hard to say that the data involved in the humor utilized frames at all, much less that one replaced another that was false. Is there a frame for the (likely novel, to the participants) experience of being handed similarly hefty weights while blindfolded? Is there another frame for being handed weights of very different heft while blindfolded? We think, instead, that it was simply an inferential belief—an expectation—that was at the core of the humor experience for those participants. The frame (if it could be called such) for this experience did not change at the moment of humor; only one expectation did.

While his mechanics of comprehension differ from ours significantly, Minsky's broader proposal for humor does mirror our idea of humor as a cognitive cleanup mechanism. His concept of "cognitive censors" points to humor as a kind of machinery for preventing mistakes. The types of mistakes are different (his, "inappropriate comparisons"; ours, just beliefs, though they derive from logic), and the imagined mechanisms are strikingly different: his, a "heuristic control of logic," a metalogic implemented as an array of millions of learned logical censors applied through series of tests for preconditions in order to "suppress unproductive mental states"; ours, simply the detection of an improper commitment. Despite the differences, we consider the Minsky model to be probably our closest kin because of its theme of cognitive cleansing. But, let's make the difference[10] a little clearer: The concept of "cognitive censors" says that we discover millions of preventative rules of logic over our lives, which describe thoughts and inferences that we have experienced and learned about and should try to avoid having again. On this view, humor happens when such rules are broken—when we do have such "prohibited" thoughts, we are delighted. There is a focus in this theory on "ineffective or destructive thought processes," but we don't see humor as being related to the learning about or detection of such structured fallacies. This is a very subtle point: Though humor *is* related to mistakes that happen in *belief* caused by *assumptions* in *inference*, these mistakes are not signs of *improper reasoning*, and they are not subject to censorial early detection and prevention. On

---

10. There are quite a few other dissimilarities—for instance, Minsky assumed his theory worked not alone but in conjunction with Freud's taboo-censors to provide for all humor. For Minsky, humor always includes a pinch of childlike spice: the delight in being *naughty* and getting away with it. While we agree that this aspect enhances much humor, we claim that it is not a crucial ingredient.

our view, humor shows us that a resulting belief that we arrived at in comprehension happened to be wrong, not that the reasoning we used to get there is systematically wrong. In fact, the reasoning we used to get there usually (though, perhaps, not always) is in some way *correct* reasoning. Though inherently risky, the heuristic inferential thought that we normally use is, statistically, more likely to be right than not. It provides correct beliefs most of the time, through assumptions that are usually valid and inferences that usually work. Two goldfish in their tank *should* usually be interpreted as being in a fish tank. Detecting the mistake this time, in the pun, does not mean that next time you should be more careful—you should still assume next time that "their tank," when paired with "fish," means a fish tank. Taking these risks is an unavoidable consequence of using the tool that all of our successful reasoning crucially depends on; we have, in fact, no other choice.[11] Such risk taking does make for mistakes, yet correctly taken risks are not the kinds of mistakes that we can learn to avoid—not something we could develop a rule-list of cognitive censors to protect us from. No tool, humor or otherwise, can teach us how to make probabilistic assumptions without ever failing. Rather, *we have to learn to live with the failings of our minds, and to detect their consequences after they occur.* Humor is a backup system that discovers some (though not all) of those occasional—but inevitable—times when depending on such a risky system just happens to fail.

A tempting oversimplification of our epistemological theory of humor is that it is about falsified beliefs. Some other recent theories have also focused on beliefs (e.g., LaFollette and Shanks 1993)[12] and even on falsified beliefs (e.g., Jung 2003). Any model along these lines is, like ours, also a variant of the incongruity resolution family—and in fact such models are typically retellings of Schopenhauer's incongruity between a conception and a perception. Sometimes, presumably in recognition that Schopenhauer's model is an underspecification, theorists propose additional constraints such as those recommended by Wyer and Collins (see above,

---

11. The alternative—the ideal of deductive certainty in a nonideal world—threatens us with either infinite processing or the failure to have any thought at all.

12. LaFollette and Shanks, although right in the casual speculation at the end of their paper that humor theory will eventually inform epistemology and philosophy of mind, are, we think, far off base in their description of humor—for them, a high-speed oscillation or "flickering" of the mind between two sets of beliefs while maintaining the proper "psychic distance" from the stimuli, which "provides a space within which to flicker" (1993, p. 333). We think it is clear how our model differs from this.

p. 203) or those put forward by Jung (2003). Jung's "inner eye theory of humor" will be the last family member with which we compare the epistemological theory.

For Jung, humor is caused by a falsified belief (FB), with the additional constraints of "empathy" (E) and something he calls "sympathetic instant utility" (SIU). These three constraints are each "a necessary condition and . . . the three criteria are jointly sufficient to explain all laughter" (Jung 2003, pp. 220–221). Jung exploits a couple of good intuitions (falsified belief and the intentional stance) that are reflected in our work as well, but he has overlooked some others, and those he has noticed have not been put together in quite the right way. Since Jung's theory is only a theory of the "trigger mechanism" of humor, we will compare only that portion of our theory with his.

By *empathy* we take Jung to mean the ability to take the intentional stance: "To laugh at a joke requires understanding the desires or the beliefs of the joke-teller and those of the characters in the joke" (Jung 2003, p. 219). He uses the term "theory of mind" (which we criticize above, p. 144), cites the mirror-neuron literature (Gallese et al. 1996; Rizzolatti et al. 1996), and often claims that "a laugher understands the mental states held by" agents in the joke. Of course he is right that theory of mind or the intentional stance is always used when perceiving any humor situation in which there are other agents, but he has no analysis of the ways in which using the intentional stance provides for the perception of a false belief, the ways in which first-person humor does *not* require the intentional stance, and the epistemological differences between first- and third-person knowledge of mental states that explain the relaxed conditions for third-person humor.

Jung uses "sympathetic instant utility" to mark whether we are pleased with the outcome of a situation for people. In his words, "In a simple generalization, when good things happen to those the laugher likes and bad things happen to those whom she dislikes, the state is satisfactory to her and her SIU is positive while when bad things happen to people she likes and good things happen to people she dislikes, the state is dissatisfactory to her and her SIU is negative" (2003, pp. 219–220). This bears an interesting resemblance to our use of Boorstin's perspectives (see chapter 8), which can sometimes modulate humor, but on our theory, the deliverances of the different Boorstinian eyes are only occasional modifiers of humor, not part of the trigger mechanism at all. This can be readily seen in first-person humor in which there is no one to empathize or sympathize with (aside from one's own fallible self) and no one to receive "instant utility." For instance, consider simple puns whose humor turns only on misinterpretations, such as this one:

(77)   A cardboard belt would be a waist of paper.

Both Jung's account and ours feature falsified beliefs, but Jung's is under-specified, simply claiming that there is always a falsified belief. As we've explained, many falsified beliefs do not provide humor (even if they are accompanied by empathy and sympathetic instant utility). For instance, imagine you are at the airport waiting for your daughter's arrival, and you get a call from her saying she's been bumped from her oversold flight; you will have to wait another two hours for her to arrive on the next flight. You settle down to read your novel, making the best of an annoying situation. A few minutes later she calls back to say another passenger relinquished a seat to her on the original flight. You're relieved, but not amused, even though your belief about waiting two more hours is falsified, you get sympathetic instant utility, and you "understand the mental states held by" everyone involved.[13] To identify the trigger mechanism for humor, one must specify what kinds of beliefs there are, what kinds of fallacies can occur in beliefs, and which kind of fallacy in which kind of belief can lead to humor. Also missing from Jung's theory is any mechanism for falsifying beliefs that would help to differentiate between the triggers for first- and third-person humor. So we see Jung's theory as somewhat close in spirit to the cognitive trigger part of our model, based on similar intuitions, but incomplete in some regards and mistaken in others.

There is one other theorist who deserves special mention. Graeme Ritchie has been looking at and writing about humor theories for a number of years (e.g., Ritchie 1999, 2006), and has been the only writer (we've found) who accepts incongruity resolution theories but also openly notes their incompleteness. Let's hold our theory up to Ritchie's salutary caution.

E.   Graeme Ritchie's Five Questions

"Life is like a bridge."
  "In what way?"
  "How should I know?"
—Minsky (1984)

---

13. This example is not funny, on our model, because the falsified belief was not introduced covertly. It was a case of misinformation. It was an active belief that was committed to, but the commitment was not due to a leap to a conclusion.

Occasionally, theorists in a field find themselves spiraling around some very deep intuition about their subject, without being able to see or say exactly how that intuition is related to their phenomenon. In "Developing the Incongruity Resolution Theory" Graeme Ritchie (1999) makes the point that I-R theorists have long had an intuition of just this sort. He analyzes the models of both Suls and Shultz as applied to textual and narrative (mostly joke) humor stimuli, and poses—but does not answer—five questions which together compose the core questions: "What kind of incongruity is funny?" or "What is it about incongruity that is funny?" He suggests that answering these questions would be a major step forward for humor theory, and we agree. Here are our answers:

(Q1) What makes one potential interpretation more obvious than another?

In classical incongruity resolution theory, one interpretation is initially taken to be the case, and another supplants it later. Ritchie wants to know why each is chosen when it is. The interpretation replacement structure of I-R is a subclass of the model given in this book. The first interpretation, under our model, is caused by an inferential assumption based on the hearer's world knowledge and the joke's setup. Clues in the setup of a joke may lead one interpretation to seem to be the more likely given the context, and so the assumption is "automatically" (i.e., covertly) made. It is the most likely comprehension structure given the partial data. Note that *even when one is in joke-swapping mode*, and hence *expecting* just this kind of error to be induced, one cannot help but make the faulty inference, if the joke teller is talented. To reuse the goldfish pun yet again, when we are told "Two goldfish were in their tank," the use of "tank" with reference to "fish" most frequently refers to a fish tank; thus, given no disambiguating information, we choose the statistically likely meaning (in the context of the word "fish") for the ambiguous word "tank" (in other cases, it may just be a primed meaning, instead of a probable meaning, that is activated). When we realize that this belief was false, it is often because a new interpretation that can describe all the available data without contradiction and in a way that is consistent with existing knowledge has supplanted the old one. In jokes, this is usually handed to us by the joke's designer (either a creative person or memetic evolution or both) who has discovered just what information will make the new interpretation more consistent. *Obviousness* is the property shared by whatever inferences are generated by the unconscious triage mechanisms that mediate the time-pressured heuristic search that is constantly generating our expectations.

(Q2) How difficult to assimilate must a piece of text be in order to stimulate a search for another interpretation? How can this search be guided by the portion of text that caused the reassessment?

First, not all humor comes from a reassessment of a portion of text. We can laugh at the Three Stooges knocking each other down, a form of humor that requires no reassessment whatsoever. We will rephrase Ritchie's question, in light of our model, as "what causes us to recognize that a model in a mental space is insufficient?" Consistency-checking in mental spaces is not just frequent; it is an involuntary component of the process of generating mental spaces in the first place, so generating a mental space is *ipso facto* doing something approximating an exhaustive search for contradictions. In many cases of humor, a more wholly consistent evaluation of the available data will show us that the initial construction of the space is faulty (if it fails to include some data that the new evaluation does include), but in other cases we may not have a more consistent evaluation; we will simply be shown that the mental space is faulty by contradiction within itself.

(Q3) What does it mean for two interpretations to differ in an amusing way (as opposed to merely not being the same)?

This question was formulated based on intuitions of previous incongruity resolution theories that do not apply to our model—notably, that the humor is in the stimulus. The amusement is the sense of discovering the false committed active belief. It is often, but not always, two interpretations of something that bring this to light. In fact, the two interpretations are *always* "merely not the same," as Ritchie says. It is not that they "differ in an amusing way"; it is *the way the difference is discovered* that is amusing. The humor lies in what their difference points out about the mistake the audience has made.

(Q4) What factors make an interpretation inherently more amusing?

Nothing intrinsic to any one interpretation makes it more amusing, any more than something intrinsic to an ink trail makes it an authentic Abraham Lincoln signature. What makes it authentic is that he, Lincoln, made it. What makes an interpretation amusing is that the audience made it in the course of discovering a mistake. It is the discovery of a mistake in a mental space that pleases us, and the pleasure takes the form of mirth when the mistake arose from a surreptitiously introduced inference. (This suggests that in the limit, *any* sentence could in principle serve as a funny punch line to some joke, setting aside issues of ponderousness of setup, attention span of listeners, and the like.[14])

(Q5)   What combinations of these factors combine to produce humor?

Ritchie suggests that his last three questions may boil down to the same thing, but that if this is so, it needs to be established. He is right. Again, like the previous two questions, humor is produced not by interpretations, but by what (in some cases) a difference in interpretations points out. In other cases, though, other factors may lead us to the mistake.

---

14. It is said that Dorothy Parker was once asked, "Can you make a joke about horticulture?" Without missing a beat, or so the story goes, she replied, "You can lead a whore to culture, but you can't make her think."

11 The Penumbra: Nonjokes, Bad Jokes, and Near-Humor

Q: What's wrong with lawyer jokes?
A: Lawyers don't think they're funny and other people don't think they're jokes.

Humor, whatever it is, is a product of evolution, both genetic and cultural, so there will very likely be some quasi-humorous or pseudo-humorous phenomena that bear deep similarities to prototypical humor—and in fact are ancestors, descendants, or components of the genuine article. It is always a mistake to think that the aim of such a search is a perfect set of *necessary and sufficient conditions* that define the *essence* of all humor and admit of no undecidable penumbral cases. Biologists can't define *mammal* with that kind of imagined Socratic precision—where, in the transition from reptiles through therapsids to true mammals do we "draw the line"?—and humor will probably exhibit the same sort of systematic family resemblances with no nonarbitrary boundaries. However, by looking more closely at four of the dimensions of variance that delimit some of these boundaries, we can try to sharpen the edges a little more.

First, of course, are the individual differences—the knowledge-relativity of humor. Not everyone finds the same things funny, or, at least, people find them funny to differing degrees, or at different times while taking different perspectives (recall the perspectival asymmetry between first- and third-person humor). A lawyer may not see the humor in the joke above, for instance. In chapter 3 we showed that humor is knowledge-relative, but we didn't say why this should be so. Humor is knowledge-relative because the core of the matter is the validity of working-memory belief constructs, which vary between individuals. Second, even within an individual, humor ranges in degree. Some jokes are just funnier—to you—than others are. The conditions for humor, which we first laid out in chapter 7, need to be augmented to explain this gradient. We provide two answers below. Third, there are boundary cases which folks find funny, yet for which they have difficulty saying, even casually and nontheoretically, what's funny about them (though there almost certainly are other cases yet to be explored, our theory explains all the ones we've looked at, and we will show how shortly). And fourth, humor often overlaps with related phenomena. Jokes are memes evolved for enjoyment. There are many kinds of memes that have been selected for their enjoyment value only, but it is not important (to their cultural fitness) just which kinds of enjoyment they evoke. Those that evoke the most enjoyment—of any kind—are the most likely to be transmitted, provided that they are structured in memorable (if possible, *unforgettable*) ways. In becoming enjoyment packages, memes have not always been selected for which joys they cause; any joy that will get it passed on will do. And so we have the various close kin of humor: riddles, puzzles, witty rhymes, and clever aphorisms.

There are no reasons why a single meme shouldn't take advantage of more than one of the cognitive pleasures that help them copy themselves into the future, so we find much overlap in these categories of humor-kin. Most *jokes* these days, in fact, have their humor inextricably bound together with pleasures of other kinds—simply because this is possible, and makes it a more potent item. Some of these related pleasures are very similar to mirth, such as other epistemic emotions: joy in insight, the *Aha!* of discovery or problem solving, and the appreciation of wit. Others are related simply by common association, such as Schadenfreude and recognition of superiority, and, of course, sexual titillation.[1]

A. Knowledge-Relativity

A sax player dies and goes to the pearly gates. St. Peter says "sorry, too much partying, you have to go to the other place." The elevator doors open and he goes into a huge bar. All the greatest are on stage on a break. Satchmo. Count Basie, Miles Davis. He goes over to Charlie Parker and says, "Hey this can't be Hell; all the best are playing here." Charlie says, "Hey man, Karen Carpenter is on drums!"

We each have idiosyncratic beliefs, shaped both by culture and by our personal histories. And, for any particular belief, each person's instantiation of it will be shaped slightly differently, with a range of aspects accented

---

1. Dirty jokes are the chocolate candies of humor, you might say. It is remarkable that hot, unsweetened chocolate was drunk like black coffee for several millennia before somebody thought to sweeten it by mixing some sugar with the cocoa powder. The equally bright idea of mixing basic humor with the multidimensional pleasures of (the merest contemplation of) sex came much earlier in the history of human self-stimulation.

in diverse ways and having distinct likelihoods of priming in the same circumstances. In addition, we each have idiosyncratic propensities to epistemic caution when activating beliefs in various domains. These individualities cause us to construct our mental spaces idiosyncratically and thus give us each distinct susceptibilities to mirth during any given event. There are central tendencies, stimuli that can evoke mirth in a broad cross-section of a culture, but there are also outliers like the very in-group jazz joke above. Most of the jokes in this book should be accessible to our contemporaries, but below are some examples that probably are not. These come from Bubb's (1920) *The Jests of Hierocles and Philagrius*, which contains sundry jokes many of which are still comprehensible, from a number of sources dating from as far back as the fifth century AD and likely told in oral tradition for centuries before.

(78) A pedant ordered a silversmith to make a lamp, and when the latter enquired how large he should make it, he replied, "Large enough for eight men."

(79) A pedant was tying on some new sandals. When they squeaked he paused and said, "Do not squeak or you will injure your two legs."

These two jokes, likely, once turned on some kind of homonymy (in the original Greek) or cultural information that today's casual reader (including the authors) do not have available. Likewise, we are all familiar with "inside" jokes which we either cannot easily or do not want to explain to an outsider, or for which we have been the outsider who was not privy to the implicit beliefs that the joke requires. There are some jokes, too, which we might get because we know *of* the beliefs necessary, even if those beliefs aren't our own.

(80) How do you know you're at a bulimic bachelor party?
    When the cake jumps out of the girl!

Many of us have heard of the idea of a bachelor party where a hired dancer jumps out of a (very large) cake. But for those of us who have never witnessed this (and the authors presume that's most of us, these days) the likelihood of activating this belief when hearing the setup of the joke is near zero, though we can usually access it when it is forcibly primed by the punch line.

This is another good example of a joke on its way to extinction. As fewer people automatically activate the girl jumping out of the cake when they hear of the bachelor party, the audience for this joke will shrink. And, of course, it is no use explaining what bachelor parties used to include.

It is hopeless for analysts to try to find the false belief in a joke they did not understand (such as in jokes 78 and 79 above). No amount of textual deconstruction or stimulus analysis will reveal the boundaries of humor, since, as our definition shows, humor is that which causes a false belief to be detected *in a mind*, and this not only allows for knowledge-relativity, it predicts it, and explains why the category boundary is fuzzy.

Although we have used jokes and other examples to describe our model and to show how it works at a high level of abstraction, at some point the analysis of humor will have to move beyond these individually variable objects and look for its proper object of study as a neurochemical process in the brain. In the meantime, the analysis of humorous events can continue on the same foundation that comedians and other designers and purveyors of humor have always relied on—the assumption that any more or less unified population, any gathered audience, as a result of having had similar experiences in the world, will share enough beliefs (and covert structures of association between them) to generate much the same processes of JITSA when targeted with well-aimed setups.

B. Scale of Intensity

> When I was growing up we had a petting zoo and, well, we had two sections, a petting zoo and heavy-petting zoo, for people who really liked animals a lot.
> —Ellen DeGeneres

We all know the difference between a good joke and a bad joke even if we each have our own unique sorting mechanisms for this distinction. The bachelor party joke is a bad joke, in our opinion. Just as there are degrees of sadness, different flavors of pain, and both mind-blowing orgasms and so-so orgasms, so too are there different grades of mirth. The level elicited in a circumstance is driven, we suspect, by at least two factors. The first is (something along the lines of) the *amount* of false belief invalidated on the occasion. If, for instance, the misinterpretation of a single word (e.g., "tank" in the goldfish pun) is the hinge, mirth will be low. If, on the other hand, a sly bit of trickery leads to major misdirection, when the dénouement comes the mirth should be much greater. A different measure of "quantity" of belief also contributes: We already mentioned bipersonal humor, which occurs simultaneously from the first-person and third-person perspective, but two persons—the audience plus a character in the story—is not the limit. In fact, the more the merrier. For each character whose belief is dislodged alongside the laugher's own, the mirth should be increased commensurately. We gave examples of this in chapter 9 (section D). Here's another:

(81) After a heavy night of drinking at the local bar, a drunk stumbles into a Catholic church and slowly makes his way into the confessional booth. There, the priest patiently awaits the man to begin his confession. After a few minutes of silence, the priest politely taps on the window . . . nothing. The priest taps again and this time clears his throat a bit . . . still nothing. At this point the priest begins to lose his patience and bangs on the window. Finally the drunk yells out: "Ain't no use knocking, there ain't no paper over here either!"

In this joke, the drunk's belief that he is in a toilet, and the priest's expectation that there is a confessor in the confessional are broken simultaneously with the audience's belief, which is in line with the priest's. Three mistaken beliefs crashing in unison make the mirth stronger than any one belief on its own.

The second factor in distinguishing the level of humor is that of the *additives*, spicy sources of other positive emotions that are provoked during otherwise mild humor. It has long been known that emotional arousal can be achieved by a wide variety of interventions, and the emotions experienced can be strongly influenced by the cognitive state of the subject at the time (Schachter and Singer 1962). Moreover, as has more recently been shown, arousal can be transferred from one emotional modality to another. In a famous experiment, the anxiety induced by walking on a bridge over a chasm was reinterpreted as physical attraction to the experimenter (Dutton and Aron 1974), and subsequent experiments have not only replicated that effect but demonstrated its presence even when the subjects are informed in advance (Foster et al. 1998). Cantor, Bryant and Zillmann (1974) and Zillmann (1983b) applied this finding directly to humor, showing that any arousing experience, whether it be a positive or negative emotional episode,[2] can increase the reported intensity of subsequent mirth, so long as enough time has passed that the arousal can be misattributed, and not so long that it has entirely dissipated.

We conjecture that the most effectively transmitted joke-memes have exploited just such a transfer effect by combining the basic mechanism of humor perception with such hot-button topics as sex, violence, death,

---

2. Other findings by Zillmann (Zillmann, Katcher, and Milavsky 1972) indicate that even the arousal of physical exertion (such as that caused by running on a treadmill) can be transferred to psychological effects.

excrement, and racial perception, creating emotional priming that heightens one's susceptibility to mirth. The result is a more potent cocktail of
types of arousal, enhancing the effect of humor in much the way chocolate
or coffee enhances the effect of sugar.

This is a straightforward effect of what is known in artificial intelligence
as the credit-assignment problem: It is not a simple cognitive task to distinguish which part of a complex set of events leading to a reward or
punishment is the proper cause. The next two jokes don't exhibit the
potent cocktail of multiple emotions but do vividly illustrate the credit
assignment problem:

(82) A 6-year-old and a 4-year-old are upstairs in their bedroom. "You
know what?" says the 6-year-old. "I think it's about time we started
cussing." The 4-year-old nods his head in approval. The 6-year-old
continues, "When we go downstairs for breakfast, I'm gonna say
something with 'hell' and you say something with 'ass,' okay?" The
4-year-old agrees with enthusiasm.

When their mother walks into the kitchen and asks the 6-year-old
what he wants for breakfast, he replies, "Aw, hell, Ma, I guess I'll have
some Cheerios." *Whack!* He flies out of his chair, tumbles across the
kitchen floor, gets up, and runs upstairs crying his eyes out, with his
mother in hot pursuit, slapping his rear with every step. She locks him
in his room and shouts, "And you'll stay there until I let you out!"

She then comes back downstairs, looks at the 4-year-old, and asks
with a stern voice, "And what do *you* want for breakfast, young man?"

"I don't know, Mom," he blurts out, "but you can bet your ass it
won't be Cheerios!"

(83) A pedant was looking for his book for many days but could not
find it. By chance, as he was eating lettuces and turned a certain corner
he saw the book lying there. Later meeting a friend who was lamenting
the loss of his girdle, he said, "Do not worry but buy some lettuces and
eat them at the corner, when you turn it and go a little ways you will
find it." (Bubb 1920)

The brain has two crude solutions available to help with the credit-
assignment problem, and it seems to use both. The first is Hebbian:[3]

---

3. Named for Donald Hebb (1949), whose learning rule is often expressed as if it governed
dendritic connections between neurons—"what fires together wires together"—but which has
come to be much more widely applied in models of learning.

Reward everything "in sight" but don't look too widely, and then leave it up to statistical regularities over time to sort out proper accreditation for patterns of events. The second solution involves metacognition: If a causal "hypothesis" (right or wrong) can be temporally associated with an emotion and this association is (rightly or wrongly) rewarded with that emotion or also with the *Aha!* emotion of discovery or insight, this labels the thought that preceded the emotion as credit-worthy. Unlike the first solution, the second solution can also be used to accredit memory after the fact—either in imagination or in attentive repetition of the event.

We will classify some of the related phenomena, the close kin to humor, shortly, but first we want to point out how misattributions involving some of these related phenomena can have an effect on the intensity of mirth. Experiences of insight, Schadenfreude, and the like each cause some level of positive emotion. Likewise, many of the socially proscribed or taboo contents of a joke can be arousing in their own right. If a thought triggers not just humor, but also some of these other emotions at the same time, then the total arousal level will be higher, yet the brain does not have the resources to determine which blanket reward is caused by which effect of the stimulus. When we feel the humor, and are asked to report on how funny a joke may be, we may mistake the cumulative effect of all the positive emotions aroused for the magnitude of a single factor: humor. Sometimes, if we are conscious of it, when a joke makes us laugh only a little, we may note that it "was a really good joke" nonetheless. This explicit distinguishing of comedy from other sources of pleasure is especially apparent sometimes when we've heard a good joke before. Once one has lost one's virginity for a joke, the pleasures of connoisseurship and nostalgia can replace the more intense pleasure of the first hearing.[4]

To recap, humor varies on a scale of intensity. There are two factors that contribute to this scale: the amount of false belief, and the level of concomitant, yet misattributed, emotions. In the limit, as both of these variables approach zero, an event drops out of the humor category.

---

4. Clark (1970) gives an account of humor as incongruity plus another "amusement." By such an account, mirth per se does not actually exist, but rather is the intersection between cognitive detection of incongruity and some kind of enjoyment. We believe in mirth; it is not just an appearance created out of various other kinds of pleasure in particular cognitive contexts, but we do think it is intricately augmented by them.

C. Boundary Cases

You tickle my fancy—and I'll tickle yours!

You've outdone yourself—as usual.

—Raymond Smullyan

It should be clear that while the model we are building owes a lot to incongruity-resolution models of humor, it purports to account for types of amusement that escape the narrower focus of the earlier attempts, and grounds humor in an explanatory framework that, for the first time, really can explain why there should be such a phenomenon as humor in the first place. Do any other species have a sense of humor? It is obvious that *florid* humor and laughter is one of the distinctive marks of just one species, *Homo sapiens*, but since risky future-generation is a task for any brain, we might expect to see a variety of related phenomena in other species. We do find play behavior in the young of many mammals, and its role in rehearsing and honing their anticipatory skills has long been asserted, plausibly, but with scant prospect of finding detailed confirmation. Nothing that resembles shared amusement (at the pratfalls of group members, or in response to antics, for instance) has been reported, so whatever it is that generates our hunger for comedy seems to be lacking in even our closest relatives. In human beings we do find several phenomena that typically elicit laughter but do not in any obvious way involve incongruity resolu- tion: playing peek-a-boo, trust falls, roller-coaster rides, and tickling.

Well before an infant can get a verbal joke she may exhibit a delight almost amounting to an addiction for the simple game of peek-a-boo, in which an adult or other child briefly hides behind an occluder, and then is suddenly revealed—"Peek-a-boo!"—to peals of laughter. Why should infants enjoy this pastime so much? This is, one might speculate, a glimpse of the first stirrings of the anticipation machinery that will soon swing into high gear and carry the child through life on waves of accurate predictions. What better way of jump-starting the system than by exploit- ing the child's innate curiosity and using the visual experience of occlu- sion and object permanence as a rehearsal, especially when the object is a smiling face? Anthropologists and developmental psychologists have found peek-a-boo and variations thereof around the world (Göncü, Mistry, and Mosier 2000), but in some cultures, visual and vocal interactions between mother and child are much more limited than in others (Gratier 2003), and peek-a-boo may be entirely absent from the normal child's experience in these settings. It would be interesting to learn if there are measurable differences in the maturation of anticipation-generation in these children.

A trust fall is an exercise in which you allow yourself to fall backward (often with your eyes closed) and trust that a partner will catch you. You usually start to panic partway down, and then when your partner does catch you, you may laugh with relief. It is not the relief that causes the laughter, though, it is the overgrown commitment to the belief that your partner has failed. Repeated exposure to trust falls obtunds the laughter because the expectation that you will *not* be caught is no longer generated in the active mental space. Similarly, the moment at the top of the first peak on the roller coaster, when your body's anticipation-generators predict a frightening plunge, triggers a neural alarm that sets off a flood of adrenaline, but soon, if you are not too frightened, you may burst out laughing with relief. The belief that you were going to die is, thankfully, disproven.[5]

At first glance, tickling might seem to be a problem case for our model. What is cognitive or computational about tickling? A number of its attributes render tickling unique among sources of humor, making it is as much a difficulty for our account as it is for *any* account of humor elicitation. For one thing, there is the fact that mirth can be evoked consistently over an extended period of time, instead of as a momentary episode as in most cases of humor. No simple belief-correction—no mere recognition that something is false—can stop the mirth in tickling and in fact, unlike any joke ever told, the longer it continues the funnier it seems to get. For another thing, it doesn't seem that high-level reasoning is involved. Whatever thoughts and beliefs take part in tickling are very low-level, very tacit, very automatic. If the mistaken belief in tickling were an obvious, consciously accessible and verbalizable one, then the issue would not be so enigmatic! For a third thing, tickling is aversive—it is the only kind of mirthful circumstance that we actively try to avoid. As has often been noted, you can't tickle yourself,[6] and Blakemore, Wolpert, and Frith (2000)

---

5. We've certainly oversimplified the very complex sets of thoughts that happen over an entire two-minute roller-coaster ride. There are surely several different false physical commitments that one may come to as one's body is tossed about faster than one can predict. Analyzing them all is an exercise left to the reader.

6. To be precise, you can't give yourself *gargalesis*—the laughter-inducing kind of tickling we usually think of as related to humor. But, you can self-induce *knismesis*, which is the kind of uncomfortable tickling sensation felt when an insect crawls on your skin or even when you drag a feather lightly across your skin (Hall and Allin 1897).

review recent studies that strongly support the hypothesis that the "forward model" made by the motor system when one attempts to tickle oneself is in effect too good at generating anticipations of the effects. Like the inept joke-teller who "telegraphs the punch line," the forward model of the would-be self-tickler prevents any conflict from arising, and hence sweeps away any grounds for mirth. Most tellingly, Blakemore et al. demonstrate that interfering with the predictive fidelity of the forward models made by subjects enables self-tickling. Note, though, that the failure to anticipate the precise locations and pressures of finger touches in a tickle cannot be the sole reason for humor. These are not the kinds of things we should be able to predict. If it were the cause of the mirthfulness in tickle, then similarly difficult-to-predict, other-created stimuli (such as *clapping* in an unexpected pattern on your belly, or, in another modality, perhaps just finding someone humming a tune you haven't heard before) should, but as we all know do not, create the same kind of tickled response in us. Also, tickling is location specific, so an unanticipated series of touches, pokes, scratches, and squeezes to the forearm typically does not result in tickling, though the same treatment on the soles of the feet usually does. Lack of prediction is a necessary but not a sufficient condition for tickling. Blakemore et al.'s findings don't explain why we are tickled; nevertheless, a successful account of tickling should explain their findings along with the other anomalous features of this tactile form of humor.

An insightful suggestion by Ramachandran and Blakeslee (1998) explains tickling as a form of humor under a version of traditional incongruity theory. Their idea is that the incongruity is between the sense of being attacked and that of being touched by a friend or lover. Most incongruity explanations, and ours is no exception, are capable of being adapted to Ramachandran and Blakeslee's model, but, as you'll see, we need to take care with how we go about servicing such an adaptation. Of course, as you well know by now, we are not satisfied with a simple incongruity in the stimulus; our tale will need to explain the dynamic effects of such an incongruity in the mind. In this case, we might say that we have a belief that rises to momentary commitment (one belief or the other—"I'm being attacked" or "I'm being caressed"—either one might suffice to begin with). But as soon as we are committed to the belief that we are either under attack by our friend or intimately engaged, the opposing sense can come into epistemic conflict with that belief, and, in fact, the humor can be continuously evoked by dislodging each of these beliefs over and over again in alternation. Although such rapid alternation could explain the constancy of mirth in tickling and it may at first seem parsimonious with our account, we are somewhat concerned about this explanation. Should we be fooled so easily? And then fooled again and again each moment later? Why wouldn't we, in our experience with having been tickled before, approach either or both of those beliefs with epistemic caution, not committing to either one strongly enough to find oneself fooled? And why do we not notice a conscious alternation in belief? In contrast, we actually seem to feel a simultaneity between the humorousness and the aversiveness of tickle with neither feeling pausing to allow space for the other (Harris and Alvarado [2005] also give facial-action-coding evidence of this basic phenomenological observation).

The realization that you are not being attacked by your friend—the recognition that this is instead a *tickle*—would render the "I am being attacked" belief false and would *perhaps* be humorous once *if* you had really committed to your friend attacking you instead of tickling you. We don't think that's likely. Nevertheless, even if it happened, after resolving it once you would not be able to come to that belief again—not in this tickle episode, and not likely ever again. If this kind of high-level belief was what was active in tickling, the first tickling would, perhaps, be hilarious, but like a first-person joke you've heard before, continued or subsequent tickling would be ruined. Since we know that isn't true, we need to look deeper.

Although the alternation hypothesis didn't seem to hold, the Ramachandran and Blakeslee model is based on good insights about the phenomenology of tickling. Our next (and final) suggestion is a different adaption of their model that is consistent both with our theory of humor elicitation and with the idiosyncratic distinguishing facts about tickling that we've just reviewed.

As we said, similarly difficult-to-predict touch is not funny. And difficult-to-predict sensation in other modalities is not funny either. There is something very specific about the modality of touch in tickling, but it is not entirely the result of prediction. Tickling is a very precise *kind* of touch. We all know how to tickle someone *and* how to touch them without tickling them. In particular, tickling is a form of aversive touch. The fact that we typically ask "why does tickling make us laugh (when it's not very funny)?" rather than "why do we try to avoid being tickled (if it's so funny)?" indicates that our default view is that the feeling of tickling is aversive, and that something further about the belief structure in that experience is what we cannot help but find funny.

We think dissociating the humor and the aversion can help illuminate the relevant beliefs that create each component separately. Notice that if you are tickled by someone but you don't know (and don't suspect!) that it is a person, you feel no mirth or anything like it. What we suggest makes the difference is *the recognition of intentional human touch*. Try this thought experiment: Imagine yourself alone in an unfurnished, unlit room with a number of small holes in the corners of the walls and along the floor. You've locked the door, and you lie down on the floor. Suppose that, after some time, you suddenly feel the exact tactile sensation of being tickled, perhaps on your side, perhaps on the bottom of your foot or perhaps in the pit of your arm. If you are certain that no one else is there and still think this is funny, we think you're crazy—it's horrifying! Notice, too, that the clear recognition of human touch could easily make this situation humorous. If someone else was there, and you could tell that they'd reached over and touched you, you would know it rather instantly as a tactile joke.

The very particular kind of touch we call tickling—the rather localized sensation of multiple points of contact moving with a semiregular yet unpredictable organic rhythm—is a tactile pattern that, before humans invented tickling, was commonly caused only by small animals or large insects crawling on your skin (this kind of occurrence was not uncommon prior to the very recent invention of rather well-sealed homes).[7] Consider also the tickling-like sensation of a small insect walking among the hairs on your skin (which humans sometimes replicate with a feather touch to the back of the neck, for instance). People also say this tickles, though it is usually less intense. The lever-like behavior of these hairs allows them to amplify small movements on the surface of your skin, providing strong enough signals to activate internal sensors at the base of the hairs—those sensors, using the hairs as triggers, are, in a rough manner of speaking, insect detectors. It is significant to notice that not every touch of those hairs (e.g., brushing against a wall, wearing clothes) can create this sensation. It requires a very particular pattern to elicit that feeling—a pattern that is reliably created by insects, though also occasionally created by droplets of sweat or other means. Likewise, the neurological detection mechanism that makes the patterns of strong tickling aversive can be called (again, very roughly speaking) rodent detectors. Or scorpion detectors. Or wild-boar-planning-to-eat-your-belly-while-you-sleep detectors.

Obviously, there is a very good reason why this kind of touch should be neurally coded (whether through learning or innate structuring) as aversive. Once we feel this kind of touch (whether or not there is an insect or

---

7. Gregory (1924) offers a similar hypothesis, but rather than insects or rodents, he says it is exposure in hand-to-hand combat that was the threat that this feeling warns us against. Black (1984) finds that the most ticklish parts of our bodies also have the strongest protective reflexes.

rodent actually there) the immediate reaction of brushing at that area indicates a belief. What is the belief? As we noted before, it isn't easily verbalizable. It certainly isn't as precise as "there is a rat scratching the sole of my foot." You aren't committed to there being a rat there every time you are tickled. We think Ramachandran and Blakeslee's idea, "I am under attack," is closer to the right answer. Perhaps something general like "there is something nasty and alive on my skin" gets at the right kind of description. This is a tacit, unarticulated kind of belief, founded much more directly in our sensory nervous system than higher-level beliefs (about mathematics, for instance). It is not pure sensation (the pure sensation is the touch itself), but *logical* inference may not be involved either. The belief that there is something nasty there is created closer to the level of perception. Such built-in dispositions of lower-level perception, in being prerational processing, are very susceptible to illusions that can commit us to beliefs. We take up the general issue of illusions in more detail later in this section.

When tickling hijacks our basic rodent-sensors, we are fooled into making a heuristic leap to the belief that there is something nasty there that we need to get rid of. This is the active covertly entered committed belief that is not true. Because the illusion is so powerful, and because a tickler can reactivate it by just moving their hands again, we commit to this belief over and over, and each time it is invalidated by the clear recognition that we are simply being tickled.

In short, tickling is a cognitive bug—an aspect of our phenomenology that serves no purpose of its own but rather is a by-product of humor and some built-in structures of our defensive neurophysiology, each of which is good for something on its own. This is not to say that we haven't learned to use tickling for a purpose—the enjoyment it creates has often been cited as a tool for social bonding, and there's no reason why such a mirthful accident couldn't be commandeered by willful agents (us) intending to take advantage of such natural predispositions.

So, does this reframing of Ramachandran and Blakeslee's original suggestion now answer to all the questions of the unusual status of tickling? Let us review. First, we think it explains the fact that everyone finds the "reason why tickling is funny" to be ineffable. The belief construction is *perceptual*—it is still a constructed belief, but its construction is done at a level lower than conscious reasoning. This also explains why we can't avoid the humor in tickling by recognizing a false high-level inference. High-level beliefs have only post hoc epistemic power over perceptual beliefs; they cannot stop the formation of perceptual beliefs, they can only question their status after they exist. When you look at the picture that has no woman in it (in fig. 11.1), you cannot stop yourself from seeing a

Figure 11.1
Sunrise in the Nature Reserve, reprinted with permission from Sandro Del Prete.

woman there even if you are told ahead that she is not there. The only power the high-level belief has is in telling you that it's not really true, after you've already seen her.

This relative impotence of higher-level beliefs may also explain the persistence of humor in tickling, both in the consistent extended nature of each bout, and in the repeatability of this first-person form of humor. You can't stop yourself from coming to the same false belief over and over as your tickler continues to move their hand. Each move makes it a different stimulus, retriggers a new sensation, slightly to the left . . . now above . . . then below . . . each of which while similar to the first is not the same. Powerless to defend yourself against the misinterpretation, you are, again and again, forced into a false belief—an aversive false belief at that—that you know is false even before it forms.[8]

As for why you can't tickle yourself, our view accepts Blakemore et al.'s explanation. Others can tickle us because their carefully designed movements replicate a truly aversive stimulus in our ecological/evolutionary history.[9] We can't tickle ourselves because, unless you remove predictability, our self-prediction doesn't allow us to be fooled by our own attempts. Contrary to first appearances, though, this isn't what makes tickling funny; it's what makes it aversive! This also explains why other unpredictable touch or unpredictable nontactile stimuli are not ticklish or humorous— there is no built-in rodentoceptor-like system in these other modalities, so we are not driven to the illusory belief that something is wrong. Lastly, this brings us to our explanation of the aversive nature of tickling: It is simply an artifact of the original nature of the stimulus which is illusorily evoked by the tickling. In addition to this answer, we might speculate

---

8. In the jargon of cognitive science, we label such low-level beliefs as *cognitively impenetrable*. Even when you know better, at a higher level, they continue to exert their influence.

9. Recently, subjects who thought they were being tickled by a *machine* (though they were only being deceived) were found to produce as much smiling, laughing, and squirming as when they thought they were being tickled by a human (Harris and Christenfeld 1999). This arguably stands in opposition to social theories of tickling, but is consistent with our view, as it is not actually the human but rather the *known* that can dislodge our rodentoceptor-based beliefs. An interesting further experiment to test part of our conjecture would be to observe subjects for a laughter response when they are tickled by a human, the tickling-machine, or an actual rodent or tarantula through a hole but are uninformed about what is touching them. We would expect no laughter in any of these cases.

further that the arousal from the mirth, the aversive touch, and the either intimate or brutal contact with your tickler will all fuel each other, intensifying the emotional impact of the event in a kind of a feedback process.[10]

The hypothesis we have just offered extends the Darwin–Hecker hypothesis by providing a specific mechanism by which comedy and tickling both impart mirth. We offer no evidence yet, other than our arguments above; however, the hypothesis is testable.

Harris and Christenfeld (1997) recently found evidence that they think argues against the Darwin–Hecker hypothesis. Although they found a correlation between susceptibility to tickling and comedy, they also found that experience of either tickling or comedy does not "warm up" a subject for the other experience. According to Harris and Christenfeld (1997; see also Harris 1999), if similar mental states are held, then cross-modal "warming up" would be predicted. There are only two systems that are currently well-documented forms of "warming up" in the human brain. The first is priming related to spreading activation—this consists of contents, typically concepts and perhaps subconceptual content activating related concepts and features. The second is transfer of arousal. Certainly, the underlying content in Harris and Christenfeld's experiment (physical touch and video of comedic social interaction) has no conceptual similarity, so neither the low-level perceptual nor high-level conceptualization of

---

10. As we've mentioned, a tickler can continuously attack a victim and when this is done the tickled person is often driven into hysterics by the emotional cocktail it produces. But there is another kind of mirthful hysteria, worth mention, that we are all familiar with too. Recall times when you knew you shouldn't laugh but just couldn't help it; times when you tried to stifle it but just couldn't contain the overwhelming mirth! Various kinds of feedback are the cause of this emotional buildup. For instance, there is feedback from the recursive intentional stance modeling of your laugh-stifling compatriots and of their modeling of you— each fueling each other as furtive glances let everyone know that we're all on the same internal page. Sometimes it goes further than this, though. The fact that you are laughing at something can be funny, itself, because of context. If it's funny that you find something funny (when you aren't supposed to), then it will be funny that you find it funny that you find something funny, and so on, thus creating these positive feedback loops of uncontrollable hilarity that occasionally overcome a junior high classroom. Such feedback loops, or other related cyclically dynamical situations, may be what cause laughing epidemics such as the astonishing months-long event in 1962 in Tanganyika (as reported in Provine 2000). Also, the outtakes of situation comedies often feature episodes where one actor muffs a line and then the whole cast is reduced to giggles for an extended period of time, as take after take dissolves into uncontrollable laughter. Someone seeing only the later rounds of this recursion would fail to see anything funny.

these stimuli should have a priming effect on the other. If what they share is only the discovery of an overcommitted false belief, note that this discovery is *process*, rather than content, and it is uncertain whether such a base process might have any kind of priming effect. Perhaps, then, what warms an individual up for comedy is simply their arousal state. Further experimentation may shed some light on the prospect, but, to determine a transfer of arousal effect between comedy and tickling will require careful dissociation of timing and valence effects, since comedy consists primarily of mirth, whereas tickling has a highly aversive component.

The drawings of "impossible objects" such as the devil's tuning fork (fig. 11.2a), the Penrose triangle (fig. 11.2b), and the artwork of M. C. Escher constitute an interesting class of almost-humorous visual stimuli, pointed out to us by Donald Saari. Consider how they do seem to meet our five

(a)

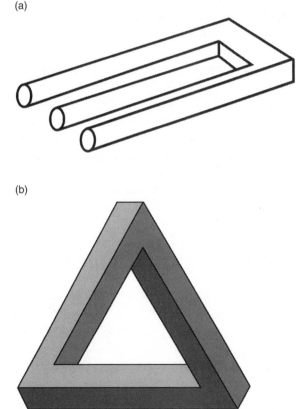

(b)

Figure 11.2

conditions. When you first look at the Penrose triangle, for instance, you automatically assume that this is a two-dimensional rendering of a normal three-dimensional object. That assumption is (1) an active element that is (2) covertly entered and (3) "taken to be true," but then discovered to be (4) false in your current mental space, and of course however surprising this is, it is (5) not accompanied by any strong negative emotion. So why don't we laugh? Well, people often do laugh the first time they find themselves fooled by such an image, and, as usual, context can make a big difference. It is one thing to encounter the devil's tuning fork in a book called *Visual Illusions* and another in a book called *Easy Woodworking Projects*. They may also find it confusing at the same time, though that confusion comes from the irreconcilability of the contradictory elements, while the humor comes from the fact that this very irreconcilability dislodges the premature belief that this was a visually stable and consistent object. (Notice that this explanation goes quite against the standard incongruity-resolution interpretation, which would likely assess the humor as a result, somehow, of the incongruent elements of the stimulus itself.)

Rather than *unstable*, like the Penrose triangle or the devil's tuning fork, another class of visual illusions, including the Necker cube (fig. 11.3a) or the well-known duck-rabbit (fig. 11.3b), are what we can call *bistable*. In these images, instead of having your assumption of its possible reality broken, you have one stable interpretation of the image broken by another. These might also be humorous, but typically less so, even on a first viewing, because the second stable interpretation does not actually invalidate the first. You won't have necessarily made a mistake to believe that you are looking at a duck. What may be at risk would only be a covert but committed belief that there is only one way to perceive this object.[11] So, when it is humorous, the recognition is not "oh, it's not a duck!" but rather "oh, there's another way to see it!"

Our original concern still stands, however: Typically these images do not make us laugh. Why not? The occasional humor in these objects is a fortune of virginity, soon lost with experience. In short, these are jokes that are too predictable, jokes for which we telegraph the punch line to ourselves before it can hit us. We approach things in this category with

---

11. Another way to possibly increase the humor would be to press a viewer into committing to a belief that can be shortly invalidated: "What do you see?" "A duck." "You see a duck, right?—there's no rabbit in that picture?" "No, no rabbit. A duck. . . ." When the rabbit is now apprehended, it may be funnier than if the viewer only believed that there was only one way to see this picture.

(a)

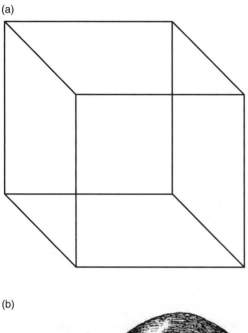

(b)

Figure 11.3
Reprinted with permission from Wrights Media.

epistemic caution after having seen them before, not committing to what we know won't be true. Everyone knows there are two interpretations to the Necker cube, and seeing one of them does not commit us to no longer believing the other one exists; likewise, seeing the duck does not preclude us from believing we can see the rabbit.

There are too many classes of visual illusion to discuss, but we will look at one more complicated case that has important relevance to our model. We already mentioned this kind of illusion in our discussion of tickling earlier—these are illusions for which you are committed to a belief at a very low level: The almonds really aren't moving (fig. 11.4a), but it's hard not to believe they are, and the chess pieces are the same shade of gray in both images (fig. 11.4b)!

These are visual effects over which you have no conscious control. So, while we know they can be funny on a first viewing (as we entertain false inferences that static pictures don't move, for instance), we should ask ourselves why they don't constantly evoke unbearable mirth the way tickling does. Sure, an actually steady picture isn't moving to new positions again and again, but nonetheless when you look away and look back, you are struck anew with a convincing belief that the almonds are moving; but you don't find it funny again each time, like you do with tickling.

On the continuum from sensation, through perception, and then tacit automatic inference, finally to conscious logical inference, we think the mistaken assumption in tickling lies somewhere between perception and tacit automatic inference. The motion of the almonds, on the other hand,

(a)

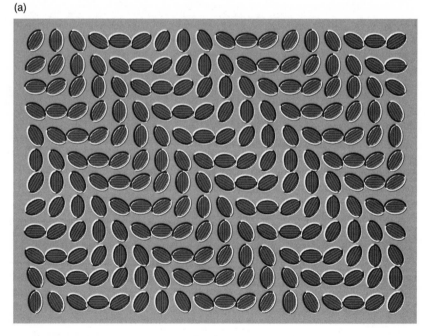

Figure 11.4
(a) Reprinted with permission from Akiyoshi KITAOKA. (b) Reprinted by permission from Macmillan Publishers Ltd: Nature (Image segmentation and lightness perception), copyright Barton L. Anderson, Jonathan Winawer (2005).

(b)

Figure 11.4
(continued)

is much closer to sensation—you don't question that you see them moving (if it works for you—some viewers claim not to see any apparent motion).

Thus, while tickling can commit you to a false belief, you can also dislodge that false belief with other rather direct and in fact less inferential measurement—looking and feeling that area to determine that there indeed is no rat, scorpion, or snake there. The commitment to motion in the almonds, being so extremely low level, is unquestioned. When faced with the knowledge that images on paper don't move, the data from the visual sense have greater epistemic strength. Yes, they *are* moving. The same reason explains why we don't find motion picture video (the illusion of motion due to a rapid succession of still images) to be funny. This is all predicted rather nicely from our (still rough) epistemic reconciliation chart on page 116.

Visual illusions, tickling, peek-a-boo, and trust falls are all first-person forms of physical humor. Nonverbal humor—various kinds of physical humor being the major subcategory—requires no language and ranges from the antics of Laurel and Hardy or the Three Stooges through the subtle silent miming of Jacques Tati or Rowan Atkinson, to visual puns and paradoxes such as figure 11.8 below, and the false belief in these kinds of humor often depends, directly or indirectly, on an appreciation of agents' purposes. In slapstick, when someone runs into a brick wall or a carpenter swings a ladder into the face of an assistant, this is obvious enough; the audience recognizes the faulty model or models of those purposeful agents. The carpenter story is particularly funny if, say, Larry turns around with a long ladder over his shoulder, Moe sees it coming but expects it will hit Curly first, and then Curly ducks such that Moe gets hit in the face.[12] Moe's improper commitment to his own safety is probably the most important mistaken inference made there, and we debug it in our simulated third-person mental space.

Not all physical humor depends on a mistaken model in the actor; sometimes the actor exposes a mistaken or impoverished model in the audience, as when Jack Lemmon, cooking supper in his bachelor kitchen

---

12. This is a good example of how our model differs from superiority theory. The superiority theorist is happy to see Moe get hit in the face. They will argue along the lines that we don't like Moe, we think him a stooge, and we feel better than him when we see him get knocked down. However, if we change the circumstance just a little, Moe needn't get hit, and the humor remains: Curly ducks and then Moe with a shocked expression . . . also ducks, just in time. In this case, Moe has still overcommitted to Curly shielding him and this committed belief was disproven—his shocked expression shows us that.

for Shirley MacLaine in *The Apartment*, suddenly (and bafflingly) grabs his tennis racquet—and then uses it to strain the spaghetti over the sink. (MacLaine doesn't have to witness this deed, let alone be puzzled—as we are—by it, though a reaction from her can boost the humor.) In figure 11.5b the designer has tried to trick us into believing the chair has a purposeful goal that we are observing; when we realize that's not true, we laugh.

At first glance, it seems that physical humor need not involve any human agent involved in a mistaken assumption, but this is an illusion, which we can bring out by looking at a minimal case. We watch a movie of a volcano, on some desolate moon (not an animal or agent in sight), growing, growing, bulging, rumbling, shaking, and then . . . *sploot, plop!* A drop-sized spurt of lava pops out of the gaping summit and lands ignominiously on the slope. We laugh. What an anticlimax! Indeed, the humor in this presentation lies in the fact that it exploits the Gricean maxim: Be relevant (Grice 1957). Any presentation is a communicative act that we expect to repay our attention. An utterly pointless sequence is surprising just in its pointlessness, and when we see the buildup of the volcano, we anticipate something rather spectacular to reward our attention. As usual in humor, when no other agent is in sight, we ourselves are the agent who has fallen for the mistaken assumption. Another Gricean joke, though in this case verbal, is the following bit of non sequitur, which rests both on the maxim of relevance and the maxim of quantity:

(84) Tom: Why is a teacup like an antelope?
     Dick: I have no idea.
     Tom: Neither do I. I can't imagine why anyone would think so!

This is like the riddle about what was green and had seventeen legs, back in chapter 7. Here, the listener, following Grice's advice, expects there to be a point to the question. Breaking these and other Gricean maxims can often create a humorous situation—witness: calling "Bingo" after just three numbers have been drawn from the cage and then recanting with a slyly guilty smile (the maxim of quality [truth]). The beliefs that we are implicitly, yet actively, committed to in Gricean humor are not about the content, but rather about the medium of communication. Hofstadter (Hofstadter and the FARG 1995, p. 46) suggests as a kind of joke the idea of a jigsaw puzzle where some (or all) of the pieces don't fit together. If funny, this is analogous to a Gricean joke—the puzzling participant has overcommitted to a belief that the manufacturer has abided by the standard of creating solvable puzzles.

(a)

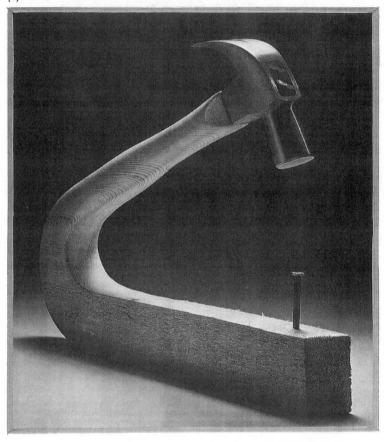

Figure 11.5
(a) "Bent Hammer." Reprinted by permission of Malcolm Fowler. (b) *Oops—A sculpture* by Jake Cress. Reprinted by permission of Jacob Cress.

Riddles form a broad category that firmly crosses the boundary between humor and problem solving, with exemplars at both extremes: one-liner jokes in the form of riddles, and utterly unfunny puzzlers that may need paper and pencil and much head-scratching to solve, as well as every shade in between. The flavors of delight upon figuring out, or being told, the answer are similarly arrayed in a spectrum. We will concentrate on funny riddles. The defining format of the riddle is asking a "simple" question; all riddles are dramatically brief, the better to grab and hold the attention of the listener. A question "automatically" pushes the listener

(b)

Figure 11.5
(continued)

into answering mode, initiating a search through world knowledge by JITSA spreading out from the key terms in the question. This reflex response commits the listener, covertly, to the task of finding an answer. And in a good joke-riddle this is typically a mistake, a cognitive *over*commitment: the "solution" would almost never be found by a diligent and imaginative search since (1) it is so distant in search space from the starting point, and (2) it is—probably—not the only good solution, and (3) there is no possibility of gradient ascent (clues to show your search is getting closer to the summit). You're playing a game you cannot hope to win, since riddles are probably composed backward: Funny answers are thought up first, and then impossibly remote questions contrived for them.

(85)   What is the main reason Santa is so jolly?
       He knows where all the bad girls live.

(86)   What is the difference between a Harley and a Hoover?
       The position of the dirt bag.

Riddles are held in low esteem by many adults, not only because they are the ur-humor of childhood, where the answers are typically the simplest of puns, all too easily guessed by adults, but also because the riddle format is almost a cheat: It achieves its primary purpose of getting the audience to create and furnish the desired mental spaces with such a crude and hackneyed cognitive tool: the question. The best riddles enhance the pleasure by not just relying on a pun in the answer (e.g., the two meanings of "bad girl" and "dirt bag") but by adding a dollop of sex or Schadenfreude or outgroup derision. Puns are not the only source of humor in the answers:

(87)   Why does O. J. Simpson want to move to Alabama?
       Everyone has the same DNA.

You would never guess "the" answer, and this riddle manages to hit a triple: sex, Schadenfreude, and two flavors of outgroup derision, thanks to its sly exploitation of a widely shared stereotype of a celebrity.

Another interesting subvariety of physical humor is humor in music, which can invoke exaggeration, parody, and even the violence of slapstick. Think of Haydn's Surprise Symphony (Jackendoff [1994, p. 171] and Huron [2006], for instance, find other witty passages in Haydn). Humor in music is a particularly clear example of violated expectations, but not all surprise in music is humorous. Indeed, Huron (2006) argues persuasively that most if not all excellence in music involves the artful alternation of fulfilled expectations and unexpected (not entirely predictable) variations. Humor arises here, we maintain, when one is lulled into an *overcommitment* of expectation, so that the unexpected element is clearly outside the envelope of acceptable but still somewhat unpredictable variation. In this it is close kin to the humor in caricature and parody.

How does the humor in caricatures get explained on our theory? They apparently involve no timing, no withheld information, no narrative at all, and yet they can provoke a smile or even a belly laugh. But look more closely, and in slow motion. Our brains never stop trying to produce future, generating expectations about everything, involuntarily using all the resources available. Recognition of faces, and even the identification of objects, depends to some degree on a (still ill-understood) process of coding by "departures from the norm." This can be seen clearly in the pioneering work of linguist Susan Brennan (1982), who created a simple computer program that could automatically turn out quite good caricatures from simple full-face (and realistic) line drawings of real people's faces. The program compared the candidate face to the anonymous, androgynous average or mean face, utterly unmemorable and bland. It did this by identifying key points in the face—tip of nose, distance between eyes, height of forehead, width of mouth, and other less easily described but significant features—and measuring their distance and direction from the corresponding points on the vanilla face. This defined vectors where the real face departed from the mean face, which could then be drawn in caricature by multiplying all or some of these vectors to create 5 percent caricatures and 10 percent caricatures, and so forth. More subtle and sophisticated graphics programs (e.g., Mo, Lewis, and Neumann 2004) for morphing photographs of faces, exaggerating their departures from the bland average, have since been developed, and the best of these produce results that are both "instantly" recognizable and amusing. A 5 percent caricature is not only barely distinguishable from a faithful likeness; it is more easily and quickly identified by those who know the person than the faithful likeness is (Mauro and Kubovy 1992). Larger exaggerations are quite reliably amusing, and huge departures are typically seen as grotesque but still recognizable. The output of these programs is not as witty and incisive as the work of the best artists, but it does suggest that they are working more subtly at the same task. The best caricatures also make further points, not merely exaggerating distinctive features but implying further commentary on the target. The well-known caricature of Charles Darwin epitomizes the art, exploiting an exaggerated distortion of Darwin's theory in addition to his facial features, showing how at least the added value in a caricature can depend on relatively ephemeral world knowledge in the same way a narrative joke usually does.

Why does the stimulation of the identification system trigger mirth? According to our model, it is because however swift the process is, it takes time, and as soon as the initial processing triggers a tentative identification, this creates expectations about what the next micro-step will reveal, and when these are violated, this is a standard case of covert assumptions being undone by subsequent developments. There is a rapid interplay between recognition, which creates expectations, which are violated, which creates corrections, which lead to reconfirmation of identification, which creates new expectations, and so forth. You've outdone yourself as usual. This temporal process is more obvious in the case of comedians who "do impressions," contorting their faces and adjusting their voices to create four-dimensional caricatures of celebrities. The initial identification is both supported and challenged by the details that follow, creating a succession of conflicts that require continual adjustment. Why, though, do caricatures and comedic impressions depend on exaggeration instead of diminution? Why wouldn't *un*caricatures, sliding back toward the mean, be just as funny? They too would involve violations of expectations. Yes, but they would also subvert the presumption of identification upon which carica-ture depends. ("For a moment, it looked a bit like Nixon, but the impres-sion evaporated.")[13]

It may well seem improbable that an experience as momentary and "unified" as looking at and recognizing a caricature could involve viola-tions of what might be called micro-expectations, but remember that Huron (2006) argues persuasively that central features of the phenomenol-ogy of listening to music have just such an explanation. All of the micro-emotional responses to these expectations can occur within a few hundred milliseconds, and some of the effects are so evanescent that they are con-sciously undetectable (see, e.g., Huron 2006, p. 36). Unconscious emo-tional responses? Is that not a contradiction in terms? No. No more than splittable atoms. The term *atom* actually means indivisible or unsplittable

---

13. This case also usefully illustrates the difference between presumption and conviction; you don't ever *believe* you are looking at Nixon (any more than you *believe* that three nuns walked into a bar with a moose . . .), but the presumption that this is Nixon is uncritically and unre-servedly in force within the mental space where the humor happens. See also Ramachandran and Rogers-Ramachandran 2006, where they compare caricature to the *peak shift* phenomenon in which animals respond more intensely to stimuli that exaggerate the feature of difference on which they have been trained.

Figure 11.6

in the Greek in which it was first coined, but it turns out the paradigmatic atoms—of oxygen, nitrogen, . . . uranium, and plutonium—are composite after all. Instead of giving up the word—in the atomic age—physicists decided to jettison its original meaning. A similar theoretical advance in psychology and neuroscience can find plenty of conceptual elbow room for unconscious emotional responses, if they are clearly the same sort of phenomenon as the more familiar, indeed obtrusive, emotional responses, and owe their imperceptibility to their being subthreshold in intensity or duration or both. These *nearly* conscious ingredients of experience can play important dynamic roles in heightening the (conscious) sense of surprise, or pleasure, or dissonance, or weirdness—or humor.

Stretching the boundaries further, we find some kinds of humor that are a bit more difficult to explain on our theory, but the harder to explain, the more satisfying these cases are when they fall into place within the theory. At the edges of the category of the humorous are phenomena that some would simply exclude, but we want our theory to be as inclusive as possible. Children laugh at deformity and the grotesque. Adults, too, laugh at untold categories of oddity. Carroll (1999, p. 154) gives an illustration: "Juxtaposing a tall, thin clown and a short, fat one may invite comic laughter, but it is hard to see how such laughter can be traced back to a contradiction."

The humor in Carroll's example cannot necessarily be attributed to agency in the clowns or even their status *as* clowns. If we buy a box of apples and open it at home, it may be slightly funny (if at all) to find one extremely small apple among the bunch; but it may be funnier to find one extraordinarily large one and one astonishingly small one. Did the large one absorb the mass of the smaller? What is it about this kind of unlikely combination that can make us laugh?

There are intrinsic statistics to our knowledge. When something is unlikely, we don't calculate the statistics—we simply know (or, rather, feel) that it is unlikely. The statistics have been precalculated for us, in our experience with the world such that our knowledge reflects the likelihood of events, and when these likelihoods are contradicted we are surprised. But, careful: It is not the contradiction with a static likelihood that causes humor here. Recall, humor must happen in a dynamic—active—belief structure. We do not actively contemplate *not* seeing a short, fat and a tall, thin clown together. We just suddenly see them both. One possibility is that seeing something very unlikely—something that sets off our novelty detectors—causes us to actively think about its likelihood, whereupon we build a mental space that contains the thought that "this shouldn't exist."

That post hoc mental space is then falsified by the double take—reviewing the sensory facts that this does in fact exist "right in front of your eyes."

We explore another possibility: In seeing something so unlikely, we often think that someone is playing a joke on us. But, who? In the case of the clowns it may be them, or the show's designer. But, not if it is a short, fat man and a tall, thin woman walking, as a couple, down the street together; and not in the case of the unusual apples. We learn, early in life, that the most likely answer to why things that should not happen randomly do nonetheless occur is that someone willfully arranged for their occurrence. Barring knowledge of any other possible cause, imputing agency is, in fact, also the most *likely* assumption. Of course, making such ad hoc folk theories blindly is a mistake—there are many unlikely things that, though a person can't easily explain them, do have reasonable, nonintentional natural causes. Figure 11.7a is one of Andy Goldsworthy's sculptures made of many gathered and sorted natural stones, and figure 11.7b shows one of nature's own rock sculptures, made by cycles of freezing and thawing in the Arctic.

Seeing human (or superhuman) agency in natural arrangements is a very compelling and very pervasive mistake.[14] One possible source of humor in unlikely occurrences is in making this attribution, and then realizing that a false belief lies therein—recognizing that we have no good basis for assuming the odd couple's joint image was designed for the sake of statistical surprise or for assuming someone chose to put these two apples in our box.

But, we can look further too. There may not actually be another mind, but when we have imputed willful design on the scene and imagined that some demon or god (or person) has methodically put the situation together since chance alone couldn't have done the job, the implicit presence of another mind in our mental space opens up numerous possibilities for false beliefs. The humor may be in your recognition of the imagined agent's (nonexistent) trick on yourself or it may be from that fictional agent's perspective, but it could be even more complicated. Remember, the presence of one mind makes for basic humor, but the presence of two minds allows for far more complexity. Think of the giddiness you feel when you just anticipate someone falling for a trick you've arranged. Then move it up a level, and imagine sharing the feeling of someone else in that position—you might watch a situation in which Jim has arranged a trick on Dwight. Now turn it back on itself and make it self-referential—imagine

---

14. It is in fact the same mistake made by those who don't believe in evolution.

(a)

Figure 11.7
(a) Reprinted by permission of Andy Goldsworthy. (b) Reprinted by permission of
M. Kessler, B. Murray, and B. Hallet.

Jim arranging a trick on you. Even if you don't fall for it, you can imagine
yourself falling for it. You might say to Jim, "That would have been a good
one," while bemusedly pondering who else you both might play the same
trick on. You needn't have actually had a false belief to imagine your
counterfactual self having had a false belief from the third person. Some
of the best humor doesn't consist of a told story, but just someone saying
something that encourages us to impute a wildly false belief to the speaker.
Such a belief imagined can be the source of the humor without ever being
expressed.

We can imagine other theoretically possible exploitations of the humor
mechanisms that have not yet been regularly instantiated in our experi-

(b)

Figure 11.7
(continued)

ence or in the work of comedians. Recall the possibility that Lindsay, who forgot to go to the ATM, may experience private third-person humor—laughing at herself retrospectively, a case of humor-upon-reflection rather than humor-in-the-moment. This need not be lengthy reflection but could occur only milliseconds after the event. The more reflective one is, the more raw material for humor one generates, and it may well be that communicative geniuses will soon invent novel means of conveying such private sources of mirth to wider audiences. The opportunities for humor are as boundless as the opportunities for thought—and for taking cognitive pratfalls as you think. It may be that a closer inspection of many instances of first-person humor will reveal that they are more astutely classified as reflexive third-person-humor with oneself as butt—even though they are, to casual introspection, indistinguishable from paradigm cases of first-person humor. The use of the intentional stance exponentially increases the complexity of thinkable thoughts. As a result, mental spaces constitute a fertile ecology for a plenitude of niches for diverse mechanisms of intentional traits such as humor, and we should not be surprised to find some of the extremophiles in this landscape behaving in heretofore unimagined ways, consistent with our theory.

D. Wit and Other Related Phenomena

> I always like to know everything about my new friends, and nothing about my old ones.
> —Oscar Wilde

We've discussed examples that are well within the bounds of humor, and other examples (such as proto-humor, Gricean humor, and the humor in oddity) that are scarcely within the category of humor, but there are also important phenomena which lie just outside these bounds and are easily confused with them. As we have already noted, the mixture of pleasures induced by most artful concoctions of humor are not easily teased apart, and Schadenfreude, the related joy of triumph, the thrill of breaking taboos, and the pleasure of lustful thinking (our list is not exhaustive) are not mirth, but all may loiter with—and seem to increase—mirth at various times. The appreciation of wit, or the display of sheer cleverness, is such a close relative to mirth that it may seem indistinguishable, but we can help you see the difference by using the same method favored by wine experts teaching neophytes how to identify wines: Let them sample the ingredients separately and in close temporal juxtaposition before inviting them to appreciate anew the pleasures of the combination. Some of Oscar Wilde's famous observations are indeed funny, sometimes funny enough to provoke laughing out loud in a solitary reader. But others, just as sublime, are more thought-provoking than laugh-provoking, and an appreciative sigh or eyebrow raising is the more likely response. That is a response to wit in the absence of humor. Here is a brief list, starting with pure wit, dabbling in comic reversals, and ending with a pun:

(88) If you want to tell people the truth, make them laugh, otherwise they'll kill you.

(89) One should always play fairly when one has the winning cards.

(90) The only thing worse than being talked about is not being talked about.

(91) I am not young enough to know everything.

(92) Work is the curse of the drinking classes.

(93) I can resist anything but temptation.

(94) Morality, like art, means drawing a line someplace.

Visual puns, such as those shown in figure 11.8, are not really puns. They aren't funny—we think you will agree—they are just a little bit clever. Both creating them and solving them make us feel good, but it's not humor that we're feeling (no false belief is disconfirmed); it is wit.

Many jokes and most witticisms are both clever *and* funny, which is why these two species of emotion are often conflated. Together, there is increased arousal (recall our earlier discussion of transfer and misattribution), which may be felt by the comprehender as increased humor. Here, in our opinion, is a clever joke:

(95) A trucker driving along on the freeway sees a sign that reads "Low Bridge Ahead." Before he knows it, the bridge is right in front of him—he tries to brake, but his rig gets stuck right under the bridge. Cars are backed up for miles. Finally, a highway patrolman arrives. The cop gets out of his cruiser, walks over to the truck driver, and says with a smug look, "Got stuck, huh?" The truck driver replies, "No. I was delivering this bridge and ran out of gas."

The humor and the wit here are not separable—they both arise from the trucker's reply. To see this, subtract features one by one and see what happens. The cop need not be smug and need not ask if the driver got stuck. Suppose instead the cop walks up cautiously, asks "what happened?,"

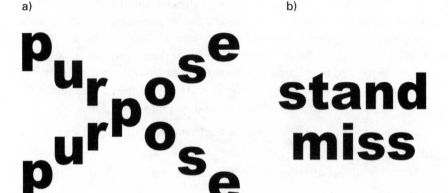

a)

b)

c)

d)

Figure 11.8

and gets the same response. Still funny. Or imagine that the cop walks up, and capably takes control, calling a towing company, the highway bridge department, etc., to arrange for a resolution of the problem, but during this process, the trucker simply offers his creative story: "Who would've guessed I'd run out of gas delivering this bridge right here?" It's still funny, if perhaps a little less so. Instead of being the butt, the cop himself could even laugh. As is often the case, the cleverness and the humor are both in one place; singlehandedly, the trucker's comment sets up a false reality that is nearly consistent with the plainly visible facts and then induces us (or the cop) to build the actual reality disconfirming the false one. The way the trucker does so is very creative. As if that wasn't enough, the implication of the cop's smugness makes the comment an insult to him too, adding another kind of joy—disparagement of an outgroup member— which just makes the joke better.

Examples of wit and humor together abound. Here is another drawn from Bubb's *The Jests of Hierocles and Philagrius*:

(96) A shrewd fellow having stolen a young pig was fleeing. When he was overtaken, he placed the pig on the ground and giving it a thwack, said, "Root there, and not in my possessions." (Bubb 1920)

It is obvious why wit and humor are so similar: They both require careful thought and are directed toward proper event comprehension. Cleverness is, after all, also the exploitation of some subtleties of knowledge, carefully employing the directives of insight and other epistemic emotions.

In many cultures, perhaps in all, there are tales of a folk hero, typically a young man, who lives by his wits (these have traditionally all been male, but modern writers have redressed the balance somewhat with Mary Poppins and Pippi Longstocking), thwarting all the villains, deflating the pompous, confounding the arrogant, and generally providing the youth in that culture with a wealth of inspiring stories of clever self-reliance and one-upmanship. Examples are Till Eulenspiegel stories in Germany, Jack tales in Appalachia ("Jack and the Bean Stalk" is just one of hundreds, including versions of many other folk tales with different title characters), Br'er Rabbit in the South, and, with a slightly different edge, Nasrudin Hodja in the Middle East. Nasrudin is not a young man, but he has a subversive side that appeals to youth everywhere. Some of these stories are downright funny, but many are more tales of cleverness overcoming evil— thrilling, but not laugh-inducing. Trickster jokes are their cousins, definitely funny, but leaning also on the appreciation by the audience of the ingenuity of the protagonist. This is, in effect, the other great source of pleasure to be had in third-person humor: Either you take delight in your own superiority over the characters, or you admire—and hope to emulate—the cleverness of the hero, who sees better ways—better than you can see—to induce the emblematic errors of humor in those he encounters.

Solving riddles is one of the tasks such heroes excel at. Here is an example. Once you solve it, you may be amused at the tacit assumptions in your thinking that made it difficult to solve.

(R3) There are three lightbulbs up in an attic and three unlabeled light switches inside the front door, controlling those lights, up two flights of stairs. You can switch the switches any way you like before heading upstairs to see the results, but you can make only one trip to the attic. Now, how do you match up which switch goes with which bulb? (Assume you are alone and there is no way of sending information between attic and basement.)

The fact that humor depends, as we have shown, upon a false belief makes it often an ideal tool to use when pointing out others' false beliefs. As Bertrand Russell once said,

> People often make the mistake of thinking that "humorous" and "serious" are antonyms. They are wrong. "Humorous" and "solemn" are antonyms. I am never more serious than when I am being humorous.

The laugh that may accompany finding the solution to the puzzle is possibly the result of three separate emotional reactions: a smidgen of humor from the recognition of your own mistaken assumption, the personal joy of triumph over a challenge, and even some of the superiority theorist's favorite additive, the pleasure that comes from a winning move in a competition. As Gore Vidal once put it, in a fine example of his own wit, "It is not enough to succeed. Others must fail." Not really funny, but you may find yourself chuckling.

E.   Huron on the Manipulation of Expectations

> A girl went out on a date with a trumpet player, and when she came back her roommate asked, "Well, how was it? Did his embouchure make him a great kisser?" "Nah," the first girl replied. "That dry, tight, tiny little pucker; it was no fun at all." The next night she went out with a tuba player, and when she came back her roommate asked, "Well, how was his kissing?" "Ugh!" the first girl exclaimed. "Those huge, rubbery, blubbery, slobbering slabs of meat; oh, it was just gross!" The next night she went out with a French horn player, and when she came back her roommate asked, "Well, how was his kissing?" "Well," the first girl replied, "his kissing was just so-so; but I loved the way he held me!"

Can you make people fall to the ground in a quivering faint just by manipulating their expectations? Yes, as Marjoe Gortner (1972) shows in his documentary, *Marjoe*, about the tricks of the trade of revival preachers. First, you use music and highly emotional rhythmic preaching to create a general mood of near delirium; then comes the laying on of hands, which has a demanding temporal recipe: You exhort the person—it works best on women, it seems, but men can also be enraptured—to lift up her hands to the Lord Jesus and look up to Heaven; then you quite explicitly fill her mind with expectations (for instance, "I believe He's going to touch you right now"), and then you *suddenly* and firmly put your hand on her forehead while calling out "in the name of Jesus!"—a surprising shock even though she was expecting *something* special. With any luck she will collapse (into the waiting arms of the preacher's assistants, who gently place her on the floor and put a modesty cloth over her twitching legs, taken from the handy stack of such cloths set out in advance). It doesn't always work, of course; at any revival meeting only a few of the saved will have been brought to *just the right pitch* of emotional anticipation, and in many cases the timing of the hands may be a few milliseconds off the optimal value, which no doubt varies from person to person. But it works well enough to be a standard part of the stagecraft.

What is this curious susceptibility *for*? Not for anything, probably; it is just a seldom-encountered glitch in the cobbled-together system of human emotions, a weak spot that somebody once discovered by accident. The trick has been passed on, by imitation or explicit instruction, to generations of preachers, who each try to make it their own, tuning it to their particular styles, trying to improve the hit-rate. It presumably exploits the partial independence, and different time courses, of two kinds of expectation, one vividly conscious (Jesus is—maybe—going to touch me) and the other unconscious or subliminal (the *preacher* is about to put his hand on my forehead). The earlier-than-expected arrival of the stimulus triggers an emotional firestorm that temporarily incapacitates the person. Some people may acquire a taste for such rhapsodies and (unconsciously) tune themselves up for the preacher's hand, becoming ever more sensitive, more readily aroused by the touch. This is an extreme—and relatively primitive—instance of what is a much more general phenomenon, if David Huron (2006) is right.

Huron claims that the joy of music, the tension, the relief, the awe, and the surprise, can be accounted for as the predictable results of techniques of *expectation-management* that have been refined over the centuries by musicians. His title says it well: *Sweet Anticipation: Music and the Psychology of Expectation*. Like us, he sees the brain as an anticipation machine, and emotions as "motivational amplifiers" that "encourage organisms to pursue behaviors that are normally adaptive, and to avoid behaviors that are normally maladaptive" (Huron 2006, p. 4). The system isn't perfect, and "nature's tendency to overreact provides a golden opportunity for musicians" (p. 6). All of the arts, he suggests, involve "manipulation of expectations" (p. 356), and in the case of music, he offers a remarkably detailed set of hypotheses, supported by experimental evidence, about just how this manipulation occurs and what neurophysiological dispositions it taps. A heavily compressed summary of his "ITPRA" model will give you the flavor (but the details left out are fascinating).

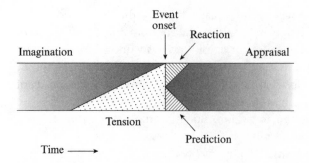

Figure 11.9
Schematic diagram of the time-course of the "ITPRA" theory of expectation. Feeling states are first activated by imagining different outcomes (I). As an anticipated event approaches, physiological arousal typically increases, often leading to a feeling of increasing tension (T). Once the event has happened, some feelings are immediately evoked related to whether one's predictions were borne out (P). In addition, a fast reactive response is activated based on a very cursory and conservative assessment of the situation (R). Finally, feeling states are evoked that represent a less hasty appraisal of the outcome (A). (From David Huron, *Sweet Anticipation: Music and the Psychology of Expectation*, The MIT Press, ©MIT 2006, figure 1.1.)

There are, he says, at least five distinct emotional *responses* that, together, modulate all our expectations over very brief time intervals: Imagination, Tension, Prediction, Reaction, and Appraisal. Imagination is just the urge to anticipate and has an indefinitely long duration. As a specific anticipated event of interest looms, a preparatory Tension, orienting the person to deal with it, arises; then as soon as the event happens (or doesn't) a *yes!* or *no!* response records whether one's Prediction was right, followed by "quick and dirty" Reaction evaluating whether this is a *good or bad* thing, followed in turn by a more measured Appraisal of the outcome. All this can happen in less than a second. One of Huron's innovations, as mentioned before, is his characterization of "micro-emotions" (p. 25) that occur too swiftly and subliminally to be consciously isolatable in experience, while playing a decisive role in the *qualia* of the experience.[15] Booth

---

15. Huron is cognizant of the philosophical traditions that infect the concept of qualia with dubious ideology (Dennett 1991 and elsewhere), but he plunges in undeterred and demonstrates that far from being ineffable and atomic to analysis, many of the qualia of scale tones (*do, re, mi, fa, sol* . . .) fall into clear groupings (determined by open-ended interviews of ten musicians and two nonmusicians) and that these groupings can be accounted for: "scale tones acquire distinctive *qualia* as an artifact of learned statistical relationships" (Huron 2006, p. 174).

(1969) offers quite the same idea, four decades earlier—we describe his use of the notion of microemotions in the comprehension of literature, on pages 280–282. The most interesting—for our purposes—of these micro-emotions exhibit what Huron calls contrastive valence:

> Pleasure is increased when a positive response follows a negative response. While surprise is biologically bad, surprise nevertheless plays a pivotal role in human emotional experience. Surprise acts as an emotional amplifier, and we sometimes intentionally use this amplifier to boost positive emotions. (p. 39)

Think of this "limbic contrast" as Huron's backstage trampoline, a typically unseen downer that makes the subsequent upper all the more delightful. The negative component can happen too swiftly and evanescently to be directly introspectible, but its presence can be extrapolated from the effects achieved when slight variations in the triggering stimuli are presented. And why should this enhancement effect occur? Because, Huron suggests, the initial negative reaction prepares for the worst with an anticipatory endorphin release, but no pain follows (since it's a false alarm), so the body gets a little surplus endogenous opiate for nothing (p. 23)! Huron notes that Kant "characterized laughter as arising from 'the sudden transformation of a strained expectation into nothing.' The key here is the contrast between the fast *reaction response* and the slower *appraisal response*" (p. 29). The parallels with our model of humor are obvious.[16]

So if you find that you want to say you are "addicted" to music—or humor—that may be more literal than metaphorical. It has been known for many years that long-distance runners often develop symptoms that look like addiction, in their craving for the "runners' high" that ensues after miles of painful running, and is caused by the body's massive release of endorphins—endogenous morphines. On Huron's view of music, and it may carry over to humor, these are safer, quicker, less painful ways to get a much smaller, but still delightful, dose of nature's painkiller without suffering any pain for it to neutralize.

---

16. We learned of Huron's work at the Tufts University conference on Music Language and the Mind (July 11, 2008) at which Dennett presented a sketch of our model, and learned, in the discussion, that it bore a striking similarity to Huron's model of music. Huron makes it clear in his own discussion of humor (not just humor in music) that much of what he says about music should carry over to humor. We disagree with some elements of Huron's treatment of humor, as noted in passing here, but since Huron is working on his own theory of humor (personal communication, 2008), we will refrain from detailed discussion of our differences in advance of publication of his settled views.

So, while wit, Schadenfreude, and enjoyable contents can increase mirth through addition of positive valence, Huron's limbic trampoline may increase it by *contrast with negative valence*. The source of the negative valence that we are thinking of could be a number of things. A well-developed joke may often impose just a moment's confusion upon the listener before the resolution of that confusion points out where the mistaken commitment had been made. Other situations may induce concern—say, a file you've been working on isn't in the folder you expected it in, and then you recall you recently moved it. If the situation ends up being humorous, if you momentarily commit to believing you've lost your work before recalling that you saved it elsewhere, the moment's concern about possibly losing the file should act as a trampoline for the enjoyment of the mirth when you realize the file is safe. These cases are interesting context-based modifiers of the microdynamics of humor, but the most common downer that precedes the reward of mirth is simply the disappointment that there's been a mistake in comprehension. The mere fact that anything has gone wrong at all, the recognition that there was an improperly committed belief in a working memory space, may supply a micro-emotional twinge of distress. This is the downer of mirth. If this conjecture is right, the qualia of mirth will be intimately tied to Huron's trampoline.

In problem solving, the assumptions active in the relevant mental space are (mostly) overtly entered and registered, in effect. You know you're making these assumptions, at least "for the sake of argument," so you are perplexed, perhaps, by the conflict you have discovered, but not surprised that there is a conflict. Recognition of a conflict may have been what put you into problem-solving mode. If you resolve the conflict, *Eureka!* You experience the joy of discovery, and will come back another day to solve another problem. Humor, in contrast, may sneak up on you. Humor poses a problem that you don't know you have until you've solved it—or rather, *almost* until you've solved it. There is that evanescent moment when the recognition of the mistaken commitment flashes (with negative valence) before the relief and reward of mirth floods in, enhanced by the contrast.

Just as the *qualia* that distinguish the musical tonic (*do*) from the "leading tone" (*ti*) are generated by an interplay of anticipatory emotional flood and ebb, so (on our conjecture) the *qualia* of mirth turn out to be generated as by-products of the normal operation of your epistemic emotions. We conjecture that the mirth reward system is not simply the discovery reward system with different temporal dynamics, though that is possibly its ancestral version; the mirth system may have evolved into a distinct and parallel reward system, duplicating much of the machinery with variations, much the way our innate capacities to feel the pain of intense heat and the pain of sharp objects have come to occupy distinct circuits—with different "qualia" experienced. No sooner did these new by-products become salient and appreciated by our reflective ancestors than they began to be enhanced, harnessed, exapted to purposes for which they proved to be well fitted. The primitive mirth response, born of an accidental juxtaposition of timing differences in the modulation of the mind by emotions, became a target of exploitation by a different kind of artist, not a musician but a composer of funny things, a comedian. Many of the most salient features of (modern, nonprimitive) humor are all but invisible when we look at the mechanism they exploit, but without that mechanism, there would be no humor.

12 But Why Do We Laugh?

A. Laughter as Communication

A professor gave his class an assignment for over the weekend, and said the only acceptable excuses for not handing it in on Monday would be if you were sick or a close relative died.

One student raised a hand and asked "What about sexual exhaustion?"

The professor patiently waited for the other students' supportive laughter to subside and then replied, "Maybe you should consider using the other hand!"

Bergson (1911) claims that any other emotion will nullify humor, but this is too strong. Humor might be an unwelcome interruption to someone engulfed in the glories of listening to a Beethoven string quartet or in the afterglow of great sex, but if the remark was funny, one would probably laugh in spite of oneself (or so we are inclined to think). Emotions interfere with one another when they have an opposite valence, but even here, they don't simply antagonize each other, and a state of negative affect can actually pave the way for a heightened appreciation of humor, as when anxiety or anger is turned to amusement by a well-aimed witticism. A negative emotion may not actually interfere with humor itself, but rather just the pleasure that accompanies it or the laughter used to express it. In the limit, it is possible, we think, to recognize and even evaluate a bit of humor without taking any pleasure in it. For instance, a professional gag-writer in the midst of a harrowing tooth extraction could note an unwittingly comical turn of phrase uttered by the dentist and make a mental note to try to work that line into a routine, all without cracking a smile, let alone laughing.

The question remains, though: In normal circumstances, why do we laugh out loud when things are funny? The answer might be that this is just a stubborn by-product of the way we are wired, serving no function at all, but since there are clear costs to having such a built-in disposition, one should wonder why evolution hadn't uncovered a path to weeding it out. Could it be paying for itself in some subtle way? Recall Frank's (1988) suggestion that some emotions motivate us into beneficial commitments we might not choose rationally. Part of his point is that the involuntary *expression* of emotions also provides benefits unavailable via deliberate behavior. Blushing, for instance, by exposing the secret intentions of somebody contemplating indulging in a taboo behavior, can enforce a certain level of socially induced mind control. One who learns that one's poker face can be betrayed by a blush may be motivated thereby to avoid that awkward prospect by avoiding *even thinking about* such behaviors. One who succeeds in this policy of private self-control can then be more "open" in public, gaining trust from the community (and thus continued membership therein), which in the long run provides a greater benefit than the immediate rewards of cheating. The recognized risks of blushing (from embarrassment and guilt) could have been great enough to drive considerable efforts of self-mastery, since the cost of detected cheating, in early social groups, may have been death or at least ostracism.[1]

In sum, we are forced by both the physiological sensations of our emotions *and* their involuntary outward expressions into more beneficial courses of action (from the gene's eye point of view), even when they do not look more beneficial to our superficial rationality. However, we must not overlook the fact that, like every evolved trait, the emotions have costs in addition to benefits. The traits that exist today have been selected for because, on the whole, the benefits outweighed the costs in our ancestral lineage even if the costs have been heavy in particular instances. Take anger and its concomitant expression, for example. On Frank's account, anger expression evolved as a way to notify conspecifics that the person who is angered is not one to be cheated; the emotion arises when one feels that a resource has been unfairly taken, and it triggers behaviors, often violent ones, that can both deter others and possibly terrify the current cheater into making amends. The witnesses of anger come to realize that the costs of cheating may be higher than they expected given the dangerous behavior of the angered person. That said, we also all know that we sometimes

---

1. This is just one example of the way a "handicap" can prove, over evolutionary time, to be a "crutch," by forcing organisms to adopt an otherwise too expensive tactic. For a thoughtful reevaluation and revision of Frank's account of emotions as signals, see Ross and Dumouchel 2004a,b, and Frank 2004.

regret what we do when angry.[2] Being quick to anger—and being *known* to be quick to anger—can dissuade others from cheating you, but in some circumstances the emotion can also cause you to lose more than you gain. Each of the emotions that has been coded for by natural selection, including the epistemic emotions, motivates behaviors that are—or were—on the whole, useful, but which may in certain circumstances diminish the fitness of the organism.

In the light of Frank's account of the emotions, consider the fact that laughter is normally involuntary. Is there a hidden benefit to laughing that we would not—or could not—choose rationally? The fact that it is involuntary makes laughter a curious variety of *communication*, since information we broadcast by involuntary behavior (trembling when afraid, shivering when cold, stumbling when drunk, etc.) is rightly viewed in general as not so much communication as unintended self-betrayal. Curious, but not unique. Smiling, for instance, has been shown to be not just a sign of happiness, but rather a communication of happiness—it happens robustly only when we are facing someone able to receive the signal (Fridlund 1991, 1994; Kraut and Johnston 1979; Fernandez-Dols and Ruiz-Belda 1995; Provine 2000). The same sensitivity to the presence of an audience—or even an implied or imagined audience (Fridlund 1991)—is exhibited in laughter. Fridlund suggests this "implicit sociality" is the main reason that solitary laughing occurs. What is not so clear is what this communication—this normally involuntary communication—is for. What benefit could accrue to us from communicating our having made (and recognized) a mistake in judgment? Even though an agent who has felt humor has recovered from her mistake, nonetheless it seems like an exposure of infirmity to admit that there was a mistake in the first place. Why broadcast to the world, "I made a mistake in reasoning!"? Why not just keep it private?

Communication occurs when a signal made by an agent reliably influences the behavior of those receiving the signal to the inclusive benefit of the genes of the agent creating the signal (Wilson 1975; Dawkins 1982, 1989). The optimal strategy for a communication system appears to be one

---

2. Anger in particular is one emotion that we suspect has reduced utility in our modern culture. These days the social, economic, and public legal system manage arbitration of unfairness for us. We no longer need to bare our teeth as often as we may once have. That is, of course, not to say that there is no use for anger anymore. See Gibbard 1990 for a good discussion of the optimal "tuning" of emotions in a modern society.

where you communicate what you know will be received (Oliphant and Batali 1997). When a bird sings, a person hearing it may pay attention and be stimulated thereby to whistle a tune. Or a hunter might shoot at the bird. Neither is a case of communication since the bird does not transmit information to the people that causes them to behave reliably in a certain way that is beneficial to that bird's genes' likelihood of replication. When a conspecific approaches because of the song, in contrast, this is communication—this is behavior that is reliably evoked by the expenditure of energy to create that signal *and* there is a benefit to the communicator from the behavior of the second agent that "pays for" the expenditure. A young bird's scream may reliably beckon its mother for protection or a mature bird's song may reliably beckon a potential mate. Interspecific communication is not impossible, of course: When a rattlesnake warns a mammal not to approach, or when a honeyguide bird leads hunters to a beehive, these behaviors meet the conditions for communication. The evolution of communication as a behavior is not without its perplexities. E. O. Wilson (1975, p. 176) observes that "communication is neither the signal by itself, nor the response, it is instead the relationship between the two." But Maynard Smith points out (1997, p. 208) the paradox of this: "It's no good making a signal unless it is understood, and a signal will not be understood the first time it is made." For a discussion and resolution of this and related concerns, see Hauser 1997.

What behavior would conspecifics perform if given the information that you have detected a mistaken model? As we just noted, it is not likely that the function of laughter is to alert them to an infirmity in your own mental capacity. Informing them of this would probably cause them to infer that they have elevated opportunities to cheat you out of your food or dupe you into cuckoldry. A more realistic answer to the question is suggested by the play theories of laughter.

Play is an enjoyable behavior, and this enjoyment is likely to be the emotional motivation for us to pursue playlike types of behavior regardless of the fact that such behavior may increase both our risk of being caught unawares by a predator and our risk of hurting ourselves from playing too hard. The fact that we (and quite a number of other animals) are motivated to play suggests that there must be some other benefit that outweighs this risk. There is a growing consensus among researchers that the purpose of play behavior is to sharpen the mind's physical, cognitive, and emotional skills (Fagen 1993; Byers and Walker 1995; Spinka, Newberry, and Bekoff 2001; Einon and Potegal 1991; Potegal and Einon 1989). It is a form of practice—practice in using the body you have for the basic purposes that it was designed for. Practice in mental skills is a way for both positive and negative instances to be introduced to a cognitive system so that the system can build or refine hypotheses, or make them more readily accessible. We accept this explanation of the prevalence of play as a critical component of the developmental processes that yield mature competences.

Social play—which can hone the same skills as other play, as well as social skills—has been shown in research to facilitate nonaggressive competitiveness. The suggestion made by play theories is that laughter is a tool to facilitate nonaggressive play (Van Hooff 1972; Provine 2000; Gervais and Wilson 2005). Most of the evidence comes from primate studies. When tickled and chased, apes and especially chimps produce a "play face" that is often complemented by a type of vocal panting (Darwin [1872] 1965; Provine 2000). This panting, which appears to be the phylogenetic precursor to laughing, has been shown to facilitate the maintenance of a playlike state between conspecifics (Flack, Jeannotte, and de Waal 2004; Matsusaka 2004; Gervais and Wilson 2005) and has been found to be more relevant than the play-face itself for chimps' recognition of each others' playful intentions (Parr 2004; Gervais and Wilson 2005). This recognition would allow both parties to continue to hone their skills together without unnecessary and risky aggressive escalation. The play theorists conclude that laughter was originally a signal of nonaggression, and Gervais and Wilson (2005) go on to venture that (human) humor later evolved out of this use of laughter.

We would like to offer a slightly different proposal based in part on Ramachandran and Blakeslee's (1998) explanation of tickling as described earlier. Recall their suggestion that tickling is a swift and involuntary alternation between perceptions of attack and friendly touch. As this happens in a first-person, present-moment, sensory mental space based on reality, the experience does not require the cognitive tools that are necessary to elaborate either theory of mind or fictional mental spaces. Tickling should be an effective type of (proto-)humor in species without theory of mind as well as in young humans who have not yet fully developed their theory of mind. We suspect that the panting and play faces seen in chimpanzees were thus already in place in our ancestors when they began to develop the more elaborated forms of humor, made possible by the recursive growth of higher-order intentional-stance thinking.

This does not yet answer the question of why apes and humans (and, perhaps even rats [!], though we should be careful with our attribution—see Panksepp and Burgdorf 1999, 2003) emit laughter when tickled or chasing/being chased during play. Ramachandran and Blakeslee answer that laughter descended from a "false alarm" signal. Many species that live in groups have alarm calls that are used to warn the members of one's group of impending dangers. Thus vervet monkeys have distinct and identifiable eagle alarms, snake alarms, and leopard alarms, for instance, and many birds have predator alarms of varying specificity (Cheney and Seyfarth 1990), and, in fact, some of these alarm calls may emerge without cultural exposure (Hammerschmidt, Freudenstein, and Jürgens 2001; see also Seyfarth and Cheney 1997). The behavioral response to these alarm calls ranges from "orientation responses" and heightened vigilance to headlong flight. Some species, including chimpanzees, also have a "never mind, the coast is clear" signal that cancels a *false* alarm. For instance, a group of apes or early hominids that panics from the expectation that a rustling in the grass is due to a stalking lion can be relieved of their worry by the vocalization of one who determines that there is actually no threat there. According to Ramachandran's theory, just such a signal is the evolutionary ancestor of laughter, which also appears able to emerge without cultural exposure (Eibl-Eibesfeldt 1989) and which appears to have similarities in both form and usage patterns with alarm calls (Deacon 1989; Preuschoft and van Hooff 1997; Provine 1996, 2000). Its original use was to notify a group of relatives that they needn't be anxious about some topic of current concern; its meaning has been broadened so that now it communicates detection of a resolution to an incongruity. This is an interesting possibility. It accounts independently for the pleasure felt in laughter (which may be separate, on this account, from the pleasure felt in perceiving humor) and for the contagion of laughter, since spreading the "false alarm" signal is a useful habit. We suggest another possible explanation for the contagion of laughter below.

Perhaps the false-alarm theory of laughter and the play theorists' explanation, which says that laughter is a ritualized form of panting used as a signal of nonaggression during play, can be welded together. The play theory gives a very clear explanation of how the staccato form of the laughter sound developed (Provine 2000). But if tickling is a kind of humor, as Ramachandran suggests (and we agree), then the question arises why laughter would be the response to this kind of humor and few others. The answer may be that humor in our predecessors has been—and in chimps still is—coextensive (or nearly so) with play behaviors. Perhaps the underlying meaning it conveys not only to other play participants but also to concerned onlookers (mothers in particular) is "Don't worry! This isn't dangerous aggression." Chimps' play behaviors, aside from tickling, are pretty much restricted to chasing (playing tag, in effect) and wrestling, and chimps laugh primarily when they are about to be caught or attacked or just after they have been caught or attacked during these competitive exercises. These are exactly the moments when a mental space of safety and control becomes eradicated by the reality of being captured. In playing tag, for instance, we try to outwit each other—we try to expect what another will do, model their model, anticipate their moves, and catch them. This typically involves deception on the part of the one being chased and prediction on the part of the chaser. I may build a model of the circumstance, then predict that if I bob this way, and weave that way, I can get away from you (or I can catch you). This game of tag, or hide and seek, is a "toy model" of the primordial contest of predator vs. prey, or the competition between rivals for mating opportunities, and as such, it is a contest of "producing future" by using a rudimentary application of the intentional stance. Playing tag is chess for chimps. Either the chaser's model or the chasee's model will get invalidated by every occurrence of capture or of slyly slipping away. An animal in that situation may laugh at his own faulty model, or perhaps with a bit of theory of mind, at that of his opponent. If tickling and chasing are the primary manifestations of humorous circumstance, and laughing associated with these had an early benefit in the reduction of aggression, or reduction of anxiety about the prospect of aggression, then laughing at all forms of humor may just be a vestige of this early behavior. (On the other hand, though it may have evolved to reduce aggression, we discuss in the next section how the modern version of laughter rather than being vestigial may have been co-opted to encourage other kinds of behaviors in conspecifics).

The literature on the evolution of alarm calls has been marked by controversy, but current models suggest that there is no need for a group-selectionist explanation. (See, e.g., Dawkins 1989, pp. 168–170; Zahavi 1996; Bergstrom and Lachmann 2001.) The same reasoning supports the claim that the behavior of canceling one's own alarm call, or sending a "relax, the coast is clear" signal when one's group of conspecifics is aroused to an alert state by some anomaly, would in many circumstances be fitness enhancing to those who had this instinctual behavior in their repertoire. The extension of the application of such a signal to cover play behaviors is a small step, since those behaviors are potentially misread as deadly serious. As play behaviors became more sophisticated, and occasions for genuine alarm receded, the vestigial instinctual calls survived as reliable and contagious "feel good" signals.

B. Co-opting Humor and Laughter

Laugh alone and the world thinks you're an idiot.
—American Proverb

Nothing shows a man's character more than what he laughs at.
—Johann Wolfgang von Goethe

When we have read a book or poem so often that we can no longer find any amusement in reading it by ourselves, we can still take pleasure in reading it to a companion. To him it has all the graces of novelty; we enter into all the surprise and admiration which it naturally excites in him, but which it is no longer capable of exciting in us; we consider all the ideas which it presents rather in the light in which they appear to him, than in that in which they appear to us, and we are amused in sympathy with his amusement which thus enlivens our own.
—Adam Smith ([1759] 1976)

Once this rudimentary form of proto-humor and its attendant laughter was in place, it was available to be co-opted by evolution for other purposes. And, in fact, the broad range of ways we see humor and laughter used today stands as testament to the fact that this trait must have been co-opted for quite a few additional purposes. Nonetheless, whatever retooling laughter has undergone, it still plays the role of a communication, and so it will still be useful to ask: What is the behavior, which laughter reliably elicits in the receiver, that benefits the laugher? Let us first consider in particular the hypothesis that sexual selection played a major role in shaping—enhancing and refining—and multiplying the occasions on which laughter was the natural response. The basic claim is that humor evolved into a social tool that could be used to great advantage in the competition for mates.

The first step in the argument is to assess the relationship between laughter and cognitive ability and knowledge. The acquisition of knowledge has an obvious evolutionary purpose: to create the expectations that guide the organism's behavior. In organisms simpler than us, these anticipations tend to be stereotyped and local, permitting them to avoid immediate threats and track the simpler patterns in their environment that portend good or ill to them. In us, the arms race of anticipation-generation has created an unremitting pressure on us to become virtuoso expecters. Everybody anticipates, in mental spaces, as much of the relevant future as possible, to the best of their ability given the specific knowledge they have already collected. We aspire to decide on the basis of "all things considered," but of course we must always truncate our considerations in order to meet the deadlines of effective action. So each of us is engaged in a never-ending round of *heuristic search*, building partial, and risky, structures—mental spaces—that depend on *jumping* to conclusions—as deftly as possible. Our particular "choices" (and these must almost always be unconscious, or unconsidered) are to some degree idiosyncratic, depending on what experience we have had, and what matters most to us at the moment. Whenever a mental space is created upon perception of some information, it must be the case that it is swiftly populated by all the inferences (to a reasonable recursive inferential depth) that are available from existing knowledge. This is what *understanding* the new datum consists in: integrating it with what you already know.

Our model has it that the humor response is always triggered by the detection of a false belief in a mental space. Since we each can be expected to have tried to optimize our use of our inferential capacities to create these mental spaces, every such false anticipation reveals something about the limits of our useful knowledge about the domain involved. Clearly, then, when you laugh as a result of the detection of humor, you *unintentionally* reveal something of strategic interest about your knowledge (and your largely unconscious methods of putting it to use). Agents that take the intentional stance toward you will often be able to determine what you had falsely anticipated—and to some degree, then, what you know. Both knowledge and ignorance are valuable strategic secrets. A comedian telling jokes about marijuana, for instance, typically confronts a sharply divided audience of slyly knowing laughers and others sitting in uncomfortable clueless silence. And an unstifled giggle or raised eyebrow in response to a subtle double entendre can betray one's "dirty mind" to the vicar, or to the parents of one's beloved. In even more serious circumstances, a counterintelligence agent could slip a referential joke revolving around the structure of some secret information into a conversation, and watch for any lips that curl up.

Keeping up with the competition in the knowledge acquisition sweepstakes puts a premium on *recently discovered* information. (A "quidnunc"— from the Latin for "what now?"—is a person obsessed with the very latest news. We all have—and should have—quidnunc tendencies, since the latest news creates an information gradient that may be exploited by others at our expense.) If we partition a person's information store into the latest news on the one hand and familiar—tried and true, hackneyed, trite—information on the other hand, which will be, on our model, more vulnerable to mistaken inferences? Will it be the least-digested, newest information, or the long-neglected, maintenance-deferred, taken-for-granted information? The answer is not clear, but humor helps us to explore the question. Some humor seems to depend on our unthinking reliance on overfamiliar patterns of inference. Other humor capitalizes on the relatively unexplored implications and presuppositions of novel topics. Developmental research has shown that it is the most recently mastered items that often give rise to greater mirth during childhood (McGhee 1971), though if these children are frequently making mistaken inferences with this new information, this raises the question of what we mean by "mastery"; the same may not hold for adults or those who have *truly* mastered a domain. Nevertheless, the level of cognitive accessibility for pieces of knowledge will have biasing effects on the ways in which that knowledge is integrated into JITSA-built mental spaces and thus on its likelihood of participating in humor.

Young children also seem more susceptible to tricks for which older children and most adults have mastered metacognitive avoidance techniques.

Answer quickly: What do cows drink?

The first thing that comes to mind for many is "milk." And, if you almost said it just now, you might have amused yourself a bit. But cows don't drink milk. Well, *calves* do, but cows usually drink water. The tendency to think of milk here (even if meta-awareness and top-down control helps you avoid saying it) betrays the automatic JITSA behavior of the mind—we just can't help it when thinking of cows and drinking at the same time. A similar little trick sometimes heard in the schoolyard is this one:

A: What is the most popular drinking soda?
B: Coke.
A: What's something that's funny?
B: A joke.
A: What's the word for the white part of an egg?
B: The yolk. Wait, no! It's the . . .

Usually the interrogating child laughs at the other child's mistake. The word for the white part is "albumen," but it's not a common word, especially among school children. Again, child B is primed by "Coke" and "joke," which helps the spreading activation in their mind settle on the only word for a part of an egg that they can think of . . . which happens to rhyme, too.[3]

The relative immunity adults have to childish humor clearly reflects a difference in the cognitive accessibility of various mistaken inferences, an effect that manifests further in the pride that people often take in their connoisseurship of more abstract and sophisticated forms of humor.

Then there is the robust phenomenon of expert, "in-joke" humor, which exploits and delights in the discrepancy between the mental spaces of novices and experts. A person's sense of humor will reflect not only their quick-witted ability to detect logical flaws and work on resolving them, but also both the domains of knowledge that they hold and the most recent levels of cognitive mastery that they have within those domains.

If the intellectual disparity between audience and butt is too great, the result is not as funny, since the comparison is so one-sided to begin with. In effective humor you want the butts of your jokes to be approximately equal in cleverness to the audience—there's no mirth in pointing out the "stupidity" of (real) idiots, or infants, or cows, for instance. This is why moron jokes lose their allure once childhood is over. There are exceptions, for cases of spectacular idiocy, as in this true story, recounted some years ago by a professor friend of one of the authors whose office phone rang one day:

"Hello."
"Hello, are you a biologist?"
"Yes."
"I've got a bet on with my buddies. Here's the question: Are rabbits birds?"
"Um, no."
"Aw shit!" [hangs up]

Laughter is a hard-to-fake signal of cognitive prowess—and weakness. It is not surprising, then, that humor-detection has come to play a central role in human communication. Aside from fabricated (non-Duchenne) laughter and stifled laughter, our every roar and giggle broadcasts something about our cognitive abilities and knowledge. But once there exists the option of subtly communicating cognitive mastery, it is a trivial step

---

3. They also know "shell" but that depends on thinking of the egg as a whole object rather than a cooked object. We suspect it crosses their minds but is less strongly activated because of children's prototypical interaction with eggs (i.e., they eat them, their *parents* cook them).

to begin using that information to one's own advantage. Laughter may be a hard-to-fake signal, but faking is not impossible, and an arms race of exploratory provocation and detection has ensued. The game-theoretic aspects of humor communication begin here.

When we encounter a new person, we immediately adopt the intentional stance and begin fleshing out a portrait of the person as a knower and believer, an agent with desires, tastes, weaknesses, and all manner of attitudes. Without resorting to exhaustive questionnaires and invasive little social psychology experiments, we aim a few quick probes that will highlight the crucial points of knowledge and attitude that interest us. Humor is a particularly efficient and reliable—though not foolproof—quick probe. The role of humor as a relatively hard-to-fake or costly signal in mate assessment is thus not hard to discern (see Miller 2000 for a clear account).

The next step on the escalator is also quite obvious. If the intentional stance allows you to model others by provoking laughter in them, others must be similarly modeling you. This recognition opens the door to the search for ways of manipulating these others by contriving to control your laughter or at least suppress or mask particularly revealing instances, and to emphasize flattering instances of "involuntary" laughter. Like the peacock caught on the treadmill of ever rising standards, you will invest heavily to make yourself look like a more desirable mate by displaying your humor feathers as best you can. You will try to stifle laughter when it might reveal your limit of cognitive mastery, and you will exaggerate laughter when you think it may express a level of mastery that you do not have. (There is an old job-interviewer's ploy of telling an entirely nonfunny "joke" to see if the aspirant will chortle gleefully—one of the countermeasures in the arms race.) You will work harder to detect the humor in situations as quickly as possible, taking barely conscious pride in being the first one to laugh. You may, without knowing it, acquire a habit of laughing when others laugh, just to make them believe that you understand what is going on, even when you have not received the stimulus that evoked their laugher. Here, then, is another mechanism that could explain the contagion of laughter. While there may well be a genetically inherited predisposition to laugh whenever you hear laughter—and Ramachandran's false-alarm theory could explain this—it may also be true that a socially evolved and transmitted habit is spread under the pressure of this arms race. There would be *two levels* of contagion: The contagious *habit* of laughing when others laugh would underlie the contagious spread of laughter on particular occasions among people who had acquired that habit. And finally, given enough time, this culturally transmitted uniformity in habit could be driven, by the Baldwin effect, into the genome after all. (For a recent survey of the Baldwin effect see Weber and Depew 2003.) Those who most readily *acquire* the habit of laughing when others laugh will be those in whom the tendency is already present in the form of a partial genetic predisposition, and with steady selection pressure, this predisposition will become ever more easily triggered. Over only a few hundred generations this could establish an "instinct" for joining in the laughter—like the "language instinct" itself (Pinker 1994). It goes without saying that these considerations also provide a natural account of the existence and persistence of non-Duchenne laughter in our species.[4] Once commonplace, non-Duchenne laughter may come to serve a number of uses too, from group cohesion and hegemony to social lubrication or Hinde's (1985a,b) ethological notion of emotional expression as a form of negotiation, and more. A thorough discussion of these topics is beyond the scope of our work, but see Provine 2000 for a good introduction.

Returning to the question of communication—how is laughter a form of action at a distance?—one answer, as we've detailed, is that it may have been exapted from its ancestral version to help a laugher enhance their reputation of intellectual capacity in the minds of potential mates and competition. Owren and Bacharowski propose a slightly different use (also readily predicted by the strategic stance we give above): We use laughter as a way of "inducing positive affect in the perceiver in order to promote a favorable stance toward the laugher" (Owren and Bacharowski 2003, p. 183). One way this might happen is through the creation of the enjoyment of mirth. But another way may be through laughter as a form of praise or admiration. Several studies have found differential humor production and appreciation between members of social status categories, with those of higher perceived status being more profligate producers (e.g., Coser 1960; Keltner et al. 1998; Greengross and Miller 2008).[5] Whether a laugher provokes belief or affect, or more likely both, in a recipient—that is, whether the sender gives a recipient beliefs about the laugher or beliefs about the laugher's beliefs—they have generated a likelihood of some kind of more favorable treatment from the recipient.

Perhaps the most pervasive of the ways we have co-opted humor is the least competitive. We are referring to the commonplace behavior of

---

4. One might ask why, if it is deceitful and thus induces or hides some false beliefs, isn't non-Duchenne laughter funny itself? The answer is yes—it can be: Recall the joke about the German from chapter 3.

5. The flipside of this is, of course, the use of humor for hegemonic purposes.

shooting the breeze. Although it is often riddled with instances of superiority humor as well as instances of all the aforementioned ploys and strategies, one of its main purposes is relatively benevolent, done in the spirit of economic surplus. Many times when we sit around with friends, chewing the fat, there seems to be no overarching communicative goal to the conversation taking place. As we all know, the actual goal is simply *enjoyment*, and one of the kinds of enjoyment widely employed at such a time is humor. The pastime of permeating casual conversation with witticisms not only serves the simple selfish goal of flaunting one's wit, but is also a method of trade in the currency of social capital. We value friends who can make us laugh; they provide us with a valuable recreational drug—the endogenous mind-candy of mirth—and that value is cashed out in good will and reciprocity—though those who are less skilled at humor creation or purveying pay their friends back in other kinds of social capital. The value of this social capital is made more tangible when compared with its industrial counterpart: Professional comedians, like musicians, pornographers, and confectioners in their own fields, have refined their skills at providing a kind of enjoyment, and instead of trading them for social capital, use their talents to earn cold hard cash.

C. The Art of Comedy

If you're reading this and don't think it's funny, maybe your timing is off.

"Who is the greatest Polish comedian?"
  "I am."
  "And what is the secret of your suc-"
  "Timing!"

I've been doing a lot of abstract painting lately,
extremely abstract.
No brush, no paint, no canvas,
I just think about it.
—Steven Wright

We have spoken in very general terms about the way cultural evolution, including more or less insightful human tinkering, could design supernormal stimuli that pack a bigger punch than those usually found in nature. Supernormal stimuli can occur by coincidence or accident, of course, in the everyday environment, but unless there is a mechanism—some form of cultural evolution—to replicate, and thus preserve, these happy accidents, they tend to go extinct with a single burst.

In *Guns, Germs, and Steel* (1997), Jared Diamond argues that, to a first approximation, in every culture on every continent, human exploration over the millennia has discovered *all* the local edible plants and animals, including many that require elaborate preparation to make them non-poisonous. Moreover, the people have domesticated whatever local species have been amenable to domestication. We have had the time, intelligence, and curiosity to have made a near-exhaustive search of the possibilities—something that can now be proved by genetic analysis of domesticated species and their nearest wild relatives. This process of trial-and-error prospecting for edible foods (and potent medicinal herbs and the like) was simultaneously a process of prospecting our own inner constitutions; finding out what tasted good and bad, what tasted particularly yummy, what made you nauseated, sleepy, alert, hallucinatory, or sexually aroused. Homing in on the best sources of pleasure, the best techniques of preparation, the best overall experiences was a search that did not require any technical knowledge of chemistry or nutrition, or understanding of human digestion, metabolism, or neurophysiology. Practical know-how preceded theoretical understanding by millennia, and could be the product of variable measure of utterly insightless trial-and-error, unimaginative repetition of what one's elders did, canny and even systematic titration of techniques by ingenious innovators, and serendipitous breakthroughs that then would spread like a new virus through whole populations (Boyd and Richerson 2005; Richerson and Boyd 2005; Dennett 2006). Moreover, this incessant exploration of one's own sensations could also provoke permanent changes in one's own constitution, stretching the boundaries of the acceptable, and raising or lowering the thresholds of pleasure. There are acquired tastes in every dimension, and the price of acquiring one novel taste may often be losing the capacity to be thrilled by the pleasures of one's youth.

We propose that the development of comedy in human culture follows this pattern exactly. The initial, raw, comedy-in-the-wild consisted of one's own inadvertent mental goofs and the pratfalls of others, tickling one's funny bone in private. You had to be there, as the saying goes. But eventually, the human practice of trading narratives, itself an exploratory process of developing prowess, compensated for this insulation by making the best experiences vicariously available to all, and even, on the best occasions, improving on the original stimulus. In successful cases, art outdoes nature: You *didn't* have to be there, and in fact, the episode is funnier in the (re-) telling than in its original form, all distracting features abandoned, and only the pure, distilled comic essence transmitted. At that point, humor could free itself from the *objets trouvés* of real-world experiences more or less truthfully recounted and invent fictions ad lib.

But how could a narrative be *more* effective than seeing the event in the wild? What aspects of design and delivery could heighten the likelihood and intensity of stimulated mirth? Think of a joke (for instance) as a narrative bound in the first place by all the rules of good storytelling, humorous and otherwise. Narratives intended to impart edifying morals, such as Aesop's fables, are streamlined little delivery vehicles; each element plays a role in setting up the lesson. There are no digressions or distractions. Narratives intended to convey knowledge of important historical events direct the audience's attention to the key facts using a variety of devices, but also include crowd-pleasing extraneous details that add verisimilitude (Barber and Barber 2004). Good storytellers appreciate (unconsciously or not) that a liar often gives himself away by too streamlined and perfect a tale—a few intrusive and pointless additions can reassure the audience of the teller's childlike candor and lack of guile.

Jokes, in this arena of competition for the attention and pleasure of the audience, can be seen to be like little psychology experiments. One of the cardinal rules of experimentation with human subjects is that the experimenter must withhold information about the hoped-for effect, since subjects will otherwise be unable to refrain from making unwanted contributions and adjustments to the process under study. After the experiment, the "naïve subjects" can be debriefed and let in on the joke, in effect. In a joke, the withholding of information until the punch line is the feature that more or less ensures that the key elements will be covertly entered into the mental space, a necessary condition for mirth to occur. In the wild, this covert entry occurs when it occurs, and mirth results only when circumstances are propitious; in a narrative, the audience can be fairly reliably kept in the naive state until the right moment. Of course a poor joke teller may telegraph the punch line or a particularly sophisticated audience may "get it" too early, spoiling the sought-after effect. What works for one audience may be ineffective for another. The art of the comedian is in large measure a matter of delivering highly reliable supernormal stimuli to subjects who are kept in the naive state until the proper moment.

Among the artificial improvements created by comedians are double punch lines, jokes that hit the audience with one delight after another. As the laughter is dying down after the first strike, a second volley is delivered.

(97) A man goes to the camel market to buy a camel and is told by the salesman that for $100 he can have a good camel, and for $150 he can get a camel that goes 50 percent farther on a single fill-up of water. The man expresses interest in the more expensive option when the salesman explains that the extra $50 is for a method that you can use on all your camels. How does it work? The salesman explains:

"Look at that camel at the oasis just finishing drinking. His head is under water and with his hind legs like that, his balls are out in the open. Watch the camel closely, and *just* before he pulls his head out of the water, take these two bricks and *wham!* right on his balls. He'll suck in 'shshshshshlooop!' and that will put on board 50 percent more water!" [as the laughter is dying down] "But doesn't that hurt?" "Not if you hold your thumbs back like so."

Michael Close (2007, pp. 23–24) provides us with an improved descendant of the Aggie cruise joke, which actually has *three* punch lines:

(98) Kowalski sees an enticing ad in the newspaper—Two Week Cruise to Bermuda, Only $79! He goes to the travel agency listed in the ad and purchases the $79 ticket. On the morning of the cruise, he arrives at the dock, walks up the gangplank, and shows his ticket to the steward. The steward looks at the ticket and blows a whistle; suddenly two big burly guys grab Kowalski and drag him below decks, where he is chained to an oar, next to an Armenian fellow.

As the day goes on, the hold of the ship fills up with people who have purchased the $79 cruise ticket. By three o'clock every seat is occupied. A big man comes in and sits down at a large drum. A man with a whip appears. A heavy "Boom, boom, boom" resonates through the hold as the drummer pounds out a cadence. Everyone grabs hold of the oars, and, under the prodding of the man with the whip, the unfortunate passengers row the cruise ship to Bermuda.

The trip takes three and a half days. When the ship docks in Bermuda, the steward comes down to the hold, "We're going to unchain you; you can leave the ship and have fun on the island. But be back here in seven days." The hold empties out in seconds.

A week passes and, of course, the $79-ticket passengers fail to return to the ship. But the cruise line was prepared; they send out squads of big, burly guys who track down the passengers, dragging them kicking and screaming back to the hold. They are again chained to the oars; the drummer takes his position, and "Boom, boom, boom," they row the ship back to New York.

By this time, Kowalksi has become good friends with the Armenian. As they are being unchained he says to him, "It is unbelievable that this type of inhuman treatment still exists in the world. This was a living nightmare. But I have to admit it: That guy was a hell of a drummer. [1] Do you think we should tip him?" [2]

The Armenian says, "Well, we didn't last year." [3]

Just as saccharine can supplant calorie-carrying sugar as the stimulator of our sweet tooth, and pornography can supplant actual coupling as the stimulator of the libido, so humor can jettison the serious business of error-cleansing that paid for the evolutionary invention and development of the funny bone, and get on with providing it with heightened and vicarious delights, supernormal stimuli generated by techniques that have been optimized by "intuitive" humor-engineers for centuries. Jokes, cartoons, caricatures, parodies, and other humorous artifacts are, then, like designer drugs, created deliberately, but with scant understanding of the underlying machinery that makes them work, and then delivered to the senses, rather than eaten, inhaled, or injected. Saccharine and other artificial sweeteners are like slugs that work when put in a coin slot: Their functional structure is practically indistinguishable by the "sweet tooth machinery" from sugar, so they trigger the payment of a reward for nothing actually valuable (from the point of view of the environmental conditions that prevailed when our sweet tooth evolved). Much humor is probably in the same category: It has the right structure to trigger the reward system without providing the benefit the system was designed for. Probably most of the errors our humor sentries detect and disarm are not all that dangerous, all that subversive to our data integrity, so if it weren't for the serious errors those sentries intercept on fairly rare occasions, the system wouldn't pay for itself and would be likely headed toward extinction. So contrary to the advertisements that bombarded us on television a few years ago, you *can* fool Mother Nature. All the arts are engaged in delivering artificial, supernormal slugs to pump extra rewards from our reward systems, and of course we don't mind, because we love the rewards for themselves, not for any distant genetic benefit they may still provide us.[6]

---

6. And once again, such by-products or spandrels can, of course, be immediately exapted to play further genuinely adaptive roles, either by genetic or cultural evolution. Our point is that it is a (quite common) mistake to assume that the survival of humor (or music, or

Comedians know to target their audiences with content that resides in highly accessible knowledge stores, where it is more quickly activated. So they tailor their routines to fit the crowd: stock market jokes for business-people, jokes about spouses for crowds of married folks, bathroom humor for children (of all ages), and sex, death, and current affairs for almost everyone. It requires just as much intuition to use these kinds of content to enhance humor—through transfer and misattribution of arousal (Dutton and Aron 1974; Cantor, Bryant, and Zillmann 1974; see also this vol., pp. 217–218)—as to create the humor itself. How do such inventors of humor direct their design efforts? By large amounts of trial and error, adjusting their wording, their timing, their facial expressions, to see what combination gets the heartiest laughter—a handy metric, delivered by a collection of black boxes whose inner workings they need not understand (except "intuitively") in order to be guided by its volume. They use them-selves as their first test beds, trying to gauge the effects on others by extrapolating from their own felt twinges of mirth, and one of the occu-pational hazards of this intense reflexive process is the phenomenon described by Carr and Greaves (2006, p. 80): "In the process of researching this book we must have sifted through over twenty thousand jokes, mostly in solitary silence. About halfway through the process Lucy [Greaves] went temporarily 'joke-blind'—an affliction that renders the suf-ferer incapable of distinguishing a funny joke from a hopeless one. Jimmy [Carr], already acclimatized to the strange and rarefied air of the high joke country, was completely unaffected."

The results of this process of testing and refining are a well-cultivated sense of the subtlety of an audience's perception structure, a polished understanding of joke structure, and, of course, *timing.*

Why does timing matter? Well, it only matters sometimes.[7] Some jokes are funny no matter who tells them; you can slow them down or speed them up significantly without appreciable effect on their potency. But

---

pornography, or dance, or . . .) would be jeopardized unless it contributed directly to genetic fitness somehow. In the case of humor, the (free-floating) rationale of humor could be shifting slowly away from data-integrity protection to sexually selected prowess-demonstration. The latter couldn't exist until and unless the former laid the foundations with a strongly supported reward system.

7. As noted in chapter 3, all humor depends on timing effects in some way, as they are generally ruined when told out of *order*—a property of time and position. But the most interesting curios-ity of timing in humor is that the same potentially hilarious remark or punch line, just a few seconds late, may lose all ability to amuse. Knowing just how and when these effects will occur is where the true art of subtlety lies.

there are other jokes that seem to *require* the artful touch of a master of subtlety and timing. When you retell such a joke to your friends and they don't laugh, you find yourself apologizing—"Well, you should have seen Eddie Izzard deliver it; he makes it hilarious!"

What does Izzard do differently than the rest of us? A master comic uses a variety of semantic tools to control the JITSA of an attentive audience. A well-timed glance, an expression of confusion or surprise or shame, or just a single word or gesture that refers to an earlier joke, can be used to significantly alter the spreading of semantic activation in an audience's mind. Well-known comics exploit shared beliefs about their quirks of personality (Jack Benny's stinginess, George Carlin's anarchistic streak, Joan Rivers's vanity) to prompt automatic assumptions in their audiences; in such cases, we have slim chance of repeating the joke with much success, even when we preface the retelling by citing our source.

And then there is timing—the most ineffable of all the qualities of joke delivery, and yet, well-predicted and laid out quite simply by the model of humor we've already described: During the process of JITSA, to make an improper commitment an audience will often require just enough time to make the necessary faulty inference without enough time to double-check it. Wait too long, and activation spreads further, increasing the chance that some conflicting piece of information will bring the key belief into epistemic doubt.[8] Once that occurs, the chance for humor is doomed. Too little time and the inference that leads to an improper commitment might never be made, as the mind is moving on to the next parts of the delivery and leaving the trail of JITSA surrounding the possible joke quickly fading into obscurity. These tools of timing are standard apparatus for professional rhetoricians, too—leading an audience down a path, activating contents just strong enough and long enough for them to seem coherent within their context, but not giving the listener enough time to bring in further context in order to determine whether or not what they are listening to is sound. In this way, a skilled rhetorician and a comedian are quite the same. The difference is that the comedian, soon after, lets you in on how they have misled you, while the orator has no such intention.

---

8. This creates a caveat for our theory also: For any possible instance of humor, there *may* be a timing effect that can help or hinder mirth elicitation. The dependency is on whether or not the key belief that would cause humor is put into epistemic doubt before being disconfirmed, or whether it is directly disconfirmed. Returning a belief to a condition of epistemic doubt *uncommits* it and thus abolishes its candidacy for humor.

Over the centuries there have been "instinctive" comedy creators with little accessible insight into their own "genius," and thoughtful, self-reflective comedy creators, with no discernible advantage gained from their attempts at theory. It is not surprising that comedic talent, like talent in art and music, has a reputation for being unanalyzable, ineffable, a gift that should not be disassembled, since it cannot be put back together again.[9] Magicians, in contrast, have been more methodical analysts of their methods, and the best are often erudite scholars of the history of their art.

What is the difference between stand-up comedians and stage magicians? The best magicians incorporate humor into their acts to great effect, and both practitioners depend on exquisite timing. The best of both, moreover, specialize in leading the minds in the audience down quite specific paths, imperceptibly nudging here and luring there, controlling people's thought processes to an amazing degree. As the magician Jamy Ian Swiss observes, in an insightful article detailing many of the triumphs of such mind control by magicians, "The fact is, there is no room for solipsism in magic. If the only mind you can imagine is your own, then the only person you will end up consistently fooling is yourself—and many spend lifetimes in magic doing just that" (Swiss 2007, p. 41). He quotes the magician Roberto Giobbi: "A magic effect doesn't take place in the hands of the performer, or on the platform he is standing, or in the props he is handling, but solely in the heads of the spectators" (ibid., p. 42). If this is so, and we think it is, then there are really just two main differences: Both comedians and magicians create conflict out of clarity, so the confusion you feel is *not their fault* but some misstep of your own, and the first difference is that magicians—when trying to amaze, rather than amuse (they do both!)—leave out important details that would help you debug it, and usually you have to just give up. You are left with a deep conflict, made palatable and even enjoyable by the magician's manner. Comedians, in contrast, give you just enough information that in most cases will dispel your momentary confusion. The second difference, of course, is that comedians typically work their brand of sleight of mind without any props, but only words and gestures.

---

9. It would be interesting to see if there are notable patterns discernible in the history of humor creation, like the patterns we find in musical composition, poetry, etc. What progressions (or even progress!) in style or content can be charted? How important is structural or thematic novelty? This investigation of details of cultural evolution is, however, beyond the scope of this book.

"On the other hand, maybe humor shouldn't be analyzed."

Figure 12.1
From <http://www.CartoonStock.com>.

D. Comedy (and Tragedy) in Literature

A panhandler approached a pedestrian on Broadway and asked for a small loan, to tide him over. The pedestrian replied haughtily: "Neither a borrower nor a lender be.—William Shakespeare." Said the panhandler: "Fuck you.—David Mamet."

What's the difference between a park bench and an English major?
A park bench can support a family of four.

There is a huge body of scholarly work on comedy in literature already, and it would be very interesting to show how our theory applies to this wealth of material, but for us even to begin to step into that discussion would fill another book (or two!). Rather than try our hands at such a task, we prefer to offer a few words of guidance, and a few caveats, to those who are more qualified for it.

If, as we expect, science begins to bear out our theoretical claims, we invite literary analysts and rhetoricians to apply our theory in their analyses. It would be interesting to see convincing analyses of how different authors have constructed various stimulus-delivery devices—not just sentences or short narratives but book-length passages, full of interludes and asides serving to distract a reader or create tangential priming effects that either influence tacit, covert commitment to various beliefs or, in third-person humor, portray those mistaken commitments in others. It would also be interesting to see how authors use different types of dénouement— sometimes instantaneously dramatic, other times in punctuated steps—to bring to light these overcommitted jumps to conclusions. And, of course, we expect to see virtuoso exploitation of the intentional stance. An author may craft the circumstances of humor not just in the reader's mind or in the characters' minds, but also in the reader's expectations about the narrator's intentions, or about the author's intentions about the reader's interpretation of the narrator's intentions, and so on. There is no end to the ways a creative author can construct humorous circumstances, though they will all depend, in some way, we claim, on the demolition of a belief commitment.

A note of caution: Such analyses, whether done under the framework of our theory or another theory, should not be expected to bring us much closer to an understanding of the nature of humor unless they attend to the dynamics of the emotional and cognitive effects induced in the brains of in the audience. Studying the stimulus-delivery devices (more traditionally known as the works of art) by themselves will never provide more than a superficial understanding of why they are vehicles of humor. (Nothing could be "intrinsically funny.")

Among the questions such analyses could illuminate are these: Why are some authors considered—by some people—to be funnier than others? What categories of comedy appeal to what tastes and why? What are the features by which we recognize the distinctive comic style of an author? When and why does the detachment of the voyeuristic perspective (Boorstin 1990; see our discussion above, pp. 140–141), which is more or less standard for jokes, get replaced by a more empathic perspective? The playwright Neil Simon, for instance, avoids jokes and wisecracks, and evokes humor from the untoward consequences of imbalances and weaknesses in characters for whom we care:

"When people care, even the slightest joke will get a big laugh, for they'll be so caught up in what's going on," he told *Playboy*. "If they *don't* care and are *not* caught up, you need blockbusters every two minutes and even that won't fulfill an audience." (Quoted in Lahr 2010, p. 73)

The answers to these and other questions are not going to be simple or singular, and they probably depend more on the traditional tools of literary analysis than on the cognitive mechanics of humor, though there will have to be some interplay. The fact that different comic styles all converge upon a central mechanism for humor does not make articulating their differences any easier—try taxonomizing styles of clothing, all of which are constrained in one way or another to cover some parts of the human body. Likewise, there are as many goals and motives for creating comedy as for cooking. Some folks create humor simply because they enjoy the reputation of being a funny person. Some put humor into their work for educational purposes—an offering of mind-candy to their readers to seduce their attention or to break down ill-examined presuppositions—or for sheer entertainment, only meant to increase enjoyment (and sales). Others have political agendas, and are satirizing social roles and habits with the intent of changing the balance of power in some domain—gender or class or income or ethnicity or, for that matter, academic discipline. Again, we think the traditional tools of literary analysis will have—and already have had—more to say on these topics than our theory does.

Many literary theorists have stressed the importance of what takes place in the minds of the audience or readers—"reader response" theorists are the paradigmatic school—and it is now possible to go beyond the informal concepts and introspective methods available to traditional analysts in the arts and humanities; we can start using concepts of cognitive science as a foundation for the analysis of literary achievement. Looking for events in the mind, and taking the JITSA view seriously, has consequences for understanding many of the effects authors generate—sometimes wittingly, other times not so wittingly. For instance, the distinguished Shakespeare expert Stephen Booth (emeritus professor of English literature at the University of California, Berkeley) argues for two important notions which we find particularly harmonious with our work. The first is the *ideational pun*, and the second is his view on tragedy.

An ideational pun, or "almost-pun," according to Booth's coinage, is "an interplay between an idea and word that could—but does not—express or relate to that idea" (Booth 1977, p. 465). An ideational pun provokes an event in the mind that *approaches* the status of humor, and which—if one reflects on it—one thinks must be funny somehow, but isn't sure how.

As Booth stresses, ideational puns are near or below the threshold of awareness; they do not draw attention to themselves, and hence any effect they
achieve is subtle. We have stressed the importance of consciousness in the
process of detecting the contradictions, which is a precondition of humor;
so ideational puns are not outright humor and do not of themselves incite
laughter, but they do incite microemotional twinges that sometimes let
you know they are there (especially if, like Booth himself, you are attuned
to their existence). Occasionally a reader might notice the almost-pun,
make conscious sense of it, perhaps even extrapolate to find it funny, and
then even wonder whether the author had intended it. From our perspective, this is an entirely optional issue; poets, like comedians, may have
little insight, let alone self-conscious intentions, about why and how
they achieve the effects that they have learned to produce. Booth puts it
this way:

> I mean to suggest by my commentary that Shakespeare uses syntactically and
> logically impertinent ideas, ideas latent in words because of their habitual uses in
> other contexts, in rather the way he uses rhythm and rhyme—that he "rhymes"
> ideas, and "rhymes" ideas with sounds, and makes rhythm-like patterns in which
> extra-syntactical meanings link to sounds or other extra-syntactical meanings
> or to meanings active in the syntax to give his sonnets extra-logical coherence.
> Shakespeare plays to the mental faculties that under cruder conditions cause us
> to make and understand puns. (1977, p. 371)

Let's use Booth's last phrase here to illustrate his point. Is he deliberately
creating the confusion between the verb *play* (the primary or intended
meaning) and the familiar association of *Shakespeare's plays* and, in a
context where he has just made a gibe about the "wanton ingenuity of
disciples of the new criticism," does his juxtaposition of *faculties* and *cruder*
echo that gibe and subliminally discredit the discoveries (or hallucinations)
of cruder academicians? For simplicity, let's make up a dead-obvious
example of an ideational pun:

The garden has flourished under their care, but now as Janina and her
lover part forever, she sees the tulips' leaves are wilting.

A straightforward analysis might note the obvious symbolism, the parallel
between their love story and the tulip's ebbing vitality, but what is more
interesting to someone attuned to Booth's perspective is what happens in
the reader's mind: The possessive *tulips'* has phonetic copies of the words
"two" and "lips," which, in the JITSA of a comprehender's mind will be
initially activated meanings. Normally, these activations would fade fast as
the disambiguation would be instantaneous, but since the situation

involves *two* lovers parting (and probably kissing, since that is a ready default fill-in when we hear of such a parting) there would be some priming, some pressure on hearing *tulips'*—even if it's not quite enough pressure to make a full misinterpretation—to activate the meanings for *two* and *lips* all the way to conscious strength. Into the bargain, we can add that the word "leaves" has a second interpretation as a verb, with similar cross-priming effects due to homonymy and the context. (It doesn't end there, of course.) No false interpretation is fully committed to; no full humor happens, but much of the same neural dynamics involved in humor is occurring, and the reader, without realizing it, may feel that there are more connections than necessary—more meaning than seen on the surface. That's why Booth calls it an "almost-pun."

Booth's second point in harmony with our view is his claim about the role of microemotions in Shakespeare's works (and all good literature, really). In his 1969 book, *An Essay on Shakespeare's Sonnets*, he describes how a reader's emotions *evoked by the experience of reading*, on a miniature scale, can reflect the semantic content of the work and deepen the experience of it. For example, regarding Sonnet 33, he says, "Each violation of the reader's confidence in his expectations about a syntactical pattern evokes a miniature experience for the reader that mirrors the experience of betrayed expectations which is the subject of the poem" (Booth 1969, p. 55). There is a series of microemotions, perhaps just beneath the threshold of consciousness, which color one's reading of the poem even if even if one cannot say how or why. Likewise, in a later book, he uses this notion to describe the role of "indefinition" in tragedy, and more specifically, in *King Lear*: "Shakespeare presents the culminating events of his *story* after his *play* is over. . . . The play makes its audience suffer *as* audience; the fact that *King Lear* ends but does not stop is only the biggest of a succession of similar facts about the play" (Booth 1983, p. 23). Like his view of ideational punning, this claim has the flavor of JITSA. For Booth, tragedy has a thoroughgoing dependence upon the repeated experience of microemotional confusion and uncertainty, evoked by the *indefinition* introduced by inconclusive acts and speeches. For Booth, tragedy is not so much a part of the content of a story as it is an experience in the audience of the consistent evocation and reevocation of these other epistemic emotions throughout the story. He says, "I submit that the tragedy of the play *Macbeth* is not of the character Macbeth and that it does not happen on the stage. The tragedy occurs in the audience, in miniature in each little failure of categories and at its largest in the failure of active moral categories to hold the actions and actors proper to them" (ibid., p. 109). It is the sum of all these little epistemic disappointments of "indefinition" that gives us a constant feeling of uncertainty throughout the play, and then leaves us lingering long after with a feeling we name *tragedy*.[10]

Our discussion of Booth's work is meant to provide an example of *one* of the ways we expect our theory to join forces with the researches of literary critics and theorists. We wish to forestall a familiar defensive response among thinkers in the humanities: we are not out to *replace* or *refute* their projects but rather to *underpin* and *enlarge* their perspective by going into psychological and biological details that they have ignored or postponed.[11]

E.   Humor That Heals

First the doctor told me the good news—I was going to have a disease named after me.

—Steve Martin

What do you give a man who has everything?
Antibiotics.

—Carr and Greeves (2006)

The idea of humor that heals is not new, as indicated by an old proverb: "Laughter is the best medicine," a version of which ("a merry heart doeth good like a medicine") dates back at least as far as the King James Bible (Proverbs 17:22, King James Bible; as cited in Martin 2001). However, finding doctors who take this adage seriously may be a fairly recent change. In 1971, Dr. Patch Adams and a group of friends established a medical clinic—the Gesundheit! Institute—founded on the principles of positive attitude, which notoriously included humorous entertainment as a form of treatment for their patients. The institute is still running today.

Others suggest laughter as a more preventative kind of treatment. Dr. Madan Kataria began the first Laughter Yoga Club in 1995 in India, though

---

10. An example that might be easier for modern audiences to grasp is the feeling you have after a movie that has left you with a number of questions and loose ends. There is so much epistemic dissatisfaction about this movie that you can't take it lightly, whether or not its *content* was dramatic or comedic. The effect is best coupled with dramatic content, but there is nothing wrong with mixing a certain amount of humor in as well.

11. Huron (2006) makes an eloquent plea for the same alliance of disciplines.

now there are chapters worldwide. Members of thousands of these clubs gather together regularly and go through breathing and laughing exercises. If nothing is funny, they even coerce themselves into non-Duchenne laughs until the situation appears so farcical that they are compelled to natural contagious laughter, which they continue to sustain for quite some time and which they believe improves their medical constitution. Keltner and Bonanno (1997) have shown that laughter—though only Duchenne laughter—predicts swifter recovery from bereavement. An interesting result, but keep in mind that causality could go either way here, and it is uncertain whether such laughter is simply a signal for the underlying mirth reward, another social sharing reward, perhaps both, or even some other factor. Whether humor and laughing actually have an effect on health is controversial, though many have speculated on the topic, and we will continue, cautiously, in that tradition of speculation.

Norman Cousins, longtime editor of the *Saturday Review*, who strongly supported the notion of emotions in healing, has become something of a folk legend since supposedly curing himself (he suffered from ankylosing spondylitis, a painful inflammatory arthritis of the spine) by self-medicating with a cocktail of vitamin C and laughter. Perhaps inspired by the telling of his story (Cousins 1979), many have explored, both scientifically and personally, the notion of humor that heals. However, the scientific evidence has been inconclusive. Numerous theories (e.g., Fry 1977, 1994; Kataria, Wilson, and Buxman 1999) and studies (e.g., Dillon, Minchoff, and Baker 1985; Lefcourt, Davidson-Katz and Kueneman, 1990; Lefcourt et al. 1997) have attempted to support this idea. However, in reviews of this literature and much more, Martin (2001, 2004) has disputed that there is any evidence of a health benefit to humor, supporting only the possibility that laughter provides some measure of analgesia. It's perhaps unsurprising that positive affect (laughter) should have a reducing or attenuating effect on negative affect (pain) under the unified formulation of emotions and other affective sensation that we argue for in chapter 6, keeping in mind the valence-competitive nature of emotions and their nature as perceptual stimuli competing for attention. Martin (2001, p. 514) even notes that "similar [analgesic effect] findings are obtained with [other] negative emotions . . . suggesting that the observed analgesic effects may be due to general emotional arousal regardless of affective valence." This is not to say that we should thoroughly discount the notion of humor that heals, only that the evidence to date has been weak. Martin's complaints are primarily methodological, and resolving them may allow for a more careful inquiry.

Our own addition to the speculations about humor that heals is unrelated to pain, and instead based on the fact that mirth is emotionally asymmetrical. Typically an emotion and the contents that elicit it are closely related—dangerous things cause fear, and beneficial things cause joy. But the positive affective state of mirth can be triggered by contents that are positive, negative, or even neutral, causing sometimes surprising effects (recall the positive emotions from violent video games or the laughter at tragedies mentioned in chapter 9). This feature of mirth, rare among emotions, can be—and probably has been—exploited in a number of ways. In his 2003 book *Deep Survival*, Laurence Gonzales describes how fighter pilots seem to use a form of dark humor as a tool to keep from panicking during dangerous takeoffs and landings on aircraft carriers. Joking about the disastrous—using the negatively valenced content to create a positively valenced emotion—gives them the necessary levity to perform their dangerous job. Another possibility that we hinted at earlier is that the positive affect can be used to disrupt a feedback loop of negative affect and negative contents.

The feedback loop is a classic recursive problem—a process whose output increases (or, at least, repeats) its own input (with a magnitude greater than any damping factors) is bound to continue forever until disrupted.[12] We are all familiar with feedback loops between microphones and speakers, but cognitive versions of this phenomenon exist too: For instance, the song that is stuck in your head is self-activating—given the cyclical nature of tunes, humming the last stanza often compels you to start over at the

---

12. Here is a joke exemplifying the idea of feedback, adapted from Cathcart and Klein (2007):

It was autumn, and the Indians on the reservation asked their chief if it was going to be a cold winter. Raised in the ways of the modern world, the chief had never been taught the old secrets. To be on the safe side, he advised the tribe to collect wood. A few days later, just to be sure, the chief called the National Weather Service and asked whether they were forecasting a cold winter. The meteorologist replied that, indeed, he thought it would be. The chief advised the tribe to stock even more wood.

A couple weeks later, the chief checked in again with the weather service, "Does it still look like a cold winter?" he asked. "It sure does," replied the meteorologist, "it looks like a *very* cold winter." So the chief advised the tribe to gather up every scrap of wood they could find.

A couple of weeks later, the chief called the Weather Service yet again and asked how the winter was looking at that point. The meteorologist said, "We're now forecasting that it will be one of the coldest winters on record!"

"Really?" said the chief. "How can you be so sure?"

The meteorologist replied, "The Indians are collecting wood like crazy!"

beginning. A more troubling kind of cognitive feedback loop happens with depressing thoughts—in this case, the negative emotion from the initial thought lingers in the mind and may compel one to review what has caused this feeling. Such a review stimulates negative thoughts (perhaps the same one, perhaps others) in spreading activation, which further engenders negative emotions. The cycle may then continue from there.[13]

A feedback cycle of such negative content can be psychologically damaging, and if related behavior follows, even physically damaging. In some cases, humor may be just the necessary cure for this kind of cycle: If those same negative thoughts can be turned around, by a humorous transposition, to engender the positive emotion of mirth, then there is a chance that the feedback cycle could be, if not permanently broken, at least temporarily blocked. The hypothesis of humor as a "distraction from negative affect" has also been offered by Strick et al. (2009). They showed this kind of distraction to work in the short term, and we think it may be able to scale up to be applied to the kind of emotional feedback loop of moods that we describe here. There may be some justification, then, in the old quip that "laughter is the best medicine"—humor just may play a role in healing depressive cycles.

---

13. We don't claim that this feedback cycle is the cause for clinical depression, though there is no reason why, in some cases, it might not be partially involved. Clinical depression more likely turns on a more general affliction of the emotional motivation system. Sadness in depressed patients may be a resultant *tendency*—an emotional disposition caused by witnessing themselves in such an undermotivated state—"Why am I like this?" such patients ask themselves in confusion, indicating metacognitive disappointment due to the state.

13 The Punch Line

And so these men of Indostan
Disputed loud and long,
Each in his own opinion
Exceeding stiff and strong,
Though each was partly in the right,
And all were in the wrong!

—John Godfrey Saxe *The Blind Men and the Elephant: A Hindoo Fable* (1873)

The fable about the blind men and the elephant is replayed often in science and philosophy. The many theories of humor that have been raised over the years (see chapter 4) have not been all wrong—they each described some important aspect of the elephant. Each has been wrong only in declaring itself an alternative to all the others. Taking the Hindu fable to heart, and recognizing that we are all in the position of the blind men when looking at nature, can help us realize that all that is missing is a way of unifying the various descriptions of the elephant—of joining the parts that each theorist has wrapped his hands around—to show that they all are right.

Humor involves a mental space that contains a false belief, a mistaken construction, and hence indicates that someone is the maker of that mistake. The laugher is always the one who has just discovered the mistake, and when the mistake-discoverer is also the mistake-maker, one might suppose that the appropriate emotional response would be chagrin or dismay or even shame or anger, but nature has arranged to tilt the balance in favor of glorying in the discovery, as Hobbes says, instead of sulking. The laugher, as the mistake-discoverer, will typically feel some degree of superiority over whoever made the mistake, and that could be, as Hobbes said, either another person, or a previous version of oneself. The superiority theorist thus gets some vindication, for there is always a factor of judgment in humor: This is obvious in the cases of humor that inspired the superiority thesis, the genre in which there is another person or group that is the butt of the joke. In cases of impersonal humor, the superiority enjoyed is one's later self over one's earlier self; one has discovered a bug and repaired it; one is suddenly a little bit better, a little bit wiser, a little bit more in the know. Furthermore, superiority theory gave us the insight that the (misattributed) joys of Schadenfreude, or insult to a competitor or outgroup, adds to the joy of humor. Incongruity-resolution theorists will find their insights deeply embedded and generalized within our model—incongruity is a common way to lead one into either making or discovering a mistaken commitment—and it should come as no surprise that surprise theorists will also find some vindication. Surprise is the response when a specific expectation is broken, and the recognition that a committed active belief is false is exactly that. First-person humor should be surprising, and in the third person, if the false belief we discover in another is not one we ourselves would have committed to, we still often find it surprising that the third person would have committed to it. The rapidity of change is what gives us the sense of surprise in humor. It is not surprise itself that brings humor into existence, however, but rather the fact that the engendering episode often contains a structure whose sudden debugging causes coincident surprise. To make it clearer: If the debugging wasn't rapid, if instead it was a slow dawning, then the intermediate stage of that dawning—the act of *doubting* the belief—would *remove the commitment* preemptively before we had the evidence to actually destroy it. Shortly later we discover the falseness of the now not-committed belief, but that is not enough to cause humor. There would be no instantaneous discovery. Even release (and ambivalence) theorists can find some support for their intuitions in this model. Huron's trampoline, the vanishingly brief negatively valenced emotional response that heightens the positive rebound, applies to humor as it does to music. And not only do we agree that the core of humor is the positive emotion that attends the debugging, but when there is anxiety or confusion or some other negative affect in the prehumorous circumstances, the humorous discovery very probably does bring a measure of relief, and hence can be expected to have been appreciated by would-be therapists over the ages, in the same way that they have recognized the analgesic properties of herbs and treatment rituals. Comedians, musicians, confectioners, pornographers, and shamans are only five varieties of practitioners who have figured out, by trial and error, how to exploit the underlying biases in our nervous systems to achieve effects their clients crave.

A. Twenty Questions Answered

Analyzing humor is like dissecting a frog. Few people are interested and the frog
dies of it.
—E. B. White

We can see now why each of the traditional theories of humor was produced. Each was right in some rather deep way. Each clued us in to some
important aspect of the way humor operates. Now that we've presented
our model, let's see how it answers the questions we posed as desiderata,
and assure ourselves that we have a full explanation of humor. At this
point, many of our answers will sound rather repetitive, and some of them
perhaps even mundane and obvious. Nonetheless it is worth checking our
list to ensure we've answered them all cohesively.

✓1. *Is humor an adaptation?* Humor is one part of the emotional mechanism that encourages the process that keeps data integrity in our knowledge representation. This process ensures that we reduce the likelihood of
making faulty inferences and fatal mistakes. Without a trait like this, a
cognitive agent as complex as we are would be practically guaranteed a
quick death.

Tooby and Cosmides point out that evolutionarily acceptable explanations for human engagement in aesthetic activities, such as the creation
of and engagement with fictions, fall into two categories: The first (which
they endorse) is that these activities serve (or once served) an adaptive
purpose that may be difficult to suss out. The second possible explanation
is that these behaviors are an accidental not-too-damaging by-product of
other adaptive functions. We basically agree with their arguments for
putting the arts into the first category: These things do help in "organizing
the brain both physically and informationally" (Tooby and Cosmides 2001,
p. 14). The building of mental spaces and the manipulation and organization of data done therein allows for stable and *reliable* knowledge. We claim
further that the process of directing these mental "aesthetic" behaviors is
performed by another set of traits: the epistemic emotions.

Our theory of humor, however, bridges both of Tooby and Cosmides'
categories of evolutionary explanation. There is, we claim, an original
adaptive purpose for mirth and the epistemic emotions—to encourage a
particular task of knowledge maintenance—and this puts these traits firmly
into Tooby and Cosmides' first category, along with the other fictions and
arts. But that original function recedes into the background when one

considers the countless hours that humans devote to humor consumption today. Jocular memes, some designed by inadvertent mutation and differential cultural replication—folk funnies, you might call them—and some the products of intelligent (re-)design by comedians, have hijacked the innate funny bone machinery and exploited it to further their own proliferation. Our resulting humor addiction (see questions 3 and 17 below) is not particularly debilitating, and brings lots of pleasure to us—which matters more to us than our genetic fitness, of course.

✓2. *Where did humor come from?* The simplest organisms that can learn anything ("Skinnerian" as opposed to "Darwinian" hard-wired organisms; Dennett 1975, 1995, pp. 373–383) have an innate feature of their nervous systems that "rewards" or reinforces any circuit that captures some local regularity in the environment and directs an appropriate response to it, seeking the good and fleeing the bad. Such organisms can thereby acquire useful habits in their own lifetimes, but they don't really *represent* their options (to themselves) because they have no mental space in which to "consider" them; they just execute them whenever they are called. A more advanced brain builds up something more like a mental model, a structure that can store information about the world to be consulted as necessary ("Popperian" creatures). It is here that the simplest form of data integrity checking must arise. If new input contradicts what is stored in the model, something must give, and something must sort out, fallibly, what stays and what goes. Later in evolution came a mind with the ability to keep multiple mental spaces, opening the door to "Gregorian" creatures, capable of entertaining fictions and counterfactuals (Fauconnier and Turner 2002) and "theory of mind" (the intentional stance), as well as creativity and problem solving along with the more sophisticated forms of humor that we see today.

As we have seen, laughter, our most salient response to humor, probably shares ancestry with the play panting and false-alarm calls of chimpanzees and other primates, but amusement at the plight of others, or more elaborate forms of nonlinguistic humor such as practical jokes, have not been observed—though it must be granted that there is always a chance that observers have not known what to look for, or how to interpret what they have observed. The controversy over whether, or to what extent, chimpanzees "have a theory of mind" (Premack and Woodruff 1978) has been waged for twenty years without resolution (Dennett 1983, 1998; Savage-Rumbaugh and Lewin 1994; Povinelli and Eddy 1996; Tomasello, Call, and Hare 2003; Griffin and Dennett 2008), but on even the most *romantic* (as contrasted with *killjoy*; Dennett 1983) interpretation of the experimental work to date, chimpanzees have at best a rudimentary appreciation of the minds of others, and thus the breadth of humor that is due to social circumstance and others' perspectives (which is the bulk of humor) is lost to them, and presumably to all other species. Chimpanzees have considerable powers of expectation, but nothing (as best we can tell so far) to rival ours, so if they engage in time-pressured heuristic search, it is presumably a simpler and lower-dimensional search space. Perhaps, then, they do have a humor-like mechanism designed by evolution to maintain data integrity, but if so, it shows no signs of explosive elaboration like ours. We concur with Deacon: "I suspect that implicit in the notion of humor there is a symbolic element, a requirement for recognizing contradiction or paradox, that the average chimpanzee has not developed" (Deacon 1997, p. 73).

Additionally, we may be the only species with the ability to create mental spaces for any context other than the present reality. Our ability to maintain fictions or counterfactual scenarios in a number of mental spaces gives us much more opportunity for humor. If apes have a humor-like mechanism that operates in the first-person present perceptual reality for them, they have no provision for communicating any discoveries they make, and hence no practice—beyond their play behaviors and false-alarm calls—to which to attach laughter.

✓3. *Why do we communicate humor?*   The communication of humor may have begun as a way of causing our conspecifics to know that we were only half-serious with them during mock-aggression and play. The effect was that these joint behaviors would not aggressively escalate in violence. Later, laughter was co-opted for usage in more complex social circumstances, especially the mate-attracting display of intellect and the trading of social capital in various manners. Telling and retelling humorous stories and other jokes is a form of humor communication that evolved (culturally—there is no need to posit a comedian gene) to exploit this semivoluntary communicative disposition of laughter. In telling a joke, we show that we appreciate a particular instance of humor—and think our listeners will, too. (Telling somebody a joke is as much flattery as showing off.) Humor evolves into a medium for the display of intelligence and mutual knowledge and opinion.

Jokes, as memes (or "rogue cultural variants"; Richerson and Boyd 2005), can then hitch rides on this well-designed and well-maintained information highway. Exploiting the intrinsic appetite for humor that evolved by genetic selection, these quasi-independent informational entities can foster their own replication (rehearsal in the individual and eventual retelling) independently of any fitness advantage they specifically offer to their hosts. Like Internet spam, stupid and disgusting humor that would be unlikely to favorably impress a potential mate, or even a rival or ally, can thrive in this medium, "bad habits" that are hard to erase and annoyingly infectious. And such rogue cultural variants can go on to create their own escalating arms races, in emerging cultural ecosystems that take on a life of their own (as illustrated in the recent film *The Aristocrats*).

✓4. *Why do we feel pleasure in humor?* The pleasure of mirth is an emotional reward for success in the specific task of data-integrity checking. This is designed (by evolution) to motivate us to persist in this particular cognitive behavior in the future. Mirth is thus related to, and is often accompanied by, the pleasure of discovery, but they are distinct: They reward distinct cognitive behaviors. This perspective draws our attention to a striking and unexpected linkage: Our playful love of humor and our serious allegiance to the Law of Noncontradiction have a common ancestor in the evolution of an effective control system for our time-pressured heuristic search engines: our brains.

✓5. *Why do we feel surprise in humor?* The explicit razing of a previously committed belief in a mental space can be nothing if not surprising. In the first person, then, humor should always be at least mildly surprising, and, much of the time, it will be surprising in the third person too.

✓6. *Why is judgment a ubiquitous component in the content of humorous stimuli?* When a mental space is invalidated there is always a subjective component of rightness or wrongness delivered by the logic employed: After all, a mistake has been made and uncovered. All humor, therefore, makes judgments. The fact that in much humor there is also a judgment of nobility/ignobility arises from the further exploitation of humor for socially competitive purposes.

✓7. *Why does humor often get used for disparagement?* In the armamentarium of human competition, scorn, insult, and mocking are well-tested weapons. Putting someone down by *humorously* demonstrating an infirmity in their cognitive capacities efficiently makes the humorist *and the addressed audience* look superior in comparison, enlisting the audience as like-minded allies and at the same time making the humorist appear good natured, not just angry or aggrieved. This is a common use of humor in modern society, but not its original or even secondary purpose, which is more plausibly the demonstration of intellectual prowess (with or without a target or butt of the joke) to potential mates and allies.

✓8. *Why does humor so often point to failures?* Because that's exactly what it does: It points out failures and mistakes in a mental model. It also brings remedies for those mistakes along with them, but the remedies are only a common side effect. The identification of failure is central to humor.

✓9. *What is the role of nonsense or incongruity in humor?*   The sense of nonsense comes from the exposed (if typically unarticulated) contradiction that must underlie any faulty inference in a mental space.

✓10. *If incongruity causes humor, how does it do it?*   It is not incongruity in a stimulus that causes humor; it just happens to be the case that incongruity in a stimulus often plays a part in the discovery of a faulty mental space and its deconstruction.

✓11. *Why is it that we only laugh at humans or anthropomorphized objects?*   Only a mind is furnished with the necessary components for humor. Either you are laughing at something in your own mind, or you are laughing at something that has a mind or to which we might counterfactually attribute a mind.

✓12. *What is right about Bergson's claim that mechanical behavior is humorous?*   The mechanical, as Bergson intended it, happens when someone acts repeatedly on an assumption that is not true in all circumstances. The person has not just a faulty mental space, but a persistent habit of making the same faulty mental space over and over again. The larger fault is the failure to detect and debug this bug-making bug. This form of repetitious humor thus exploits our capacity to "go meta" and notice the patterns in others' representations of their worlds that are suboptimal. Our capacity to generate ever higher metalevels of mental spaces is impressive, but still finite, and any persistent failure we uncover by this process of ascent strikes us as "mechanical."

✓13. *Why can humor be used as a social corrective?*   Humor works as a social corrective because it points out mistakes, sometimes rather publicly. In order to avoid this publicity of our shortcomings, we attempt to avoid risking making such mistakes, and thus humor relatively gently encourages revisions of behavior.

✓14. *What is similar that unites the broad variety of types of humorous stimuli?*   This should be obvious by now. All types of humorous stimuli contribute to a mental space being constructed and subsequently being found to contain an overcommitted belief.

✓15. *How does play relate to humor?*   While the many variations of play have their own purposes, some forms of play, including tickling and other games (notably chasing), are probably the earliest forms of (proto-)humor; they involve broken expectations and suddenly revised models, yet do not require a full-blown theory of mind. It is also likely that social play is the original source of laughter, which evolved into the natural expression of humor detection.

✓16. *What is the relationship between problem solving, discovery and humor?* The similarity, noted by Deacon, Koestler, and others, between "Ha-ha!" and "Aha!," derives from their common co-occurrence and the similar mechanics of problem solving often used in both. Though each may crop up unaccompanied, it is not uncommon for the solution of a gap in comprehension (which causes the feeling of discovery) to facilitate humor. The newly added jigsaw puzzle pieces from problem solving may complete a part of the puzzle, and at the same time add a new contradiction which helps to pinpoint a mistaken belief—a previously misplaced piece of the puzzle—thus causing mirth.

✓17. *Why do we desire humor so intensely?* We have a powerful appetite for humor because the emotional reward it provides was designed to foster the habit of searching for surreptitiously included mistakes in our mental spaces. Evolution had no idea that we would eventually turn this desire into an addiction to comedy that supports a multibillion dollar industry of television production, cartoons, books, comedy clubs, and the like. Sugar tastes good and humor feels good. We trade, sell, and buy artifacts such as jokes, cartoons, and movies, which capitalize on the fact that we get joy from debugging. We then can use them to *create* bugs in our mental spaces, which we can then enjoy debugging in a sort of mental masturbation, rewarded not with orgasm but with mirth.

✓18. *What is the peculiar specificity often found in humor?* The mental models that can be created in a mind are specific to the knowledge that person has. Any humor that is created in an individual mind is subject to the constraints of the knowledge that is available there. Humor does not depend on actual truth; it depends on consistency. (Some mental spaces are largely fictional, but they still have their mutually shared default assumptions; witches ride brooms, not hockey sticks, and dragons breathe fire, not snowflakes.) Thus, a person could laugh at something that is not funny to the general population if that thing were found to be inconsistent in some way with some part of that person's knowledge representation.

✓19. *What is the generality in humor?* Many things are common knowledge for humans, since we live in the same world. We are likely, to a large extent, to have very similar knowledge structures and to use these to develop very similar mental spaces. So it is not surprising that we will all find many of the same things funny.

✓20. *Why are there gender differences in humor?* The assessment of intelligence certainly plays a role in sexual selection, and as humor became more and more used for purposes of sexual competition, the gender divide of the trait would tend to have widened. However, this is almost certainly more of a social effect than an innate difference—a debugging mechanism that serves epistemic purposes will be equally useful for both genders. Provine's (2000) data show a bias for males to compete more aggressively in humor creation and females to compete among themselves in humor connoisseurship. But, if this evidence does not necessarily indicate a greater *capacity* for humor in men than women, what is responsible for it?

We mentioned before that the art of unconscious prospecting will equally apply to Dutton and Aron's (1974) transfer of arousal as it does to hidden rewards such as mirth, or more tangible overt rewards such as sweetness. Individuals may tacitly learn, through causing various kinds of arousal and enjoyment *in others*, that their efforts are repaid in attention, friendliness . . . or even *attraction*. These recompenses reward the prospector and encourage repetition of the act that brought them on. We thank an anonymous reviewer for bringing to our attention that this kind of prospecting is most likely used, not just by comedians and between friends as we said earlier, but also by males in pursuit of females.

Despite the recent empowerment of women caused by a growing feminist movement, the profound biological differences between males and females due to differential reproductive costs (Trivers 1972) still cast their shadows in our modern culture: For the most part, males actively pursue the attention of females. Any activity that can induce in a female a more favorable stance toward a male will be useful to the goals of pursuit, and so males—more than females—may learn, through this reinforced behavioral prospecting, that humor production is an effective strategy because of transfer of arousal. Their ensuing exploitation of this strategy would certainly produce the gender differences we see in Provine's data.

Here is how transfer of arousal could play a role in courtship-by-humor (much as in Dutton and Aron's original bridge experiment): The positive arousal in a humor appreciator caused by the mental event of satisfactory detection of an overcommitted false belief could be transferred (with imprecise credit-assignment) to positive arousal about the person one is with during this event. Our earlier point about sexual competition still holds—members of both genders should be likely to judge each other's intellectual capacity through observation of both humor production and appreciation, and this tool should be used in mate selection. However, the transfer-of-arousal-in-pursuit effect offers a better account of the strong bias toward more male humor production.

Another suggestion, by Carr and Greeves (2006), may play a role as well. They say, quite bluntly, "[Men] don't want women to be funny. They won't let women make them laugh" (p. 154). The idea is that men tacitly know that humor production is a signal of intelligence, and that creating a culture of suppression of such signals from women will give them an advantage. In order to enforce their desired gender roles (mostly unconsciously) through humor, male competitive aggression plays out not just in making better jokes than the other guy, or using jokes to disparage the other guy, but also in creating an environment in which men will be seen as more capable (more witty) and women as subservient—better positioned in the humor realm as appreciators of men's wit. All the more reason to applaud the women who brave the stand-up stage, despite this social force.

B. Could We Make a Robot with a Sense of Humor?

Yesterday my friend's computer beat me at chess, but it was no match for me in kick-boxing.
—Emo Philips

The question is not whether intelligent machines can have any emotions, but whether machines can be intelligent without any emotions.
—Minsky (1986)

A fine way to test a theory is to build an instantiation of it and see if it works as advertised. We are nowhere near ready to write the code and install it in a robot, but we can expose the strengths and look for weaknesses in our theory *sketch* by thought-experimentally considering that task in enough detail to clarify the specs for a humorous robot. Suppose, then, we set ourselves the task of engineering a robot that not only told jokes and sought them out, but responded to humor with *genuine* laughter. (It might respond to social pressures with robot-Duchenne laughter as well, but our goal would be to make it capable of genuine amusement and hence genuine laughter.)

A trivial and unsatisfying "solution" to this problem would be to develop a standard modern machine-learning algorithm that could use syntactic and semantic features as cues to detect (with a high probability) whether a joke or other event would be judged humorous according to the hypothesis it developed from its training set, and then output a laugh or other signal if (and only if) humor were found. Such a system, it seems, would "behave the way we do" but only superficially. Even if it were, amazingly, good at *generating* humor for human consumption, it would not, it seems, *appreciate* the humor it detected or generated, and its laughter would be hollow indeed. Our theory shows what is missing: The cognition required to discover humor must be motivated by an emotional drive, and the system of emotions that thus controls cognition must exist for a computational reason—not merely as a facade to satisfy the skeptics. (It would be an interesting exercise to write a computer program for doing, say, long division problems of the sort that give people trouble simply because of their size, and then giving it a human-like fallible memory of the multiplication table, distractability, and competing tasks that could lead it into error. It might provide a persuasive model of difficult concentration—the sort that twelve-year-olds may or may not muster when solving such problems—but this difficulty would be artificially imposed on it, for the sake of the modeling exercise.) In short, the robot would have to be in an epistemic predicament something like ours: under time pressure, drowning in a combinatorial explosion of possibly relevant anticipation-candidates, and hence—*hence*—obliged to take risks that lead to unsupervised and unflagged insertions of bugs that could later thwart its serious goals.

We must resist the temptation to divide the emotional and cognitive components and model them separately, engineering the cognitive aspect by creating an agent that can maintain data consistency in its knowledge representation and then engineering the emotional aspect by creating an agent that can get a good feeling from hearing jokes and engaging in socially mediated enjoyment. This separation would be self-defeating, since the emotional aspect needs a trigger to turn it on *appropriately*, and that trigger must come from the detection of the right kind of (mis-) information by a cognitive process with the right kind of demands on it. Suppose it were possible to design a cognitive agent that had so much computing speed at its disposal that it could "automatically" maintain data-integrity without any trade-offs that obliged it to take risky shortcuts (impossible in reality, but suppose it). The punch line of every joke would be "telegraphed" to it. While it might have a model of its human companions that enabled it to see the point of human humor, and even create it (the way a sophisticated author of children's books might have a deft touch at creating effects that would delight or move children without being in the least bit moved by them), it would have none of the cognitive frailties escape from which grounds the positive emotion that would permit it to *enjoy* humor for itself. It would find Oscar Wilde and Robin Williams to be slow-witted belaborers of obvious connections—and would respond to their most hilarious moments the way we quick-witted adults do to the most inane of children's riddles.

If, on the other hand, our artificial cognitive agent faced the same sorts of overwhelming epistemic demands we do, and its designers solved the problem with an emotionally driven competitive reward system somewhat like ours, it would be in a position to "know from the inside" how delightful humor can be, even if its own brand of humor was as practically incommunicable to us Westerners as Korean humor (see chapter 3, section E)—and for the same reason: We don't share enough deep background "knowledge." So if the goal of our endeavor were to engineer something that had the capacity to create and appreciate humor across cultural borders with humans—a machine that could join us at social events or theater productions and laugh together with us, tell jokes, and make witty commentary—then we might be in for a disappointment. The model of the world that exists in the knowledge structure of an agent depends crucially on the set of sensors with which the agent detects the world, and the perceptual architecture behind them. Slight differences in perceptual structure will gather subtly different assessments of the gross regularities of the world—analogous to the way color-blindness or differences in olfactory sensitivity can skew our individual human perceptual worlds, but in every dimension of difference that is perceptible—and these broad differences in perceptual structure can have a profound impact on an agent's model of the world. Not only would our artificial cognitive agent require a phenomenological worldview that is drastically similar to the human view to find most of the same things funny, it would also require a desire to censor and flaunt its humor feathers in the way humans do for each other so that it would laugh in the same ways. This is the germ of truth behind the clichés about the "Martian" sensibilities of robots—or people from other ethnic or social or occupational backgrounds. When interacting cross-culturally, people often attribute either irrationality or awkwardly false beliefs to members of another culture when they behave in ways that do not make sense to us, or laugh at something that we cannot find funny. It is unlikely, then, that anything that is not structurally equivalent—or very close to equivalent—to humans will have the same sense of humor as humans.

It should now be clear why we claimed at the beginning that the problem of engineering artificial humor is AI-complete. Humor is dependent on nearly all the skills and tools of general cognition, but those skills and tools are also, in us if not in all conceivable robots, dependent on the specific architectural structures that underlie our sense of humor. Our limitations as anticipation-generators are not just a historical happenstance, a weakness of the neurochemical implementation that evolution discovered for our cerebral computer architecture, but rather an inevitable feature of our finitude, no matter how our control systems were engineered. As long as an agent has less than complete information about the world it inhabits, it must proceed heuristically, and the task of maintaining data integrity in the wake of that risky leaping needs to be controlled by some process that can compete successfully with the other demands on the agent's resources. We are not attempting to prove that there is no *conceivable* way this control could be implemented other than by something like the epistemic emotions that govern us (perhaps pseudo-emotions that meet the same computational needs), but perhaps this is so. In that case, we would have to conclude that *Star Trek*'s character, Data, is actually a cognitive perpetual motion machine, not really possible in the universe as we know it. Be that as it may, we do claim to have produced a model that explains both the data on humor and our responses to it and supports the folklore that finds a connection between a sense of humor and practical, social intelligence.

If we ever set out to produce a robot that has epistemic capacities strong enough to perform the kind of reasoning we do, we must endow it with something like humor and the other epistemic emotions.

Epilogue

There are two kinds of people in this world: Those who require closure

This completes our attempt to lay the groundwork for an empirical theory of humor and the brain, explaining why humor exists, how it arises from our brain's activities, and why comedy is an art. Like earlier work on humor, ours attempts to find and describe patterns in the wealth of humor phenomenology, but unlike earlier theorists, we have tried to ground our speculations in a realistic model of the cognitive and emotional processes occurring in human brains, and also to account for why and how such remarkable phenomena could have evolved in the first place.

If we are right, the hope of distilling the essence of humor just by studying the history and structure of humorous texts and other artifacts and stimuli is systematically forlorn, like studying the molecular structure of glucose in search of its intrinsic sweetness. Just as the diverse set of green things share only the property of having a common effect on normal human color vision systems, the even more diverse set of funny things can be identified only by their similar effects on properly tuned normal human cognitive and emotional systems. And since those systems vary widely in individual human beings, exquisitely sensitive to differences in culture and experience, the prospect of a one-size-fits-all recipe for humor-creation is close to nil. Indeed, as we have shown, since the scope of humor will always keep pace with, and even on occasion accelerate the expansion of, the scope of human thought, its domain is ever shifting, growing in some areas and contracting in others, as species of humor go extinct for want of suitably furnished brains to inhabit.

There are many ways of studying the brain. David Huron (2006) has shown that the phenomena of music make excellent probes for studying the dynamics of human brain activity, because culture over the centuries has prospected the brain's auditory sensitivies and found ways of amplifying the effects in human responses, highlighting some of the foibles and predilections of our cognitive machinery. Humor, we argue, is a similarly valuable source of highly refined stimuli to explore the brain's powers.

Humor proves to be an ideal instrument, in fact, for examining the penumbral, covert elements in anybody's conscious states (their mental spaces), since although they cannot be introspected without interfering with them by raising their profiles in consciousness, we can often argue with confidence from readily observed effects to covert causes: You simply could not be amused by joke J if you didn't already know that p, and your knowledge or belief has to be active but covert. You may not realize (until someone like us comes along and dismantles the joke in slow motion) that you "entertained" these propositions at all, and may sincerely deny having been conscious of them, but if they weren't activated enough to generate your failed expectation, you would not now be laughing. Humor, then, can be used as a sort of cognitive sonar probe that generates perceptible echoes of otherwise "invisible" mental contents.

Putting subjects in scanners and then telling them jokes to see what lights up is a well-begun research effort, but it is only the first wave of informal exploration, laying the foundations and locating the landmarks for more telling experiments that will test actual models of the cognitive processes involved. The model we have sketched has been deliberately noncommittal at this early stage about many measurable dynamical and structural features, but the way has been paved for putting more detailed versions to the test, against their own variations, and, of course, against any other models that are proposed. Any model worth testing in the lab should first be shown to be capable of handling the mountains of evidence already assembled about what makes people laugh. We are swimming in empirical data—the libraries full of comedies, cartoons, jokes, and carica-tures that have accumulated over the centuries—and a lot can be inferred from this variety about the constraints on *any* acceptable model of humor appreciation. As centuries of frustrated theorists demonstrate, it is hard to come up with a hypothesis that has any hope of covering all that ground, so the first order of business is, as we think we have demonstrated, to canvass the existing proposals, extract the insights from them, and try to construct a skeletal theory that *could* do justice to it all. This project by itself already casts long shadows over ideas about how the brain operates, strongly favoring models that rely on emotional dynamics to control all aspects of cognition, and motivating the search for larger-scale, more neu-rally realistic models of just-in-time spreading activation. Our sketch has deliberately remained neutral about the options here, content for the time being with the task of setting some of the performance specs for a successful model. In the meantime, there are plenty of ways to test our model, which puts some quite severe restrictions for what can be funny: Find something manifestly unfunny that the model predicts to be funny, or find something funny that evades our model in one way or another. We look forward to seeing if the theory can meet this challenge.

References

Ainslie, G. 2001. *Breakdown of Will*. New York: Cambridge University Press.

Alexander, R. D. 1986. Ostracism and indirect reciprocity: The reproductive significance of humor. *Ethology and Sociobiology* 7 (3–4):253–270.

Anderson, J. 1983. A spreading activation theory of memory. *Journal of Verbal Learning and Verbal Behavior* 22:261–295.

Anderson, J. R. 1976. *Language, Memory, and Thought*. Hillsdale, NJ: Lawrence Erlbaum.

Apter, M. J. 1982. *The Experience of Motivation: The Theory of Psychological Reversals*. London: Academic Press.

Aristotle. 1954. *The Rhetoric and Poetics*. Trans. Rhys W. Roberts. New York: Modern Library.

Arnold, M. B. 1960. *Psychological Aspects*, vol. 1: *Emotion and Personality*. New York: Columbia University Press.

Arroyo, S., R. P. Lesser, B. Gordon, S. Uematsu, J. Hart, P. Schwerdt, K. Andreasson, and R. S. Fisher. 1993. Mirth, laughter, and gelastic seizures. *Brain* 116:757–780.

Ashraf, A. B., S. Luceya, J. F. Cohn, T. Chena, Z. Ambadara, K. M. Prkachin, and P. E. Solomona. 2009. The painful face—pain expression recognition using active appearance models. *Image and Vision Computing* 27:1788–1796.

Attardo, S. 2001. *Humorous Texts: A Semantic and Pragmatic Analysis*. Berlin: Mouton de Gruyter.

Azim, E., D. Mobbs, B. Jo, V. Menon, and A. L. Reiss. 2005. Sex differences in brain activation elicited by humor. *Proceedings of the National Academy of Sciences of the United States of America* 102:16496–16501.

Bain, A. 1875. *The Emotions and the Will*, 3rd ed. London: Longmans & Green.

Barber, E. W., and P. T. Barber. 2004. *When They Severed Earth from Sky: How the Human Mind Shapes Myth*. Princeton: Princeton University Press.

Baron-Cohen, S., A. M. Leslie, and U. Frith. 1985. Does the autistic child have a "theory of mind"? *Cognition* 21 (1):37–46.

Bartlett, F. C. 1932. *Remembering*. Oxford: Oxford University Press.

Bergen, B., and S. Coulson. 2006. Frame-shifting humor in simulation-based language understanding. In "Trends & Controversies: Computational Humor," ed. Kim Binsted. *IEEE Intelligent Systems* 21 (2):56–69.

Bergson, H. 1911. *Laughter: An Essay on the Meaning of the Comic*. Trans. Cloudesley Brereton and Fred Rothwell. New York: Macmillan.

Bergstrom, C. T., and M. Lachmann. 2001. Alarm calls as costly signals of antipredator vigilance: The watchful babbler game. *Animal Behavior* 61:535–543.

Binsted, K. 1996. Machine humour: An implemented model of puns. Ph.D. thesis, Department of Artificial Intelligence, University of Edinburgh. Retrieved July 1, 2006, from Binsted-McKay company website: <http://www.binsted-mckay.com/KimBinsted-PhDThesis.pdf>.

Binsted, K., and G. Ritchie. 2001. Towards a model of story puns. *Humor: International Journal of Humor Research* 14 (3):275–292.

Black, D. W. 1982. Pathological laughter: A review of the literature. *Journal of Nervous and Mental Disease* 170:67–71.

Black, D. W. 1984. Laughter. *Journal of the American Medical Association* 252 (21):2995–2998.

Blackmore, S. J. 1999. *The Meme Machine*. Oxford: Oxford University Press.

Blakemore, S.-J., D. Wolpert, and C. Frith. 2000. Why can't you tickle yourself? *NeuroReport* 11:R11–16.

Bloom, P. 2010. *How Pleasure Works: The New Sciences of Why We Like What We Like*. New York: W. W. Norton.

Boorstin, J. 1990. *Making Movies Work: Thinking Like a Filmmaker*. Los Angeles: Silman-James Press.

Booth, S. 1969. *An Essay on Shakespeare's Sonnets*. New Haven: Yale University Press.

Booth, S. 1977. *Shakespeare's Sonnets, Edited with Analytic Commentary*. New Haven: Yale University Press.

Booth, S. 1983. *King Lear, Macbeth, Indefinition, and Tragedy*. New Haven: Yale University Press.

Borges, J. L. [1944] 1962. *Ficciones*. Trans. Anthony Kerrigan. New York: Grove Press.

Bower, Gordon H. 1981. Mood and memory. *American Psychologist* 36 (2):129–148.

Boyd, R., and P. J. Richerson. 2005. *The Origin and Evolution of Cultures*. New York: Oxford University Press.

Boyer, P. 2001. *Religion Explained: Evolutionary Origins of Religious Thought*. New York: Basic Books.

Breazeal, C. 2000. Sociable machines: Expressive social exchange between humans and robots. Sc.D. dissertation, Department of Electrical Engineering and Computer Science, MIT, Cambridge, Massachusetts.

Brennan, S. 1982. The caricature generator. Master's thesis, MIT Media Lab, Cambridge, Massachusetts.

Brennan, S. 1985. Caricature generator: The dynamic exaggeration of faces by computer. *Leonardo* 18 (3):170–178.

Bressler, E., and S. Balshine. 2006. The influence of humor on desirability. *Evolution and Human Behavior* 27 (1):29–39.

Bressler, E., R. A. Martin, and S. Balshine. 2006. Production and appreciation of humor as sexually selected traits. *Evolution and Human Behavior* 27 (2):121–130.

Brewer, M. 2000. Research design and issues of validity. In *Handbook of Research Methods in Social and Personality Psychology*, ed. H. Reis and C. Judd. Cambridge: Cambridge University Press.

Broadbent, D. E. 1958. *Perception and Communication*. London: Pergamon.

Brooks, R. 1991. Intelligence without representation. *Artificial Intelligence* 47:139–159.

Bubb, C. C. 1920. *The Jests of Hierocles and Philagrius*. Cleveland: Rowfant Club.

Byers, J. A., and C. Walker. 1995. Refining the motor training hypothesis for the evolution of play. *American Naturalist* 146:25–40.

Byrne, A. 1993. Truth in fiction: The story continued. *Australasian Journal of Philosophy* 71:24–35.

Call, J., and M. Tomasello. 2008. Does the chimpanzee have a theory of mind? 30 years later. *Trends in Cognitive Sciences* 12, 5:187–192.

Cannon, W. B. 1927. *Bodily Changes in Pain, Hunger, Fear, and Rage: An Account of Recent Researches into the Function of Emotional Excitement*. McGrath.

Cantor, J. R., J. Bryant, and D. Zillmann. 1974. Enhancement of humor appreciation by transferred excitation. *Journal of Personality and Social Psychology* 15:470–480.

Carr, J., and L. Greeves. 2006. *Only Joking: What's So Funny about Making People Laugh?* New York: Gotham Books.

Carroll, N. 1999. Horror and humor. *Journal of Aesthetics and Art Criticism* 57 (2):145–160.

Cathcart, T., and D. Klein. 2007. *Plato and a Platypus Walk into a Bar . . .: Understanding Philosophy Through Jokes*. New York: Penguin.

Chalmers, D., R. French, and D. R. Hofstadter. 1995. High-level perception, representation, and analogy: A critique of artificial-intelligence methodology. In Douglas Hofstadter and the Fluid Analogies Research Group, *Fluid Concepts and Creative*

Analogies: Computer Models of the Fundamental Mechanisms of Thought. New York: Basic Books.

Chambers, C. G., M. K. Tanenhaus, K. M. Eberhard, H. Filip, and G. N. Carlson. 2002. Circumscribing referential domains during real-time language comprehension. *Journal of Memory and Language* 47:30–49.

Chambers, C. G., M. K. Tanenhaus, and J. S. Magnuson. 2004. Actions and affordances in syntactic ambiguity resolution. *Journal of Experimental Psychology* 30 (3):687–696.

Chapman, A. J., and H. C. Foot, eds. 1976. *Humour and Laughter: Theory, Research, and Applications.* London: Wiley.

Chapman, A. J., J. Smith, and H. C. Foot. 1980. Humour, laughter, and social interaction. In *Children's Humour,* ed. P. E. McGhee and A. J. Chapman, 141–179. New York: Wiley.

Cheney, D., and R. Seyfarth. 1990. *How Monkeys See the World.* Chicago: University of Chicago Press.

Chislenko, A. 1998. Theory of humor. <http://www.lucifer.com/~sasha/articles/humor.html>.

Chwalisz, K., E. Diener, and D. Gallagher. 1988. Autonomic arousal feedback and emotional experience: Evidence from the spinal cord injured. *Journal of Personality and Social Psychology* 54:820–828.

Clark, A. 1997. *Being There: Putting Brain, Body and World Together Again.* Cambridge, MA: MIT Press.

Clark, A., and D. J. Chalmers. 1998. The extended mind. *Analysis* 58 (1):7–19.

Clark, M. 1970. Humor and incongruity. *Philosophy* 45:20–32.

Clarke, A. In press. *A Closer Look at . . . Information Normalization Theory.* Cumbria: Pyrrhic House.

Close, M. 2007. *That Reminds Me: Finding the Funny in a Serious World.* Self-published.

Cohen, T. 1999. *Jokes: Philosophical Thoughts on Joking Matters.* Chicago: University of Chicago Press.

Collins, A. M., and E. F. Loftus. 1975. A spreading-activation theory of semantic processing. *Psychological Review* 82 (6):407–428.

Coser, R. L. 1960. Laughter among colleagues: A study of the social functions of humor among the staff of a mental hospital. *Psychiatry* 23:81–95.

Coulson, S. 2001. *Semantic Leaps: Frame-Shifting and Conceptual Blending in Meaning Construction.* Cambridge: Cambridge University Press.

Coulson, S., and M. Kutas. 1998. Frame shifting and sentential integration. UCSD Cognitive Science Technical Report 98-03.

Coulson, S., and M. Kutas. 2001. Getting it: Human event-related brain response to jokes in good and poor comprehenders. *Neuroscience Letters* 316:71–74.

Cousins, N. 1979. *Anatomy of an Illness as Perceived by the Patient: Reflections on Healing and Regeneration.* New York: W. W. Norton.

Craig, A. D. (Bud). 2003. A new theory of pain as a homeostatic emotion. *Trends in Neurosciences* 26 (6):303–307.

Crawford, M., and D. Gressley. 1991. Creativity, caring, and context: Women's and men's accounts of humor preferences and practices. *Psychology of Women Quarterly* 15 (June):217–231.

Currie, G. 1986. Fictional truth. *Philosophical Studies* 50:195–212.

Currie, G. 1990. *The Nature of Fiction.* Cambridge: Cambridge University Press.

Damasio, A. 1994. *Descartes' Error: Emotion, Reason, and the Human Brain.* New York: Grosset/Putnam.

Damasio, A. 1999. *The Feeling of What Happens: Body and Emotion in the Making of Consciousness.* London: William Heinemann Harcourt.

Damasio, A. 2003. *Looking for Spinoza: Sorrow, and the Feeling Brain.* London: William Heinemann Harcourt.

Darwin, C. [1872] 1965. *The Expression of the Emotions in Man and Animals.* New York: Oxford University Press.

Dawkins, R. 1982. *The Extended Phenotype.* New York: Oxford University Press.

Dawkins, R. 1989. *The Selfish Gene,* 2nd ed. Oxford: Oxford University Press.

Dawkins, R. 1993. Viruses of the mind. In *Dennett and His Critics,* ed. B. Dahlbom, 13–28. Oxford: Blackwell.

Deacon, T. W. 1989. The neural circuitry underlying primate calls and human language. *Human Evolution* 4:367–401.

Deacon, T. 1997. *The Symbolic Species.* New York: W. W. Norton.

De Groot, A. M. B. 1983. The range of automatic spreading Activation in word priming. *Journal of Verbal Learning and Verbal Behavior* 22:417–436.

Dennett, D. C. 1975. Why the law of effect will not go away. *Journal for the Theory of Social Behaviour* 5:179–187 Reprinted in Dennett 1978.

Dennett, D. C. 1978. *Brainstorms: Philosophical Essays on Mind and Psychology.* Cambridge, MA: Bradford Books/MIT Press.

Dennett, D. C. 1983. Intentional systems in cognitive ethology: the "Panglossian Paradigm" defended. *Behavioral and Brain Sciences* 6:343–390.

Dennett, D. C. 1984. Cognitive wheels: The frame problem in AI. In *Minds, Machines, and Evolution,* ed. C. Hookway, 128–151. Cambridge: Cambridge University Press.

Dennett, D. C. 1987. *The Intentional Stance*. Cambridge, MA: Bradford Books/MIT Press.

Dennett, D. C. 1988. Quining qualia. In *Consciousness in Modern Science*, ed. A. Marcel and E. Bisiach, 42–77. Oxford: Oxford University Press.

Dennett, D. C. 1990. Memes and the exploitation of imagination. *Journal of Aesthetics and Art Criticism* 48 (spring): 127–135.

Dennett, D. C. 1991. *Consciousness Explained*. Boston: Little, Brown.

Dennett, D. C. 1995. *Darwin's Dangerous Idea*. New York: Simon & Schuster.

Dennett, D. C. 1996a. Producing future by telling stories. In *The Robot's Dilemma Revisited: The Frame Problem of Artificial Intelligence*, ed. K. Ford and Z. Pylyshyn, 1–7. Norwood, NJ: Ablex.

Dennett, D. C. 1996b. Consciousness: More like fame than television. Published in German translation as "Bewusstsein hat mehr mit Ruhm als mit Fernsehen zu tun," in *Die Technik auf dem Weg zur Seele*, ed. Christa Maar, Ernst Pöppel, and Thomas Christaller, 61–90. Reinbek: Rowohlt.

Dennett, D. C. 1996c. Hofstadter's quest: Review of Hofstadter and F.A.R.G., *Fluid Concepts and Creative Analogies*. *Complexity Journal* 1 (6):9–12.

Dennett, D. C. 1998. *Brainchildren: Essays on Designing Minds*. Cambridge, MA: Bradford Books/MIT Press.

Dennett, D. C. 2005. *Sweet Dreams: Philosophical Obstacles to a Theory of Consciousness*. Cambridge, MA: Bradford Books/MIT Press.

Dennett, D. C. 2006. *Breaking the Spell: Religion as a Natural Phenomenon*. New York: Viking.

Dennett, D. C. 2007a. Heterophenomenology reconsidered. *Phenomenology and the Cognitive Sciences* 6 (1–2)..

Dennett, D. C. 2007b. Instead of a review. *Artificial Intelligence* 171:1110–1113.

Dennett, D. C. 2007c. A daring reconnaissance of red territory. [Review of Humphrey 2006.] *Brain* 130:592–595.

Dennett, D. C. 2007d. What could a neuron "want"? On edge.org, Edge Question: "What Have You Changed Your Mind About?" <http://www.edge.org/q2008/q08_11.html>.

Dennett, D. C., and K. Akins. 2008. Multiple drafts model. Scholarpedia.org 3(4):4321. <http://www.scholarpedia.org/article/Multiple_drafts_model>.

Descartes, R. [1649] 1988. The passions of the soul. In *Selected Philosophical Writings of René Descartes*, ed. and trans. J. Cottingham, R. Stoothoff, and D. Murdoch. Cambridge: Cambridge University Press.

de Sousa, R. 1987. *The Rationality of Emotion*. Cambridge, MA: MIT Press.

Diamond, J. 1997. *Guns, Germs, and Steel: The Fates of Human Societies.* New York: W. W. Norton.

Dillon, K. M., B. Minchoff, and K. H. Baker. 1985. Positive emotional states and enhancement of the immune system. *International Journal of Psychiatry in Medicine* 15:13–17.

Dolitsky, M. 1992. Aspects of the unsaid in humor. *Humor: International Journal of Humor Research* 5 (1/2):33–43.

Duchenne (de Boulogne), G.-B. [1862] 1990. *The Mechanism of Human Facial Expression.* Trans. R. A. Cuthbertson. New York: Cambridge University Press.

Dutton, D. G., and A. P. Aron. 1974. Some evidence for heightened sexual attraction under conditions of high anxiety. *Journal of Personality and Social Psychology* 30:510–517.

Eastman, M. 1936. *Enjoyment of Laughter.* New York: Halcyon House.

Eibl-Eibesfeldt, I. 1973. The expressive behavior of the deaf and blind born. In *Social Communication and Movement,* ed. M. von Cranach and I. Vine, 163–194. London: Academic Press.

Eibl-Eibesfeldt, I. 1989. *Human Ethology.* New York: Aldine de Gruyter.

Einon, D. F., and M. Potegal. 1991. Enhanced defense in adult rats deprived of play fighting experience as juveniles. *Aggressive Behavior* 17:27–40.

Ekman, P. 1992. An argument for basic emotions. *Cognition and Emotion* 6:169–200.

Ekman, P. 1999. Basic emotions. In *Handbook of Cognition and Emotion,* ed. T. Dalgleish and M. Power. Sussex: John Wiley.

Ekman, P. 2003. *Emotions Revealed.* New York: Times Books.

Ekman, P., and W. V. Friesen. 1971. Constants across cultures in the face and emotion. *Journal of Personality and Social Psychology* 17:124–129.

Ekman, P., and W. V. Friesen. 1978. *Facial Action Coding System: A Technique for the Measurement of Facial Movement.* Palo Alto: Consulting Psychologists Press.

Ellsworth, P. 1994. William James and emotion: Is a century of fame worth a century of misunderstanding? *Psychological Review* 101:222–229.

Elster, J. 1996. Rationality and the emotions. *Economic Journal* 106:1386–1397.

Elman, J. L. 1991. Distributed representations, simple recurrent networks, and grammatical structure. *Machine Learning* 7:195–225.

Elman, J. L., E. A. Bates, M. H. Johnson, A. Karmiloff-Smith, D. Parisi, and K. Plunkett. 1996. *Rethinking Innateness: A Connectionist Perspective on Development.* Cambridge, MA: MIT Press.

Fagen, R. 1993. Primate juveniles and primate play. In *Juvenile Primates: Life History, Development, and Behavior,* ed. M. E. Pereira and L. A. Fairbanks, 182–196. New York: Oxford University Press.

Fauconnier, G. 1985. *Mental Spaces: Aspects of Meaning Construction in Natural Language*. Cambridge, MA: MIT Press.

Fauconnier, G., and M. Turner. 2002. *The Way We Think: Conceptual Blending and the Mind's Hidden Complexities*. New York: Basic Books.

Feldman, J. A. 1989. Neural representation of conceptual knowledge. In *Neural Connections, Mental Computation*, ed. L. Nadel, L. A. Cooper, P. Culicover, and R. M. Harnish, 68–103. Cambridge, MA: MIT Press.

Fernandez-Dols, J. M., and M. A. Ruiz-Belda. 1995. Are smiles a sign of happiness? Gold medal winners at the Olympic Games. *Journal of Personality and Social Psychology* 69:1113–1119.

Flack, J. C., L. A. Jeannotte, and F. B. M. de Waal. 2004. Play signaling and the perception of social rules by juvenile chimpanzees (*Pan troglodytes*). *Journal of Comparative Psychology* 118:149–159.

Fodor, J. 2004a. Having concepts: A brief refutation of the twentieth century. *Mind & Language* 19 (1):29–47.

Fodor, J. 2004b. Reply to commentators. *Mind & Language* 19 (1):99–112.

Fodor, J., and Z. Pylyshyn. 1988. Connectionism and cognitive architecture: A critical analysis. *Cognition* 28:3–71.

Foster, C. A., B. S. Witcher, W. K. Campbell, and J. D. Green. 1998. Arousal and attraction: Evidence for automatic and controlled processes. *Journal of Personality and Social Psychology* 74:86–101.

Francis, R. C. 2004. *Why Men Won't Ask for Directions: The Seductions of Sociobiology*. Princeton: Princeton University Press.

Frank, M., and P. Ekman. 1993. Not all smiles are created equal: The differences between enjoyment and nonenjoyment smiles. *Humor* 6: 9–26.

Frank, M., P. Ekman, and W. V. Friesen. 1993. Behavioral markers and recognizability of the smile of enjoyment. *Journal of Personality and Social Psychology* 64:83–93.

Frank, R. H. 1988. *Passions within Reason: The Strategic Role of the Emotions*. New York: W. W. Norton.

Frank, R. H. 2004. In defense of sincerity detection. *Rationality and Society* 16 (3):287–305.

Franklin, S. 2007. A foundational architecture for artificial general intelligence. In *Advances in Artificial General Intelligence: Concepts, Architectures and Algorithms, Proceedings of the AGI workshop 2006*, ed. Ben Goertzel and Pei Wang, 36–54. Amsterdam: IOS Press.

Franklin, S., and F. G. Patterson, Jr. 2006. The LIDA Architecture: Adding new modes of learning to an intelligent, autonomous, software agent. *Integrated Design and Process Technology, IDPT-2006*. San Diego, CA: Society for Design and Process Science.

Fredrickson, B. L., and R. W. Levenson. 1998. Positive emotions speed recovery from the cardiovascular sequelae of negative emotions. *Cognition and Emotion* 12:191–220.

Fredrickson, B. L., R. A. Mancuso, C. Branigan, and M. M. Tugade. 2000. The undoing effect of positive emotions. *Motivation and Emotion* 24:237–258.

French, R. 1995. *The Subtlety of Sameness: A Theory and Computer Model of Analogy-making.* Cambridge, MA: MIT Press.

Freud, S. [1905] 1960. *Jokes and Their Relation to the Unconscious.* Trans. J. Strachey. New York: W. W. Norton.

Freud, S. 1928. Humor. *International Journal of Psycho-Analysis* 9:1–6.

Fridlund, A. J. 1991. Sociality of solitary smiling: Potentiation by an implicit audience. *Journal of Personality and Social Psychology* 60:229–240.

Fridlund, A. J. 1994. *Human Facial Expression: An Evolutionary View.* San Diego, CA: Academic Press.

Fridlund, A. J., and J. M. Loftis. 1990. Relations between tickling and humorous laughter: Preliminary support for the Darwin–Hecker hypothesis. *Biological Psychology* 30:141–150.

Fried, I., C. L. Wilson, K. A. MacDonald, and E. J. Behnke. 1998. Electric current stimulates laughter. *Nature* 391:650.

Friend, T. 2002. Dept. of Humor: What's so funny? A scientific attempt to discover why we laugh. *New Yorker*, November 11, 78–93.

Frijda, N. H. 1986. *The Emotions.* Cambridge: Cambridge University Press.

Fry, W. F. 1977. The respiratory components of mirthful laughter. *Journal of Biological Psychology* 19:39–50.

Fry, W. F. 1994. The biology of humor. *Humor: International Journal of Humor Research* 7:111–126.

Gallese, V., Fadiga, L., Fogassi, L., and Rizzolatti, G. 1996. Action recognition in the premotor cortex. Brain 119:593–609.

Gazzaniga, M. S. 2008. *Human: The Science of What Makes Us Unique.* New York: HarperCollins.

Gervais, M., and D. S. Wilson. 2005. The evolution and vunctions of laughter and humor: A synthetic approach. *Quarterly Review of Biology* 80:395–430.

Gibbard, A. 1990. *Wise Choices, Apt Feelings: A Theory of Normative Judgment.* Cambridge, MA: Harvard University Press.

Gigerenzer, G. 2008. Why heuristics work. *Perspectives on Psychological Science* 3:20–29.

Gigerenzer, G., and D. G. Goldstein. 1996. Reasoning the fast and frugal way: Models of bounded rationality. *Psychological Review* 103:650–669.

Goldstein, J. H., and P. McGhee. 1972. *The Psychology of Humor.* New York: Academic Press.

Goldstone, R. L., and L. W. Barsalou. 1998. Reuniting perception and conception. *Cognition* 65 (2):231–262.

Göncü, A., J. Mistry, and C. Mosier. 2000. Cultural variations in the play of toddlers. *International Journal of Behavioral Development* 24 (3):321–329.

Gonzales, L. 2003. *Deep Survival: Who Lives, Who Dies, and Why.* New York: W. W. Norton.

Gopnik, A. 1998. Explanation as orgasm. *Minds and Machines* 8:101–118.

Gopnik, A., and A. N. Meltzoff. 1997. *Words, Thoughts, and Theories.* Cambridge, MA: Bradford Books/MIT Press.

Gopnik, A., and H. Wellman. 1994. The "theory theory." In *Domain Specificity in Culture and Cognition*, ed. L. Hirschfield and S. Gelman. New York: Cambridge University Press.

Gortner, M., 1972. *Marjoe.* Film. Sarah Kernochan, Howard Smith, directors.

Grahek, N. 2007. *Feeling Pain and Being in Pain*, 2nd ed. Cambridge, MA: Bradford Books/MIT Press.

Gratier, M. 2003. Expressive timing and interactional synchrony between mothers and infants: Cultural similarities, cultural differences, and the immigration experience. *Cognitive Development* 18:533–554.

Greengross, G. (under review). Does making others laugh lead to mating success? Verbal humor as a mental fitness indicator. Under review for *Evolution and Human Behavior.*

Greengross, G., and G. Miller. 2008. Dissing oneself versus dissing rivals: Effects of status, personality, and sex on the short-term and long-term attractiveness of self-deprecating and other-deprecating humor. *Evolutionary Psychology* 6 (3):393–408.

Greenspan, P. 2000. Emotional strategies and rationality. *Ethics* 110:469–487.

Gregory, J. C. 1924. *The Nature of Laughter.* New York: Harcourt Brace.

Grice, P. 1957. Meaning. *Philosophical Review* 66:377–388.

Grice, P. 1969. Utterer's meaning and intention. *Philosophical Review* 78:147–177.

Griffin, R., and D. C. Dennett. 2008. What does the study of autism tell us about the craft of folk psychology? In *Social Cognition: Development, Neuroscience, and Autism*, ed. T. Striano and V. Reid, 254–280. New York: Wiley-Blackwell.

Griffiths, P. E. 1997. *What Emotions Really Are.* Chicago: University of Chicago Press.

Griffiths, P. E. 2002. Basic emotions, complex emotions, Machiavellian emotions. In *Philosophy and the Emotions*, ed. A. Hatzimoysis, 39–67. Cambridge: Cambridge University Press.

Gruner, C. R. 1997. *The Game of Humor: A Comprehensive Theory of Why We Laugh.* New Brunswick, NJ: Transaction Publishers.

Gustafson, D. 2006. Categorizing pain. In *Pain: New Essays on Its Nature and the Methodology of Its Study*, ed. M. Aydede. Cambridge, MA: MIT Press.

Hall, G. S., and A. Allin. 1897. The psychology of tickling, laughing, and the comic. *American Journal of Psychology* 9:1–42.

Hammerschmidt, K., T. Freudenstein, and U. Jürgens. 2001. Vocal development in squirrel monkeys. *Behaviour* 138:97–116.

Harris, C. R. 1999. The mystery of ticklish laughter. *American Scientist* 87:344–351.

Harris, C. R., and N. Alvarado. 2005. Facial expressions, smile types, and self-report during humor, tickle, and pain. *Cognition and Emotion* 19:655–699.

Harris, C. R., and N. Christenfeld. 1997. Humour, tickle, and the Darwin-Hecker hypothesis. *Cognition and Emotion* 11:103–110.

Harris, C. R., and N. Christenfeld. 1999. Can a machine tickle? *Psychonomic Bulletin & Review* 6 (3):504–510.

Haugeland, J. 1985. *Artificial Intelligence: The Very Idea.* Cambridge, MA: MIT Press.

Hauser, M. D. 1997. *The Evolution of Communication.* Cambridge, MA: MIT Press.

Hauser, M. D. 2000. *Wild Minds: What Animals Really Think.* New York: Henry Holt.

Hebb, D. O. 1949. *The Organization of Behavior: A Neuropsychological Theory.* New York: Wiley.

Hecker, E. 1873. *Die Physiologie und Psychologie des Lachen und des Komischen.* Berlin: F. Dummler.

Herrnstein, R. J. 1970. On the law of effect. *Journal of the Experimental Analysis of Behavior* 13:243–266.

Hilgard, E. R. 1980. The trilogy of mind: Cognition, affection, and conation. *Journal of the History of Behavioral Sciences* 16: 107–117.

Hinde, R. A. 1985a. Expression and negotiation. In *The Development of Expressive Behavior*, ed. G. Zivin, 103–116. New York: Academic Press.

Hinde, R. A. 1985b. Was "the expression of emotions" a misleading phrase? *Animal Behaviour* 33:985–992.

Hobbes, T. 1840. *Human Nature*. In *The English Works of Thomas Hobbes of Malmesbury*, vol. 4, ed. W. Molesworth. London: Bohn.

Hofstadter, D. R. 2007. *I Am a Strange Loop*. New York: Basic Books.

Hofstadter, D. R., and the Fluid Analogies Research Group. 1995. *Fluid Concepts and Creative Analogies: Computer Models of the Fundamental Mechanisms of Thought*. New York: Basic Books.

Hommel, B., J. Müsseler, G. Aschersleben, and W. Prinz. 2001. The theory of event coding (TEC): A framework for perception and action planning. *Behavioral and Brain Sciences* 24:849–937.

Humphrey, N. 2006. *Seeing Red: A Study in Consciousness*. Cambridge, MA: Belknap Press of Harvard University Press.

Hurley, M. 2006. The joy of debugging: Towards a computational model of humor. Honors dissertation in Cognitive Science, Tufts University, Medford, Massachusetts.

Huron, D. 2006. *Sweet Anticipation: Music and the Psychology of Expectation*. Cambridge, MA: Bradford Books/MIT Press.

Hutchins, E. 1995a. *Cognition in the Wild*. Cambridge, MA: MIT Press.

Hutchins, E. 1995b. How a cockpit remembers its speeds. *Cognitive Science* 19:265–288.

Izard, C. E. 1971. *The Face of Emotion*. New York: Appleton-Century-Crofts.

Jackendoff, R. 1987. *Consciousness and the Computational Mind*. Cambridge, MA: MIT Press.

Jackendoff, R. 1994. *Patterns in the Mind*. New York: Basic Books.

Jackendoff, R. 2002. *Foundations of Language*. New York: Oxford University Press.

Jackendoff, R. 2007. *Language, Consciousness, Culture: Essays on Mental Structure*. Cambridge, MA: MIT Press.

James, W. 1884. What is an emotion? *Mind* 9:188–205.

James, W. 1890. *The Principles of Psychology*. New York: Henry Holt.

Jung, W. E. 2003. The inner eye theory of laughter: Mindreader signals cooperator value. *Evolutionary Psychology* 1:214–253.

Kaas, J. H., and T. M. Preuss, eds. 2007. *Evolution of Nervous Systems*, vol. 4: *The Evolution of Primate Nervous Systems*. Oxford: Elsevier.

Kamide, Y., G. T. M. Altmann, and S. L. Haywood. 2003. The timecourse of prediction in incremental sentence processing: Evidence from anticipatory eye movements. *Journal of Memory and Language* 49 (1):133–156.

Kant, I. [1790] 1951. *Critique of Judgment*. Trans. J. H. Bernard. New York: Hafner.

Kataria, M., S. Wilson, and K. Buxman. 1999. Where East meets West: Laughter therapy. Workshop presented at the meeting of the International Society for Humor Studies, June, Oakland, California.

Keith-Spiegel, P. 1972. Early conceptions of humor: Varieties and issues. In *The Psychology of Humor*, ed. J. H. Goldstein and P. E. McGhee, 3–39. New York: Academic Press.

Keltner, D., and G. A. Bonanno. 1997. A study of laughter and dissociation: The distinct correlates of laughter and smiling during bereavement. *Journal of Personality and Social Psychology* 73:687–702.

Keltner, D., R. C. Young, E. A. Heerey, C. Oemig, and N. D. Monarch. 1998. Teasing in hierarchical and intimate relations. *Journal of Personality and Social Psychology* 75:1231–1247.

Kirsh, D., and P. Maglio. 1994. On distinguishing epistemic from pragmatic action. *Cognitive Science* 18:513–549.

Koestler, A. 1964. *The Act of Creation*. London: Hutchinson.

Konner, M. 1982. *The Tangled Wing: Biological Constraints on the Human Spirit*. London: William Heinemann.

Kosslyn, S. M., G. Ganis, and W. L. Thompson. 2001. Neural foundations of imagery. *Nature Reviews: Neuroscience* 2:635–642.

Kraut, R. E., and R. E. Johnston. 1979. Social and emotional messages of smiling: An ethological approach. *Journal of Personality and Social Psychology* 37:1539–1553.

Kunz, M., K. M. Prkachin, and S. Lautenbacher. 2009. The smile of pain. *Pain* 145:273–275.

Lachter, J., K. I. Forster, and E. Ruthruff. 2004. Forty years after Broadbent: Still no identification without attention. *Psychological Review* 111:880–913.

LaFollette, H., and N. Shanks. 1993. Belief and the basis of humor. *American Philosophical Quarterly* 329–339.

Lahr, J. 2010. Master of Revels. New Yorker, May 3, 70–76.

Laird, J. D. 1974. Self-attribution of emotion: The effects of expresxive behavior on the quality of emotional experience. *Journal of Personality and Social Psychology* 29 (4):475–486.

Laird, J., P. Rosenbloom, and A. Newell. 1987. SOAR: An architecture for general intelligence. *Artificial Intelligence* 33:1–64.

Lakoff, G. 1987. *Women, Fire, and Dangerous Things: What Categories Reveal about the Mind*. Chicago: University of Chicago Press.

Lakoff, G., and M. Johnson. 1980. *Metaphors We Live By*. Chicago: Chicago University Press.

Lakoff, G., and M. Johnson. 1999. *Philosophy in the Flesh: The Embodied Mind and Its Challenge to Western Thought*. New York: Basic Books.

Lakoff, G. and R. E. Nuñez. 2000. *Where Mathematics Comes From: How the Embodied Mind Brings Mathematics into Being*. New York: Basic Books.

Lange, C. G. 1885. *Om sindsbevaegelser: Et psyko-fysiologisk studie*. Copenhagen: Jacob Lunds. Reprinted in *The Emotions*, ed. C. G. Lange and W. James, trans. I. A. Haupt. Baltimore: Williams and Wilkins, 1922.

Lange, C. 1887. *Ueber Gemuthsbewgungen* 3, 8.

Lanzetta, J. T., J. Cartwright-Smith, and R. E. Eleck. 1976. Effects of nonverbal dissimulation on emotional experience and autonomic arousal. *Journal of Personality and Social Psychology* 33 (3):354–370.

Lazarus, R. S. 1984. On the primacy of cognition. *American Psychologist* 39:124–129.

LeDoux, J. 1998. *The Emotional Brain*. New York: Simon & Schuster.

LeDoux, J. 2002. *Synaptic Self: How Our Brains Become Who We Are*. New York: Penguin.

Lefcourt, H. M., K. Davidson, K. M. Prkachin, and D. E. Mills. 1997. Humor as a stress moderator in the prediction of blood pressure obtained during five stressful tasks. *Journal of Research in Personality* 31:523–542.

Lefcourt, H. M., K. Davidson-Katz, and K. Kueneman. 1990. Humor and immune-system functioning. *Humor: International Journal of Humor Research* 3:305–321.

Lenat, D. B. and R. V. Guha. 1990. *Building Large Knowledge-Based Systems: Representation and Inference in the Cyc Project*. Reading, MA: Addison Wesley.

Levinstein, B. 2007. Facts, interpretation, and truth in fiction. *British Journal of Aesthetics* 47:64–75.

Levitin, D. J. 2006. *This Is Your Brain on Music: The Science of a Human Obsession*. New York: Dutton.

Lewis, D. 1978. Truth in fiction. *American Philosophical Quarterly* 15:37–46.

Locke, J. 1690. *Essay Concerning Human Understanding*. London.

Marañon, G. 1924. Contribution a l'etude de l'action emotive de l'adrenaline. *Rev. Fran. Endo.* 2: 301–325.

Marcus, G. F. 2001. *The Algebraic Mind: Integrating Connectionism and Cognitive Science*. Cambridge, MA: MIT Press.

Marinkovic, K. 2004. Spatiotemporal dynamics of word processing in the human cortex. *Neuroscientist* 10 (2):142–152.

Martin, R. A. 2001. Humor, laughter, and physical health: Methodological issues and research findings. *Psychological Bulletin* 127:504–519.

Martin, R. A. 2004. Sense of humor and physical health: Theoretical issues, recent findings and future directions. *Humor: International Journal of Humor Research* 17:1–19.

Matsusaka, T. 2004. When does play panting occur during social play in wild chimpanzees? *Primates* 45:221–229.

Mauro, R., and M. Kubovy. 1992. Caricature and face recognition. *Memory & Cognition* 20 (4):433–444.

Maynard Smith, J. 1997. *The Theory of Evolution*, 3rd ed. Cambridge: Cambridge Universtity Press.

McCarthy, J. 1980. Circumscription—A form of non-monotonic reasoning. *Artificial Intelligence* 13 (1–2). Reprinted in *Readings in Artificial Intelligence*, ed. B. L. Webber and N. J. Nilsson, 466–472, Wellsboro, PA: Tioga, 1981; also in *Readings in Nonmonotonic Reasoning*, ed. M. J. Ginsberg, 145–152, San Francisco: Morgan Kaufmann, 1987.

McCarthy, J., and P. J. Hayes. 1969. Some philosophical problems from the standpoint of artificial intelligence. In *Machine Intelligence 4*, ed. D. Michie and B. Meltzer, 463–502. Edinburgh: Edinburgh University Press.

McClelland, J. L., D. E. Rumelhart, and the PDP Research Group. 1986. *Parallel Distributed Processing: Explorations in the Microstructure of Cognition*, vol. 2: *Psychological and Biological Models*. Cambridge, MA: MIT Press.

McGhee, P. E. 1971. Development of the humor response: A review of the literature. *Psychological Bulletin* 76 (5):328–348.

McGhee, P. E. 1976. Children's appreciation of humor: A test of the cognitive congruency principle. *Child Development* 47 (2):420–426.

McGhee, P. E. 1979. *Humor: Its Origins and Development*. San Francisco: Freeman.

McKay, J. 2000. Generation of idiom-based witticisms to aid second-language learning. M.Sc. thesis, Division of Informatics, University of Edinburgh. Retrieved July 1, 2006, from Binsted-McKay company website: <http://www.binsted-mckay.com/JustinMcKay-MScThesis.pdf>.

McKay, R. T., and D. C. Dennett. 2009. The evolution of misbelief. *Behavioral and Brain Sciences* 32: 493–561.

Melzack, R., and K. L. Casey. 1968. Sensory, motivational, and central control determinants of chronic pain: A new conceptual model. In *The Skin Senses*, ed. D. R. Kenshalo, 432. Springfield, IL: Thomas.

Mihalcea, R., and C. Strapparava. 2005. Making computers laugh: Investigations in automatic humor recognition. In Proceedings of HLT/EMNLP, Vancouver,CA.

Miller, G. 2000. *The Mating Mind: How Sexual Choice Shaped the Evolution of Human Nature*. New York: Doubleday.

Miller, G., and D. Caruthers. 2003. A great sense of humor is a good genes indicator: Ovulatory cycle effects on the sexual attractiveness of male humor ability. Paper presented at the Human Behavior and Evolution Society 15th annual meeting, Nebraska.

Millikan, R. 2004. *Varieties of Meaning*. The Jean-Nicod Lectures, 2002. Cambridge, MA: MIT Press.

Mills, C. M., and F. C. Keil. 2004. Knowing the limits of one's understanding: The development of an awareness of an illusion of explanatory depth. *Journal of Experimental Child Psychology* 87:1–32.

Milner, A. D., and M. A. Goodale. 2006. *The Visual Brain in Action*, 2nd ed. New York: Oxford University Press.

Minsky, M. 1974. A framework for representing knowledge. MIT Artif. Intell. Memo 252.

Minsky, M. 1975. Frame system theory. In *Thinking: Readings in Cognitive Science*, ed. P. N. Johnson-Laird and P. C. Wason, 355–376. Cambridge: Cambridge University Press.

Minsky, M. 1984. Jokes and the logic of the cognitive unconscious. In *Cognitive Constraints on Communication*, ed. L. M. Vaina and J. Hintikka. Dordrecht: Reidel.

Minsky, M. 1981. Music, mind, and meaning. In *Music, Mind, and Brain: The Neuropsychology of Music*, ed. Manfred Clynes. New York: Plenum.

Minsky, M. 1986. *The Society of Mind*. New York: Simon & Schuster.

Minsky, M. 2006. *The Emotion Machine*. New York: Simon & Schuster.

Mo, Z., J. Lewis, and U. Neumann. 2004. Improved automatic caricature by feature normalization and exaggeration. Paper presented at ACM Siggraph 2004. <http://graphics.usc.edu/cgit/pdf/papers/caricature_sketch.pdf>.

Mobbs, D., M. D. Grecius, E. Abdel-Azim, V. Menon, and A. L. Reiss. 2003. Humor modulates the mesolimbic reward centers. *Neuron* 40:1041–1048.

Mobbs, D., C. C. Hagan, E. Azim, V. Menon, and A. L. Reiss. 2005. Personality predicts activity in reward and emotional regions associated with humor. *PNAS* 102(45):16502–16506.

Mochida, T., A. Ishiguro, T. Aoki, and Y. Uchikawa. 1995. Behavior arbitration for autonomous mobile robots using emotion mechanisms. In *Proceedings of the IEEE/ RSJ International Conference on Intelligent Robots and Systems (IROS '95)*, Pittsburgh, PA, 516–221.

Moran, J. M., G. S. Wig, R. B. Adams, Jr., P. Janata, and W. M. Kelley. 2004. Neural correlates of humor detection and appreciation. *NeuroImage* 21:1055–1060.

Morreall, J. 1982. A new theory of laughter. *Philosophical Studies* 42:243–254.

Müller, M. 2002. Computer Go. *Artificial Intelligence* 134: 145–179.

Nerhardt, G. 1976. Incongruity and funniness: Toward a new descriptive model. In *Humor and Laughter: Theory, Research, and Application*, ed. A. J. Chapman and H. C. Foot, 55–62. New York: Wiley.

Neisser, U. 1976. *Cognition and Reality: Principles and Implications of Cognitive Psychology*. New York: W. H. Freeman.

Newell, A., and H. A. Simon. 1972. *Human Problem Solving*. Englewood Cliffs, NJ: Prentice-Hall.

Niedenthal, P. M. 2007. Embodying emotion. *Science* 316: 1002–1005.

Oatley, K., and P. N. Johnson-Laird. 1987. Towards a cognitive theory of emotions. *Cognition and Emotion* 1:29–50.

Olds, J., and P. Milner. 1954. Positive reinforcement produced by electrical stimulation of septal area and other regions of rat brain. *Journal of Comparative and Physiological Psychology* 47: 419–427.

Oliphant, M. and J. Batali. 1997. *Learning and the Emergence of Coordinated Communication: The Newsletter of the Center for Research in Language* 11(1).

Omark, D. R., M. Omark, and M. Edelman. 1975. Formation of dominance hierarchies in young children: Attentional perception. In *Psychological Anthropology*, ed. T. Williams, 289–314. The Hague: Mouton.

O'Reilly, R. C. 1998. Six principles for biologically based computational models of cortical cognition. *Trends in Cognitive Sciences* 2 (11):455–462.

O'Reilly, R. C., Y. Munakata, and J. L. McClelland. 2000. *Explorations in Computational Cognitive Neuroscience: Understanding the Mind by Simulating the Brain*. Cambridge, MA: MIT Press.

Oring, E. 2003. *Engaging Humor*. Urbana: University of Illinois Press.

Owren, M. J., and J. Bacharowski. 2003. Reconsidering the evolution of nonlinguistic communication: The case of laughter. *Journal of Nonverbal Behavior* 27:183–200.

Panksepp, J., and J. Burgdorf. 1999. Laughing rats? Playful tickling arouses highfrequency ultrasonic chirping in young rodents. In *Toward a Science of Consciousness III*, ed. S. Hameroff, D. Chalmers, and A. Kaziak. Cambridge, MA: MIT Press.

Panksepp, J., and J. Burgdorf. 2003. "Laughing" rats and the evolutionary antecedents of human joy? *Physiology & Behavior* 79:533–547.

Parr, L. A. 2004. Perceptual biases for multimodal cues in chimpanzee (*Pan troglodytes*) affect recognition. *Animal Cognition* 7:171–178.

Parvizi, J., S. W. Anderson, C. Martin, H. Damasio, and A. R. Damasio. 2001. Pathological laughter and crying: A link to the cerebellum. *Brain* 124:1708–1719.

Patel, A. D. 2007. *Music, Language, and the Brain*. New York: Oxford University Press.

Patzig, G. 1969. *Aristotle's Theory of the Syllogism*. Trans. Jonathan Barnes. Dordrecht: D. Reidel.

Penfield, W. 1958. Some mechanisms of consciousness discovered during electrical stimulation of the brain. *Proceedings of the National Academy of Sciences* 44 (2):51–66.

Penfield, W., and H. Jasper. 1954. *Epilepsy and the Functional Anatomy of the Human Brain*. Boston: Little, Brown.

Piaget, J. [1936] 1952. *The Origins of Intelligence in Children*. Trans. M. Cook. New York: International Universities Press.

Piaget, J. [1937] 1954. *The Construction of Reality in the Child*. Trans. M. Cook. New York: Basic Books.

Pickett, J., ed. 2001. *American Heritage Dictionary of the English Language*, 4th ed. Boston: Houghton Mifflin.

Pinker, S. 1994. *The Language Instinct: How the Mind Creates Language*. London: William Morrow.

Pinker, S. 1997. *How the Mind Works*. New York: Norton.

Pollock, J. 2008. OSCAR: An architecture for generally intelligent agents. In *Proceedings of the First AGI Conference*, AGI 2008, March 1–3, 2008, University of Memphis, Tennesee, 275–286. IOS Press.

Popper, K., and J. C. Eccles. [1977] 1986. *The Self and Its Brain*. London: Routledge & Kegan Paul.

Potegal, M., and D. F. Einon. 1989. Aggressive behavior in adult rats deprived of play-fighting experience as juveniles. *Developmental Psychobiology* 22:159–172.

Povinelli, D. J. and T. J. Eddy. 1996. What chimpanzees know about seeing. *Monographs of the Society for Research in Child Development* 61(2), serial no. 247.

Premack, D., and A. J. Premack. 1983. *The Mind of an Ape*. New York: W. W. Norton.

Premack, D., and G. Woodruff. 1978. Does the chimpanzee have a theory of mind? *Behavioral and Brain Sciences* 1 (4):515–526.

Preuschoft, S., and J. A. R. A. M. van Hooff. 1997. The social function of "smile" and "laughter": Variations across primate species and societies. In *Nonverbal Communication: Where Nature Meets Culture*, ed. U. C. Segerstråle and P. Molnár, 171–190. Mahwah, NJ: Lawrence Erlbaum.

Prinz, J. 2002. *Furnishing the Mind. Concepts and Their Perceptual Basis*. Cambridge, MA: MIT Press.

Prinz, J. 2004. *Gut Reactions: A Perceptual Theory of Emotion*. Oxford: Oxford University Press.

Prinz, J., and A. Clark. 2004. Putting concepts to work: Some thoughts for the twentyfirst century. *Mind & Language* 19 (1):57–69.

Prkachin, K. M. 1992. The consistency of facial expressions of pain: A comparison across modalities. *Pain* 51:297–306.

Proffitt, D. R. 1999. Inferential vs. ecological approaches to perception. In *The Nature of Cognition*, ed. Robert J. Sternberg. Cambridge, MA: MIT Press.

Provine, R. R. 1993. Laughter punctuates speech: Linguistic, social, and gender contexts of laughter. *Ethology* 95:291–298.

Provine, R. R. 1996. Laughter. *American Scientist* 84:38–45.

Provine, R. R. 2000. *Laughter: A Scientific Investigation*. New York: Viking.

Provine, R. R., and Y. L. Yong. 1991. Laughter: A stereotyped human vocalization. *Ethology* 89:115–124.

Ramachandran, V. S. 1998. The neurology and evolution of humor, laughter, and smiling: The false alarm theory. *Medical Hypotheses* 51: 351–354.

Ramachandran, V. S., and S. Blakeslee. 1998. *Phantoms in the Brain: Probing the Mysteries of the Human Mind*. New York: William Morrow.

Ramachandran, V. S., and D. Rogers-Ramachandran. 2006. The neurology of aesthetics. *Scientific American: Mind* (October).

Raskin, V. 1985. *Semantic Mechanisms of Humor*. Dordrecht: Reidel.

Ravaja, N., M. Turpeinen, T. Saari, S. Puttonen, and L. Keltikangas-Järvinen. 2008. The psychophysiology of james bond: Phasic emotional responses to violent video game events. *Emotion* 8 (1):114–120.

Reber, R., M. Brun, and K. Mitterndorfer. 2008. The use of heuristics in intuitive mathematical judgment. *Psychonomic Bulletin & Review* 15 (6):1174.

Richerson, P. J., and R. Boyd. 2006. *Not by Genes Alone: How Culture Transformed Human Evolution*. Chicago: University of Chicago Press.

Ritchie, G. 1999. Developing the incongruity-resolution theory. In *Proceedings of the 9th AISB Symposium on Creative Language: Stories and Humour*, Edinburgh, April 1999, 78–85.

Ritchie, G. 2006. Reinterpretation and viewpoints. *Humor: International Journal of Humor Research* 19 (3):251–270 (special issue on cognitive linguistics).

Ritchie, G., R. Manurung, H. Pain, A. Waller, and D. O'Mara. 2006. The STANDUP interactive riddle builder. *IEEE Intelligent Systems* 21 (2):67–69.

Rizzolatti, G., L. Fadiga, V. Gallese, and L. Fogassi. 1996. Premotor cortex and the recognition of motor actions. *Brain Research: Cognitive Brain Research* 3 (2):131–141.

Ross, D., and P. Dumouchel. 2004a. Emotions as strategic signals. *Rationality and Society* 16 (3):251–286.

Ross, D., and P. Dumouchel. 2004b. Sincerity is just consistency: Reply to Frank. *Rationality and Society* 16 (3):307–318.

Ross, W. D., ed. 1951. *Aristotle's Prior and Posterior Analytics*. Oxford: Clarendon Press.

Rozenblit, L., and F. Keil. 2002. The misunderstood limits of folk science: An illusion of explanatory depth. *Cognitive Science* 26:521–562.

Rumelhart, D. E., J. L. McClelland, and the PDP Research Group. 1986. *Parallel Distributed Processing: Explorations in the Microstructure of Cognition*, vol. 1: *Foundations*. Cambridge, MA: MIT Press.

Russell, B. 1912. *The Problems of Philosophy*. London: Henry Holt.

Russell, B. 1918. The philosophy of logical atomism. *Monist* 28: 495–527; 29, 32–63, 190–222, 345–380. Reprinted in *Logic and Knowledge: Essays 1901–1950*, ed. Robert Charles Marsh, 177–281, London: Unwin Hyman, 1956. Reprinted in *The Philosophy of Logical Atomism*, ed. David Pears, 35–155, LaSalle: Open Court, 1985.

Samson, A. C., C. F. Hempelmann, O. Huber, and S. Zysset. 2009. Neural substrates of incongruity-resolution and nonsense humor. *Neuropsychologia* 47:1023–1033.

Samson, A. C., S. Zysset, and O. Huber. 2008. Cognitive humor processing: Different logical mechanisms in non-verbal cartoons—an fMRI study. *Social Neuroscience* 3(2):125–140.

Samuels, R., S. Stich, and M. Bishop. 2002. Ending the rationality wars: How to make disputes about human rationality disappear. In *Common Sense, Reasoning, and Rationality*, ed. Renee Elio, 236–268. New York: Oxford University Press.

Savage-Rumbaugh, S., and R. Lewin. 1994. *Kanzi: The Ape at the Brink of the Human Mind*. New York: John Wiley.

Saxe, J. G. 1873. "The Blind Men and the Elephant." In *The Poems of John Godfrey Saxe*, complete ed. Boston: James R. Osgood.

Schachter, S., and J. E. Singer. 1962. Cognitive, social, and physiological determinants of emotional states. *Psychological Review* 69:379–399.

Schank, R. C. 1991. *Tell Me a Story: A New Look at Real and Artificial Intelligence*. New York: Atheneum.

Schank, R. C., and R. P. Abelson. 1977. *Scripts, Plans, Goals, and Understanding: An Inquiry into Human Knowledge Structures*. Hillsdale, NJ: Lawrence Erlbaum.

Schooler, L. J., and R. Hertwig. 2005. How forgetting aids heuristic inference. *Psychological Review* 112:610–628.

Schopenhauer, A. [1883] 1969. On the theory of the ludicrous. In *The World as Will and Representation*. Trans. E. Payne. New York: Dover.

Schopenhauer, A. 1969. *The World as Will and Representation*. Trans. E. Payne. New York: Dover.

Searle, J. R. 1980. Minds, brains, and programs. *Behavioral and Brain Sciences* 3 (3):417–457.

Sedivy, J. C., M. K. Tanenhaus, C. G. Chambers, and G. N. Carlson. 1999. Achieving incremental semantic interpretation through contextual representation. *Cognition* 71 (2):109–148.

Seyfarth, R. M., and D. L. Cheney. 1997. Some general features of vocal development in nonhuman primates. In *Social Influences on Vocal Development*, ed. C. T. Snowdon and M. Hausberger, 249–273. Cambridge: Cambridge University Press.

Shammi, P., and D. T. Stuss. 1999. Humour appreciation: A role of the right frontal lobe. *Brain* 122:657–666.

Shastri, L., and D. Grannes. 1996. A connectionist treatment of negation and inconsistency. In *Proceedings of the Eighteenth Conference of the Cognitive Science Society*, ed. Garrison Cottrell, 142–147. Mahwah, NJ: Lawrence Erlbaum.

Shibata, T., K. Ohkawa, and K. Tanie. 1996. Spontaneous behavior of robots for cooperation—Emotionally intelligent robot systems. *Proceedings of the IEEE International Conference on Robotics and Automation*, Minneapolis, Minnesota, 2426–2431.

Shultz, T. R. 1976. A cognitive-developmental analysis of humor. In *Humour and Laughter: Theory, Research, and Applications*, ed. A. J. Chapman and H. C. Foot, 11–36. London: Wiley.

Smith, A. [1759] 1976. *A Theory of Moral Sentiments*. Ed. D. D. Raphael and A. L. MacFie. Oxford: Clarendon Press.

Smith, J. E., V. A. Waldorf, and D. L. Trembath. 1990. Single white male looking for thin, very attractive. . . . *Sex Roles* 23 (11–12):675–685.

Solomon, R. C. 1976. *The Passions*. New York: Doubleday.

Solomon, R. L., and J. D. Corbit. 1974. An opponent-process theory of motivation: I. Temporal dynamics of affect. *Psychological Review* 81 (2):119–145.

Soussignan, R. 2002. Duchenne smile, emotional experience, and autonomic reactivity: A test of the facial feedback hypothesis. *Journal of Personality and Social Psychology* 2:52–74.

Spencer, H. 1860. The physiology of laughter. *Macmillan's Magazine* 1:395–402.

Sperber, D., and D. Wilson. 1986. *Relevance: Communication and Cognition*. Oxford: Blackwell.

Sperber, D., and D. Wilson. 1995. *Relevance: Communication and Cognition*, 2nd ed. Oxford: Blackwell.

Sperli, F., L. Spinelli, C. Pollo, and M. Seeck. 2006. Contralateral smile and laughter, but no mirth, induced by electrical stimulation of the cingulate cortex. *Epilepsia* 47:440–443.

Spinka, M., R. C. Newberry, and M. Bekoff. 2001. Mammalian play: Training for the unexpected. *Quarterly Review of Biology* 76:141–168.

Spivey, M. J. 2007. *The Continuity of Mind*. Oxford: Oxford Universiuty Press.

Spivey, M. J., M. K. Tanenhaus, K. M. Eberhard, and J. C. Sedivy. 2002. Eye movements and spoken language comprehension: Effects of visual context on syntactic ambiguity resolution. *Cognitive Psychology* 45:447–481.

Sterelny, K. 2003. *Thought in a Hostile World: The Evolution of Human Cognition.* Oxford: Wiley-Blackwell.

Stock, O., and C. Strapparava. 2005. HAHAcronym: A computational humor system. In *Proceedings of the ACL Interactive Poster and Demonstration Sessions*, 113–116, Ann Arbor, June. Madison, WI: Omnipress.

Strack, F., L. Martin, and S. Stepper. 1988. Inhibiting and facilitating conditions of the human smile: A nonobtrusive test of the facial feedback hypothesis. *Journal of Personality and Social Psychology* 54:768–777.

Strick, M., R. W. Holland, R. B. van Baaren, and A. van Knippenberg. 2009. Finding comfort in a joke: Consolatory effects of humor through cognitive distraction. *Emotion* 9 (4):574–578.

Suls, J. M. 1972. A two-stage model for the appreciation of jokes and cartoons. In *The Psychology of Humor*, ed. J. H. Goldstein and P. E. McGhee. New York: Academic Press.

Suls, J. M. 1977. Cognitive and disparagement theories of humour. In *It's a Funny Thing, Humour*, ed. A. J. Chapman and H. C. Foot. London: Pergamon Press.

Swinney, D. 1979. Lexical access during sentence comprehension: (Re)consideration of context effects. *Journal of Verbal Learning and Verbal Behavior* 18:645–659.

Swiss, J. I. 2007. Empathy. *Antinomy* 11:41–47.

Tanenhaus, M. K., J. M. Leiman, and M. Seidenberg. 1979. Evidence for multiple stages in the processing of ambiguous words in syntactic contexts. *Journal of Verbal Learning and Verbal Behavior* 18:427–440.

Tanenhaus, M. K., M. J. Spivey-Knowlton, K. M. Eberhard, and J. C. Sedivy. 1995. Integration of visual and linguistic information in spoken language comprehension. *Science* 268 (5217):1632–1634.

Thelen, E., and L. B. Smith. 1994. *A Dynamic Systems Approach to the Development of Cognition and Action.* Cambridge, MA: MIT Press.

Thompson, J. 1941. Development of facial expression of emotion in blind and seeing children. *Archives de Psychologie* 37:1–47.

Thorndike, E. L. 1898. Animal intelligence: An experimental study of the associative processes in animals. *Psychological Review Monograph Supplement* 2 (8):1–109.

Thorndike, E. L. [1911] 2000. *Animal Intelligence*, 2nd ed. New York: Hafner. Transaction Publishers.

Tinbergen, N. 1951. *The Study of Instinct.* Oxford: Clarendon Press.

Tinbergen, N. 1953. *The Herring Gull's World.* London: Collins.

Tomasello, M., and J. Call. 1997. *Primate Cogition.* Oxford: Oxford University Press.

Tomasello, M., J. Call, and B. Hare. 2003. Chimpanzees understand psychological states: The question is which ones and to what extent. *Trends in Cognitive Science* 7:153–156.

Tomkins, S. S. 1962. *Affect, Imagery, and Consciousness*. New York: Springer.

Tooby, J., and L. Cosmides. 2001. Does beauty build adapted minds? Toward an evolutionary theory of aesthetics, fiction, and the arts. *SubStance* 30(1):6–27.

Treisman, A., 1960. Contextual cues in selective listening. *Quarterly Journal of Experimental Psychology* 12:242–248.

Trivers, R. L. 1971. The evolution of reciprocal altruism. *Quarterly Review of Biology* 46 (1):35–57.

Trivers, R. L. 1972. Parental investment and sexual selection. In *Sexual Selection and the Descent of Man*, ed. B. Campbell, 1871–1971. Chicago: Aldine.

Turing, A. M. 1950. Computing machinery and intelligence. *Mind* 59:433–460.

Tversky, A., and D. Kahneman. 1974. Judgment under uncertainty: Heuristics and biases. *Science* 185:1124–1131.

Tversky, A., and D. Kahneman. 1983. Extensional versus intuitive reasoning: The conjunction fallacy in probability judgment. *Psychological Review* 90:293–315.

Uekermann, J., I. Daum, and S. Channon. 2007. Toward a cognitive and social neuroscience of humor processing. *Social Cognition* 25:553–572.

van Hooff, J. A. R. A. M. 1972. A comparative approach to the phylogeny of laughter and smiling. In *Non-Verbal Communication*, ed. R. A. Hinde, 209–243. Cambridge: Cambridge University Press.

van Gelder, T., and R. F. Port. 1995. It's about time: An overview of the dynamical approach to cognition. In *Mind as Motion: Explorations in the Dynamics of Cognition*, ed. R. F. Port and T. van Gelder. Cambridge, MA: MIT Press.

Veatch, T. C. 1998. A theory of humor. *Humor: International Journal of Humor Research* 11 (2):161–215.

Vogt, B. A. 2005. Pain and emotion interactions in subregions of the cingulate gyrus. *Nature Reviews: Neuroscience* 6:533–544.

Watson, K. K., B. J. Matthews, and J. M. Allman. 2007. Brain activation during sight gags and language-dependent humor. *Cerebral Cortex* 17(2):314–324.

Weber, B. H., and D. J. Depew, eds. 2003. *Evolution and Learning: The Baldwin Effect Reconsidered*. Cambridge, MA: MIT Press.

Weisfeld, G. E. 1993. The adaptive value of humor and laughter. *Ethology and Sociobiology* 14:141–169.

Wild, B., F. A. Rodden, W. Grodd, and W. Ruch. 2003. Neural correlates of laughter and humour. *Brain* 126:1–18.

Wild, B., F. A. Rodden, A. Rapp, M. Erb, W. Grodd, et al. 2006. Humor and smiling: Cortical regions selective for cognitive, affective, and volitional components. *Neurology* 66:887–893.

Wilson, E. O. 1975. *Sociobiology: The New Synthesis*. Cambridge, MA: Belknap Press of Harvard University Press.

Wiseman, R. 2002. *LaughLab: The Scientific Search for the World's Funniest Joke*. London: Arrow.

Wittgenstein, L. 1953. *Philosophical Investigations*. Ed. G. H. von Wright, R. Rhees, and G. E. M. Anscombe. Trans. G. E. M. Anscombe. Oxford: Blackwell.

Wolfe, T. 1965. *The Kandy-Kolored Tangerine-Flake Streamline Baby*. New York: Farrar, Strauss & Geroux.

Wyer, R. S., and J. E. Collins, II. 1992. A theory of humor elicitation. *Psychological Review* 99 (4):663–688.

Yamamoto, M. 1993. Sozzy: A hormone driven autonomous vacuum cleaner. *Proceedings of Mobile Robots* VIII:162–165.

Zahavi, A. 1996. The evolution of communal roosts as information centers and the pitfall of group-selection: A rejoinder to Richner and Heeb. *Behavioral Ecology* 7:118–119.

Zajonc, R. B. 1980. Feeling and thinking: Preferences need no inferences. *American Psychologist* 35:151.

Zajonc, R. B. 1984. On the primacy of affect. *American Psychologist* 39:117–123.

Zigler, E., J. Levine, and L. Gould. 1967. Cognitive challenge as a factor in children's humor appreciation. *Journal of Personality and Social Psychology* 6 (3):332–336.

Zillmann, D. 1983a. Disparagement humor. In *Handbook of Humour Research*, ed. P. E. McGhee and J. H. Goldstein, 85–107. New York: Springer-Verlag.

Zillmann, D. 1983b. Transfer of excitation in emotional behavior. In *Social Psychophysiology: A Sourcebook*, ed. J. T. Cacioppo and R. E. Petty, 215–240. New York: Guilford Press.

Zillmann, D., A. H. Katcher, and B. Milavsky. 1972. Excitation transfer from physical exercise to subsequent aggressive behavior. *Journal of Experimental Social Psychology* 8:247–259.

Ziv, A. 1984. *Personality and Sense of Humor*. New York: Springer-Verlag.

Index

Cartwright-Smith, J., 22n, 318
Caruthers, D., 319
Casey, K. L., 70n, 319
Catch trials, 181
Cathcart, T., 112, 178, 285n, 307
Causation, theory of, 18, 78
Censor model of humor, 44, 51, 52, 204–206
"Central conundrum" of humor, 26
Chair sculpture. *See Oops!*, sculpture
Challenged expectations, 183, 184
Challengers (beliefs), 184, 185
Chalmers, D. J., 65, 77n, 85, 154, 307, 308
Chambers, C. G., 99, 308, 324
Channon, S., 129n, 327
Chaplin, Charlie, x, 7, 146
Chapman, A. J., 35, 308
Chasing, in play, 152, 261–263, 293
Cheating, 75, 76n, 82, 198–199, 258–259
Chena, T., 305
Cheney, D. L., 262, 308, 325
Chess, ix, x, 66, 83n, 88, 93–94, 107, 188, 191–192, 232, 263, 296
Chevrolet brain, 12, 126
Children, humor and mirth in, 32, 35, 38, 42, 58, 157, 180, 220–221, 242, 266–267, 275, 298. *See also* Infants
Chimpanzees, 90, 125–126, 261–263, 290–291
play in, 145, 261
theory of mind in, 145
Chislenko, Alexander, xii, 159n, 308
Chocolate, 1, 2, 214n, 218
Christenfeld, N., 39, 228, 315
Chwalisz, K., 69, 308
Circular definition, 24. *See also* Definition, circular
Clark, A., 65, 85, 154, 308, 322
Clark, M., 219n, 308
Clarke, A., 127, 308

Classifying humor, 143, 156, 280. *See also* Humor, taxonomy of
Cleverness, 120, 123, 198, 246–249, 267. *See also* Wit
Close, M., 160, 273, 308
Closure, 107–108, 301
Coffee, 105, 107, 214n, 218
Cognition, xii, 63, 66, 70n, 73, 79, 83–91, 95, 97, 100–101, 104, 117, 120, 154, 297, 298
distributed, 154
embodied, 69, 85, 89–92
extended, 154
Cognitive accessibility, 266–267
Cognitive agent, 289, 297–298
Cognitive anchor, 203
Cognitive architecture, 17, 18, 65, 76, 86, 89, 94, 117, 123–125
Cognitive behavior, 77–78, 80, 86, 292. *See also* Behavior, covert
Cognitive bug, 225
Cognitive censors, 52, 204–206
Cognitive collusion, 154
Cognitive elaboration, 204n
Cognitive emotions, 66, 81, 85, 87. *See also* Epistemic emotions
Cognitively impenetrable belief, 227n
Cognitive mastery, 266–268
Cognitive mechanisms, 26, 103n
Cognitive processes, 66, 70, 301–302
Cognitive processing, 5, 61, 62
Cognitive scaffolding, 65
Cognitive science, 4, 39n, 66, 83–84, 280
Cognitive theory, 6, 57
Cohen, T., 33–34, 308
Coherence, 15, 62n, 98, 124
Cohesion, group, 269
Cohn, J. F., 305
Collins, A. M., 101, 308
Collins, J. E., II, 17, 49, 50, 173, 202–204, 206, 328
Color-blindness, 18, 298